THE
KATYN
MASSACRE 1940

THE
KATYN
MASSACRE 1940
HISTORY OF A CRIME

THOMAS URBAN

Pen & Sword
MILITARY

AN IMPRINT OF PEN & SWORD BOOKS LTD.
YORKSHIRE - PHILADELPHIA

© Verlag C.H. Beck oHG, Munich, 2015

First published in Great Britain in 2020 by
PEN & SWORD MILITARY
an imprint of
Pen & Sword Books Ltd
Yorkshire - Philadelphia

Copyright © Thomas Urban, 2020

ISBN: 978 1 52677 535 1

Typeset in 10/12.5 & Times New Roman
by SJmagic DESIGN SERVICES, India.

Printed and bound in UK by TJ Books Limited.

Pen & Sword Books Ltd incorporates the Imprints of Pen & Sword Books Archaeology,
Atlas, Aviation, Battleground, Discovery, Family History, History, Maritime, Military,
Naval, Politics, Railways, Select, Transport, True Crime, Fiction, Frontline Books,
Leo Cooper, Praetorian Press, Seaforth Publishing, Wharncliffe and White Owl.

For a complete list of Pen & Sword titles please contact

PEN & SWORD BOOKS LIMITED
47 Church Street, Barnsley, South Yorkshire, S70 2AS, England
E-mail: enquiries@pen-and-sword.co.uk
Website: www.pen-and-sword.co.uk

Or

PEN AND SWORD BOOKS
1950 Lawrence Rd, Havertown, PA 19083, USA
E-mail: uspen-and-sword@casematepublishers.com
Website: www.penandswordbooks.com

Contents

Foreword to the German Edition (2015)

Katyn is one of the glaring ciphers of the twentieth century, a mass murder that had a powerful and lasting effect. The murder of some 4,000 Polish officers, most of them reservists with academic careers, by Stalin's secret police in the spring of 1940 was much more than a war crime. The name of the small village in western Russia is representative of the Kremlin's attempt under Stalin to exterminate the Polish elite in order to extend the totalitarian system of the Soviet Union to Poland. The murder order concerned not only Katyn, but also other places where a total of around 25,000 Polish officers and officials were killed.

The term 'Crime of Katyn' in today's Polish terminology includes the victims of the other mass graves that became known only half a century later, because the village west of Smolensk was the first place where it became apparent. They are therefore also taken into account in this book.

Katyn also stands for the lie as a core element of the system shaped by Lenin and Stalin, which turned all moral categories upside down: anyone who spoke of Soviet perpetrators was persecuted, punished and, in the worst case, liquidated. Not least because of the Katyn lie, the system imposed by Moscow, which called itself socialism, could not gain a foothold in Poland. Far beyond the conflict-laden history of Polish–Russian relations, Katyn also stands for the striving for truth against lies, for freedom against oppression, for culture and civilisation against brute force and murder.

The struggle for the 'truth about Katyn' became a constant in the Polish dissident and democracy movement, from which the Solidarity trade union emerged. This struggle got a hagiographic touch, Katyn as the place where absolute evil has destroyed the good, namely the flowering of the nation. More than ever, the crime and memory of it took on a mythical and sacral dimension when the Polish presidential plane crashed near Smolensk in 2010, on the way to a commemoration of the seventieth anniversary of the Katyn massacre.

In the search for motifs, two positions face each other: in Poland in particular, it is considered genocide, while some Western European and American historians define it as class murder. But there are objections to these clear classifications: Stalin also had tens of thousands of Poles who were simple peasants workers deported to the depths of the Soviet Union, i.e. from the 'classes' that were to become the ruling classes according to pure doctrine.

The importance of ethnic and national categories in Stalin's thinking is demonstrated by some of his sayings and, above all, by his actions: he certified the Poles and the Russians to be 'of the same blood', namely the Slav one. Although he was Georgian, he thus followed Pan-Slavic ideas. The Russians were the 'greatest of all peoples of the Soviet Union' – an echo of the 'Third Rome' of the Russian Orthodox Church.

Stalin boasted to the representatives of the Polish government in exile that he 'destroyed' the allegedly German-friendly Ukrainians – and as far as their cultural elite was concerned, he actually made a good deal of progress along this path. He claimed control of the Ukrainian inhabitants of what was then eastern Poland, who were Polish citizens before the war and whose homeland had never belonged to Russia. One of the late consequences of his brutal policy is the bloody conflict between Moscow and Kiev today.

In the tradition of the tsarist empire, Stalin also saw the Jews as a 'national minority'. The last major waves of cleansing during his lifetime, the campaign against 'cosmopolitans' and the 'medical conspiracy', were primarily directed against the Jewish intelligentsia in the Soviet Union, and were therefore also culturally and ethnically motivated.

He also had entire ethnic groups deported, such as the Volga Germans, Chechens and Crimean Tatars. Distrusting the other peoples, he placed Russians in key positions in all Soviet republics and satellite states. In Warsaw, the Soviet Marshal Konstantin Rokossovsky became Polish Defence Minister, a humiliation of the Poles.

In his ideological writings, Stalin justified the solution of political problems through violence with the teachings of Karl Marx, as the revolutionary Lenin had already done. Stalin and the members of his Politburo who were involved in the Katyn murder thought in terms of enemy categories and conspiracy theories, true to Lenin's dictum 'Who, whom?' – Who will defeat whom?

Whether they pursued a social goal in Lenin's sense other than securing their own position of power is controversial among historians. Whether they were driven by desire to kill and boundless criminal energy, omnipotence fantasies or cold calculation, is too. It was probably something of each.

It has been proven that Stalin was increasingly paranoid and that his secret service boss Beria had a perverse nature. They and their accomplices in the leadership of the party and the secret services claimed for themselves the right to decide on the life and death of opponents. Apparently, they were convinced that they had to do something necessary in the Katyn case as well.

In an attenuated manner Stalin's successors, from Khrushchev to Andropov, acted in the same way. They, too, claimed the right to dictate thinking and lifestyle to their citizens and to send deviants to the Gulag or psychiatric clinics, accepting their death. Their secret services were not subject to any social control and were instruments of terror – now strongly subdued, far less comprehensive and also more predictable.

But while Lenin openly preached the 'red terror', and while the communist press in the Russian Civil War and the first years after the Bolsheviks seized power led open campaigns for the destruction of capitalists, tsarists and priests, Stalin's totalitarian regime gave itself the appearance of a constitutional state: constitution, elections, judicial procedures and international agreements imitated democratic states. Orwellian efforts of camouflage and deception, secrecy and propaganda were enormous, especially in the Katyn case.

Even the last Soviet leader, Mikhail Gorbachev, who tried in vain to modernise the giant empire, adhered to this lie for a long time against his better knowledge. Only long after he had lost control did he admit at least a part of the truth. But it was too late to keep the Poles in the Eastern bloc.

Thus the saying attributed to Gorbachev came true: 'Life punishes those who are late.' Katyn has proven to be an explosive device with a long time delay. It is part of the tragedy of the failed reformer Gorbachev that his policy has only opened the floodgates to the broad stream of coming to terms with the past, which ultimately also carried him away. For the flood of reports of crimes on behalf of the Communist Party undermined the entire basis of legitimacy of its rule.

This book is based on eyewitness reports, documentaries and analyses of the fate of the Polish officers who disappeared in the Soviet Union. Most of them were published in Poland, a considerable part in Russia. In the case of Katyn, the Kremlin under Vladimir Putin is trying to construct a Russian–Polish community of victims: there are many times more Soviet citizens shot during the Stalin era buried in Katyn Forest than Polish officers. In Poland, Putin's speeches are not seen as a step towards reconciliation, but rather as an attempt to negate Russia's responsibility as the legal successor of the Soviet Union.

Katyn is as absent from Russian textbooks as Soviet terror in the post-war annexed territories and occupied countries. Instead, the Poles, the Balts, the Western Ukrainians and the other peoples from the former Soviet bloc in Moscow are accused of being ungrateful, because the Red Army paid a high blood toll for their liberation from the yoke of Hitlerism.

But the fact that the Red Army also acted as rude occupiers, and that Moscow's secret services led a Stalinist terror regime with deportations and countless political murders in almost all of post-war Eastern Europe, is almost completely suppressed in today's Russia.

This book also takes a look at the Western Allies' dispute over Katyn, which was not a minor matter: It influenced the relationship between British Prime Minister Churchill, US President Roosevelt and Stalin.

In recent years, several thousand pages from an investigation by the US Congress have been made available, and the Foreign Office in London has also published comprehensive documentation on the Internet. The discovery of the mass graves by the Germans in the spring of 1943, when the war, despite Stalingrad, seemed far from over, demanded that Britain, as the protective power of the Polish government in exile, and the United States take a stand.

The government in exile accused the Soviet Union of the crime, so it was a serious conflict between two of the Western Allies. Both Churchill and Roosevelt opted for realpolitik: the anti-Hitler coalition must under no circumstances be endangered and they ignored and consequently isolated the Poles in exile. In the collective memory of the Poles, this was cynical and immoral, a betrayal that preceded the even greater one of Yalta, when the Western powers approved Stalin's future rule over Eastern Europe.

The documents show a more differentiated picture: Roosevelt and his most important advisors were firmly convinced of Stalin's sincerity ('Uncle Joe'); they were blinded and naive.

Unlike them, Churchill had no illusions about the character and aims of the Soviet regime. But he and his experts on Eastern Europe did not see a clear picture of what had happened in Katyn. It made them uncertain in their assessment that Goebbels' Katyn campaign was based mainly on the reports of two coroners of dubious reputation: one was SS-Standartenführer, the other the chairman of a National Socialist medical association.

In the first two decades after the war, numerous articles about Katyn appeared in Western Germany, which can be read as justification for the Wehrmacht's attack on the Soviet Union: the opinion was propagated that Stalin was barbaric not only with his own people, but also with neighbouring peoples; it was therefore justified to protect Europe from the Bolsheviks.

But this wave of articles died down as a result of the Auschwitz trials in the mid-sixties and a major debate on guilt broke out in Germany. More and more reports on the German scorched earth policy, on massacres of civilians, on the fate of Soviet prisoners of war occupied the German public.

Indeed, a presentation of the mass murder of Katyn and its consequences is in no way suitable to relativise the German war of annihilation in Eastern Europe. Rather, Katyn cannot distract from the National Socialist crimes.

This idea comes from Rudolf-Christoph von Gersdorff, who supervised the exhumation of the victims as a General Staff officer of the Central Army Group in the Smolensk region. It was precisely at this time that Gersdorff and Lieutenant Fabian von Schlabrendorff, also stationed in Smolensk, made two attempts to eliminate Hitler with a bomb attack.

Both played a very important role in the failure of the Soviet plan to impeach Katyn to the Germans at the Nuremberg trials. It would have been the crowning glory of the Katyn lie if this plan had been successful in Nuremberg. Apparently, there wasn't much missing. For the first time this book describes the role of the two well-known members of the anti-Hitlerite resistance in the battles over the truth about Katyn.

* * *

During my twenty-four years as a correspondent on the Vistula, the Dnieper and the Moskva, I have reported time and again on this coming to terms with the mass murder.

I spoke to the prelate Stanisław Niedzielak, who under communist rule had founded an illegal association of relatives of the Katyn victims. In January 1989, some months before the collapse of the communist regime in Poland, he was murdered, probably by the secret police SB.

I was a member of the press delegation that accompanied Polish prime minister Tadeusz Mazowiecki, the cautious intellectual from Solidarity, into the snowy Katyn Forest in November 1989, two weeks after the fall of the Berlin Wall.

There was such a strong frost that water and wine were frozen in the chalice during the funeral mass under the open sky. But the Polish priest was prepared: he stirred some drops of vodka into it. In Moscow, I talked to prosecutors and historians. It was also research into family history: a great uncle of my wife, Ewa, whose family comes from the former Polish town of Tarnopol, today's Ukrainian Ternopil, is on the official list of victims.

That is why we participated in meetings and conferences of the victims' association. Some of our acquaintances from this circle were among the victims of the Smolensk plane crash. This book is also dedicated to them.

Foreword to the English Edition (2020)

The mystery of the Katyn massacre has been solved for a long time. Polish historians, with the support of a small group of Russian colleagues, have accurately reconstructed the prehistory and course of the mass murder. The first chapters of this book are mainly based on their fundamental analyses and the documentation they have produced. The publications of these historians, who have achieved great things under sometimes adverse circumstances, are listed in the bibliography and the notes.

This book, however, focuses on the immediate consequences of the discovery of the mass graves in Katyn Forest by Wehrmacht soldiers in 1943: the propaganda campaigns and political manoeuvres with which each side tried to bring the world public on its side and above all, exert influence on the governments in London and Washington.

It thus also examines why the Polish government in exile in London, which very quickly had a clear picture of the Soviet perpetration, could not assert itself with this view. The London Poles were even denounced as supporters of the Hitler regime, not only in the Kremlin-controlled Soviet press, but also in most American and British newspapers. In today's words, one would say that the 'fake news', the false news spread by the Soviet propaganda apparatus, was extremely effective.

There are two main reasons for the success of the Kremlin's Katyn campaign. The first reason is well known and obvious: it was the Nazi propaganda minister Joseph Goebbels who brought the subject to the world public. Goebbels was a notorious liar and manipulator in the service of a criminal regime; there was no reason for the politicians and journalists of the Western Allies to believe him this time. In this sense, the Polish exiles in London became victims of Goebbels' fatal reputation.

The second reason for the Kremlin's success was the fundamental misjudgement of the Soviet regime by the most influential American and British correspondents in Moscow and by the White House administration in Washington during Roosevelt's term. Almost all of the Anglo-American correspondents who came to Moscow in the 1930s described the construction of the Soviet Union with great sympathy and closed their eyes to the dark side. As it became known decades later, some of them were on the NKVD's list of informants. At least three of the Western correspondents accredited in Moscow took part in Comintern agitation courses; their readers, of course, knew nothing about it.

It was these sympathisers of the Stalin regime who uncritically adopted the Soviet version of Katyn and thus strongly influenced international public opinion. Another factor was that before their trip to Katyn most of them had already visited other mass graves in the Soviet hinterland, where the German perpetrators were beyond doubt, such as the canyon of Babi Yar near Kiev. The influence of the correspondents was enormous, the reports by the British press agency *Reuters*, for example, were reprinted during the Second World War by a total of 4,000 newspapers in many countries, also in other languages.

But there is no evidence that any of these Western correspondents deliberately lied. On the contrary, they were all firmly convinced that they were reporting Katyn correctly. The same was true of the White House: thousands of American documents on Katyn, from diplomatic dispatches to intelligence analyses, have been posted on the Internet in recent years. They show that the opinions of the experts were divided, even among the US ambassadors in Moscow during the Stalin era: two saw strong evidence of Soviet perpetration, while two others accused the Germans. The latter enforced their view in the White House. But there is not a single indication that Roosevelt deliberately spread the untruth about Katyn; rather, the documents and memories of contemporaries suggest that he was firmly convinced of the Germans' guilt because he believed in Stalin's honesty.

For the first time, this book sheds light on who influenced the White House decisions in the Katyn case, from diplomats to press commentators. Many of them saw the Stalin system as a hope for humanity, just as thousands of intellectuals around the world mistakenly did.

Churchill, unlike Roosevelt, had no illusions about Stalin, but he was not sure how to evaluate the contradictory information from Berlin and Moscow. Although he saw himself as the patron of the Polish government in exile, his political leeway was limited because he was not supported by Washington. Pro-Soviet forces had prevailed in the White House.

The alleged witnesses on the Soviet side deliberately lied – out of fear – at the manipulated presentation of the Soviet investigative commission to Western correspondents and at the trials of German war crimes in Leningrad and Nuremberg. Decades later, Gorbachev, the last head of the CPSU, also deliberately lied – for political reasons – when he first claimed that there were no files on Katyn in Moscow; later he had to admit part of the truth.

Katyn has also left its mark on the work of several writers, including the controversial American poet Ezra Pound. His famous colleague George Orwell even advocated the translation of a Polish book on Katyn after the war in London, but without success – no British publisher was interested in the uncomfortable subject at the time.

While these are rather marginal aspects, this book can answer one of the important questions about the history of the struggle for the truth of Katyn: why did the Soviets fail to put Katyn on the list of German war crimes at the Nuremberg International Military Tribunal, even though the White House and the entire Western press were firmly convinced of the German perpetration at the time?

The answer comes from the papers of the American general William Donovan ('Wild Bill'), who was head of the military secret service OSS in the Second World War: the German Hitler opponent Fabian von Schlabrendorff, who was involved in two failed attacks on the Führer and experienced the end of the war in a concentration camp, had convinced Donovan of the Soviet guilt.

Schlabrendorff had been an officer of the Army Group Centre in Smolensk and had been friends with another member of the resistance movement, Lieutenant Colonel Rudolf-Christoph von Gersdorff, who had supervised the exhumations in Katyn Forest. Gersdorff had informed him of all the details. Since Schlabrendorff had provided the Americans with information about German war crimes in Nuremberg, he was absolutely credible for Donovan. For this reason, the hitherto unknown contribution of the German Hitler opponents to the controversies surrounding Katyn is presented in detail here for the first time.

* * *

The present book is not identical to the position adopted in *Katyn 1940: History of a Crime* published in 2015 in German by the publishing house C. H. Beck in Munich. That book does not contain the detailed analyses of the press campaigns and the secret service documents, because most of these materials were not yet accessible at that time. However, the German edition also emphasises that Katyn would not have come about without the Wehrmacht's attack on Poland. At the same time as the Soviets carried out the mass murders in Katyn and elsewhere, the Germans also murdered thousands of members of the Polish elite.

Chapter 1

Attacks from West and East

On 17 September 1939, the Red Army crossed Poland's eastern border on a broad front. The military leadership in Warsaw, which for seventeen days had concentrated entirely on the attacks of the Wehrmacht from the West and North, was completely surprised by this. At first, the government was even convinced that the Red Army should rush to help the oppressed Poles. The Soviet ambassador in Warsaw had contributed to this assessment: just a few days earlier he had proposed organising supplies for the Polish armed forces over Soviet territory, it was a ruse to lull Warsaw.[1]

Indeed, the Polish leadership did not see through this deception. The Polish forces in the east of the country were ordered not to take up the fight against the Red Army. But the Red Army treated the Poles as enemies. Soviet aircraft dropped leaflets urging Polish soldiers to disarm and kill their officers. The Soviet secret service, the NKVD, took action itself: it shot dozens of Polish officers who had not even taken up the fight and negotiated to hand over their garrisons after handing over their weapons.[2]

Towns and villages were under fire, even if it was not necessary for military reasons. The Red Army and the Wehrmacht left a trail of devastation in their blitzkrieg against Poland. On 22 September, a joint victory parade of Wehrmacht and Red Army troops took place in Brest Litovsk. The commander on the German side was the later famous tank general Heinz Guderian. The Polish government and the army command had already left for Romania by this time.

The division of Poland had been agreed in the Secret Additional Protocol to the German-Soviet non-aggression pact, which Foreign Minister Joachim von Ribbentrop and Viacheslav Molotov, People's Commissioner for Foreign Affairs, had signed in the Kremlin on 24 August 1939 in the presence of Joseph Stalin. In this way, the Soviet Union thwarted the efforts of the British government to neutralise Nazi Germany through a network of treaties among the neighbouring states. Stalin commented on the Wehrmacht's first successes, which had invaded Poland on 1 September 1939, with the words that 'another fascist state' was going to disappear.

On the night of 17 September, when the Red Army was already at the Polish–Soviet border, Molotov had the Polish ambassador in Moscow, Wacław Grzybowski, summoned from his bed and asked to come to the Foreign Ministry.

At 2a.m. Molotov's deputy Vladimir Potemkin read to the diplomat the note invalidating the 1932 Polish–Soviet non-aggression pact. Potemkin, a specialist in ancient Hebrew, was an old comrade-in-arms of Stalin. Now he told Ambassador Grzybowski that the Polish state had disintegrated with the government's flight to Romania. The Soviet Union therefore considered itself obliged to protect the Ukrainian and Belarusian population on the territory of the former Polish state. Grzybowski protested and refused to accept the note.

At 4a.m. the tanks of the Red Army rolled over the border. After two weeks the resistance of the last Polish troops, which had taken up the fight despite the instructions from Warsaw, was broken. Molotov wrote shortly afterwards that the 'Bastard of Versailles' had disappeared.

The miracle of the Vistula

In the spring of 1919, the Versailles Conference had conceded a large increase in territory at the expense of the German Reich to the Polish state, which had only emerged a few months earlier after 123 years of division.

The question of Poland's eastern border remained unanswered, however, because there were still battles in this part of Europe. There were still formations of the Reichswehr, and the Russian Civil War raged between the White Forces and the Red Army. Polish and Ukrainian troops also fought against each other.

Using maps across language borders, British Minister of Foreign Affairs George Curzon proposed a line that largely followed the course of the Bug and San rivers as Poland's future eastern border. But Marshal Józef Piłsudski, the commander-in-chief of the Polish armed forces, sought a confederation under Warsaw's leadership, which would include Lithuania and large parts of Belarus and Ukraine. He had in mind a new edition of the former European great power Poland–Lithuania, which in the second half of the eighteenth century, due to its internal weakness, was divided by its neighbours Prussia, Austria and Russia.

For this reason, Piłsudski rejected the Curzon line, which was based on ethnic criteria. When Red Army units occupied the Lithuanian capital, Vilnius, he went on to counterattack and regarded Russia as Poland's main enemy. His troops made huge gains and moved into Kiev in early May 1920. But the Poles could only stay in Kiev for a few weeks, the Red Army drove them away again and now advanced westwards. In August 1920 it stood on the Vistula.

However, the Polish forces under Piłsudski's command were able to destroy the Red Army not far from Warsaw. In the 'Miracle on the Vistula' the Poles had succeeded in encompassing the units of Russian commander Mikhail Tukhachevsky from behind. The later Soviet marshal blamed Political Commissioner Joseph Stalin for the defeat, as the latter had previously withdrawn some of the red troops on his own authority. In return, the Poles again advanced far to the east and were able to dictate their peace terms after a ceasefire.

In the 1921 Riga peace, Poland established its new borders including the western regions of present-day Belarus and Ukraine. Some of it was 250 kilometres east of the Curzon line. In the eastern regions of the Republic of Poland, however, Belarusians and Ukrainians made up the vast majority of the population, only about one third was Polish. In some districts not even every tenth was Pole.

However, Warsaw set a strict course of polonisation, accompanied time and again by severe political repression. The consequence was that, the Ukrainians in the eastern regions of the country particularly, rejected the Polish authorities.

Soviet propaganda tried to exploit this mood for itself. The Riga Agreement was called a 'dictated peace'. In Moscow, however, not only Tukhachevsky, but also several members of the Politburo blamed Stalin for this serious setback in the 'struggle for the world revolution'. During the Great Purges of 1936 to 1938, Stalin was to take bloody revenge on all his critics. The defeat on the Vistula also reinforced his view that bourgeois Poland was Soviet Russia's main enemy.

When Stalin had consolidated his autocratic rule, he also tackled the 'Polish problem'. He saw a constant threat in the Polish minority in the western districts of the USSR. In the 1930s a total of 135,000 Poles who were Soviet citizens were arrested, almost half of them were shot.

Stalin's feelings of hatred and distrust of the Poles were so great that he had liquidated almost all members of the Polish Communist Party who had fled persecution by the nationalist leadership in Warsaw to the Soviet Union. Of some 3,800 Polish CP members, fewer than 100 survived the Great Terror in Soviet exile.

In the autumn of 1939, Stalin crushed the Republic of Poland together with Nazi Germany, his biggest ideological enemy to date. Now the Soviet propaganda, which had so far despised the German Reich as 'fascist', called the Poles fascists.

But the allies Hitler and Stalin were unable to wipe out Poland under international law. In Paris, a Polish government in exile was formed, which was diplomatically recognised by France, Great Britain, the USA and many other democratic states as legal successor to the previous Warsaw leadership.

Sikorski's revenge

However, not a single minister from the pre-war cabinet belonged to the government in exile. Most of them were in internment camps in Romania at that time. Poland had a common border with Romania in its south-eastern corner during the interwar period. This is where most ministers and the Armed Forces High Command fled when the total military defeat against the German and Soviet aggressors became apparent after the Red Army invaded on 17 September.

Although Romania was formally a neutral state and under international law should have allowed Poles to pass through to France, their ally, the Polish government members were interned under German pressure, as were the generals – except for one: Władysław Sikorski.

He had also been a prominent politician in the interwar period, but he had not held public office for years, because he had completely divided himself from the rulers. Before the First World War Sikorski had belonged to armed forces that fought for the rebirth of the Polish state. He joined Piłsudski, the founder of the new Polish Army after the First World War. In the Polish–Soviet war of 1920 Sikorski was already a general; his troops contributed to the defeat of the Red Army commanded by Tukhachevsky in the 'Miracle of the Vistula'.

Sikorski was promoted to chief of staff. After a government crisis, the Sejm, the parliament in Warsaw, even elected him prime minister in 1922. He saw Poland's foreign policy future in a close alliance with France, and also advocated cooperation with Soviet Russia. But he stayed in office for only five months, then he was toppled by the Sejm and took over various army commands again.

Sikorski alienated himself from Piłsudski when the latter seized power with a coup d'état in 1926 and established an authoritarian regime. Sikorski was ordered to the army reserve, which was tantamount to involuntary early retirement.

Finally, he was given the opportunity to study at the French military academy in Paris; then it was said that the French secret service had recruited him. After his return, Sikorski published articles about national security and the military. He predicted that the Polish armed forces would have no chance against the Wehrmacht, which was highly armed under Hitler, but the General Staff in Warsaw rejected his analyses.

Immediately after the Wehrmacht attack on Poland on 1 September 1939, he asked for a command post, but was denied it. When the Polish defeat became apparent, he left for Romania, as did many active generals. He managed to contact the French embassy in Bucharest and immediately got a visa to leave for France.

General Władysław Sikorski, prime minister of the Polish government in exile.

Thanks to his contacts in Paris, Sikorski won the fierce battles among Polish emigrants for the post of head of the government in exile. He declared his main goal as the fight against the German Reich until the liberation of the homeland. To this end, an army in exile would be formed.

According to Sikorski, the underground groups that were formed in occupied Poland should unite and be subordinate to the government in exile. He made it clear that the Poles were also at war with the Soviet Union.

Sikorski campaigned in Paris and London in support of Finland in the war against the Red Army.[3]

The exiled prime minister succeeded in getting almost all of the 18,000 Polish soldiers interned in Romania to emigrate to France. Later, several thousand Poles arrived in France by other means. He also assumed the offices of Minister of Defence and Chief Commander of the Exiled Armed Forces. The French provided accommodation and, together with the British, equipment.

However, Sikorski and his followers took care that high officials of the pre-war government did not occupy important positions. He blamed the pre-war leadership for the total military collapse of September 1939. He set up a commission to 'investigate recent events in Poland and determine their causes', and even a trial was prepared. Many officers, who according to the first investigations were partly to blame for the disastrous war preparations, were interned on French soil.

Sikorski also maintained his irreconcilable line when the Wehrmacht, in its blitzkrieg in the summer of 1940, broke up the French army and the British units rushing to its aid.

Together with the fleeing British, the Polish army in exile, which had not taken part in the fighting, was able to cross the Channel into England. The new prime minister, Winston Churchill, had previously made Sikorski an offer to establish his government in London.

Neither Berlin nor Moscow recognised the government in exile. Instead, they built up their own power structures in occupied Poland and took action against the Polish elite. Both German and Soviet occupying forces presumed the power of disposal over life and death of the people in divided Poland.

'Special treatment' and liquidation of the 'Pans'
The Germans annexed the western and northwestern regions of Poland. The rest of Poland occupied by them was henceforth called the General Government. The former head of the legal department of the NSDAP, Hans Frank, resided as governor general on the Wawel, the old royal castle in Krakow.

The SS hunted not only Jews, for whose murder the term 'special treatment' was conceived, but also the Polish upper class and intellectuals. Several thousand land and factory owners, teachers and professors, lawyers, doctors, engineers and clergymen were murdered. Most of the survivors from these groups were sent to concentration camps. More than two million Poles had to perform forced labour for German companies.

The 'Special Criminal Law for Poland' took away all legal protection. There were draconian punishments for the slightest offence and the death penalty for 'anti-German statements'. Poland's private property could also be confiscated at any time. The German authorities requisitioned radio sets, cameras, binoculars, musical instruments and bicycles on a massive scale.

The two Nazi leaders Heinrich Himmler (left) and Hans Frank had the task of destroying occupied Poland both socially and economically.

The Germans closed all higher education institutions in Poland, the University of Krakow became a German university, and a few Polish professors were allowed to continue working there as assistants of German professors. In the eyes of SS leader Heinrich Himmler, the Poles were 'Slav subhumans'; he allowed only a four-class elementary school for them. Poland should be destroyed as a cultural nation. For this reason the occupying forces systematically transported art objects from museums and churches to Germany. Libraries and archives were destroyed.

At the same time, the Germans allowed the publication of Polish-language newspapers. They had to acclaim the Wehrmacht's successes and to praise the 'new order' in the General Government. Hitler ordered Frank 'to make the area a heap of rubble in its economic, social, cultural and political structure'.

At a secret police meeting in Krakow, Frank explained to his top officials and the higher SS officers in the General Government: 'The Polish leading class is to be liquidated.'[4] Frank ordered the AB action, AB stood for '*Ausserordentliche Befriedung*' (extraordinary pacification). Some 5,000 Polish intellectuals fell victim to it.

In the regions occupied by the Red Army, the Soviet administration had initially hardly appeared. Marauding gangs marched through the villages and hundreds of Polish landowners were brutally murdered, as were civil servants and police officers. It was only after the collapse of public order that Soviet officials took over the territories with a hard hand.

On 22 October 1939, five weeks after the invasion of the Red Army, elections were held in the occupied territories. The candidates were nominated by Soviet officials. Many criminals were added to the candidate lists and in this way the moral principles of the predominantly deeply religious population were deliberately mocked. Uniformed officers and soldiers of the Soviet secret police, NKVD, stood in the polling stations. All in all, more than 90 per cent of the votes went to the candidates who called for the occupied territories to join the Soviet Union.

On 1 November 1939, the Supreme Soviet in Moscow responded to requests for membership and declared all inhabitants of the territories Soviet citizens. As a result, the men were subject to military service. Anyone among the local Poles and Ukrainians who wanted to evade military service in the Red Army was sent to the Gulag or shot immediately as a deserter.

Soviet officials headed the administration; most of the former officials were arrested as representatives of 'fascist Poland'. The NKVD organised a network of street officials who had to spy on the private lives of the citizens.[5]

All churches and synagogues were closed, all priests who had not gone underground in time were arrested, Roman Catholic Poles as well as Greek Catholic (Uniate) and Orthodox Ukrainians were arrested; also the rabbis were subjected to cruel persecution. The NKVD murdered several hundred priests, and almost all of the survivors were sent

'Liberation of the brother peoples of Western Ukraine and Western Belarus': the stamp shows how enthusiastically the allegedly liberated inhabitants of the eastern regions of Poland read the Red Army leaflets. In reality, a time of terror began for the inhabitants of the region.

to the Gulag. The new Soviet authorities also declared all church organisations and associations as well as Talmud schools dissolved.[6] Even Polish sports clubs were now illegal, replaced by new Soviet clubs named Dynamo, Spartak or Tractorist.

Sovietisation of Eastern Poland

Polish was no longer the official language, it was replaced by Ukrainian and Russian. The authorities issued Soviet passports. Without a passport there was no work permit, no residence permit, no tickets.

'Class enemies' did not get a passport: businessmen, house and landowners, also '*kulaks*', farmers with their own farms. They were immediately expropriated. The majority of them were added to the deportation lists. The small farmers had to form *kolkhozes*, and those who resisted were arrested.[7] All companies were nationalised irrespective of their size. In this way millions of people became impoverished in a very short time, especially as the Soviet authorities also declared all savings assets state property.

Within a few weeks, Soviet officials ploughed over society as a whole. As during the Great Purges in the Soviet Union from 1936 to 1938, the NKVD demoralised the Polish and Ukrainian population through indiscriminate arrests.

According to historians, about a tenth of the population in Poland's eastern regions found themselves in completely overcrowded prisons. Executions without a court ruling were the order of the day. Many people tried to cross the green border into the General Government.

But the border line was guarded by military patrols with dogs and illuminated at night with spotlights. Anyone caught by the Soviet military attempting to escape risked being deported to a labour camp. German soldiers patrolled on the side of the General Government.

Gestapo and NKVD officers met regularly to regulate their cooperation. Both governments agreed not to tolerate any 'Polish agitation' directed against the other side. Several of these meetings took place in German-occupied Krakow and Zakopane and in Lwów (Lviv), controlled by the Soviets.[8] During boozy evenings the Gestapo and the NKVD officers toasted the 'Führer' and Stalin. A colonel of the NKVD was accredited to Governor General Frank in Krakow.[9]

It was long speculated whether the German and Soviet measures against the Polish elite were coordinated because the AB action in the General Government and the mass executions of Polish officers by the NKVD took place shortly after such a meeting in Zakopane in March 1940.

But Polish historians now rule out the possibility that both sides would have exchanged information about it. Rather, the files indicate that both sides continued to distrust each other. When People's Commissioner Molotov, whose delegation included deputy NKVD leader Vsevolod Merkulov, was received by Hitler at the Reich Chancellery in Berlin in November 1940, both sides had already started secret preparations for a German–Soviet war.[10]

The Soviets also saw deportations as an effective means of destroying Polish society. After four waves of arrests, almost one million inhabitants of the annexed areas had to make the arduous journey to Siberia, Kazakhstan and the mining areas on the Arctic Circle. Among them were 16-year-old Wojciech Jaruzelski, the future Polish head of state, and his parents. Among the deportees were also tens of thousands of Jews; the NKVD had targeted especially Zionists.[11]

The food supply during the transports, which often lasted several weeks, was miserable and completely inadequate; a total of about 100,000 of the deportees died on the involuntary journey to the east. Trains also ran in winter. A contemporary witness's report states:

> Frost, 35 to 40 degrees. People were brought here all night, then held in the wagons. A mother had a baby at the age of a few months. The child died in the unheated wagon. When the soldiers opened the door and gave the people some hot water, the woman threw the dead child right into the NKVD officer's face. The little stiff body fell between the tracks. The officer called two soldiers, they took the body, and that was it.[12]

At the destinations, the guards specifically tore families apart. Often the deportees had to build their own shelters, log cabins or burrows. Men had to do hard labour, children were sent to special camps where they were educated in the spirit of communism. The worship of Stalin was at the centre of the teaching programmes.

Adults also had to regularly attend meetings at which Poland was branded an exploiting state and the Catholic Church as an institution of idiots. The food was poor and there was usually no medical care. Life expectancy in the camp was less than one year.[13]

The Soviet authorities left the homes and houses of the deportees entirely to Russians, who until then had only made up a small fraction of the population in the annexed areas.[14] The metropolis of Lwów (Lviv) had never before been under Russian rule in its history. Russians also took over the management of the larger companies, as well as party cells, which were founded everywhere.

The news of the mass repressions also came to the attention of Western governments. Sir Owen O'Malley, British ambassador to the Polish government in exile, wrote in an analysis in diplomatic language:

> It is difficult to escape the conclusion that, even if the Soviet Government did not humiliate the Poles by treating them as an inferior race, as the Germans undoubtedly have done, the amount of human suffering inflicted by them on the Polish race was not less than that inflicted by Nazi Germany during the same period.[15]

Chapter 2

Caught in a Devastated Monastery

At the beginning of the Second World War Poland had mobilised almost one million soldiers, headed by 98 generals. These commanded 40,000 officers; just over half, 21,500, were reservists, the vast majority of whom had a university education. During the fighting in September and October 1939 almost 2,000 Polish officers were killed, among them four generals. Nearly 420,000 Polish soldiers, including 18,000 officers, were taken prisoner of war by the Germans.

The Red Army, which invaded Poland from the east, took 180,000 Polish prisoners. In the following weeks, the NKVD arrested another 60,000 Poles who had served in the armed forces but had returned to their homes in eastern Poland after the end of the fighting. Among them were about 10,000 officers, whom the Red Army handed over to the new Administration for Prisoners of War run by the NKVD.[1]

NKVD First Lieutenant Pyotr Soprunenko, responsible for the Polish prisoners of war, was ordered from Moscow to intern several groups of people in camps: officers, spies, state and military officials, police and gendarmes, provocateurs, secret police agents, active members of anti-Soviet parties and organisations, landowners, princes, professors, journalists, doctors, artists.[2]

International law did not allow for the subordination of prisoners of war to the authorities for 'internal security', as the NKVD was formally considered. However, the Soviet Union had not signed the 1929 Geneva POW Convention.

Of the 8,500 captured Polish officers, more than 6,000 of them were reservists, including 800 doctors, and were distributed to three NKVD camps: Kozelsk, Ostashkov and Starobelsk. In addition, there were 6,500 police and gendarmerie officers as well as officer cadets, and officials of the judicial service and the military administration. Tens of thousands of sergeants and soldiers – the exact number could not be determined – were deported to remote areas of the Soviet Union for forced labour, above all to the Arctic Circle, Siberia and Kazakhstan. The press informed the Soviet population that the Polish soldier or policeman was 'a brutish and merciless murderer'.[3]

Soprunenko proposed to the People's Commissioner for Internal Affairs, Stalin's Georgian compatriot Lavrentiy Beria, that all prisoners of war over 60 years old, as well as all invalids and seriously ill persons, be released.

But Beria did not respond to this proposal.[4] However, contrary to his original orders, three princes were released among the Polish officers. The British, Italian and Romanian governments, urged by their relatives and some celebrities, had fought independently for them. At the request of the Reich embassy in Moscow, 562 prisoners of war, who were ethnic Germans, were handed over to the Wehrmacht; the majority were sick, wounded and disabled.[5]

The Kozelsk camp, some 250 kilometres south-west of Moscow, was located in a monastery and its outbuildings that had been dissolved and looted by the Bolsheviks. In the first months of 1940, the number of Polish prisoners of war was around 4,500, more than two-thirds of whom were reservists, almost all of whom belonged to the intellectual elite. Among them were several dozen university professors and about 100 publicists and journalists.

Among the prisoners of Kozelsk were four generals, about 400 staff officers, 3,500 captains and lieutenants, and 500 cadets. In addition, there were about 60 top officials who were not members of the army.

The monastery grounds were surrounded by a two and a half metre high fence reinforced with barbed wire, patrolled at night by guards with dogs. Some of the shelters were heavily polluted, especially the sanitary facilities, as is even stated in an NKVD report. The prisoners also slept in the churches, chapels and vaults. A house in the grounds, in which the highest staff officers were quartered, was jokingly called 'Hotel Bristol' in allusion to a noble Warsaw hotel. In the lodgings for the mass of lower officers ranks were about twenty men per 25 square metres.

The medical care provided by the NKVD was miserable, but the camp commander allowed the Poles to organise themselves. Among them were fourteen medical professors and several hundred doctors. They performed operations under primitive conditions and without medication; they also set up a dental practice. Sickness levels, however, remained high.[6]

Secret masses and lectures on psychology
Among the prisoners were sixteen chaplains. Despite a strict ban, several of them regularly held services. The only woman in the camp, the pilot Janina Lewandowska, who was shot down during a reconnaissance flight, helped in their preparation. Separated from the men, she slept in a shed under the stairs in the 'Bristol'. She baked sacramental bread for the secret masses and also took part in religious discussion groups.[7]

Two handwritten newspapers appeared in the camp: *Merkury* with four issues and *Monitor* with fifteen. But the editors were denounced; they received twenty days of detention for 'propaganda of Polish patriotism'. The newspapers were confiscated and probably burned.[8]

In the oppressive climate of Kozelsk, spiritualism was booming, small groups met at night for spiritualist meetings. Above all, however, the quarrels among the

Military pilot Janina Lewandowska was the only woman among the Polish officers in Soviet captivity.

prisoners and nervous breakdowns increased. So a 52-year-old ensign of the reserve, in the civil profession of locksmith, hanged himself. He left no notes; his comrades found two photographs of his children in his jacket pocket.[9]

An almost equal group of Polish officers, 3,900, was deported to the Starobelsk camp not far from the large industrial zone of Lugansk in the east of the Ukrainian Soviet Republic. The camp was located in the grounds of a former nunnery surrounded by high walls. The main church had five-storey beds.[10] Among the prisoners of Starobelsk were eight generals and 380 staff officers.

Here, too, services were held secretly, not only Catholic, but also ecumenical, a completely new experience for many of the faithful. The Chief Rabbi of the Polish Armed Forces, Baruch Steinberg, was particularly committed. One of the few officers who survived the camp wrote later:

> The great and powerful need for common prayer was demonstrated by the participation of many prisoners of Mosaic, Protestant and Orthodox confessions in Catholic services. ... On some Friday evenings we went together to a shabby shed where hundreds of Jews under the guidance of their clergyman Dr. Steinberg prayed fervently.[11]

Ostashkov, the third NKVD camp for 'Polish public enemies', was located some 300 kilometres northwest of Moscow in a plundered monastery that stood on an island in a large lake. More than 5,000 policemen were interned there, including 300 officers, border guards, secret service personnel and prison staff. Here, too, the quarters were completely overcrowded with 1.5 square metres allocated per person.

One of the police officers had been arrested and deported with his 8-year-old son; the NKVD files do not reveal why the child was there. Father and son were separated when the camp was evacuated. An NKVD officer explained that there were thousands of orphans of enemies of the people in the Soviet Union, and that this was inevitable. The father was shot and the son survived the war.[12]

Common to all three camps was that there was not enough room to sleep; also, there were not enough cots, mattresses, straw sacks or blankets. Many prisoners had to lie down on the ground to rest, in some shelters they slept in shifts. Baths and laundries were either not available or mostly not ready for operation. On some days in January 1940 it was below 40 degrees; it was bitterly cold in the camps – the buildings were not heated.

The kitchens lacked the most basic equipment; there was a lack of bowls, plates and cups, and the water supply also functioned poorly. The prescribed amounts per person for food, which the NKVD had already estimated to be very low, were never reached. There were no fresh fruit and vegetables; many of the prisoners suffered from symptoms of vitamin deficiency.

The staff of the camps withheld some of the officially recorded food. In Kozelsk there was a strike because of the poor quality of the white cabbage soup. Two NKVD officers spooned up the soup to test it, and found that the standards had been met, even if the soup tasted bitter and smelled like fish. In their report to Soprunenko, they called the protests of the Poles an 'enemy demonstration'.[13]

Many of the reports to the NKVD headquarters in Moscow dealt with violations of camp discipline. There were fights, thefts in the kitchen, the spread of unspecified 'provocative rumours' and card games for money.[14] But the guards almost encouraged the prisoners to do so. Representatives of the state jewellery trade and black traders were allowed to the camp grounds; they bought watches or exchanged zloty for roubles.[15]

Once a month the prisoners were allowed to send letters to their families. The address they had to give was the 'Gorky Resort', the name of the village and a post office box: 12 for Kozelsk, 15 was Starobelsk and 37 Ostashkov. The mail was censored. According to the letters received from their wives, many of their relatives believed that the prisoners were doing really well.[16]

In all three camps, Polish officers organised language courses, Russian was particularly in demand, as well as evening lectures, during which the scientists among them reported on their areas of expertise, from literature and music to medicine and psychology; one topic was 'On the child's smile'. In Starobelsk, the painter and writer Józef Czapski, who had lived in Paris, spoke about French painting and literature.[17] Later, he became a key figure in the Katyn case.

However, the lectures of the political officers of the NKVD, the politruks, took up much more space. The programme included Soviet feature films on the construction of socialism or important Russian military leaders, propaganda films on the five-year plan, the literacy campaign in the Soviet Republic of Turkmenistan or lectures on the blessed work of the revolutionary leaders Lenin and Stalin. However, it did not escape the attention of the NKVD instructors that most Poles were not interested in this kind of political indoctrination and even used the propaganda brochures as toilet paper.[18]

Beria instructed the camp authorities to draw up detailed dossiers on each of the prisoners. Their political views should be explored as well as their position in the Polish elite and their contacts abroad. The aim was to divide them into groups: 'counterrevolutionaries' hostile to the Soviet Union, advocates of cooperation with the Soviet Union and those undecided, who could perhaps be drawn to the Soviet side.[19]

The NKVD interrogators were very thorough; some interviews lasted for three full days and each statement was recorded. Probably the majority of Poles did not understand the intention behind these interviews. Most of them were proud of their position in society and the military, and they did not keep their own political positions behind the scenes.

In Kozelsk, the group of interrogators was led by Major Vasily Zarubin. He did not introduce himself under his name, but was later identified by survivors in photographs. Zarubin had previously been an NKVD officer in Denmark, then deployed in Paris, where he controlled the infiltration of the Russian emigrant community and was involved in the kidnapping of a former Tsarist army general to Moscow. Under the false identity of a Czech businessman, he built up a network of informants in Berlin in the mid-1930s. Officially, he represented the US film production company Paramount in Berlin; the cover-up had got him a Russian emigrant in Hollywood who had been recruited by Soviet foreign espionage.[20]

In Berlin, Zarubin also survived the period of the Great Purges from 1936 to 1938, and in autumn 1939 he was part of the NKVD contingent that organised the Soviet terror in eastern Poland. But at that time Beria suspected him of being an agent of the Gestapo. On the website of the Russian foreign secret service, SVR, which sees itself in the tradition of GPU, NKVD and KGB, it is noted today that he came through the investigation 'with great dignity'.[21]

Vasily Zarubin decided in the Kozelsk camp which Polish officers were executed and which survived. Later he was deployed as a Soviet spy in the USA.

One of the survivors of Kozelsk, the economics professor Stanisław Swianiewicz, described Zarubin as an educated person with impeccable manners, he had behaved correctly towards the prisoners. In one-on-one conversations, he had dinner with the prisoners of interest to him; he even served oranges.[22] Zarubin brought about 500 books for the camp library, including many foreign-language works, for instance an original edition of Churchill's *The World Crisis*.

Asked about the future of Polish officers, Zarubin ambiguously declared: 'You would lose your mind if I told you. I assure you that would be inhuman. It's better if you don't know what we want to do with you.'[23]

In the Ostashkov camp, students of the NKVD Academy took part in the interrogations as part of their training.[24] In Starobelsk, the painter Czapski, who was cavalry captain of the reserve, had difficulty convincing his interrogators that he was not a foreign spy of the Polish government: the Soviet secret police officer asked him what government task he had had during his stay in Paris, for example, that of drawing up a sketch of a road network. Czapski explained to him that you could buy maps in any kiosk there – in the Soviet Union they had been declared secret material in campaigns against alleged enemy spies and had long since been removed from the sales offer.[25]

'The highest sentence: shooting'

The political balance of the interrogations in the camps was negative in the eyes of the NKVD leadership. The overwhelming majority of Poles saw the Soviet attack on their country in September 1939 as aggression. They criticised the alliance between Moscow and Hitler's Germany and hoped for help from the Western allies. They stressed their duty to their homeland and did not want to acknowledge the achievements of the communist regime. Some said they hoped for the rebirth of a Polish state that would extend from the Baltic Sea to the Black Sea.[26]

Only a few of the captured Poles spoke freely with the Politruks, were interested in the USSR and agreed to take part in a joint Polish–Russian fight against Hitler. This topic was already discussed in the NKVD camps at the beginning of 1940, although the Soviet Union and the German Reich were in actual fact still allies at that time.[27]

Soprunenko reported to Beria that his interrogators in Ostashkov had recruited 103 informers among the camp inmates. In Kozelsk they held recruitment talks with 32 of the prisoners, 20 of them reported about their own comrades.[28] They denounced an attempt to escape: three officers had got themselves civilian clothes and hoarded rusk; they were at the fence when the guard picked them up at the last moment. They were placed in solitary cells.[29]

The interviews by NKVD specialists also served to prepare criminal proceedings under Soviet law: Polish officers who were active in military defence or judicial officers who brought proceedings against communists were to be punished as enemies of the Soviet Union. The documents show, for example, that Polish police

The head of the secret service Lavrentiy Beria (left) and his deputy, Vsevolod Merkulov, organised the executions of Polish officers.

officers involved in actions against the 'revolutionary movement' in Poland in the years before the war were convicted under the Criminal Code of the RSFSR, the Russian Socialist Federal Soviet Republic.[30]

Beria's deputy, Vsevolod Merkulov, ordered Soprunenko to prepare the transfer of about 400 'counterrevolutionaries' among the inmates of the three camps to remand prisons for further trials: prison guards, spies, provocateurs, judicial officers, landowners, merchants and large landowners.[31] These 400 prisoners were deplored by their comrades because NKVD prisons were feared as torture rooms.

Based on Soprunenko's reports, Beria estimated the chances of recruiting the captured Polish officers to the Soviet Union as extremely slim. Instead, the NKVD interrogators had consistently attested to their hostile attitude towards the Soviet Union. In addition, news came from the Polish government in exile, which at the time resided in Paris: the Polish prime minister and commander-in-chief, General Sikorski, had announced that he would send a brigade of his soldiers to the Finnish–Soviet Winter War to fight against the Red Army. Ultimately, this did not happen because both sides concluded a truce.[32]

On 5 March 1940 Beria submitted to the Politburo a four-page draft for a secret order to the NKVD on how to deal with the Polish enemies. He named two groups under the control of the NKVD: 14,736 persons in the camps and 10,685 political prisoners in the prisons of 'the western districts of Belarus and Ukraine', i.e. the former eastern Polish territories annexed by the Soviet Union.

First Beria gave an assessment of the situation: 'The POW officers and policemen in the camps try to continue their counterrevolutionary activities, they engage in anti-Soviet agitation. Each of them is just waiting for release to take an active part in the fight against the Soviet power.'

In the letter he listed Polish prisoners by rank, occupation and political opinion. Among the camp inmates were listed 144 'civil servants, landowners, priests and new settlers'. Among the prison inmates the NKVD had identified 347 'spies and miscellaneous' and 5,345 'members of c-r organisations' – 'c-r' meant 'counterrevolutionary' and included every kind of critical attitude towards Stalin's system. Beria proposed an 'inescapable' measure for these 'persistent, incorrigible enemies of the Soviet power', the number of which he rounded up to 14,700 and 11,000: 'the application of the highest sentence – execution'.

Beria explained that there was no provision for the defendants to participate in the trials: the judgements on the individual prisoners should be taken 'without summoning those arrested and without reading out the accusations, without establishing the conclusion of the investigations and without a final verdict of guilt'. In other words: without any proceedings, without defence, without legal protection.

The members of the Politburo confirmed their agreement by signing across the first page of Beria's paper: J. Stalin, K. Voroshilov, V. Molotov and A. Mikoyan. In block letters were also written on the edge of the sheet: Kalinin – for it, Kaganovich – for it. Apparently they had given their consent by telephone. Thus the death sentence had been passed on 25,700 Polish citizens, most of whom belonged to the educated elite.

Like Stalin, the five co-signatories had great experience with the physical liquidation of political opponents: Kliment Voroshilov had ordered mass executions in the Russian Civil War; as People's Commissioner for Defence he signed the death lists with the names of 142 commanders during the bloody cleansing in the Red Army.

In the early 1930s, Vyyacheslav Molotov, as head of government, was responsible for implementing collectivisation in agriculture, sending hundreds of thousands of landowners (*kulaks*) to the Gulag. The resistance, especially in the Ukraine, was broken by an organised famine with several million deaths. During the Great Purges he co-signed at least 342 death lists, each with 100 names.

Lazar Kaganovich was also responsible for suppressing resistance to collectivisation in Ukraine and the Northern Caucasus. He ordered thousands shot; during the Great Purges he signed at least 189 death lists, thus sealing the execution of some 19,000 'enemies of the people'.

Anastas Mikoyan also placed his name on NKVD death lists; together with Beria he carried out purges in his home country, Armenia, killing thousands of his compatriots and deporting tens of thousands to Central Asia or Siberia. Mikhail Kalinin also signed many of these lists as well as decrees that allowed the NKVD the mass terror.

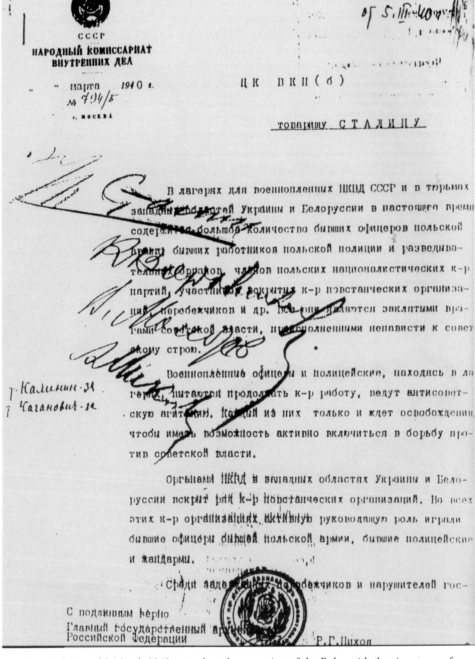

Beria's letter of 5 March 1940 regarding the execution of the Poles with the signatures of Stalin and other members of the Politburo was kept secret until 1992.

On 5 March 1940, the Politburo confirmed the 'Decision No. 144', according to which 25,700 Poles were to be shot. Beria's deputy, Vsevolod Merkulov, was commissioned with the implementation of this secret order.

The son of an officer of the Tsar's army, he had belonged to the Soviet secret police for almost two decades and had participated in countless murders. Beria had personally taught him lessons in torture, and under his supervision Merkulov quickly learned to torture prisoners physically and mentally. He supervised Laboratory X near Moscow, where human experiments with poison injections were carried out. He had an unusual hobby: he wrote two plays under a pseudonym, which were also performed. In addition, he distinguished himself as an author of eulogies praising Stalin and Beria. For the latter he also wrote the speeches.[33]

Only two days after the execution order, Beria signed an order for the 'ten-year banishment' of relatives of the 25,700 Poles sentenced to death without their knowledge. From mid-April 1940, around 60,000 women, children, siblings and parents were deported to the Kazakh steppe, where no accommodation was prepared for them.

Most of them initially lived in simple huts, tents or burrows. Thousands did not survive the first winter with temperatures up to 45 degrees frost. Their homes in the territories annexed by the Soviet Union were formally expropriated and given to well-deserved Red Armists and members of the Communist Party.[34]

Chapter 3

Journey to Death

Vsevolod Merkulov ordered the commanders of the three camps to prepare the 'removal of the POWs in accordance with the issued sentences'. The camp inmates were to be given the impression that their release to their hometowns was imminent. NKVD officers specifically hinted at this in order to calm the prisoners in view of the preparations for the evacuation of the camps: Poland should become a strong country again; together they wanted to destroy German fascism. In mid-March, the captured Poles were no longer allowed to send letters on the grounds that the distribution to transit camps on their way home was not regulated.[1]

The camp commanders had to prepare lists with 250 names each for the transport. This was the specified group size for travel by train. The trains were provided by the People's Commissariat for Transport, headed by the experienced deportation organiser Kaganovich. However, several Polish officers from Jewish families whose places of origin were in the General Government applied to remain in the Soviet Union. Most of these requests were, however, ignored.

Some of the guards also spread the idea that the Poles should emigrate to neutral third countries. Hardly anyone among the prisoners imagined that it would be a journey to death, nor was it a topic of conversation. Two of the Polish officers overheard the conversation between NKVD people: 'If they knew where they were being taken, they would probably not laugh so much.' The two Poles concluded that their guards were convinced that the prisoners were better off with them than in a German camp.

As there was great uncertainty about the destinations of the transport, the Polish officers agreed before departure to leave clues about the route in the wagons. Although these were cleaned each time, some of the scribbles were preserved. These were prison cars with ten cells for originally six people each. However, during the transportation, which lasted at least two days, up to twenty people were crammed into one cell. There was usually nothing to eat.[2]

The destinations of the transports from the camps Ostashkov and Starobelsk became known only half a century later: the army officers, policemen, gendarmes, border guards and judicial officers interned in Ostashkov travelled 180 kilometres east to the city of Kalinin (today: Tver), named after one of the signatories of Beria's murder plan. The officers from Starobelsk were brought about 250 kilometres to the northwest to Kharkov in Eastern Ukraine, a centre of the Soviet armaments industry.

In the case of the Kozelsk camp, however, there was one witness: the captain of the reserve Stanisław Swianiewicz, who was a professor of economics in the civil profession. The destination of the trains from Kozelsk was Gnezdovo station about ten kilometres west of Smolensk. The linear distance of the two places was 250 kilometres, but the railway line made a wide bend, so that the distance was 450 kilometres. The journey was repeatedly interrupted for hours in order to give priority to regular or military transport.

When Swianiewicz looked through a ventilation hole after a day and a half's drive, he recognised the domes of the Russian Orthodox Cathedral of Smolensk. He knew the city; he

The Polish officers from the Kozelsk camp were taken to a remote siding at the Gnezdovo railway station, which is on the Moscow–Berlin long-distance line.

had visited it repeatedly during the time of the tsarist empire. Half an hour after arriving in Gnezdovo, an NKVD colonel arrived, tall and 'with the red-blue face of a butcher', as Swianiewicz wrote in his memoirs. The colonel exclaimed his name and told him that he could not continue on the journey, that he was destined for transport in another direction. The professor was taken back to an already empty car.

Through the ventilation hole he could observe the further events at the railway station: a cordon of NKVD soldiers with bayonets had surrounded the train. A small bus with white painted windows drove backwards to a train coach. Through the door in the back of the bus, thirty people entered, then it continued across the road into the forest. After half an hour the bus came back empty, the next group of thirty men got on it. However, Swianiewicz did not imagine that his countrymen went to the forest for their execution.

A little later came a 'black raven', as the windowless vans of the NKVD were called, to pick up Swianiewicz. The NKVD guards explained to him that his

The professor of economics Stanisław Swianiewicz became one of the most important witnesses for the version of the Soviet perpetration in Katyn.

comrades were lucky: 'They will be sent to their families.' The driver locked him in one of the six cells of the car and brought him back to Smolensk, where he was the only prisoner in the cell wing. After one week he was transferred to Lubyanka, the NKVD headquarters in Moscow.[3]

The NKVD experts were interested in his study, published shortly before the war, on the economic policy of the Third Reich with special consideration of the arms industry. Since Swianiewicz refused to cooperate with the NKVD, he was sentenced to eight years in prison as a spy under Soviet criminal law.[4]

At the Gnezdovo railway station, some trains stood for more than twenty hours until all Polish prisoners of war were unloaded. The bus with the whitewashed windows made its tour between the platform and the forest up to ten times a day for four weeks, as later Russian residents reported.[5]

The Polish Major Adam Solski, who kept a diary during the imprisonment, secretly noted on 9 April 1940, immediately after leaving the bus:

> The day began at dawn in a very peculiar way. Ride with the prison car in cells (horrible), we were brought somewhere into the forest, a kind of holiday home. Intensive body search. They took the watch that indicated 6.30/8.30, asked for the wedding ring that was taken, as well as roubles, belt, pocket knife.[6]

Probably a few minutes after this entry Solski was dead. The NKVD men who shot him and his companions near a small elevation called 'Goat Hills' were not interested in his notes; they were found three years later during the exhumation of his body. Since then they have been regarded as important evidence in clarifying the question of the date of death and the perpetrators.

NKVD soldiers apparently led the Polish officers individually to the edge of a mass grave and shot them there. Quite a few tried to resist in the last moments of their lives: about one in five went to their deaths tied up, and in many cases their uniform coat was pulled over their heads and tied up. The NKVD guards also struck the victims with rifle butts and stabbed them with their bayonets.[7]

Killing like on a conveyor belt

There are no eyewitness accounts of the mass murder a few steps away from the Dnieper and a training and holiday home of the NKVD, the so-called Dnieper Manor. But not all the prisoners who came by train from Kozelsk died in the forest.

A small group was taken to the NKVD headquarters in Smolensk and shot in the basement, including the military chaplains. There were eleven Roman Catholics, one Orthodox and one Ukrainian-Uniate priest, one Protestant pastor and one rabbi; two others could not be identified later.[8] On the mass graves, gardeners planted two-year-old pines as a camouflage, which were brought in by a tree nursery.

There are three eyewitness accounts of the murder of the Poles in the Smolensk cellars. In the early 1990s, the retired NKVD prison guard Pyotr Klimov told an investigator how the liquidation of alleged enemies of the people took place:

> In the small basement room there was a trap door above the drain shaft. A victim was introduced, the trap door opened, his head placed on the edge of the opening, then they shot him in the back of the head or in the temple (each according to his taste). ... They shot almost every day, in the evening they made it to the Goat Hills, and came back around two o'clock at night. The dead from the cellar were laid in a row, face down in the mass graves, while the others remained lying as they had fallen down.

Klimov had to wipe the blood from the weapons and wash it off the floor after every execution. The executions were led by the commander of Smolensk prison, NKVD Lieutenant Ivan Stelmakh, who had already worked for the secret police since the Bolshevik seizure of power and was involved in countless executions.

In the files it is documented that 7,931 'enemies of the people' were shot in the Smolensk district between 1928 and 1939 with Stelmakh's participation. An official evaluation attested him of the highest suitability for this activity: 'Little educated, politically illiterate, but devoted to the matter without limits.' Half a century later, NKVD soldier Kirill Borodenkov, one of his subordinates, confessed: 'Not everyone could cope with a matter like shooting people. But he did it with pleasure.'[9]

According to the report of prison guard Klimov, a Polish officer snatched the gun from one of the two NKVD soldiers who were to take him to the soundproofed execution room and shot the other. Then he barricaded himself in the basement. Klimov was an eyewitness: 'They couldn't kill him for three days, they even brought water into the cellar with the fire hose. But then they poisoned him with gas.'[10]

Even in the case of the mass murders of the inmates of the camps of Ostashkov and Starobelsk, eyewitnesses could be found half a century later: Dmitry Tokarev was chief of the NKVD in Kalinin district in 1940, Chief Sergeant Mitrofan

Syromiatnikov was supervisor in the NKVD remand prison in Kharkov. After the collapse of the Soviet Union and the fall of the party regime, both were questioned for many hours as witnesses, and the talks were recorded by a video camera.

Syromiatnikov was ordered to dig a total of fifteen pits with half a dozen NKVD men not far from an NKVD villa settlement in the Kharkov suburb of Pyatikhatki. They were supposed to be big enough for a truck to drive backwards. When the Polish prisoners arrived from the Starobelsk camp, his people first had to lock them in cells in the NKVD prison in Kharkov. A feint was supposed to lull the suspicious Poles to feel safe: they had to hand in their luggage and their roubles, but received a receipt, allegedly for the purpose of later reimbursement. Syromiatnikov then had them led upstairs in small groups of five to six men. There the completely surprised men had their hands bound together.

The veteran NKVD man further reported:

> They are led to the corridor. There I stand in the doorway. I open the door, 'May we come in?' From there the answer: 'Come in!' At the table is the prosecutor, next to him the NKVD commander. They ask: 'Surname, father's name, year of birth?' After that, you're free to go. Then suddenly: 'Pook!' – and it was over. The Commander shouted: 'Hello!' That meant taking the body away. So I went and got it. You had to tie something around their heads so they wouldn't bleed.

The former prison guard said laconically that he and the other NKVD people had worked 'like on a conveyor belt'. The dead, among them infantry captain Jakub Wajda, father of the film director Andrzej Wajda, were first deposited in a cellar room in order to take them to Pyatikhatki later that night. According to Syromiatnikov, victims of the SS task forces were buried there during the German occupation and after the war 'traitors', Soviet citizens who had collaborated with the Germans.[11] The location of the mass graves, which after the incorporation of the suburb were now located on the urban area of Kharkov, became known only in 1990.

The relatives of the disappeared inmates of the Ostashkov camp did not find out until half a century later about the mass graves in the NKVD holiday settlement, Mednoye, near Kalinin. In this case, too, the prison wing of the NKVD district administration was the scene of the crime; today, the medical institute of Tver is located there. The city got its historical name back in 1990, even before the public learned that Mikhail Kalinin, after whom it was named in the Stalin era, was one of the signatories of the execution order for the Poles.

Tokarev, the informative witness, was a major of the state security, which corresponded to the rank of a colonel in the military. He was not involved as a gunman in the executions, which took place in Kalinin for a whole month. But he

Dmitry Tokarev (left) organised the mass shootings of Kalinin. Vasily Blokhin executed them.

had to organise the transportation of the Poles and the removal of the bodies. Altogether he put thirty local NKVD men to work.

The executions were carried out by three NKVD officers, the highest of whom was Major Vasily Blokhin, who had already received several medals of merit. He was the first executioner of the NKVD headquarters; he participated as an expert in experiments with poisoned bullets that Merkulov had carried out.[12] For almost a decade, the major had commanded an execution squad with a permanent tribe of half a dozen men.

The command shot Marshal Mikhail Tukhachevsky and other military leaders during the purges in the Red Army. Blokhin personally killed the celebrated theatre director Vsevolod Meyerhold and the popular writer Isaac Babel.[13] The executions of both took place within a few days at the end of January and the beginning of February 1940 in the cellars of Lubyanka.

Two months later Blokhin and his two aides travelled to Kalinin with the order to carry out the execution order of 5 March 1940 for the Polish prisoners of the Ostashkov camp. The trio also lived in the saloon car; it stopped on a siding at the main station for five weeks. The local NKVD commander, Tokarev, learned that this was part of a major action against a total of 14,000 'counterrevolutionary Poles'. His people had to line the death cells with soundproofing material.

The prisoners, who had already been tied up, were first taken by a public prosecutor to the 'red room', where pictures, flags and wall newspapers announced the fame of the revolution leaders Lenin and Stalin. One of the Poles tried to save himself at the last moment: he revealed that he had sewn gold coins into his belt. In fact, about twenty-five to thirty gold roubles from the Tsarist period came to light.

The prosecutor took the valuable find. But the Polish prisoner, like everyone else before and after him, was led across the corridor to the death cell, where Blokhin stood behind the door and immediately pulled the trigger.

Tokarev described how the major from Moscow prepared himself for the executions: 'Blokhin put on his special clothes: a brown leather cap, a long brown leather apron, brown leather gloves with cuffs over his elbows. I was struck by this – I was faced with a hangman!'

Blokhin did not work with the failure-prone Soviet army pistols, but preferred German workmanship: he had brought a whole suitcase full of German Walther pistols with him. He had to change weapons several times in one shift, because they became too hot and threatened to fail to work. In the beginning he shot 300 men per night; after a while, he ordered the number of Poles brought daily from the Ostashkov camp to be reduced to 250.[14]

After each shift, the NKVD soldiers who had to remove the bodies received a box of vodka donated by him. Decades later, one of them said:

> Of course we drank vodka to a point of unconsciousness. After all, the work wasn't the easiest. We were so tired, we were barely on our feet. And we washed ourselves with perfume. To the belt. It was the only way to get rid of the smell of blood and decay. Even the dogs flinched away from us. And when they barked at us, it was from a distance.[15]

Orders and special rations

Blokhin had an excavator requisitioned for digging the mass graves not far from the holiday settlement of Mednoye. He brought the two excavator operators, who worked in shifts, with him from Moscow. They dug twenty-five mass graves and covered them with earth again. When the order was completed after one month, he invited everyone involved to a banquet in his saloon car. Among them were women who had done the paperwork.[16]

Also in the forest of Katyn, not far from the mass graves, dachas were built for the families of senior intelligence officers. Its inhabitants were strictly forbidden to dig the ground outside their own garden. With each snowmelt, however, soil was cleared away in the forest, so that bones came to light again and again. For this reason, new earth had to be brought in regularly by truck.[17]

Wood was also cut there for the steam baths not only of the dachas, but also of the nearby Dnieper Manor. Party VIPs from Moscow, including Kaganovich and Voroshilov, also came there on short holidays.[18]

In Pyatikhatki near Kharkov, new dachas were even built right next to the mass graves.[19] The construction of holiday homes and settlements of the NKVD in the immediate surroundings of the secret cemeteries made sense. Usually the NKVD lands were surrounded by fences and strictly guarded – outsiders had no access. The NKVD men were subject to the strictest secrecy regulations, whereby their women and children were under no circumstances allowed to find out about their official duties. Moreover, a strong corps spirit reigned among them, which did not tolerate any dissenters, who were denounced and liquidated.

Apparently NKVD men, who regarded the killing of enemies of the people as a necessary service for the state, did not find it a burden to spend their free time with barbecues and song recitals right next to the graves of their victims disguised by planting. The calculation worked: in Soviet times, none of those directly involved in the massacres ever broke this pact of silence.

The number of the Poles in the mass graves of Katyn could not be accurately determined: Polish historians put it at 4,407; the human rights organisation 'Memorial' at 4,415; according to a document of the KGB leadership it was 4,416.

In Kalinin and Kharkov the experts faced the same problem. Here, also, the pits were partly not sufficiently covered with soil, so that animals could pull bones from the ground and carry them away. Therefore, the historians have to estimate the figures: about 4,000 from the Starobelsk officers' camp in the fifteen mass graves of Kharkov-Pyatikhatki and 6,300 from the camp for police, gendarmes and judicial officers in Ostashkov in the 25 graves of Mednoye near Kalinin (Tver).

The total amount of the murdered from the three camps is thus around 14,700, as Beria had also stated. Among them were 35 chaplains, 11 generals, 1 admiral, more than 700 staff officers, almost 1,450 captains, and over 6,000 lieutenants and ensigns.[20] Most of them were reservists. Among the dead were about 800 physicians, several dozen professors of medicine, about 300 engineers, the majority of them experts of the Polish armaments industry, and 200 lawyers. Several hundred university teachers from other disciplines were also among them.[21] Up to 900 of them – the exact number could not be determined – were Jews. Among them was the chief rabbi of the armed forces, Major Baruch Steinberg; he had been taken from Starobelsk to Moscow for interrogation and then brought to the Kozelsk camp.[22]

Among the victims were some prominent sportsmen. Two of them had won Olympic medals: Captain Zdzisław Kawecki Silver with the team of eventers in Berlin 1936, Lieutenant of the Reserve Stanisław Urban Bronze in the rower with helmsman in Los Angeles 1932. A total of eight Polish Olympic athletes fell victim to NKVD firing squads in the spring of 1940. Among Katyn's dead were two former national soccer players: Reserve Lieutenant Marian Spojda, who in the pre-war years had supervised the Polish selection as assistant coach, and Captain Adam Kogut, who was the most successful scorer of the first Polish football champions Cracovia.

Beria was extremely satisfied with the course of the liquidation of the 'Polish counterrevolutionaries'. Merkulov, who led the entire action, received the Lenin Order, the highest award of the Soviet Union. On 26 October 1940, Beria signed a secret decree on the reward of the NKVD units involved. Forty-four received a special payment of 800 roubles, at that time the considerable sum of about $160. Among the beneficiaries was Blokhin, who shot the majority of the 6,300 victims of Kalinin personally. A total of 125 NKVDists benefited from premiums or even promotions, including four women.[23] There were also special rations of vodka, sausage, smoked fish and other delicacies.[24]

Presumably, the members of the NKVD commands also shared the property of the Poles among themselves: watches, money and other valuables. Eyewitnesses have observed that the luggage of the shot, mostly backpacks, was taken away on trucks. The documents do not give any information about their whereabouts.[25]

However, by no means all inmates of the three camps had fallen victim to the mass executions in the spring of 1940. In each of them, the NKVD officers had proposed several dozen POWs for further questioning. Moscow hoped to obtain useful information from them or they were possible candidates for the establishment of Polish military units under Soviet supreme command. However, they did not learn that they were isolated; they were not aware that the others were going to their deaths.

The survivors accounted for 3 per cent of the total number of Poles interned in the three camps. Most of them, a total of 394 men, found themselves in the Gryazovets camp 425 kilometres northeast of Moscow, also set up in a devastated monastery. Among them was the painter and writer Józef Czapski, for whom a German friend had campaigned via Berlin.

The NKVD sent fifteen interrogators to Gryazovets to search for Polish intelligence officers and German agents. However, they came to the conclusion that most Polish officers refused to cooperate with the NKVD and still wanted to fight for the independence of their country. After all, the NKVD had been able to recruit about 30 of the 394 informants.[26]

In October 1940, seven Polish officers who were considered pro-Soviet were brought to Moscow. There they met another group of twenty-one people from the refilled Kozelsk camp. The Poles were first distributed to Lubyanka and Butyrki Prison, where they were interrogated again, this time under the leadership of Merkulov.[27]

After days of intensive questioning, Beria personally received a small group of them, one of them was Lieutenant Colonel Zygmunt Berling. He had been dishonourably dismissed from the armed forces a few weeks before the war for embezzlement of funds and a scandal about extramarital relations, but had been recalled after the German attack.

The head of the NKVD wanted to find out what the internees thought about setting up Polish units under the Soviet command. When Berling declared that he could propose many suitable comrades from the Kozelsk and Starobelsk camps, Merkulov replied: 'They are already out of the question. We made a mistake with them, a mistake.'

So, at least one of the Polish officers present was recorded later. Merkulov is said to have made similar remarks on another occasion. But the participants in the meeting did not attach special importance to these remarks, because Beria added: 'We gave them to the Germans.'[28] Indeed, an extensive exchange of Polish prisoners with the German Reich had taken place.

Several days after the meeting, a dozen Polish officers were allowed to move into a villa in the Moscow suburb of Malakhovka. The composition of the group changed several times: some had to return to prison and new ones were added. They were now intensively attuned to the fight against the Germans under Soviet supreme command and ideologically trained. Accommodation and food were excellent, and there was also plenty of alcohol.

The Poles called the accommodation the 'Villa of Happiness'. However, it turned out that the majority did not meet the expectations of the NKVD at all: only a small group confessed their full loyalty to the Soviet Union. Among them was Zygmunt Berling, previously a prisoner in Starobelsk. He worked for the NKVD from then on.[29]

Chapter 4

Futile Search for the Missing Officers

Operation Barbarossa changed the political situation in Europe: on 22 June 1941 the Third Reich attacked the Soviet Union. The Wehrmacht moved into the eastern Polish territories annexed by the Soviet Union on a broad front. The NKVD officials, who had led a terror regime there for twenty-one months, fled in panic to the east. Before their withdrawal, they shot without any trial Polish and Ukrainian detainees; the number of victims went into the thousands. Moscow denied the crimes when the German press reported them.[1]

Within a few days the Wehrmacht achieved enormous territorial gains, hundreds of thousands of Red Army soldiers were taken captive by the Germans, most of whom were not supposed to survive: they died of starvation in the camps. Moscow had now joined forces with the British. Just two years earlier, in the summer of 1939, Stalin was not interested in this alliance, which would probably have prevented the war. Instead, he attacked Poland, Britain's ally, together with Hitler. But in the summer of 1941, Stalin had no choice. He needed military help from the British. The British immediately began supplying military equipment through their Middle East mandated territories.

Prime Minister Winston Churchill now urged a political settlement of the serious conflict between the Polish government in exile and Stalin's regime, which had previously regarded each other as enemies. Foreign Minister Anthony Eden proposed to moderate negotiations between Sikorski and the Soviet Ambassador in London, Ivan Maisky. Sikorski initially argued that for him as head of government an ambassador was not the appropriate negotiating partner, but Eden prevailed. Sikorski appeared for the first meeting in parade uniform and was visibly irritated that Maisky wore a light summer suit.[2] The negotiations were chaired by British Secretary of State Alexander Cadogan, who was well informed about the brutality of the Soviet regime. Cadogan later played his part in the controversies concerning the mass murder of Katyn.

At the beginning the political differences were enormous. The only indisputable point was the resumption of diplomatic relations. Initially, Sikorski insisted that the pre-war restoration of Poland's eastern border be included in the treaty, but Maisky blocked this on Moscow's orders. The solution of the border issue was therefore been postponed until later.

Sikorski called for the immediate return of several hundreds of thousands of deportees from the camps and places of banishment in the depths of the Soviet Union, including some 200,000 captive officers and soldiers. Maisky claimed it was only 20,000, but Sikorski cited articles in the Soviet press from the fall of 1939 that spoke of 190,000 POWs, including 10,000 officers.[3]

After consultation with Moscow, Maisky held out the prospect of an amnesty and proposed the formation of Polish forces on the territory of the USSR. Sikorski initially rejected an amnesty, as this presupposed criminal acts; instead, the sentences against Polish prisoners and deportees would have to be lifted as unlawful. But he finally gave in on this point as well.

Both sides finally agreed in the Sikorski–Maisky Agreement, as the press henceforth called it, on the release of Polish prisoners and deportees and on a joint struggle against the German Reich. Churchill and Eden were present at the signing of the contract. Moscow propaganda no longer attacked the Poles, but again, as before 1939, the Germans were called 'fascists'.

Two weeks later, a military agreement was concluded in Moscow that regulated the framework conditions: a Polish general was to head it, but under Soviet supreme command. The Polish units should also include inhabitants of areas annexed by the Soviet Union who had already been drafted into the Red Army. The British were supposed to provide the equipment over the Middle East.

However, the two agreements led to the resignation of several ministers of the government in exile. They accused Sikorski of not resolving the border issue. It was also completely unacceptable for the Polish military to be placed under Soviet command, given that the Red Army had stabbed the Poles in the back in September 1939 and established a reign of terror in eastern Poland. But Sikorski prevailed. For him, the return of hundreds of thousands of compatriots from Soviet captivity was a priority, and he hoped to be able to settle border and status issues later.[4]

Both sides agreed that the Polish brigadier general detained in Moscow, Władysław Anders, should take command of the units to be set up. Anders, who owed his family name to German–Baltic ancestors and was a Protestant, had served as an officer in the Russian Imperial Cavalry during the First World War; he spoke excellent Russian.

In September 1939 he had been captured by the Soviets; he had a bullet in one leg and could barely walk. He was taken to Moscow, where the NKVD tried to persuade him to join the Red Army. Since he refused, he was tortured so badly that he could no longer stand and walk, his gunshot wound remained untreated and worsened. Looking back, Anders wrote: 'The prison conditions were unusually harsh, my face was constantly exposed to bright lighting. My eyes were completely faded, I feared going blind.'[5]

A few days after the Sikorski–Maisky agreement, the prison guards took him out of his cell. To his surprise, he was not dragged for another interrogation, but was given crutches, and two guards supported him as he walked. The tall and strong general, formerly well trained, was emaciated, his weight dropping from 90 to 59 kilograms in prison. He was taken to a room where Beria was waiting for him. The latter informed him of his appointment as commander-in-chief of the Polish armed forces in the USSR.

The warden then paid him compensation for his personal valuables, which had been requisitioned at the beginning of his detention, and carried his suitcase to a black limousine. 'I left the prison without stockings, in a bare shirt and in long underpants with the stamp "Inner prison of the NKVD", but in the official car of the NKVD boss', he wrote in his memoirs.[6]

The Polish general learned that the location of his appointment was to be the small town of Buzuluk in the southern Russian steppe, more than 1,200 kilometres southeast of Moscow. The Soviet government promised to provide Poland with a loan of 300 million roubles to build up its new army, at the then official rate of around $60 million.[7] The reopened Polish embassy in Moscow received permission to set up twenty collection points for the Poles to be released from the camps and prisons.

The history professor Stanisław Kot was appointed Polish ambassador in Moscow; however, he spoke Russian only poorly. Together with all other foreign diplomats he had to leave the city in October 1941 because of the advance of the Wehrmacht. The Soviet Foreign Ministry was temporarily established in Kuibyshev on the Volga, which today again bears its former name, Samara. This was favourable for the Poles, as the distance between Kuibyshev and Buzuluk is only about 200 kilometres.

Poles who had been able to leave the labour camps arrived there almost daily, starving and ragged. From the Gulag in Kolyma in the northeast corner of Siberia came 160; a large number had lost fingers or toes in the hard winter and most suffered from scurvy. According to estimates by the Polish embassy, around 10,000 people had been deported to the Kolyma area.[8]

With the amnesty announced by Moscow for the Poles, the NKVD camp Gryazovets in northern Russia formally became a base of the new Polish army. Anders arrived there at the end of August 1941. He limped hard and walked with a cane, surrounded by 'smiling NKVD officers'.[9]

Anders informed his compatriots about the agreement between Moscow and the government in exile; most heard of its existence for the first time. At that time there were 448 Polish officers in Gryazovets, most of them from the Kozelsk, Ostashkov and Starobelsk camps. In small groups they could travel to Buzuluk. After a few weeks, a troop of 25,000 men stood there, which was now briefly called the Anders Army.[10]

However, the economics professor Stanisław Swianiewicz, who had observed the removal of his companions from a railway wagon into Katyn Forest in April 1940, was not among them. He had been sentenced to forced labour for espionage in the Komi region of Northern Siberia. Since Ambassador Kot was informed and even Sikorski put the Swianiewicz case on the agenda of talks with the Soviet leadership, he was released a few months later.

NKVD informers in the Polish army

Soon it turned out that only a fraction of the officers who were known to be in Soviet captivity had arrived. General Anders had expected about 9,000. The cavalry captain Józef Czapski, who was imprisoned in Starobelsk, was given the task of researching who was missing. The painter and writer, who spoke Russian very well, had great experience with such tasks: after the First World War, he had already searched in Soviet Russia for a group of Polish officers who had disappeared there. He could actually find out where they had gone: they had perished in a prison of the new Bolshevik rulers, it was officially confirmed to him. Czapski made the inmates of the three camps who had come to Buzuluk compile lists with the names of their fellow prisoners.

The Anders Army was also joined by the officers Merkulov wanted to recruit for the NKVD in a villa in Malakhovka near Moscow in autumn 1940. There, several of them, including Lieutenant Colonel Zygmunt Berling, had written a request to join the Red Army as simple soldiers in the fight against the Wehrmacht. The letter ended with the words: 'Long live Stalin, the ingenious leader of the working people and the oppressed peoples!'[11]

But Stalin did not accept this offer: he wanted to retain control of the Anders Army, therefore the officers recruited by the NKVD went to Buzuluk. There, however, some of their comrades viewed them with great suspicion. General Anders did not share these concerns, at least with Berling: he appointed him chief of staff of one of the newly established divisions.[12]

Just five weeks after taking up his post, Anders was faced with his first major task: the Soviet High Command wanted to throw the Poles into the fight against the Wehrmacht in October 1941. The general had no doubt that the chances of survival of his ill-equipped men, some of whom were still very weak physically, would be extremely low, so he categorically rejected this suggestion. He could count on the support of the British military attaché in Moscow, General Noel Mason-MacFarlane, whom Anders described as 'unusually warm and energetic'.[13]

At the end of November, Sikorski arrived in Kuibyshev for consultations with Soviet government representatives via Tehran. He then came to Buzuluk to inspect the Polish garrison. He was accompanied by Deputy Foreign Minister Andrey Vyshinsky, representing the Soviet government. Before the war, Vyshinsky had been Prosecutor General of the USSR; during the Great Purges, he had drawn up the scenarios for the show trials, he insulted the accused former party leaders, calling them 'rabid dogs, whimpering mutts, fools and snake brood'.

Sikorski and Vyshinsky jointly held the parade of Polish troops. One of the participants later described the scene:

> The soldiers started the inspection in the clothes they had. They wore mainly old, worn-out and chafed army coats, some peasant coats, furs and cotton-wool jackets, beggar rags, at their feet they had shredded boots whose soles were tied with string, or they wore no shoes at all, instead they had cloths wrapped around their feet.[14]

After the parade the officers were invited to the buffet. Previously, NKVD specialists had searched the room thoroughly for explosives and weapons. Under the direction of the NKVD, such a large buffet with meat, fish and alcohol had been created that the tables bent.[15]

In a meeting with the staff of the Anders Army, Sikorski declared that he was convinced that Stalin stood by his word. Anders and his chief of staff, Colonel Leopold Okulicki, remained sceptical. Almost all the teeth of the latter had been knocked out in NKVD custody. They told their commander-in-chief, who had experienced the war in safe French and British exile, about the repression Polish officers had endured in Soviet prisons and camps.[16]

By the end of 1941, three divisions had been set up, with a total of almost 40,000 men. But the promised British equipment arrived only slowly. The Americans, on the other hand, who formally had also been allies of the Polish government in exile since entering the war, only supplied the Red Army under the Land Lease Act, a law that envisaged the material support of the USA for the opponents of the Germans. Until the end of the war, the Soviets received 22,150 military aircraft, 12,700 tanks, 51,000 jeeps, 375,000 trucks, 35,000 motorcycles, 8,000 tractors, 2,000 locomotives, 11,000 freight cars, 200 ships, just under 150,000 firearms, more than half a million tons of explosives and 4.5 million tons of food.

Roosevelt's special envoy, W. Averell Harriman, a millionaire heir from transport companies who was later involved with the Katyn case as US ambassador in Moscow, was initially responsible for implementing the programme. His delegation included retired Admiral William H. Standley, 68 years old, former Chief of Naval Operations. The US Navy had to protect the sea transports.

Standley, who like Harriman belonged to Roosevelt's circle of friends, later described the last stage of the flight from Arkhangelsk to Moscow: the Soviet pilot had ignored the prescribed safety measures and flown to treetop level. But there was a good reason for this: apparently the Soviet air defence was not informed, because the plane was fired upon from Soviet positions.

Their return journey after one week of negotiations also began adventurously, as Standley reported:

W. Averell Harriman and Admiral William H. Standley were responsible for the transport of American weapons and military equipment to the Soviet Union. Later, both played a role in the controversies concerning Katyn.

> We left in a gale of wind on Saturday. No pilot in our country would take to the air in those conditions, but we went out. Everybody got airsick. It was a terrible storm. The reason for it was the fact that the Germans had started their attack on Moscow two days before, and Mr. Stalin wanted to get us out of there in order to avoid the embarrassment of having us stranded.

During the days in Moscow, Harriman and Standley had heard from the diplomats in the US embassy about the search for the missing Polish officers.[17]

However, under the Land Lease Act, the Polish units in the Soviet Union received nothing and the Red Army provided them with food of low quality and in insufficient quantities. The water supply was miserable like the shelters, the latrines stinking, dirty holes. Polish soldiers lived in draughty barracks or even tents in a region where average winter temperatures are –15 degrees Celsius but often drop below –30 degrees.

Apart from these logistical difficulties, more and more political problems piled up around the Anders Army. Stalin wanted to limit the Polish contingent to 30,000 men on the grounds that the British had not supplied enough military equipment. But more than 70,000 people from all corners of the Soviet Union had already arrived in Buzuluk, plus several thousand women and children from their places of exile in Kazakhstan and Siberia.[18]

General Anders also saw it as a violation of the military agreement that information sheets printed especially for Poles in the Soviet Union promoted entry to the Red Army, while at the same time the authorities prevented Polish prisoners who had been released to come to Buzuluk. Members of the Polish embassy in Kuibyshev, who protested against this practice, were even arrested as spies during inspection trips to the collection points.[19]

Ambassador Kot tried to settle these differences in a total of eight meetings with Deputy Foreign Minister Andrey Vyshinsky. Kot asked again and again about the missing officers from the three camps. But Vyshinsky repeated stereotypically that everyone had been released. Once he said emphatically: 'This problem does not exist at all.'

Kot made the same point at a meeting with Stalin and Molotov in the Kremlin. Kot, whose Russian was only fragmentary, spoke French and both sides had interpreters. At first, Stalin welcomed the fact that Poles and Russians were 'not only neighbours, but also of the same blood'. In the past, starting with the sixteenth century, Russians would have suffered under Poland and Poles under Russians. 'We must put an end to this past.'[20] Stalin said about the missing officers: 'We released them all, even the ones General Sikorski sent us to blow up bridges and kill our people.'

But Kot insisted, for example, that all officers who belonged to the staff of Anders' brigade at the beginning of the war in 1939 had disappeared. Stalin then went to the telephone and asked his interlocutor on the other end of the line whether all Polish officers had been released. As he continued the conversation with Kot, he changed the subject.

After a few minutes the phone rang, Stalin listened, ended the conversation and said to himself in a low voice: 'They say everyone had got out.' But he did not give any further explanation. Rather, he said goodbye to the Polish ambassador. Kot took the opportunity to congratulate Stalin on the successful defence of Moscow against the Wehrmacht. The Kremlin leader dismissed him with the words: 'Personally, I am keen to contribute to the reconstruction of an independent Polish state, regardless of its internal structure.'[21]

'Escape to Manchuria'

On 3 December 1941, Kot accompanied his prime minister, Sikorski, and General Anders to the Kremlin, where Stalin, again assisted by Molotov, received them extremely kindly. The Soviet newsreel filmed the welcome, and the scene found its way into a British film documentary, which is now available on the Internet.[22]

Sikorski welcomed Stalin, whom he addressed as 'Mr President', as 'one of the real creators of contemporary history' and congratulated him on the heroism of the Red Army. The further course of the meeting was recorded by a Polish embassy secretary.

Sikorski:	I would like to say to Mr President that the declaration on amnesty is not being implemented. Many of our most valuable people are still in labour camps and prisons.
Stalin:	This is not possible because the amnesty affected everyone and all Poles were released. (Molotov nods.)
Anders:	The orders are not executed where the commanders of certain camps have the duty to execute a production plan, they do not want to get rid of their best manpower, without which the execution of the plan would not be possible. (…)
Stalin:	These people should be brought to justice. (…)
Sikorski:	It is not our business to provide the Soviet government with exact lists of our people, but the camp commanders have complete lists. I have here a list of 4,000 officers who have been forcibly removed and who are still in prisons and labour camps, and even this list is not complete, because it only includes names that have been compiled from memory. I have them checked if they are not in the country we are in constant contact with. It turned out that not a single one is there, they are also not in POW camps in Germany. These people are here. No one has returned.
Stalin:	That is not possible. They have escaped.
Anders:	Where could they have fled to?
Stalin:	Well, for example, to Manchuria.
Anders:	It is not possible that they all could have fled, all the more so because from the moment of their transport from the POW camps to the labour camps all correspondence with their families has broken off. (…)
Stalin:	You know, the Soviet government has no reason whatsoever to hold even one Pole.[23]

Sikorski gave him a list of 3,825 names, but added that they were by no means all the officers he was looking for, but no more names could have been found. However, Stalin did not return to this point. Instead, he asked Anders, full of sympathy, about his imprisonment in Soviet prisons. The general said that in the beginning it was 'unusually bad and later slightly better'. Stalin, who was always well informed about the detention conditions of prominent prisoners, including torture, replied: 'Well, what can you do, those were the conditions.'

The two Polish generals informed Stalin that their forces in the Soviet Union wanted to withdraw via Iran to the British mandate in the Middle East because of the great supply difficulties and the poor accommodation. Stalin, who had long been aware of this agreement between the government in exile and the British, said according to the protocol 'in an irritated and obviously dissatisfied tone': 'I am an old, experienced man. I know once you leave for Persia, you won't come back.'[24]

The day after the Kremlin meeting, Stalin gave a dinner for the two Polish generals. He returned to the planned withdrawal of the Anders Army: 'You insulted me by not believing in our good will!' Anders noted: 'Above all, his eyes are striking: dark, dull and cold. Even when he laughs, they never laugh.'

After dinner, the two Polish generals at the government hotel received calls from ladies who offered to come to their room. Both had no doubt that they were prostitutes in the service of the NKVD. Anders warned his commander-in-chief and his companions against hidden microphones: it is best to speak only half loudly and stir with a teaspoon loudly in the glass.[25]

In February 1942 Anders was again allowed to visit Stalin. This time he was accompanied by Chief of Staff Okulicki, who had also been severely tortured by the NKVD, and about whom Stalin was probably well informed. Stalin presented a new version at the meeting: the Polish officers had fled to the area occupied by the Germans. Okulicki, however, strongly contradicted him: 'If this were the case, at least some of them would have joined the Polish underground, and the government in exile would have found out about it.' The two Poles gave Stalin a list of other names of officers who were still missing. They did not get any answer.

Cavalry Captain Józef Czapski, who came from a family of counts, also had little success with his 'Service for the Documentation of the Detention and Deportation of Poles to the USSR' set up by Anders' order. From Buzuluk, Czapski travelled to the deepest Russian province to obtain information about Polish prisoners of war. Finally, he went to Moscow to question Beria or Merkulov. But although he referred to the agreements between Stalin and Sikorski, he was treated like a simple suppliant in Lubyanka. He had to write requests and pass them through a small window in the draughty reception room. He waited a total of three weeks for an appointment there, but he was not admitted to either one or the other.[26]

Finally, an NKVD general received him in Lubyanka. He told Czapski that nothing was known about the missing Poles. He advised him to visit Vyshinsky in Kuibyshev, where the Soviet Foreign Ministry had also been relocated. Now Czapski understood that he would not receive any information from the Soviet side; he was well informed about the eight fruitless meetings between Polish Ambassador Kot and Vyshinsky.

Czapski also informed the British military attaché in Moscow, General Noel Mason-MacFarlane, about the search for the missing officers. The latter wrote in an analysis: 'We will find ourselves in a situation where we will be drawn into as mediators. ... We must stay as far away from this case as possible, and when it comes to intervening in this matter, we must remember that it is Russia, and not Poland, that can help us beat Hitler.' Mason-MacFarlane was in agreement with Czapski's assessment: 'There's no doubt the NKVD knows what happened to those Poles.' But he gave urgent advice to the British government: 'This is a matter between Poles and Russians, and I don't think we should get involved.'[27]

Czapski also showed his documentation to Admiral William H. Standley. He had become US ambassador to Moscow at the beginning of 1942 and was to monitor the implementation of the Land Lease Act, which he had helped to prepare. Standley was very interested in this riddle, many times he also talked to the Polish ambassador Stanisław Kot about it. The two were passionate card players; they met repeatedly at bridge evenings and became friends. On occasions, the new British Ambassador Archibald Clark Kerr joined the group.

Standley sent reports of the missing Poles to Washington, and during a visit to the White House he personally briefed Roosevelt. He also took every opportunity to raise the issue at meetings with representatives of the Soviet leadership. He asked Stalin as well as Molotov for information, but without receiving a concrete answer. Molotov had even reacted 'with a certain animosity': 'There is always trouble whenever Polish questions arise.'[28] After a meeting with Vyshinsky, Standley cabled to the State Department: 'I received the distinct impression that Vyshinsky was unsympathetic towards my overtures and that he might even have been resentful of our interests in Soviet affairs.'[29]

In view of the hostile attitude of Soviet politicians, Czapski tried to find support in Moscow by other means: he relied on the help of the influential writer Alexey Tolstoy, the former chairman of the Writers' Union. Tolstoy, however, could not be reached. He came from the famous count's family and enjoyed Stalin's special affection, therefore he was popularly known as 'the red count'. His portrayals of strict but just czars were read as allegories of Stalin, his novel *Peter I* was published in huge editions.

The writer Alexey Tolstoy played an important role in the NKVD's cover-up of the Katyn crime.

Tolstoy received unlimited credit from the Soviet State Bank and moved into a manor house near Moscow; he filled it with antique furniture and works of art, which he got at symbolic prices from the property of the expropriated and persecuted former elite. He also had service personnel at his disposal. In the war, he stayed away from the front. He had moved into a comfortable house in warm and well-supplied Tashkent. His role in clarifying the fate of the missing officers was still waiting for him.

Czapski systematically collected all information about their possible whereabouts: rumour had it that 1,650 Polish prisoners and a squad of 110 NKVD soldiers died in a snowstorm on their way to the Gulag of Workuta on the Arctic Circle. That hundreds were sunk on tugboats in the White Sea and the Northern Arctic Ocean. At least 750 had frozen to death in the camps on the Ob and Yenisei in Siberia. 400 Poles were shot dead in the inhospitable region of Komi in northern Russia. In July 1942 Stanisław Swianiewicz, witness of the transportation of his comrades to Katyn Forest, came from Komi. A Polish lieutenant also reported that 630 prisoners from Kozelsk worked in the penal colony Kolyma in Northern Siberia, but he could not give any names.

The arrival of economics professor Swianiewicz in Buzuluk and the information about Poles in Kolyma raised Czapski's hope that at least some of the lost officers might still be alive. However, he did not attach much importance to Swianiewicz's report on his observations on the train station of Gnezdovo near Katyn. He assumed that the Polish officers had been taken to another camp.

Czapski suggested to American diplomats that the missing officers would be detained because the Kremlin wanted to build up cadres for its own armed forces for the takeover by communists in Poland.[30] General Anders, however, who was sceptical in principle, did not share Czapski's optimism. He expressed the fear that none of the officers were still alive. When he told Sikorski about his suspicions, the latter replied: 'You don't want to claim that the Soviet government simply killed them? Absurd! Impossible!'[31]

In February 1942, the commanders of the Red Army again demanded that the Anders Army was to provide a division for the battles against the Wehrmacht. This was to be the condition for the further supply and food for the Polish troops. However, the Polish general had no doubt that the Soviet leadership regarded the Poles primarily as cannon fodder. He therefore once again rejected Moscow's request, citing the poor equipment of his soldiers. Anders informed British Ambassador Clark Kerr of his problems with the Soviet leadership. The latter declared that London would not interfere. Anders then told him that he expected the British government to put more pressure on Moscow.[32]

The Kremlin was unimpressed. Fewer and fewer food transports reached Buzuluk, so Anders had to order a rationing of the food. The Soviet authorities also continued to block the recruitment of released Poles for the Anders Army, employees of the Polish embassy were arrested on trips to Central Asia, and aid supplies for released Polish prisoners were confiscated.

From the steppe to the Promised Land

Meanwhile, some 45,000 Poles, including a large group of women and children, had arrived in the Uzbek capital of Tashkent from Siberia. The Soviet authorities, however, described their stay in Uzbekistan as illegal and prepared for their internment. Ambassador Kot repeatedly had to insist on compliance with the Sikorski–Maisky agreement and the government in exile also asked the British leadership for help. Finally, Moscow gave in. Anders even managed to set up a fourth division in Tashkent.[33]

When Czapski learned that his writer colleague Alexey Tolstoy, with whom he had previously tried in vain to make contact in Moscow, was temporarily living in Tashkent, he gave him a meal with the staff of the Polish division. While the two writers discussed poems, the young wife of the obese and short-winded 60-year-old Tolstoy danced extensively with Polish officers. During Czapski's return visit to Tolstoy's house, he promised to provide an anthology of translations of Polish poems. Tolstoy also assured General Anders, whom he met in Tashkent, of assistance in the search for the missing officers; however, it remained unknown whether he really took steps in this regard.[34]

During these months Sikorski's wife, Helena, received numerous letters in London, in which family members, mostly wives, asked for help in the search for the missing persons. Helena Sikorska subsequently wrote a letter to Eleanor Roosevelt, the wife of the US president, asking for her help in this matter. Included with the letter were copies of letters written by Polish women, together with their translation.

It is not known what impression Helena Sikorska's letter made on Eleanor Roosevelt. She received Molotov at the White House about the same time. In her memoirs she described him as a polite man and reported a curious incident: a servant of the White House found brown bread, a dry sausage and a pistol while unpacking Molotov's suitcase in one of the guest rooms. She instructed the servant to pack the suitcase again quickly.[35]

Finally, the White House ordered the US Embassy in Moscow to investigate the matter of the disappeared Polish officers.[36]

During this time General Anders had to fend off another attempt to restrain the Poles in the Soviet Union: the Kremlin proposed splitting the Anders Army into many brigades that should

The painter and writer Józef Czapski informs General Anders about the unsuccessful search for the missing officers.

separately join Soviet large formations. However, the government in exile was once again able to avert this with British support. Stalin finally accepted the withdrawal of the Poles. Given the strong anti-Soviet sentiment among Polish officers, the risk of having a potential enemy behind his own lines ultimately seemed too great for him. The march out of the Anders Army also gave him an excuse to set up his own pro-Soviet army units from the detained Polish prisoners and deportees.

For this reason Lieutenant Colonel Zygmunt Berling and thirteen other officers recruited by the NKVD left the Anders Army during the preparations for the exodus. A little later, the field court of the Anders Army ruled that they had deserted and sentenced them to death in absentia.

In August 1942, the exodus of the Polish armed forces from the Soviet Union began, which lasted until early 1943. The Polish units were transported to the Caspian Sea, where they were shipped from the north to the south shore. Neutral Iran was occupied by Soviet and British troops in September 1941 and divided into two zones of influence.

The reason was the German-friendly attitude of the Shah Reza Pahlevi, who resisted the idea of American armaments and foodstuffs being transported from the Persian Gulf via the territory of his country to the Soviet Union. Stalin had already planned to occupy the resource-rich northwestern provinces of Iran in autumn 1939 in order to annex them to the Soviet Union; Churchill wanted to secure the oil fields in the south, which British companies exploited.

So the Red Army advanced with 120,000 men from the north, British warships and fighter planes destroyed the Iranian fleet and air force, so that after three days the Shah ordered his army to stop fighting. In a letter he asked US President Franklin D. Roosevelt for support against the double attack on a neutral country. But Roosevelt had been informed of Churchill's plans and had approved them. A few days later the Shah was forced to abdicate in favour of his eldest son.

On a journey from Washington to Kuibyshev, which took him through Tehran in several stages, Admiral Standley took the opportunity to visit a camp of the Anders Army in Persia. Later he reported on the Poles who had come from the Soviet camps in Siberia and Central Asia: 'They were in all stages of malnutrition, some of them practically dying. It was a terrible situation, indicating the conditions under which the Poles had been existing, particularly the women and children, in Russia.'[37]

The soldiers of the Anders Army were placed under the command of the British High Command in Iran. A total of 70,000 soldiers, including 2,430 officers and 44,000 civilians, took part in the march.[38] Until the end, the Soviet authorities had made it difficult to allow civilians, especially women and children, to leave. However, several hundred thousand Poles remained in the Soviet Union.

Some did not make it to Buzuluk or Tashkent in time. The vast majority, however, had not even heard of the Sikorski-Maisky Agreement in the remote places of exile, although the Soviet authorities were obliged to inform all Poles.[39]

From Iran, some of the Polish soldiers were immediately brought to Iraq and deployed there to protect the British oil fields. Another group came to the British mandate of Palestine, which also included the present state of Israel. Thousands of Polish Jews already lived in Palestine and received the Anders Army very warmly. Faced with this climate, some 2,500 Jewish soldiers left their units. Most deserted; one part officially asked for release. Anders refrained from proceedings against Jewish deserters and having them searched.

The US Army sent a liaison officer to the Anders Army: Lieutenant Colonel Henry Szymanski, who came from a Polish immigrant family in Chicago and had graduated in West Point. He was a well-trained sportsman; he had participated as a wrestler in the Olympic Games of 1920 in Antwerp.

Szymanski was supposed to travel to the Poles in the Russian steppe, but he did not receive a Soviet visa. So he was assigned to the US military attaché in Cairo; from there he travelled to the locations of the Anders Army. He met Anders and his Chief of Staff Okulicki, who described the torture in Soviet prisons in detail, as well as Captain Józef Czapski. The latter gave him documentation about the search for the missing officers. Szymanski, who spoke Polish very well, now compiled a dossier on the subject and sent regular reports to his superiors.[40]

Shortly before the start of the withdrawal of Polish troops from the Soviet Union, the Foreign Ministry in Moscow had informed Polish Ambassador Kot that the whereabouts of the wanted officers had now been clarified: they had returned to Poland, fled abroad or died on their way. Many had travelled individually despite warnings from the Soviet authorities.

The government in exile did not want to believe this communication. It therefore decided to ask US President Roosevelt for help: the Poles appealed to him to press the Soviet leadership for concrete information about the fate of the officers of a common ally. But in the White House, their request was ignored. Ambassador Kot sent a total of fifty inquiries to Soviet authorities about the missing persons, without receiving a precise answer. His American colleague, Admiral William H. Standley, noticed that Kot was almost desperate and sick in this constant controversy.[41]

In the memoirs of contemporaries and in the archives there is no indication that Stalin ever expressed himself in personal conversations about Katyn. A remarkable reference, however, can be found in the memoirs of Stalin's daughter, Svetlana Alliluyeva: she describes that as a teenager during the war she accompanied her father several times to the Bolshoi Theatre for performances of Mikhail Glinka's opera *Ivan Susanin*. It is about the struggle of the Russians against the Poles advancing eastwards at the beginning of the seventeenth century.

In the third act, the hero, a Russian peasant, leads a Polish troop into a swampy area in the woods around Smolensk, from which there is no escape. According to his daughter, Stalin left the performance every time after this scene, although another act follows. Many years later she wrote: 'What did this death of the Poles in the forest mean to him? Perhaps he was reminded of the annihilation of 10,000 Polish officers captured in the forests of Katyn, secretly carried out by the Soviet leadership in 1940?'[42]

Chapter 5

Discovery of the Mass Graves

At the end of January 1943, Lieutenant Colonel Friedrich Ahrens observed a wolf digging in the deep snow in the forest of Katyn. A few steps away from the site he noticed a birch cross as it was placed on soldiers' graves. Ahrens was commander of the Signal Regiment 537 of the Army Group Centre; his staff was located in the Dnieper Manor, the former training and recreation home of the NKVD, which also had a cinema and a shooting range. He informed the officer responsible for the burial of soldiers. The latter examined the site after the frost had subsided in mid-March. Several bones were discovered, which a military doctor identified as human bones.[1]

Independently of the discovery of the birch cross by Ahrens, the military police of the Army Group Centre, whose staff was in Smolensk, learned at the same time of a mass grave of Polish officers. The railway fitter Ivan Krivozertsev, who worked in a repair facility of the Wehrmacht, had read an article about the deportation of Poles to Siberia by the NKVD in the newspaper *Novy Put* (New Path) edited for local people by the Germans. He remembered a conversation with a peasant who had told him about the shooting of Polish officers and mass graves at the 'Goat Hills' near the village Katyn. Krivozertsev was a bitter opponent of the communist regime – the NKVD had shot his father.[2] He contacted an acquaintance who worked for the Germans as an interpreter; this man informed the military police.

Several military policemen drove with the two Russians to the witness, it was 71-year-old Parfen Kiselev. The peasant led the small group to the place where he suspected a mass grave. It was the same piece of forest where Lieutenant Colonel Ahrens had watched the wolf. After the snow was shovelled to the side and a hole was chopped in the ground, the men felt a strong smell of decay despite the frost. Finally, they came across several corpses in military coats. Krivozertsev tore off a uniform button with a Polish eagle engraved on it.[3]

Kiselev, who often collected mushrooms and firewood in the forest, could also give information about who had built the birch cross: it was a group of Polish railway workers the year before, in 1942, who worked for the Todt organisation, which under the Ministry of Armament in Berlin built and maintained traffic routes. Their section had come to Smolensk to expand the railway line. They heard from the Polish wife of a Russian railwayman that there were mass graves with compatriots near Katyn. When they went into the village, they came across Kiselev, who led them into the forest. The men dug in several places and found two graves.

Kiselev later reported: 'After about an hour they returned outraged and scolding the NKVD.'[4] One of the Poles of the Todt organisation described almost half a century later that he and his colleagues had reported the gruesome discovery in the forest to their German superiors; but the latter had shown no particular interest in their description.[5]

The reports about the graves reached Lieutenant Colonel Rudolf-Christoph von Gersdorff, who was responsible for military reconnaissance and thus also for enemy observation in the General Staff of the Army Group Centre. Gersdorff sent a report to Berlin, whereupon the Army High Command ordered the graves to be opened. He also had the military police search for inhabitants of the area who could provide information about the graves. The newspaper *Novy Put* printed an advertisement in which witnesses of the executions were promised a reward.[6]

Gersdorff belonged to a group of German officers in Smolensk who had been planning an assassination attempt on Hitler for more than a year. They were outraged and horrified by the murders committed by the SS behind the combat zone against civilians, especially Jews. They also rejected the 'Commissar order', Hitler's order to shoot Politruks of the Red Army, and the propaganda of the 'Slav subhuman'. Above all, they wanted to end the war as quickly as possible.[7]

Head of the group was Colonel Henning von Tresckow. Before the war he had made contact with Hitler's opponents among the generals of the Wehrmacht who wanted to prevent a war because they believed that the German Reich would lose it. Among the conspirators of Smolensk was also his adjutant, Lieutenant of the Reserve Fabian von Schlabrendorff, whose wife was Tresckow's cousin. Schlabrendorff was a lawyer in the civil profession; he maintained connections to Hitler's opponents in the banned political parties.

On behalf of a group of Hitler opponents, Schlabrendorff, whose family had good contacts in Great Britain, travelled to London in August 1939 to inform senior officials in the Foreign Office about the secret negotiations between Ribbentrop and Molotov and the imminent German attack on Poland. But he was not taken seriously. He also met the then opposition leader Winston Churchill and explained to him that there was resistance to Hitler's plans in the German Reich.[8]

Tresckow saw the German attack on the Soviet Union as a 'Napoleon adventure' that would end badly.[9] However, he initially issued orders in the General Staff for brutal actions against 'Bolshevik partisans', to which a large number of completely uninvolved civilians fell victim. He was anti-Bolshevik and considered the measures necessary. But when he learned that women and young people were also shot in the 'fight against partisans' and that, moreover, it was only a cover for the SS for the extermination of the Jews, he tried to persuade the generals in the Army

The two German officers stationed in Smolensk, Rudolf-Christoph von Gersdorff (left) and Fabian von Schlabrendorff, failed twice in their attempt to kill Hitler with a bomb. Both later played a central role in the Katyn controversies. (© Gebr. v. Schlabrendorff)

Group Centre to resist and protest. But they did not listen to him. So he started planning the assassination of Hitler.[10] Tresckow found another ally in Count Claus Schenk von Stauffenberg, a Catholic from Southern Germany, who was briefly detached to the General Staff on the Eastern Front.[11]

Two failed assassination attempts

In Smolensk, Rudolf-Christoph von Gersdorff, who was now responsible for investigating the graves of Katyn, joined the conspirators around Tresckow. Shortly before the war he had taken part in a meeting between Hitler and a group of General Staff officers: 'The whole impression was that of a disgusting, bloated pleb.' But he almost stood alone with this opinion; most of the other officers were fascinated by Hitler. In the beginning Gersdorff was convinced that he was serving a just cause when he took part in the Polish campaign. He was horrified to learn that the Gestapo murdered Polish intellectuals and shot large numbers of Jewish civilians.[12]

In Smolensk he was confronted with news of the SS assassinations in the hinterland. After the visit of several units on the front, he noted in the General Staff's war diary in December 1941: 'I got the impression that the execution of the Jews, the prisoners and also the commissars was almost generally rejected in the officers' corps.'[13] His report had no consequences, because the generals of the Wehrmacht were afraid to confront SS leader Heinrich Himmler.

The massacres were the reason for several officers who were originally enthusiastic about Hitler joining the resistance group around Tresckow. Among them was Lieutenant Reinhart von Eichborn, who, under the command of Lieutenant Colonel Ahrens, was head of the telephone centre of the Army Group Centre in Smolensk. Eichborn had studied together with Schlabrendorff in Halle; he also spent one year at Oxford and therefore spoke excellent English. After the war, Eichborn and Ahrens were to play an important role in the propaganda war around Katyn.

After the defeat of Stalingrad at the beginning of 1943, Tresckow considered the war finally lost. However, Hitler's opponents had to take a hard blow at this very time: at the Casablanca Conference in January 1943, Churchill and Roosevelt had ruled out any negotiations with the German Reich. Both governments rejected also contact with the middlemen of the opposition against Hitler. Tresckow considered this a serious mistake by the Western Allies, which would only prolong the war.[14]

He, nevertheless, hoped for an agreement with them because he considered the Soviet system inhuman and cruel. Therefore he wanted to hold the Eastern Front until the British and Americans advanced to Germany and Central Europe. He expected nothing good from the Red Army; he thought Stalin was a mass murderer in the same way as Hitler and he feared revenge for the German war crimes.[15]

Gersdorff had obtained explosives from a Wehrmacht magazine and two British detention mines that were the size of a book. He studied the system: the mines were equipped with an acid fuse. It took between ten and fifteen minutes for the acid to eat its way through to the explosive, so the explosion was delayed. Together with Tresckow he also made experiments with explosives in the forests around Smolensk.[16]

During the days when the opening of the graves in Katyn Forest was being prepared, the conspirators suddenly had the opportunity to kill Hitler: he came to Smolensk on 13 March 1943 for a visit of the front units. First, they considered shooting him at lunch. But they rejected this plan again, because it held the risk of a gunfight between the Wehrmacht officers and Hitler's bodyguards from the SS. Besides, even days before Hitler's arrival, the Smolensk headquarters was already swarming with security personnel from the SS.

Hitler's Condor plane was accompanied by an identical plane and a fighter squadron to Smolensk. His Mercedes and other cars, accompanied by a heavily armed escort, had already arrived before after days of driving. They brought Hitler and his entourage from the airport to the city and were closely guarded around the clock. For safety reasons, Hitler never got in another car.[17]

In view of all these conditions, the conspirators decided against an immediate attack on Hitler. Rather, a bomb explosion on board the plane on the way back to the Wolfsschanze (Wolf's Lair), the headquarters in Eastern Prussia, was supposed to kill him. In this case, there could be official talk of an air accident. The British mines that Gersdorff had procured were rounded, so that they could be disguised as bottles.

Schlabrendorff described in his memoirs the lunch with the Führer:

> Hitler ate a special meal prepared for him by his cook, whom he had brought with him, and which had to be tasted before his eyes by his doctor. The process looked as if an oriental despot of prehistoric times had appeared. Seeing Hitler eat was a most disgusting sight. He supported his left hand on his thigh, while spooning in his right hand his food, which consisted of many kinds of vegetables. He did not lead his hand to his mouth, but left his right arm on the table during the whole meal, but pushed his mouth down to eat. In between he drank various non-alcoholic drinks placed in front of his plate. By Hitler's order, smoking was forbidden after eating.[18]

After lunch, Tresckow asked an officer from Hitler's company to take the bomb package disguised as a gift for a friend in Berlin: two cognac bottles. Shortly before the handover, Schlabrendorff armed the bomb's detonator. But the conspirators in Smolensk waited in vain for news of the plane crash. The bomb did not explode because it was deposited in the unheated luggage compartment where the detonator iced up. Schlabrendorff flew quickly to Hitler's headquarters at Wolfsschanze to exchange the parcel with the bomb for two real cognac bottles.[19]

Tresckow said in his circle of Smolensk friends that one must wait for the next opportunity: 'The world must be freed from the greatest criminal of all time. You have to beat him to death like a rabid dog, endangering humanity.'[20] This opportunity arose just eight days later: Hitler was to visit an exhibition of captured Soviet weapons in Berlin on 21 March 1943. It was one of the propaganda actions to lighten the mood after the defeat of Stalingrad.

The Army Group Centre had transported the exhibits from Smolensk to Berlin; Gersdorff as an expert was to provide the explanations. Before his departure, Tresckow was able to convince him that a suicide bombing would be the only way in view of Hitler's protection by the SS. Gersdorff, 38 years old at the time, was ready for it: he was a widower, his wife had died a year before and he did not have children. Schlabrendorff, who had come to Berlin from Wolfsschanze, handed over the British mines to him.

At first, everything went according the plan: the assassin was able to enter the building without control. Hitler came with his entourage. Gersdorff later noted down his impressions: 'Next to him went Göring, who in his white uniform overloaded with medals and jewellery and in red saffian boots gave the impression of a prince of operettas; moreover, he was painted with make-up in a grotesquely striking way.' First Hitler gave a speech, an orchestra played, then he took his entourage on a tour of the exhibition hall.

As planned, Gersdorff took the tour of the exhibition, activating the mine's mechanism in his jacket pocket. He now had to stay close to Hitler's side for ten to fifteen minutes until the explosion. But the Führer was not interested in the explanations about the Soviet weapons, he hurried through the hall. After only two minutes Hitler left the building. Gersdorff rushed to the toilet to defuse the bomb.

He returned to Smolensk without having achieved anything. One of his tasks was to supervise the investigation of the graves of Katyn. In the last week of March, when there was already no frost in daytime, work began. After only a few days Gersdorff received the first report: 'These are mass graves with several thousand dead.'[21]

Bayonet stitches and neck shots
Professor Gerhard Buhtz, the forensic scientist of the Army Group Centre, took over the investigation of the bodies. Buhtz, professor of forensic medicine at the University of Breslau, was a dedicated Nazi; he had been a member of the SS since 1933. In the Buchenwald concentration camp, after the autopsy of prisoners, he issued certificates stating that they had been shot 'on the run'. But after a conflict with Reich health leader Leonardo Conti, who was a senior SS officer, Buhtz had to go to the Eastern front as a medical staff officer.

In the forest of Katyn, local Russians had to excavate the earth above the dead. There were twelve layers of corpses in one of them. Most of them were officers; almost all of them wore winter clothes. According to Buhtz, the lack of insect infestation also proved that they were buried in the cold season.

In the same area the Germans also discovered older graves with hundreds of heavily decomposed corpses. An investigation of the garment remains revealed that these were Soviet production. The cause of death was a head shot throughout. It was no different with the bodies of the Polish officers. The finding was: shot in the back of the neck with the muzzle on.[22]

Buhtz gave the order to demolish a wooden house in Katyn and set it up again next to the cemetery to carry out the autopsies. Later he and his aids worked under the open sky in good weather. The recovery of the bodies was extremely difficult. There was groundwater in a grave. The corpses were, as Buhtz noted in his report, 'especially in the lower layers due to advanced decomposition firmly stuck together, so that the detachment often succeeded badly'.

At first, seven mass graves were identified, in each of which were 500 to 600 corpses. The medical professor laid down a precise procedure for the examinations:

Every single corpse was lifted onto a wooden stretcher after being uncovered, carried out of the grave and laid down in a clearing on the side

A Russian auxiliary stands in a grave with the bodies of the shot Polish officers.

of the graves. Each corpse was numbered consecutively immediately after recovery by attaching round metal marks with the corresponding stamped identification number to the victim's coat or skirt. So at times hundreds of the recovered corpses lined up side by side.[23]

Most of them had their IDs in their pockets.

Buhtz described in detail how resistance had been broken by bondage: 'The cords were knotted in such a way that the bonds automatically contracted when you try to squeeze your hands apart.' Many of the victims also had their military cloak pulled over their heads and a noose put around their necks. When a prisoner moved his head, the noose contracted.

Buhtz had found the same type of bondage in the nearby graves from the pre-war period: 'A particularly impressive example of this species is the body of a Russian man, the head was tightly wrapped with a brown sheepskin coat which was tied up with a string.' He concluded that this was a 'procedure practised by the Soviets for decades'.

As further irrefutable proof of Soviet perpetrators, his report also cited stab wounds by square bayonets, such as only the Red Army and the NKVD used. According to the report, a Polish lieutenant fiercely resisted his execution; the autopsy of his body showed a dozen bayonet stitches. Also, a greater number of victims had shattered mandibles and other bone fractures caused by blows with rifle butts. Buhtz came to the conclusion that 'the victims were driven to the place of execution by physical torments'.

With the warmer spring weather, a strong smell of decomposition emanated from the exposed mass graves. Lieutenant Colonel Ahrens, commander of the Signal Regiment 537, later complained that the 'pestilence-like stench' had even been felt in his staff building, the Dnieper Manor, several hundred metres away, and had 'continuously disturbed his well-being'.[24]

At the same time as the autopsies, the German military police questioned local witnesses, locating a total of twelve.[25] Gersdorff took part in several interrogations. Some of the witnesses reported that, since 1918, shortly after the Bolsheviks took power, the Soviet secret police had carried out executions in the forest – thousands were buried near the Goat Hills. At the end of the 1930s the area was fenced in and had since been guarded by NKVD soldiers with fierce dogs.

Five of the witnesses independently described that in the spring of 1940 Polish officers were taken to the Gnezdovo railway station in prison wagons. There they changed to buses that took the road to Katyn Forest. But none was an eyewitness to the executions, nor had anyone seen the fresh mass graves. The farmer Kiselev, who lived not far from the Goat Hills, testified: 'I cannot say what was done to the men, because no one was allowed to go there. I heard the shooting and screaming of men's voices all the way to my place.'

The locksmith Krivozertsev reported what he had observed on a Saturday in April 1940: 'About ten lorries drove with suitcases, handbags, laundry bags and coats loaded up from Katyn Forest towards Smolensk. Each truck was accompanied by two Chekists.'[26] It remained unknown where they transported the belongings of the shot Poles.

The head of the Russian local administration, Mayor Boris Menshagin, appointed by the Germans, and 250 municipal officials, were also brought to the graves. During the Great Purges under Stalin, Menshagin had been a criminal defence lawyer, then worked as an attorney for civil law and finally in the legal department of the state car repair facilities.

His relations with the German occupying forces were strained, primarily due to the camp no. 126 for Red Army POWs on the territory of the city of Smolensk. The Germans deliberately gave them too little food and the prisoners were starving, leading to cases of cannibalism. But it was beyond Menshagin's means to improve the lot of his captured countrymen. The number of inmates of the camp who died of hunger or epidemics is now estimated by historians at around 60,000.[27]

But Menshagin successfully promoted the rebirth of religious life in Smolensk, including the reopening of the cathedral. In their campaign against religion the Bolsheviks had closed 90 per cent of the 650 churches and chapels in the district;

they became storage rooms, schools or club rooms of the Association of the Godless.[28]

Menshagin himself gave lectures on the history of the Orthodox Church. This was also the line of the group of officers around Tresckow: they wanted to gain the Russian population, who had experienced the persecution of priests and faithful under Stalin, for the fight against the Bolshevik regime. Tresckow and Schlabrendorff saw their rejection of Bolshevism confirmed when they saw the graves of the murdered Poles in the forest of Katyn. On visits to Berlin they reported this to their circle of friends.[29]

Mayor Menshagin later wrote about the trip into Katyn Forest:

> Suddenly we got a strong smell of decay, although we drove through a pine grove where the air was always clean. We drove for a while and then we saw these graves. Russian prisoners

The mayor of Smolensk appointed by the Germans, Boris Menshagin, had no doubts about the perpetration of the NKVD.

of war harvested the last remains of the remaining objects. At the edge the corpses were discarded. Everyone wore grey Polish uniforms and their square military caps. Everyone's hands were tied behind their backs. And they all had holes in their necks. They were all killed with a single shot in the neck. Offside lay the bodies of two generals.[30]

The newspaper *Novy Put*, which was published under German control in Smolensk, published a total of thirty articles about the mass graves, and the NKVD was blamed for this in the comments. A commentary appeared under the headline: 'Roosevelt – accomplice to the murder of Katyn.'[31] Hundreds, if not thousands of inhabitants of the city of Smolensk were led across the area in Katyn Forest. With one of the groups came the deputy mayor, astronomy professor Boris Bazilevsky, who subsequently denounced the NKVD as the perpetrator.[32] Bazilevsky would later play an important role in the Katyn case.

The number of Soviet POWs involved in the exhumation work increased over the weeks to around 500. In the uniform jackets they brought to light other documents besides ID cards: newspapers from March and April 1940; receipts, notes, postcards and letters; here, too, the most recent ones were from April 1940.[33]

Two of the readable notebooks came from young reserve officers. A lieutenant wrote:

> I long that God makes it possible for me and all others to return to Poland. I'd finish law school there, I could work scientifically. I long to develop my character, my mind and my body. That I'm marrying a beautiful, good, dear wife, having children with her. I beg You, God, that I also have my piece of land.

A second lieutenant wrote in his notebook: 'I have received the first letter from Marysia. What luck! The long awaited letter is finally in my hands. My beloved Marysia is torturing herself there alone, and I am hanging around in my bunk.' Two days after this entry, the young second lieutenant went on the transport to Katyn.[34]

Chapter 6

Goebbels' Wedge between the Allies

Nazi propaganda minister Joseph Goebbels learned of the discovery of the mass graves in early April 1943. 'He could hardly believe the fortune that had occurred to him. He was so very much surprised that such an important news should just come to him.' With these words an employee of his staff later described Goebbels' reaction. The minister immediately informed Hitler, who ordered him to exploit the case in the German propaganda.[1]

Since the German defeat at Stalingrad three months before, Goebbels has been looking for occasions to get back on the offensive with propaganda campaigns. He had received reports of the increasingly defeatist mood because the population no longer saw 'a clear picture of war'. His speech in the Berlin Sports Palace on 18 February, in which he called for a 'total war', had not changed the pessimistic mood of the population.

In the news from Katyn he immediately saw an opportunity to drive a wedge between the Allies. He had a campaign designed to focus on the statements of eyewitnesses and photos of the exhumation work. At a meeting with his closest associates, he claimed that he would not initially inform the German public, as this could 'draw conclusions about the treatment of German prisoners of war by the Bolsheviks'.[2]

Governor General Hans Frank in occupied Krakow noted in his official diary that in addition to reports for the Polish press controlled by the Germans, film documentaries about Katyn were planned for the cinema newsreels as well as radio broadcasts, brochures, leaflets, posters, even records with reports of exhumation witnesses. The Poles should be granted a 'national day of mourning' for the murdered

The Nazi Minister of Propaganda Joseph Goebbels saw the Katyn case as a chance to provoke a conflict among the Allies.

officers, clergy should take over the 'care of the corpses', and memorials should be erected in Warsaw, Krakow and Lublin.[3]

Eventually, the decision was made to extend the campaign to the Germans; Goebbels personally obtained Hitler's permission to make a 'dramatic announcement' to the press. The campaign started with the German news agency Transocean, which had Great Britain and the USA in its sights with its English-language dispatches. On 11 April 1943, the agency reported the discovery of mass graves in Russia in which more than 3,000 Polish officers in uniform were lying face down, their hands tied. Initial investigations have shown that the murders were committed by the Soviet secret police. The total number of officers buried there was estimated at 10,000. However, this English-language Transocean message was officially completely ignored in London and Washington.

The 'nefarious crime of Katyn' became the most important report of all German radio stations on 13 April. The following day the press in the German Reich reported about it on almost all front pages, as did the newspapers in occupied Poland. On 15 April the Nazi newspaper *Völkischer Beobachter* gave its leading article the headline: 'The mass murder of Katyn the work of Jewish butchers. Judas' blood guilt grows immeasurably.'

On the same day, the Soviet agency Sovinformburo, which provided the Western Allies in particular with success stories about the course of the war and descriptions of German atrocities, both true and fake stories, reacted for the first time. The reports about the mass graves were a 'smudgy invention of Goebbels' slanderers'.

The party organ *Pravda* presented its own version: when the Germans attacked the Soviet Union in the summer of 1941, the Polish officers were interned in three camps near Smolensk. They could not be evacuated in time, the Germans captured the Poles, shot them and then used the site of archaeological research for a mass grave. In fact, such excavations had taken place since the end of the nineteenth century on the site of the former Viking settlement near the Gnezdovo railway station. But *Pravda* was completely wrong with the description of the locality: Katyn Forest with the mass graves lies ten kilometres further west. Goebbels noted in his diary: 'Something more stupid probably didn't occur to the Kremlin Jews.'[4] In a meeting at the Ministry of Propaganda he mocked according to the protocol: 'The Moscow Jews will not shy away from claiming that we put 12,000 skeletons from the second century before our time into Polish uniforms.'[5]

The American Ambassador to Moscow, Admiral William H. Standley, sent a first report on Soviet reactions to the State Department. He asked why Soviet officials had not informed him and the Poles for two years about the whereabouts of the missing officers, but now gave very specific information about their internment in camps near Smolensk in the summer of 1941.[6]

The Armia Krajowa (AK), the military wing of the underground movement in occupied Warsaw, radioed a first report on German propaganda to the government

In response to the Soviet claim that the Germans buried the murdered Poles at the site of archaeological excavations, the Völkischer Beobachter printed a cartoon entitled: The Moscow Liar Jew in a Headlock (24 April 1943).

Der Moskauer Lügenjude im Schwitzkasten

KATYN SOWJET MASSENMORDE VON 1940

„A-a-archäologische Funde ---"

in exile in London. It said that the Germans obviously wanted to drive a wedge between the Poles in the General Government and in London by warning of the Bolsheviks. The propaganda line is easy to see through: 'The Germans present themselves as defenders of Christian civilisation and act as defenders of interests and avengers of the Polish people.'[7]

After Churchill had received detailed information about the reports from Katyn, he invited Sikorski for lunch. The latter explained to him that he possessed 'plenty of evidence' of Soviet guilt. British Secretary of State Alexander Cadogan, who attended the lunch, noted in his diary that Churchill reacted very cautiously: 'We know what the Bolsheviks are capable of and how they can be cruel.'[8] But he advised Sikorski to wait for further information and added: 'If they are dead nothing you can do will bring them back.' Cadogan asked Sikorski to refrain from 'any provocation'.[9]

However, without consulting the British, the Polish cabinet decided to ask the International Committee of the Red Cross (ICRC) in Geneva for an independent investigation of the mass graves. In response to the Soviet version, the cabinet distributed an extensive statement to the press describing in detail the search for the missing prisoners of war, especially the diplomatic efforts in the Kremlin; the figures of 8,300 officers and 7,000 other persons were mentioned. The statement was factual in tone, it contained no speculation whatsoever about the causes of the officers' deaths and did not name anyone to blame for the crime.[10]

Goebbels suggested to Hitler that the Germans should also call the ICRC, and the latter agreed.[11] The German Red Cross, controlled by the Nazis, called in a telegram to Geneva for a delegation of experts to be sent to Katyn. ICRC President Max Huber, a Swiss citizen, replied after just a few hours by cable that an investigation was only an option if all parties involved wanted to do so.

Under international law Katyn was Soviet territory irrespective of the German occupation, so Moscow would have to agree.

With the telegram from Berlin to Geneva, the Nazi leadership had beaten the Poles. A representative of the Polish Red Cross (PCK) presented the note to the government in exile with the request to set up a commission of inquiry only one day later, on 17 April, in Geneva. Like the previous declarations of the government in exile, this note did not contain any suspicions or blame. Again, Huber replied that all parties involved would have to agree to the request.

The ICRC was in a weak position vis-à-vis Moscow: although the USSR ratified the Geneva Convention on the Care of the Wounded in 1929, it did not ratify the POW Convention. In addition, the Red Army invaded Poland in September 1939 without declaring war. Therefore under international law there was no state of war at all between the Soviet Union and Poland; however, this would have been the formal condition for the application of the POW Convention.[12]

However, London wanted to prevent the ICRC from being involved. The British ambassador to Moscow, Archibald Clark Kerr, telegraphed to the Foreign Office that his Polish colleague Tadeusz Romer believed the Germans' version because it matched the reports about the missing officers. Clark Kerr saw the dilemma of his government: 'Anger and unconvincing terms if the Soviet denials suggest a sense of guilt. This is disturbing for it is uncomfortable to reflect upon the consequences of an enquiry.' He warned that the Polish request to the Red Cross in Geneva could lead to a 'disaster'.[13]

On the day the note was handed over in Geneva, the government in exile met again in London. Sikorski reported on Churchill's cautious reaction and proposed to ask Pope Pius XII in Rome to mediate in the Katyn case, as well as to ask the Soviet government in a note for its consent to an investigation by the ICRC. After the meeting, Sikorski had an English-language statement published in which the Polish government protested that Berlin was using the Katyn crime for its own purposes. It said expressly: 'The profoundly hypocritical indignation of German propaganda will not succeed in concealing from the world the many cruel and reiterated crimes still being perpetrated against the Polish people.'[14]

Break-off of diplomatic relations

The Poles were well aware of the explosive nature of the situation: in the summer of 1941 they had changed from defeated war opponents to allies of the Soviet Union. In Moscow, however, the decision had obviously already been made to use the political dilemma of the government in exile to break with it. The Poles were extremely annoying to the Kremlin. They had repeatedly declared that they insisted on their eastern border from the pre-war period; this demand concerned the territories annexed by the Soviet Union in autumn 1939.

The Americans also immediately realised that Goebbels' advance was aimed at driving a wedge between the Allies. In the instructions for the Office of War

Information (OWI), which provided the media with censored news about the war, the topic was classified as 'dangerous' and should only be reported on to a limited extent and with a clear thrust: Katyn is a German 'propaganda trick'.[15] From the point of view of the Americans the new campaign of the Germans should distract from the atrocities against the Jews.

OWI was an agency with thousands of employees, responsible for the censorship of war coverage by the free media on the one hand, and for conducting campaigns to strengthen the fighting spirit and cohesion of American society on the other. At the head was a confidant of Roosevelt, the popular radio reporter Elmer Davis, one of the best paid journalists in the USA before the war. He went on air himself with a weekly commentary on world politics. Davis had direct access to Roosevelt; he pushed through the White House that the press should also publish photos of dead American soldiers, which was previously prohibited.

Davis explained the German Katyn campaign in his fifteen-minute weekly commentary to millions of American radio listeners:

> The way the Germans did this is a good example of the doctrine Hitler preached in *Mein Kampf*, that it is easier to make most people swallow a big lie than a little one … This story looks very fishy … The Germans are known to have slaughtered hundreds of thousands of Poles after the fighting was over. If they found a camp full of Polish prisoners, when they attacked Russia, it would so have been the most natural thing in the world for them to murder them, too.[16]

The US authorities also internally blocked the dissemination of information about Katyn. The liaison officer to Anders' Army in the Middle East, Lieutenant Colonel Henry Szymanski, was instructed by the Military Intelligence Service only to send reports about Katyn that indicated German complicity.[17] Szymanski had reported that his Polish interlocutors were convinced that the German radio news about Katyn was true.[18]

At the same time, the British Embassy in Moscow warned Foreign Secretary Anthony Eden that Stalin could use the Katyn conflict to marginalise London's Poles.[19] The fears were well founded: the newspaper *Izvestia* accused the Poles of having started a 'campaign against the Soviet Union' on the radio and in the press. The proof: instead of turning directly to the Soviet government for the 'lying assertions' of the Germans, the Poles called the International Red Cross. Instead of destroying the enemy of the Polish and Russian people in a joint struggle, they had stabbed the Soviet Union in the back.

Goebbels noted: 'I am extremely pleased with the development of the Katyn case. The Führer is also very satisfied. … The Führer attaches particular importance to putting the Jewish question at the centre of the subsequent discussions.'[20] The Nazi press made headlines with the slogan of the 'Jewish Bolsheviks', which Goebbels hammered into his audience at every opportunity: 'Stalin's executioners – Jews' or 'Horror at the Jewish mass murder'.[21]

According to *Völkischer Beobachter*, Goebbels' direct mouthpiece, the 'Jewish butchers' and 'GPU Jews' wanted revenge on the 'Polish lords'. Moscow's denials are 'pathetic lies of Jewish criminals', against whom the struggle 'to save Europe' must be waged: 'There is no understanding with a mentality fed by a cloaca – here there can be only extermination!'[22] Several press reports have listed alleged perpetrators with Jewish names: Chaim Feinberg, Abram Borisovich and others. These were, as later became known, smooth inventions.

The reports illustrated photos of the cemetery in Katyn Forest. Goebbels wrote in his diary: 'Let the German people see what Bolshevism is. It is better that the German people get the horror of photographs than they get the shot in the back of the neck one day because they did not recognise the danger in time'.[23]

When Goebbels received the translation of the editorial of *Pravda* on 19 April, he saw his bill paying off: Moscow attacked the Polish government in exile in the strongest terms, distressing the British as their protective power. *Pravda* claimed that their application to the Red Cross, which they had obviously agreed with the Germans, exposed the Poles as 'Hitler's helpers'. They had thus fallen into a trap of the Germans, who had nothing else in mind but to discredit the Poles as allies of the Allies.

On 21 April Stalin sent secret messages to Churchill and Roosevelt stating: 'The investigative comedy of the Hitler fascists, in which Polish profascist elements help, could not inspire confidence in any honest person.' According to Stalin the Sikorski government had apparently coordinated its actions with Hitler, thus adopting 'a hostile attitude' towards the Soviet Union.[24]

In another secret message to Churchill three days later, Stalin gave an ultimatum demanding that the Poles withdraw their application to the Red Cross. Churchill did not want to risk a conflict with Stalin. He was extremely angry at the Polish initiative, which had not been agreed with the British government. He did not hide his irritation from the Soviet ambassador in London, Ivan Maisky: 'We have got to beat Hitler, and this is no time for quarrels and charges.'[25] According to British documents, Maisky said about the Poles: 'They always mismanaged their affairs', their 'feckless government' did not want to understand that a people of 20 million should not provoke one of 200 million. It is not recorded whether Churchill disagreed with him or not.[26]

But in his answer to Stalin's secret messages Churchill stood up for Sikorski. He underlined that the Polish prime minister was under great pressure from other members of the government in exile, who accused him of being too reserved towards Moscow. 'Sikorski is anything but German-friendly', Churchill wrote. He appealed to Stalin not to break off diplomatic relations with the government in exile.

In a second letter on 25 April, Churchill made further arguments in defence of the Poles. Meanwhile, the government in exile had distanced itself from German propaganda on radio. Sikorski had also promised to prevent the Polish press in Great Britain from polemics against Moscow. The British government was examining whether it could silence Polish papers that had attacked the Soviet Union. He knew Sikorski well, Churchill said, there certainly had been 'no contact' between his government and Nazi Germany. The British prime minister finally pointed out to Stalin that Sikorski could more easily assert himself against 'Polish public opinion' if Moscow settled the question of the departure of the Poles still remaining in the USSR. Indeed, the government in exile had repeatedly insisted on this, their diplomatic démarches had remained unanswered.

But Stalin had sent another secret message to London the same day, 25 April. In it he referred to the 'public opinion of the Soviet Union, whose deep soul is outraged by the ingratitude and betrayal of the Poles' – as if there were a public opinion in a totally controlled society.

In the late evening of 25 April, Foreign Minister Molotov read a statement to Tadeusz Romer, the new Polish ambassador, who had taken up residence in a Moscow hotel. Without asking the diplomat to sit down, Molotov read a statement saying:

> The Soviet Government considers the recent behavior of the Polish Government with regard to the U.S.S.R. as entirely abnormal, and violating all regulations and standards of relations between two Allied States. ... Having committed a monstrous crime against the Polish officers, the Hitlerite authorities are now staging a farcical investigation, and for this they have made use of certain Polish pro-Fascist elements whom they themselves selected in occupied Poland where everything is under Hitler's heel, and where no honest Pole can openly have his say. ... Clearly such an 'investigation', conducted behind the back of the Soviet Government, cannot evoke the confidence of people possessing any degree of honesty.
>
> The fact that the hostile campaign against the Soviet Union commenced simultaneously in the German and Polish press, and was conducted along the same lines, leaves no doubt as to the existence of contact and accord in carrying out this hostile campaign between the enemy of the Allies – Hitler – and the Polish Government. While the peoples of the Soviet Union are bleeding profusely in a hard struggle against Hitlerite Germany, are straining every effort for the defeat of the common enemy of the Russian and Polish peoples, and of all freedom-loving democratic countries, the Polish Government, to please Hitler's tyranny, has dealt a treacherous blow to the Soviet Union.[27]

Molotov concluded by saying that for all these reasons the Soviet government is forced to break off relations with the Polish government. Romer refused, however, to accept the note. He left the building fifteen minutes after midnight. But a driver of the ministry brought Molotov's statement in a sealed envelope to the hotel in the night.

The next morning Romer asked the American Ambassador Standley for advice on how he should react to this. The admiral recommended that he send the envelope back to Molotov.[28] Romer did so; he added a letter in which he rejected the suggestion that the Polish government was working with Hitler. He also pointed out that Polish officials had been asking Moscow for information on the fate of missing officers for two years.[29]

Churchill's futile effort

While Romer was preparing to leave Moscow, American diplomats in the Kremlin delivered another letter from President Roosevelt. In it, he expressed the hope that Moscow would not break off relations with the Polish government in exile. Sikorski certainly had not made common cause with the 'Hitler gang'. He pointed out that there were millions of Poles living in the USA who are 'all bitter against the Nazis'; a large number served in the US Army.[30]

But the Kremlin ignored this letter from Roosevelt; Romer had to leave the country. US Ambassador Standley later reported: 'The way we felt there, when Mr. Romer left, taking his departure, the British Ambassador and myself went to the depot to see him off and presented going-away presents to Mr. Romer as indicating where our sympathies lay.'[31]

Goebbels saw his first goal achieved: the break between Moscow and the government in exile. Self-satisfied, he wrote in his diary:

> The opinion of all enemy broadcasters and newspapers is uniform that the break is to be regarded as a total success of German propaganda, especially of myself. One admires the extraordinary cunning and skill with which we have managed to hang a highly political question on the Katyn case. (…) Suddenly you see cracks in the Allied camp that you didn't want to admit before.

He saw very precisely the dilemma of the British government: 'Their heart is with the Poles, their mind with the Bolsheviks.'[32]

However, Goebbels had to take note that neither London nor Washington officially commented on Katyn. The *Völkischer Beobachter* commented: 'Jewry is trying to keep the revelations secret.'[33] The satirical magazine *Kladderadatsch*, published under Goebbels' control, printed a caricature of Churchill and Roosevelt sneaking through a forest, their index fingers on their mouths. The caption read: 'Silence in Katyn Forest.'[34]

The cartoonist of the British magazine Punch understood that Goebbels wanted to split the camp of the Allies.

The cartoon of the Soviet army newspaper Krasnaya Zvezda (Red Star) shows Goebbels playing the flute on a blood dripping hatchet and the London Pole dancing mazurka to it (21 April 1943).

At the end of April, the British prime minister once again campaigned in vain with Stalin for his Polish counterpart: 'We would continue our relations with Sikorski who is far the most helpful man you or we are likely to find for the purposes of the common cause.'[35] Finally, Churchill repeated the request that Moscow allow the Poles still detained in the Soviet Union to leave for Persia as well.[36]

Stalin replied to the British prime minister: Sikorski would hardly be able to prevail against the 'Hitler-friendly screamers' in his cabinet. Rumours of a new Polish government appointed in Moscow were inventions that hardly needed denial. In a letter to Roosevelt a few days earlier, Stalin had at least promised that the Poles still on Soviet territory would leave without problems.

Finally, under pressure from London, the Polish government in exile withdrew its application to the International Committee of the Red Cross in Geneva. Churchill cabled to Roosevelt: 'We have persuaded them to shift the argument from the dead to the living and from the past to the future.' The British prime minister admitted in the telegram that the development of Katyn's cause had become 'Goebbels' greatest triumph'. He wrote about the rumour that Stalin would establish its own Polish government on Soviet soil: 'We could not recognise such a government and would continue our relations with Sikorski.'[37]

In a statement, the government in exile asked why Moscow refused to agree to send a commission of the Red Cross if the Germans were the perpetrators.[38] However, the British government did not take a position on the issue. Instead, Foreign Minister Eden condemned before the House of Commons 'the cynicism which permits the Nazi murderers of hundreds of thousands of innocent Poles and Russians to make use of a story of mass murderers, in an attempt to disturb the unity of the Allies'.[39]

Stalin obviously concluded from this speech that the British wanted to keep the Katyn case secret, as the Americans had already signalled. The White House ignored the reports of the US Embassy in Moscow, which Admiral Standley later summarised in one sentence: 'It was the impression of our people in Moscow that the Russians had committed those murders.'[40] Despite the reports on Katyn, the US even increased supplies of military equipment to the Soviet Union under the Land Lease Act.[41]

Stalin concluded from the reactions of London and Washington that the Western Allies would not resist his plans for Eastern Europe. He ignored the appeals to release the Poles still detained in the Soviet Union. They were held back further, mostly in Siberia and Kazakhstan, and were only allowed to move to Poland after 1957 during the short political thaw four years after Stalin's death.

Chapter 7

The Dilemma of the Poles

The German authorities of the General Government were commissioned by Goebbels to bring Poles to Katyn, who should inform their compatriots in their homeland and report to the government in exile in London about the actions of the Soviets. In Warsaw, the staff of Governor General Frank tried to find people who could spread the message and who represented all groups of society. The choice fell just as much on intellectuals as on factory workers. Representatives of the Catholic Church of Poland, whose clergy had been mercilessly persecuted by the Germans, were also to play an essential role. The Germans thought of a special role for Polish doctors in Katyn, a very difficult and burdensome task: they should confirm the identity of the corpses.

On 9 April 1943, the secretary general of the Polish Red Cross (PCK), Kazimierz Skarżyński, was appointed by telephone to the headquarters of the German authorities. The PCK was one of the few Polish organisations that the Germans had not banned. German propaganda officers informed Skarżyński, a member of an old noble family, representatives of the trade, of women's associations and the archdiocese, briefly about the mass graves of Katyn. They were informed that a Polish delegation should fly to Smolensk the next morning to inspect the graves.

The Poles were suspicious; for two and a half years they had received almost daily reports of murder and terrorist actions by the occupiers. Astonished, they heard slogans of a necessary reconciliation between Germans and Poles, which together would have to save 'European civilisation from the barbaric East'.

While Skarżyński wanted first to discuss the proposal with the presidium of the Polish Red Cross, several of those present immediately declared that they were ready for the trip. Their arrival at Smolensk airport was filmed for the German and Polish newsreels, as was their sightseeing tour of the city accompanied by German officers and the subsequent dinner. This group included the writer Ferdynand Goetel, chairman of the Polish Pen Club and the Union of Writers before the war. He was a declared anti-communist, but considered the ban on the Communist Party and the persecution of its functionaries by the Polish authorities to be wrong.

Goetel also saw some ideas of Italian fascism as a model for Poland: the fight against capital, exploitation and corruption. He described his vision of a country with social justice, led by a strong, but intelligent leader a few months before the war in the manifesto 'In the Sign of Fascism'. He advocated emigration of Jews from Poland, but rejected German National Socialism as primitive and brutal. His books were banned by the German occupying forces. Goetel edited an underground magazine.

Immediately after arriving at Smolensk airport, the small Polish group saw a German bomber squadron returning from action behind Soviet lines. In an officers' mess, Lieutenant Colonel von Gersdorff, who was responsible for all groups of visitors, welcomed them.[1] In the evening they ate together with German officers; the meal consisted of potatoes with goulash.

Upon arrival in Katyn, German officers at the open graves spoke of the inevitable struggle 'between Western culture' and Asian barbarism, according to Goetel's report. Like the other members of the group, Goetel described his impressions to German radio reporters. He confirmed that the officers identified so far were on the list of missing persons who had entered Soviet camps as prisoners of war.

German officers asked Goetel if he knew the name of Kozelsk, which was mentioned in several of the documents found on the bodies. Goetel became convinced that the German side had never heard the name before and reported on the Polish findings about the three camps. He talked longer with Professor Buhtz, describing him as 'a representative of old Germany, an old-school man for whom the profession of doctor is an obligation'.

Goetel, who spoke Russian very well, was also able to interview the farmer Parfen Kiselev without the Germans listening in on this conversation. The old Russian confirmed his observations of spring 1940, which he had already given to the Germans for the record. In the evening after the visit to the mass graves, the Polish group was invited by the German escort officers to the theatre of Smolensk; on the program was Russian cabaret, which the Poles found tactless.

According to Goetel, the Germans moved freely in the city; there was no climate of threat. One of the officers said: 'It's quiet here.' Poland, on the other hand, is a 'danger zone for the Germans'. The night had also gone quiet; Goetel noted that there had been no shots and explosions.

Goetel, on the other hand, experienced an atmosphere of war after his return to Warsaw: the battles over the Jewish ghetto were in full swing. At the same time, loudspeaker trucks were driving through the other residential areas, announcing the news from Katyn. Goetel resisted the Germans' attempts to get him involved in their propaganda actions.[2]

A few days later a delegation of the Polish Red Cross flew to Smolensk. Secretary General Skarżyński had received the green light from the other members of the presidium. Later he wrote that, in view of the German occupation policy, he was firmly convinced at the moment that this was another propaganda campaign by the Nazi leadership.[3]

The London Poles were initially sceptical; they saw the danger that the Poles could be exploited by Nazi propaganda in Katyn. But, in the end, the argument that this might help to clarify the fate of missing officers weighed more heavily. So they instructed Skarżyński and the doctors to fly to Katyn as well. However, it was decided that the members of the delegation should not make any public statements. They should not appear on the trip to Katyn as official representatives of the PCK, but should call themselves 'Technical Commission of the Red Cross'.

The Germans attached great importance to the formation of the commission because its members were to exhume the bodies in the mass graves. Initially, it consisted of four forensic and general practitioners, and PCK General Secretary Skarżyński appointed the young Krakow university lecturer Marian Wodziński to head it. He was only 32 years old.

Six days after the meeting at Palais Brühl, the Technical Commission flew to Smolensk. Skarżyński instructed its fellow travellers to always stick together and, above all, to avoid the German press in Katyn. Soon, other experts from occupied Poland arrived, and the Commission had twelve members for a time. The Archbishop of Krakow, Prince Adam Stefan Sapieha, also accepted the request to delegate a priest to the Commission. The choice fell on his confidant Stanisław Jasiński, the long-time director of Caritas. Archbishop Sapieha told him to confine himself solely to pastoral care.[4]

The commission was first housed in a barrack on a former estate in Katyn, later in the village school, and the food came from a German officers' casino. The local Wehrmacht command had to provide several vehicles with drivers. But there was a lack of suitable working clothes at the beginning. While gowns, rubber boots and disinfectants soon arrived in sufficient quantities, there was still a shortage of rubber gloves. The pathologists examined most of the bodies with their bare hands. They also ordered 7,000 cigarettes and alcohol, some of which they gave to the Russian workers who helped with the exhumation.[5]

The Technical Commission continued where Professor Gerhard Buhtz began his investigations in March. Buhtz was a well-known figure to some of the Polish experts. Although he appeared in German uniform as a representative of the Nazi regime, they later stated that he had worked correctly, that he had never given himself up for the falsification of expert opinions.[6] The Poles also reported that Buhtz repeatedly clashed with the German propaganda officers because they wanted to announce things that were not covered by his investigations.[7]

About 150 villagers were involved in the exhumation work, and Russian prisoners of war were also deployed. Only in one of the mass graves were the shot people lying in a row, in the others they had fallen or been thrown from the edge, often the limbs were entangled. During the day, the workers recovered between 70 and 120 bodies, some of which had already fallen apart, and laid them next to the graves. There was a pervasive smell of corpses in the wood.

The Polish pathologists worked for eight weeks daily from 8a.m. to 6p.m., with a one and a half hour lunch break. The objects found during the autopsy were given the same numbers as the respective corpses and then brought to Smolensk, where German forensic scientists chemically cleaned and catalogued them. The Poles had no tools such as microscopes or laboratory cases to approximate the time of death after decomposition of the corpses. They had to limit themselves to evaluating the newspapers, letters, cards, diaries and notepads they found. Records were found on fifteen of the dead; the longest had a volume of five pages. Members of the Commission were able to copy these testimonies word for word.[8]

For every corpse a protocol was drawn up; they were also photographed. The workers then returned them to one of the mass graves, which had meanwhile been completely uncovered, and the prelate Stanisław Jasiński blessed them. Many German newspapers reprinted pictures of it, and the ten-minute documentary film for the German newsreel ended with the priest.

On the day of arrival Jasiński had already said a prayer for the dead together with the other members of the Polish delegation, but immediately afterwards he had collapsed from the stench and was perhaps overwhelmed by the terrible sight. It took the Polish doctors half an hour to bring him back to consciousness. After four days he flew back to Warsaw together with the head of the delegation, Skarżyński. He immediately set off for Krakow. He reported to Archbishop Sapieha that the Germans had asked him to make a statement on the crime for the radio. But he did not give in to this pressure; he only blessed the mortal remains of the murdered and provided spiritual support to his fellow countrymen involved in the exhumation work.[9]

The prelate Stanisław Jasiński and representatives of the Polish Red Cross pray over the graves of the murdered officers.

The Secretariat of the Red Cross in Warsaw drew up a protocol based on Skarżyński's first oral report and it was immediately sent to the government in exile. Skarżyński also sent a report to the ICRC in Geneva. The three main points were:

- The autopsy of 300 bodies shows that these officers were murdered with shots in the back of the neck, and the same type of wounds leads to the conclusion that it was undoubtedly a mass execution.
- It was not robbery, since the corpses wear uniforms and shoes, as well as medal badges, where a considerable amount of money and banknotes were found.
- According to the papers found on the bodies, the murder took place in March and April 1940.[10]

A few days later, however, members of the commission discovered German cartridge casings under the corpses and in some skulls the corresponding bullets of 7.65 mm pistol calibre. Goebbels was very concerned: 'Unfortunately German ammunition had been found in the graves of Katyn.' He ordered strictest secrecy, 'otherwise the whole Katyn affair would become obsolete'. But he soon got the all-clear: at the end of the 1920s, the manufacturer, the Genschow factory in Karlsruhe, had delivered large quantities of this ammunition to both Poland and the Soviet Union. But for Goebbels it was a sensitive topic, the press was not allowed to mention it.

Curious Wehrmacht soldiers occasionally made the exhumation work more difficult. Company by company they were transported to the cemetery to get an idea of the 'Bolshevik crimes'. The impressions should obviously strengthen their will to fight. Several tens of thousands of soldiers from the Eastern Front came to Katyn Forest, including contingents from the Waffen-SS 'Charlemagne' division and the Blue Division (División Azul), in which volunteers from France and Spain fought against the Red Army on the German side.[11]

Concentration camp for denied cooperation
It was particularly important for the Ministry of Propaganda in Berlin to bring Polish officers to the mass graves. Initially, it was planned to have representatives of the Polish Red Cross, who had been in Katyn, appear in camps for POW officers (oflag), but Skarżyński had firmly rejected this.[12]

So the Wehrmacht selected a total of six Polish officers in three oflag in the German Reich; the highest ranking was Lieutenant Colonel Stefan Mossor. Originally, a brigadier general was supposed to lead the group, but he fell ill at the last moment. Mossor had been part of the planning staff of the Polish armed forces; he was the author of 'Considerations for a strategic plan for Poland against Germany', but had also spoken indirectly in essays in favour of a political rapprochement with the Germans. He argued that Poland had no choice but to work with one of its two highly armed neighbours – and the Soviet Union was out of the question.

In Katyn, Mossor rejected attempts to persuade him be interviewed for the German newsreel; he successfully demanded that cameramen and radio people leave.[13] His comrades were allowed to examine several corpses from the mass of bodies not yet recovered for autopsy. They became convinced that they were really the disappeared Polish officers, that the bodies had not been touched before and that the uniforms had not been manipulated.[14] A Wehrmacht officer later reported that Mossor had spontaneously replied to the question as to who the perpetrators were: 'The Bolsheviks!'[15]

The group led by Mossor was brought from Smolensk to Berlin. He was first kindly invited to report on his observations in Katyn at a press conference; when he refused, SS officers threatened him with shooting. But he withstood the pressure; he agreed to describe his impressions to his comrades in the oflag. However, Mossor suspected that the executions were an arbitrary decision of a local NKVD commander, probably after a rebellion in the camp. He could not imagine that the Kremlin had ordered the mass murder.

Finally, Mossor wrote a report for the highest-ranking Polish POW in his camp. He refrained from naming the perpetrators because he assumed that the Germans would read the report. This was, in fact, the case. The Wehrmacht spread the report to other oflags. But Mossor secretly wrote another report for the Polish government in exile, which was smuggled out of the camp and actually reached London via the Polish underground – presumably the Germans knew about it, but they did nothing about it, since informing the London Poles was in their interest. In the report, Mossor expressed fears that Poland would fall wholly or to a considerable extent under Soviet rule after a defeat of the Germans. For this reason, the Polish government must work with Western countries to create a strong European organisation.[16]

Goebbels' propaganda officials had planned the same role as Mossor and his companions for the other Poles, who visited Katyn in several small groups: they were to reinforce the anti-Soviet mood among their compatriots. One group was accompanied by a reporter from the NSDAP newspaper *Ostdeutscher Beobachter* from the occupied city of Poznan. He described in drastic words the horror of the Poles when they stood in front of the mass graves.[17] On their return they reported about Katyn to their Polish compatriots in meetings organised by the Germans.[18]

Death lists for Polish witnesses

But the Polish communists, who had set up their own underground armed units, adhered entirely to Moscow's line: Katyn was an anti-Soviet provocation of the Hitlerists and the government in exile. They sentenced their compatriots, who travelled to Katyn at the invitation of the Germans, to death.[19] The Germans learned about the death sentences that were passed on participants of the trips to Katyn. When the reports about them reached Goebbels in Berlin, he arranged for some of the endangered to be given police protection.[20]

The well-known publicist Józef Mackiewicz, who was also brought to Katyn, was added to the death list of a communist underground group. Mackiewicz, a graduate biologist, had reported in the daily newspaper *Goniec Codzienny* published under German control in Vilnius about crimes committed by the NKVD after the Soviet invasion of eastern Poland. Because of his alleged collaboration with the Germans, a court of the anti-communist underground army AK in Warsaw also sentenced him to death. But the AK commander of Vilnius, who himself had witnessed Soviet terror, did not let the sentence be carried out and even had it quashed.[21]

Mackiewicz noted that the Poles were allowed to move freely in Katyn and to ask questions of the Russian population without being controlled by Germans. They were also allowed to take a close look at all documents that had been found on the victims.[22]

After his return from Katyn to Vilnius, Mackiewicz gave an interview to *Goniec Codzienny*. He not only described the exhumation work, but also reported on the things found in the bags of the uniforms during the autopsy:

> A corpse is laid on the table, the legs are a little shrunk, the head has been thrown to the side, the bullet's exit hole can be seen in the forehead. Władysław Bielecki ... The postcard is very well-preserved. The postmark shows the date: Białystok, 14.1.1940. In the side pocket the newspaper *Głos Radziecki* (Soviet Voice) of 29 March 1940. Although the paper has absorbed moisture that has caused the ink to swell, it can be clearly read: 'Comrades! To a better morning! There are new people coming to our fatherland ... Comrade Stalin ...' And so on. Next, a letter to Kozelsk. The name is illegible. A prayer book. Doctor Wodziński opens the letter, and suddenly a woman looks at us all so strangely clearly, with big eyes, she is blond, a child on her arm. ... It's his wife with the little daughter. He went to his grave with them. The bullet is still in his skull, which is rare.

Mackiewicz continued to quote from children's letters found among the dead:

> Dear Papa! We are worried because we have not received any news or letter for a long time. We sent 100 roubles and the package with the things you asked for. We're healthy and still in the same place. Don't be afraid for us! When we meet again ... Sign: Your Stacha, 15 February 1940.

And: 'Dear daddy! Thank you very much and I wish you health and all the best. I don't go to school. It's closed because of the frost. ... I collect the stamps.'[23]

The reports about the Polish delegations also reached SS leader Heinrich Himmler. He sent a suggestion to Ribbentrop: 'It occurs to me that if we were to invite Mr. Sikorski to fly to Katyn with an escort to be chosen by him, under the assurance of free escort over Spain, we would not put the Poles in an awful situation.' Ribbentrop, however, firmly rejected Himmler's proposal. According to him, 'the fundamental aspects of the treatment of the Polish question' made any contact with the government in exile impossible.[24]

The most prominent Pole the Germans brought to Katyn was the former prime minister Leon Kozłowski. But he was led alone over the cemetery; obviously he was to be shielded from the other Poles in Katyn. There were good reasons for this secrecy, because Kozłowski, professor of archaeology by profession and briefly head of government as Piłsudski's follower, was extremely controversial. After the Soviet invasion of eastern Poland, the NKVD arrested him in his hometown, Lwów, and brought him to Lubyanka in Moscow.

Since Kozłowski refused to write reports about other members of the pre-war leadership, the henchmen of the NKVD tortured him, as he later reported:

> The general asked the investigating officer whether I made a confession, he replied that I did not make a confession. Thereupon the Major began to swear, as it is only possible in Russian, and hit me in the face with his fist, the general hit me in the back with a rubber truncheon. The blows were very fast, one by one. Then I was thrown to earth and beaten again. Then I was put back on the chair and worked on with fist and rubber truncheon.[25]

Kozłowski was also systematically dazzled to such an extent that he went blind in his right eye. Because of the bad diet he fell ill with scurvy; he lost all his teeth. In a fast trial he was sentenced to death 'for anti-Soviet activities', including his participation in the Polish–Soviet war of 1920.

Surprisingly, however, he was released from prison after several weeks on death row because the government in exile and the Kremlin had, meanwhile, concluded the Sikorski–Maisky Agreement. He was accommodated in a Moscow hotel with other Poles. For the Poles, even the devastated Catholic church in the centre of Moscow was temporarily restored so that a mass could be celebrated there.

Most of the liberated Poles were taken to the Anders Army in Buzuluk. However, military service was out of question for Kozłowski because of his bad health. Without reporting to the Polish troop command, he travelled with another former inmate to his occupied homeland. In the fighting area in western Russia, the two of them passed through the lines thanks to the help of *kolkhoz* farmers, who were awaiting the Wehrmacht. The Red Army was in a chaotic retreat; the NKVD units had long since fled to the hinterland.[26]

A few days later, to the great surprise of his compatriots, Kozłowski reported on his experiences in the NKVD prison at a press conference in Berlin.[27] The London Poles, among whom Piłsudski opponents set the tone, saw his Berlin appearance as the first step towards the formation of a Polish puppet government directed by the Germans, at whose head he was to step.[28] A court of the government in exile therefore sentenced him to death in absentia for high treason. But in Berlin Kozłowski no longer played a role, since the Nazi leadership did not plan a government of its own for occupied Poland. Nor did he give a public statement on Katyn.

An analysis by the government in exile about the German Katyn campaign indicated Goebbels' attempt to justify the suppression of the ghetto uprising towards the Polish population with the formula 'Jew = murderer of Poles'.[29] The Germans announced that the relatives of the dead should receive compensation for Katyn. Representatives of the underground, however, reported to the government in exile that only a few of the family members had contacted the Germans.[30]

On 7 June 1943 work in Katyn was stopped because of the early summer temperature, the increasing smell of corpses, a fly plague and the danger of epidemics. Until then, seven mass graves had been accurately examined and an eighth one had been discovered only a few days before. The workers filled up the graves again. A wooden cross was erected on each grave. On the largest of the crosses, which was two-and-a-half metres high, members of the Polish commission placed a crown of thorns made of wire to which they had attached a metal eagle from one of the officer's caps.[31]

'Both the enemy's work'

Marian Wodziński, the head of the Polish expert group, wrote a report for the Red Cross in Warsaw. He explained that the dead had been identified as officers from the Kozelsk camp on the basis of the documents, diaries and letters found with them. The data indicated the time of the mass murder: spring 1940. The winter clothes of the dead in grave No. 1 and the summer uniforms in grave No. 8 showed that the executions took place from March to May. This is also consistent with the statements of the locals, who saw the Poles on their arrival at Gnezdovo railway station and heard screams from the forest.[32]

With the permission of the Germans, the members of the Technical Commission had copied all the documents found on the dead, but had also kept some of the objects secret and brought them to Warsaw. Archbishop Sapieha's residence in Krakow was designated as a safe place to store these objects and records. The young priest Stefan Niedzielak took on the task of smuggling them to Krakow through the strict controls at the train stations. Niedzielak would later play a role in the fight for the truth about Katyn.[33]

The results of the investigation by the Technical Commission were incorporated in the *Official Material on the mass murder of Katyn*, published by the Ministry of Foreign Affairs in Berlin in the summer of 1943. It contained a list with a short description of the 4,143 bodies, 1,328 of which could not be identified. The 273-page documentation also contained detailed information on the origin of the German ammunition found in the graves, but no references to alleged Jewish perpetrators, which had previously been widely disseminated in the press.

The Polish government in exile also received the *Official Material*, which was in the interests of the Germans. Polish experts found that four-fifths of the names of the identified victims were also on the lists of 'missing officers' handed over to the Soviet authorities in 1941 and 1942 by General Sikorski and Ambassador Kot.[34]

But the German propaganda officers in Warsaw tried in vain to set up a Polish Katyn Committee. Skarżyński countered that the Red Cross would lose the confidence of the population if it took part in it.[35] In order to prove a change in German policy towards Poland, the SS released a group of women from the Majdanek concentration camp. But Skarżyński explained to the German officers that this gesture was unconvincing in view of the still large number of death sentences imposed in occupied Poland. He also rejected the publication of an official PCK documentation.[36]

Therefore the Germans published in large numbers a thirty-two-page brochure with numerous photographs, without specifying an editor. They also distributed several million flyers with reports about Katyn throughout the General Government.[37] Goebbels was extremely satisfied with the news from occupied Poland: 'In the circles of the Polish aristocracy and the former officers, a deep bitterness is shown against the Soviets.'[38]

Governor General Hans Frank hoped that the Nazi rulers in Berlin would use the strong anti-Soviet mood among the Poles to 'bring about a change in Polish policy without shaking the prestige of the Greater German Reich'. Frank had long recognised that the mass executions in occupied Poland did not weaken the resistance movement at all, but brought it further popularity. In his opinion, this tied up too many military forces that were urgently needed on the Eastern front. In his official diary Frank wrote: 'We Germans must be grateful to fate that the graves of Katyn give us another opportunity to make concessions to the Polish people, not only in propaganda, but in fact ... to win them for German purposes'.[39]

Frank sent a forty-page memoir directly to Hitler. He criticised the failed policy in occupied Poland, which in his words absolutely had to be changed. He attacked Himmler whom he accused of causing economic chaos: the peasants defected to the partisans and mass executions of innocent people and confiscations of real estate for the SS only strengthened the enemies of the Germans. German propaganda had also proved ineffective against the 'Bolshevik infiltration'. Frank wrote that

Katyn opened up the possibility of a change of policy without being interpreted as a weakness of the German leadership.

To confirm his argument, Frank quoted from a report by the Security Police, which was subordinated to his adversary Himmler:

> The news from Katyn has not had any beneficial effects for Germany among the broad mass of the population. … It is pointed out that Germany's attitude towards Poland is no better, that there are concentration camps in Auschwitz and Majdanek, where a mass murder of Poles was also taking place.[40]

However, Frank did not mention in his memorandum that he himself was largely responsible for this policy, that he himself ordered widespread terrorist measures, which cost the lives of tens of thousands of Poles and ruined the country.

But in Berlin there was not the slightest thought of a change of course, on the contrary: after the final suppression of the ghetto uprising in May 1943, Himmler, with whom Frank had a deep mutual aversion, had the terror further intensified. Thus the campaign ordered by Goebbels in the General Government was largely ineffective and the image of the German occupying forces did not brighten in any way. On the contrary: slogans such as 'Katyn Auschwitz Unfree Hunger' or 'Katyn and Auschwitz – both of the enemy's work' were painted on the walls of houses in several Polish cities.[41]

Referring to information from the government in exile, the *Daily Mirror* printed a report about a poster campaign by the Polish underground in Krakow. The sarcastic text on the poster said:

> In view of the primitive way the Poles were killed by the Russians in the mass executions in Katyn, the Propaganda Department is organising popular excursions to the German concentration camps in Oswiecim, Majdanek, Treblinka, and other places, in order that the Poles may see themselves the modern and humanitarian means of mass executions used in these camps.[42]

The Polish underground sent an analysis of the German Katyn propaganda to London: 'The only result is the increase in hatred of the Soviets, but not the disappearance of hatred of the Germans.'[43]

Tresckow, Gersdorff, Schlabrendorff and their allies in the Central Army Group in Smolensk, who were waiting for the next opportunity to eliminate Hitler, came to the same conclusion: 'Katyn, however, could not distract us from the Nazi crimes. The persecutions of the Jews and the measures against Russians and Poles remained the main driving force behind our fight against Hitler and his regime.'[44]

Chapter 8

Failure of the Nazi Campaign
in the West

Goebbels' propagandists made special efforts to make their Katyn campaign effective abroad. They flew in medical doctors, journalists and writers from other countries – as well as prisoner-of-war officers from the armed forces of the Western Allies. In this way Goebbels wanted to discredit their alliance with the Soviet Union in the eyes of the American and British public, in particular.

The most important role was assigned to the coroners: they were to confirm that the perpetrators came from the NKVD. Goebbels instructed German Health Minister Leonardo Conti to assemble a delegation of foreign experts. In January 1940, Conti, who was SS brigade leader, had seen a demonstration in a prison in the city of Brandenburg about the effective killing of people in a gas chamber. He was one of those responsible for the euthanasia program of the Nazis. He also supervised medical experiments with typhus fever in the Buchenwald concentration camp near Weimar.

However, the efforts of the Ministry of Foreign Affairs in Berlin, which was responsible for the organisation, were not crowned with success on a decisive point: the German diplomats were unable to find physicians from the neutral states of Sweden, Spain, Portugal and Turkey for the Katyn mission, for which four days were scheduled.[1]

But at least there was a Swiss, the Geneva professor of forensic medicine François Naville, a lieutenant colonel in the reserve of the Swiss army. After consultation with the International Committee of the Red Cross and the Foreign Ministry in Berne, he accepted the invitation. When he arrived in Berlin, however, he was surprised to discover that he was the only 'neutral' in the delegation. The eleven other members came from occupied or allied countries:

- Arno Saxén, who was a military doctor for the Finnish armed forces in the rank of lieutenant colonel, arrived from Helsinki.
- Helge Tramsen from Copenhagen, 32 years old, was the youngest and the only one without a title of professor. As he reported after the war, he had

joined a resistance group. On his way back to Berlin, he was to receive documents from a contact in the Danish resistance.[2]

- Herman Maximilien de Burlet, with a doctorate in Zurich, was Chancellor of the University of Groningen and a leading member of the National Socialist Movement (NSB) in the Netherlands.
- Reimond Speleers, dean of the medical faculty in Ghent, Belgium, was also a Nazi sympathiser and an activist of the Flemish National Association (VNV).
- Vincenzo Palmieri from Naples, on the other hand, was a socially committed Catholic who had nothing in common either with the German National Socialists or the Italian fascists. He also studied in Berlin and spoke excellent German.[3]
- Eduard Miloslavich was the son of Croatian immigrants in the USA. The conservative Catholic, who had studied in Vienna, accepted a professorship in Zagreb. In the Independent State of Croatia, which in reality depended on Berlin, he became dean of the Faculty of Medicine.
- František Hájek, representative of the Reich Protectorate of Bohemia and Moravia, before the war had been dean of the medical faculty of the University in Prague, which had been closed by the German occupying forces.
- František Šubík from the University of Bratislava was head of health care in Slovakia. He was a military doctor with the rank of captain. He also made a name for himself as a poet and translator.
- Ferenc Orsós from Hungary had published articles on the determination of the time of death of corpses. He had founded a National Socialist medical association and advocated the introduction of racial laws based on the German model.
- Alexandru Birkle from Bucharest had learned German during the First World War as a volunteer of the Romanian army in Austrian captivity.
- Marko Markov, lecturer at the University of Sofia, represented Bulgaria, which was also allied with the Third Reich.

The twelve experts were accommodated for one night in the Hotel Adlon in Berlin. They chose Ferenc Orsós, a 63-year-old criminologist and medical examiner from Budapest, as their spokesperson because he not only spoke German very well, but also Russian. He had learned the language during the First World War in Russian captivity.[4]

The group took off from Tempelhof Airport in the early morning of 28 April 1943, travelling in three aircraft. In the clear blue sky, the passengers saw smoke over Warsaw. One of the flight attendants explained: 'Something has happened in the ghetto.' The Dane Tramsen wrote in his diary: 'Warsaw's city centre is one single burning pile of rubble.' In the afternoon the plane arrived in Smolensk and the delegation had dinner at the officers' mess. 'Plenty of wine and French champagne', Tramsen noted.

The next morning, Professor Buhtz led the delegation of doctors across the site in Katyn Forest. Also present was Lieutenant Colonel von Gersdorff, who five weeks earlier as suicide bomber had wanted to blow up Hitler in Berlin. Each of the coroners was asked to choose a corpse from the mass graves for autopsy, the Germans had provided all instruments and materials for it.[5]

After examining the cranial bones and the brain mass, Orsós came to the conclusion that the time of death must have been at least three years ago.[6] The professor of criminalistics Vincenzo Palmieri from Naples confirmed this assessment.

The Dane Helge Tramsen autopsied the body of a captain of the reserve. In the uniform pockets he found a small book with pictures of saints and a sheet of paper inscribed with Polish poetry verses. After the investigations were completed, Tramsen asked to be allowed to take the skull of the victim to Copenhagen for demonstration purposes.[7]

Orsós used his microscope to examine samples of the young pines that had been planted on the mass graves. He concluded from the growth rings that they

The Hungarian Ferenc Orsós questions the Russian farmer Parfen Kiselev. The Bulgarian Marko Markov (hatless) listens carefully. Markov later played a key role in the Soviet propaganda campaign.

The Dutchman de Burlet, the Belgian Speleers, the Swiss Naville and the Czech Hájek pay attention to the explanations of the German investigator Buhtz.

were five years old. But they had been replanted, as evidenced by a discoloration between the second and third annual ring; they had stood at their last place for three years, thus since 1940.

After three days in Katyn, the work of the International Medical Commission was finished. Before the return flight, the staff of the Central Army Group invited them again to lunch at the officers' casino in Smolensk. Lieutenant Colonel von Gersdorff sat between Swiss François Naville and Bulgarian Marko Markov. As Gersdorff confirmed after the war, both had 'no doubt whatsoever' about the Soviet perpetrators.[8]

However, the Commission's final report made no direct reference to the perpetrators. It was completed in Smolensk under the direction of Orsós. Young women in Wehrmacht uniforms typed it, signed by the twelve members of the delegation. A photographer took a separate picture of the page with the signatures. The text was immediately telegraphed to Berlin, where it was also translated into English and Polish. When the three aircraft made a stopover in occupied Poland on their way back to Berlin, each of the members of the Commission received a copy of the report; the photo with the signatures was attached to the text. They had been brought by a courier from Berlin.

The report cited shots in the neck as the cause of death. In summary, it described the state of decomposition of the corpses, referred to the winter clothing, the absence of mosquito bites and insect larvae and the stab wounds caused by square bayonets. The report also mentioned the letters, notes and newspapers found among the dead. All objective factors and evidence taken together would indicate that the executions took place in March and April 1940.[9]

The delegation members agreed that they would not make any comments and would not be available to the press either.[10] In Berlin, rooms were again reserved for them at the Hotel Adlon, and in the evening a visit to the opera was on the agenda. On 4 May 1943, Orsós handed over the report to Minister of Health Leonardo Conti on behalf of the delegation. After the meeting with Conti, the twelve members of the commission said goodbye to each other.

For all of them the trip to Katyn had consequences, some of them serious. The first one was Tramsen. In Berlin he met secretly with a contact of the Danish resistance. He received a package with photos of two big German water reservoirs, Moehne in Westphalia and Edersee in Hesse. Tramsen hid the photos in the upholstery of the box in which he transported the skull of the Polish officer from the mass grave of Katyn. From Copenhagen the photos were smuggled via

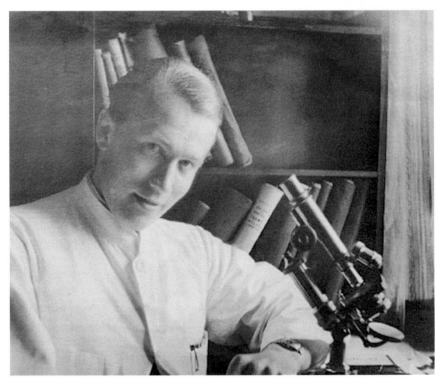

Helge Tramsen belonged to a Danish resistance group and was arrested by the Gestapo.
(© E. Jessen)

Sweden to England. Just two weeks after the Berlin meeting, the Royal Air Force bombed the dams of the two reservoirs with the aim of disrupting the power and water supply to the German defence industry.

Tramsen took part in the attack by a resistance group on a German armoury, but a Danish policeman arrested him. The Gestapo tortured him during interrogation, but left him alive on instructions from Berlin because he had been a member of the Katyn Commission. He remained in German custody until the end of the war.[11] The skull of the Polish officer, which he had cleaned immediately after his arrival, found its way into the magazine of the Forensic Institute in Copenhagen – and was forgotten there because Tramsen did not touch it anymore. It was not until 2005 that it was rediscovered there, brought to Poland and buried.[12]

After his return to Switzerland, Professor Naville was asked by a German consul to report on his observations and experiences in Katyn for the radio, but he refused. He may well give an academic lecture for colleagues.[13] This was also the view of his Italian colleague Vincenzo Palmieri. Without naming the perpetrators he published the final report of the medical commission in the popular magazine *La Vita Italiana*.[14]

Ferenc Orsós from Budapest also succeeded in resisting the pressure from the Germans: although he was a sympathiser of the Nazi regime, he refused the German embassy's request to comment on Katyn in the press. He argued that this would devalue the report of the medical commission; he was, at best, prepared to give a presentation to forensic doctors.[15]

Unlike Orsós, František Hájek, former Chair of Forensic Medicine and Criminalistics at the University of Prague, described his impressions of Katyn to the public and blamed the NKVD for the crime. The daily newspaper *České slovo*, published under German control, reported on Hájek's performances. His Slovakian colleague František Šubík did the same. He was also a writer, he had made a name for himself as a writer of patriotic poems under the pseudonym 'Andrej Žarnov'. He also translated Polish poets into Slovak; he was friends with several of them. Moreover, as a practising Catholic, he felt a connection with the Poles, which is why he was particularly committed to solving the mass murders of the officers.[16]

The Dutchman Herman Maximilien de Burlet also left no doubt that the crime was committed by the 'Bolsheviks'. A radio broadcast with him from

František Šubík accused the Soviets of the Katyn massacre in public lectures and statements to the press. (© M. Kanikova)

May 1943 is available on the Internet; for the NKVD he uses the old name GPU.[17] He also reported on his impressions of Katyn at a press conference; the German-controlled daily newspapers published detailed articles about it.[18]

According to his Belgian colleague Reimond Speleers, these were 'horrible murders that drew the attention of the entire world to the true intentions of Jewish Bolshevism'. Speleers reported on his impressions at a press conference in Brussels; he also made a lecture tour organised by the Germans, which took him to six cities in Belgium.[19] Much more reserved was the Finn Arno Saxén, who refused the invitation of the German embassy in Helsinki to give lectures and interviews about Katyn.[20]

The view of journalists and writers

Unlike the majority of the members of the International Medical Commission, who did not publicly comment on their investigations in Katyn, almost all of the foreign journalists invited by the Ministry of Propaganda wrote about it. Several groups started the journey. Most of them came from occupied and allied countries such as Norway, Serbia, Bohemia and Moravia, Italy and Hungary. The German propaganda officers paid particular attention to the correspondents from three neutral states: Sweden, Switzerland and Spain. However, the planes with the journalists did not take the shortest route from Berlin to Smolensk. Rather, they had to keep a wide arc around Warsaw, because the passengers were not supposed to see the smoke above the burning ghetto.[21]

Later, Christer Jäderlund, correspondent for the liberal daily *Stockholm's Tidningen*, reported that it was only in Smolensk that the journalists were informed of the actual purpose of the trip, namely the visit to the mass graves. Before arriving in Katyn, almost all members of his delegation were convinced that this was a new manipulation of Goebbels' propaganda machine. In Katyn, however, they understood that at least the information about the Soviet perpetrators obviously corresponded to the facts. Jäderlund was an eyewitness, as notes from the spring of 1940 were found on a body that had been examined in his presence.[22]

The correspondents ran to the autopsy tables when astonished shouts were heard from there. The Polish writer Józef Mackiewicz watched the scene:

A woman? – Yes, a woman! A female corpse in the mass of officer corpses! It wasn't clear why – but some of the journalists are taking off their headgear, which they hadn't done to the murdered men before. The Soviet prisoners of war who help with the work look crooked and curious. Silence enters. ... The journalists are worried, the Germans are consternated. One of them went to the field telephone in a makeshift barracks. ... The German authorities were so surprised and shocked by the discovery of a woman's body in Katyn that they kept this secret until the end and did not mention it in the official reports. Apparently, they feared that the improbability of the circumstances under which a woman could have reached the mass of murdered officers could become a starting point for new doubts that would undermine their credibility.[23]

It was the pilot Janina Lewandowska. The Danish scientist Tramsen took a closer look at the body: 'The head is covered with a sort of sacking, and the hands are tied on the back with a string carrying up around the neck.'

The group of journalists had to wait several days in Smolensk for their return flight. The Swede Jäderlund used the time to explore the city and its surroundings accompanied by a Yugoslavian colleague who spoke Russian. Jäderlund later reported about his conversations with Russians: They were very open-minded when he introduced himself as a Swede. They would all have been afraid of the NKVD, but also scolded the German occupying forces.[24]

Goebbels also had writers brought to Katyn to publish essays and feuilletons about their impressions of the mass graves. The Ministry of Propaganda in Berlin considered inviting the Norwegian Nobel Prize winner Knut Hamsun, who repeatedly praised Hitler and called on his compatriots to collaborate with the German occupying forces. Hamsun had appealed to the Norwegian youth to voluntarily fight against Bolshevism together with the Germans on the Eastern Front. The occupying forces supplied him with exquisite food, alcohol and tobacco out of gratitude and Goebbels raved repeatedly in his diary of Hamsun. But the idea to bring Hamsun to Katyn was dropped – he was already 84 years old.[25]

The Spanish writer Ernesto Giménez Caballero, on the other hand, did not pose a problem; he was satisfied to be involved in the Katyn campaign. Katyn as a communist crime fit the line of Franco's press, whose forces had fought against the international brigades armed by Stalin in the Spanish Civil War. Originally, Giménez Caballero had been part of circles of surrealist and futuristic artists, he saw himself as a socialist. But after a long stay in Mussolini's Italy and probably also under the influence of his Italian wife, he became an enthusiastic supporter of fascism. He campaigned for a union of 'Latin countries' under Mussolini's leadership, which should also be able to restore the Spanish empire. He took the view that his homeland had to defend itself against both Bolshevism and big business.[26] He rejected the anti-Semitism of the Nazis; rather, he took the view that the Sephardic Jews on the Iberian Peninsula had enriched Spanish culture. He considered Hitler a primitive politician of violence, and as a Catholic he also disliked the anticlericalism of the Third Reich and felt sympathy for Catholic Poland.

He published a fifty-one-page brochure about his impressions of Katyn entitled *The Slaughter of Katyn – A Vision of Russia*. In it, he justified the 'crusade' of

Franco's troops against the socialists and communists in the Spanish Civil War. He described in detail his observations in the forest of Katyn, his first impression: 'A smell that penetrates your soul'. Even campfires would not have covered the smell with resinous brushwood; many visitors would have kept cotton balls with ether under their noses. But he paid tribute to the way the Germans treated the dead: 'German soldiers formed themselves with respect in a clearing in the forest. The burial squad stood in military formation as a tribute to the fallen hecatombe of an entire army. Poor Poland!'

In Smolensk, the Spaniard noticed that everyday life continued, with Russian policemen serving at the largest intersections. He wrote with sympathy about the occupying forces: 'The German soldiers sometimes marched through these ruins in columns, singing their powerful war songs.'

In Katyn and Smolensk, Giménez Caballero was accompanied by a German officer who spoke Spanish. He had belonged to the Condor Legion, which had intervened in the Spanish Civil War on Franco's side. The writer quoted this officer as saying: 'We have always tried to separate Poland from its worst enemies: from all those who have always aimed to make Poland a Balkan wasp nest, a bayonet in the flank of Germany.'[27]

Three writers from occupied Belgium were also part of the delegation that travelled to Katyn: Ferdinand Vercnocke was an advocate of Flemish National Socialism, which was to follow closely the German Reich. He wrote an ode, 'To Hitler in Greater Germany'. Filip De Pillecyn came from the Catholic community; he saw the occupation of Belgium by the Germans as an opportunity for Flemish culture, which he saw disadvantaged in his home country by the French-speaking Walloons.[28] Pierre Hubermont, a Walloon (the French-speaking population in the southern part of his country), belonged to the Belgian Workers' Party. Originally, he had high hopes for the Soviet Union as a workers' paradise. But in 1930 he came back completely disillusioned from a congress of 'writers of the proletariat' in Kharkov. Soon he became enthusiastic about Hitler because he saw him as the leader of a workers' party.

Hubermont made detailed records of the writers' journey to Katyn, but they were never published. According to his report he was first brought to Berlin with his two Belgian colleagues, where they experienced a night of bombing. In the Kaiserhof hotel he met the Polish ex-premier Kozłowski, who also travelled to Katyn. The Polish professor became his most important interlocutor during the trip; both spoke French to each other. The Pole expressed the fear that the character of the Soviet regime would not be understood at all in Western countries: 'And that is all misfortune! You take the questions of life and death far too lightly!'[29]

On their return from Katyn to occupied Brussels, the three Belgian writers held a joint press conference, which saw a strong response in the newspapers under German control. Vercnocke wrote in Flemish an eight-page report 'I was in Katyn!' Hubermont wrote a brochure with an identical title in French. He presented the results of the Medical Commission, described his own observations and concluded: 'Just as the Soviet regime wiped out in hecatombs the nobility, the clergy and the bourgeoisie in Russia, it also killed the betrayed leaders of betrayed Poland in Katyn's bloody adventure.'[30]

French on the Eastern Front

Independent of the delegations of foreign journalists and writers flown in from Berlin, the two French publicists Fernand de Brinon and Robert Brasillach came to Katyn. The French press, controlled by the Germans, had reported little about the murder of the Polish officers until then. The most important publications were a photo of corpses from the mass grave on the front page of the Paris *Le Matin* and in the same paper a report that the Soviet secret police also executed French and British in Katyn.[31] However, it was one of many invented horror stories of German propaganda.

Count de Brinon, originally a lawyer, had become a journalist and was the first representative of the French press to interview Hitler a few weeks before his appointment as Reich Chancellor. The latter had promised France and Germany a reconciliation of interests and also found warm words for its eastern neighbour Poland: 'There is undeniably a Polish nation, and I respect its admirable patriotism.'[32] After the French defeat in 1940, de Brinon advocated close cooperation with the Germans, becoming a representative of the Vichy government as state secretary.

Brasillach, author of dramas, novels and poems, was fond of Mussolini and Franco. He was editor-in-chief of the aggressively nationalist and openly anti-Semitic magazine *Je suis partout*, which advocated the deportation of Jews. He had also emerged as president of the 'French Voluntary Legion against Bolshevism', which recruited soldiers in France for deployment on the Eastern Front in the SS division 'Charlemagne'. The inspection of these French units under the commander-in-chief of the Wehrmacht was the real purpose of de Brinon's journey to the occupied territories of the Soviet Union, during which the representatives of the Vichy government were accompanied by officers of the German garrison in Paris.

Before the journey to Russia Brasillach wrote:

> In the spring of 1940, when the Soviets were officially at peace with the whole universe, they killed thousands of Polish officers with a shot in the neck. At the same time, other Polish officers were conditionally released from the Reich or were still held captive under international law. They were prisoners of war, which is not funny, but they lived.

If the Soviet Union should win the war, he predicted a 'Katyn' for the French intelligentsia, which was currently complaining about the German occupation.[33]

On the Internet there is a report of the newsreel about this trip; it also shows pictures from Katyn Forest.[34] After the return from Russia, Brasillach published a long report entitled 'I have seen the Katyn trenches'. His leitmotif is the stench in Katyn Forest:

> What jumps in your face is the smell. The German driver had warned me: 'I couldn't eat for two days.' The people at these graves smoke to cover up that disgusting smell. ... A massive smell, a black and sour smell, the unforgettable smell of a slaughterhouse. Like from a living being, an animal that has been rotten in this earth for a long time, that no longer devours corpses. They lie there, compressed and packed together. ... Tainted flesh, such as carrion from a wild animal full of worms, the bilious stench of cowsheds that have not been aired for a long time, vomit, festering ulcers, the fermentation of seeds mix with a bitter mixture. Maybe the comparison with spoiled fish is the most appropriate. But like an enormous swarm of dead fish, with burst intestines, purulent discharge, green open wounds that have long since formed toxins.

The French delegation in Katyn: Fernand de Brinon (centre, in light coat), Robert Brasillach (second from left).

Brasillach drew a comparison to paintings from the Last Judgement of the Middle Ages. In a few words he described the work of the Russian workers:

> They have to pull the corpses apart with pitchforks and tridents, you hear a sound like tearing greasy paper. The indifferent grave diggers walk through the sand and carry the bodies around. They take them with two hooks, then they throw them at our feet, they're dry, light, like a dry herring.

Brasillach energetically rejected the version that the Germans had put pieces of evidence about the perpetrators into the uniforms of the dead:

> Can one have staged an enormous and cruel masquerade here for the sake of propaganda? But they searched the bodies before our eyes, it is really impossible to have them prepared: the clothes are completely glued to the body, they had to be removed with a knife.

Finally, the French writer concluded that there can be no doubt about the perpetration of the Soviets:

> They have understood that the Poles hate Bolshevism, and that this people, which so often acted carelessly and recklessly, with tragic care, has not forgotten the anti-Communist lesson of Piłsudski, and that beyond Piłsudski, Polish history has always been anti-Russian. The Soviets have drawn the logical conclusion from this observation: they have decapitated the Polish elite, just as they have destroyed the elites of the Baltic peoples.

The Poles had become the victims of their own 'careless leaders and Bolshevik barbarism'. However, the Bolsheviks would not have stopped at their own population, 60,000 to 100,000 Russian victims would probably also be lying in the forest of Katyn.[35] Later, Brasillach replied to the objection that the Germans had committed even greater crimes: 'Can the barbarity of some excuse the barbarity of others?'

State Secretary de Brinon said at a press conference in Paris that the mass graves were like Dante's inferno, and defended the German campaign: 'Given the size of the mass graves, German propaganda may even have failed to inform the public sufficiently. ... It is necessary for the French population to become clear about reality.[36]

Soon after the Katyn trip de Brinon went to Berlin, where he was welcomed by Goebbels. The latter noted in his diary: 'Too much of a writer and journalist to be considered for practical politics.'[37]

Americans and Britons at the mass graves

Another scandal writer of that time urged to see the mass graves was the US citizen Ezra Pound, who was considered one of the strongest voices of American modernism. Already as a young man he had gone to Europe; he lived in Ireland, England and France. The bloodshed during the First World War touched him profoundly; he blamed capitalism for it, especially Great Britain. He moved to Italy and became enthusiastic about Mussolini.

But he wavered in his attitude to Hitler: sometimes he praised him, whereas sometimes he called the Nazi regime a 'sickly and unpleasant parody of fascism'. However, his position on the Soviet Union was unambiguous: 'Stalin's regime considers humanity NOTHING save raw material.' He also had a clear opinion of Roosevelt: 'A weak man.'[38]

When the news about Katyn occupied the international press in the spring of 1943, the German diplomat Gotthardt Maucksch was asked to invite Ezra Pound to join the delegation of international writers who were to fly to Katyn. Before the war, Maucksch had owned a German bookshop in Rome; he was enthusiastic about Hitler and joined the NSDAP. In the cultural department of the German Embassy, he was responsible for translating German writers into Italian. In addition to fiction, he was obliged to offer the Italian publishers the White Paper of the Reich government, in which the German attack on Poland was justified, but this met with no interest.[39]

In his major work *The Cantos* published after the war, Pound mentioned the invitation to the journey in one sentence, but without any explanation; he misspelled the name of the German diplomat and the village of Katyn: 'Maukch thought he would do me a favour by getting Me onto the commission to inspect the mass graves of Katin.'[40]

As eyewitnesses reported, the poet was extremely interested in participating in the journey. But in the end the German embassy in Rome did not grant him a visa; he was obviously considered uncontrollable.[41]

Pound had to confine himself to a radio commentary, in which he accused the British prime minister of keeping silent about Katyn:

> Mr. Churchill knows quite as much about Bolshevik METHODS of administration as anyone else. Mr. Churchill has in the past expressed himself quite clearly on that subject. Nothing equivocal about Winston's words when referring to Russia under Bolshevik rule. The mass graves at Katyn surprised NO one.[42]

The Ministry of Foreign Affairs in Berlin recorded all these reports and comments on Katyn. But the propaganda ministry under Goebbels found that they did not have the slightest effect on the Western Allies.

Similarly, another central part of Goebbels' campaign failed: the sending of prisoner of war officers of the Western Allies to Katyn. First, the Wehrmacht was ordered to bring three British and one American general, who had fallen into the hands of the Germans. However, all four rejected the proposal, citing the Geneva POW Convention.

Finally, the Germans chose a British colonel named Frank Stevenson, a reserve officer who had worked as a teacher in South Africa before the war and also published two volumes of poetry, and the American lieutenant colonel John H. Van Vliet, a graduate of West Point. Both had been captured in the battles with the German Africa Corps. Van Vliet later reported that Stevenson was particularly interested in supernatural phenomena, and that his purse was made from an Indian's headdress.[43]

In addition, there were two other officers: the American captain of the artillery Donald B. Stewart and the British military doctor Stanley Gilder, who had basic knowledge of Russian. The eight-man group also included three privates and an English civilian arrested by the Germans on the Channel Island of Guernsey. The Channel Islands were the only British territory that came under German control. Some of the native English were deported to German camps after the British had interned Germans living in Iran.[44]

After their arrival in Berlin, the Allied officers declared that they would only accept the invitation as private individuals. They also refused to give their word of honour that they would not attempt to escape.[45] They understood that they would become part of a propaganda campaign, but did not want to miss the opportunity to get an idea of the situation for themselves. They also hoped to be taken to Spain or Portugal to travel on to their countries.[46]

In Smolensk, the Allied soldiers visited the partially destroyed city centre. The meals were taken together with English speaking German officers. The British military doctor Gilder later wrote about them: 'The German officers were as charming as only Germans can be when they have orders to be charming.'[47] After dinner at the Officers' Casino, a singer performed Broadway songs and accompanied himself at the piano. No one from the small POW group touched the liqueur that was served.[48]

The American and British officers were allowed to move freely around the cemetery of Katyn. They were asked to propose one of the bodies from a mass grave that had not yet been uncovered for autopsy. Captain Stewart later wrote in his report: 'They started to remove the boots. They said they always removed the boots and cut them open because the prisoners often had things concealed in them. They pulled off one boot, and the foot came with it from the ankle on down, leaving the bone sticking out.'

Before arriving in Katyn the American and British witnesses were all convinced that they should participate in an attempt of the Germans to conceal

British military doctor Stanley Gilder (centre) and South African reserve colonel Frank Stevenson visit one of the mass graves.

their own perpetrators. But then they made an observation that made them change their mind: 'The conclusion that we drew from our examination of those uniforms was that those officers could not have been prisoners very long at the time of their deaths. ... The boots were not worn at all.' As prisoners of war, the members of the group had experienced for themselves how quickly uniforms worn daily were in poor condition and there was no substitute for them.[49]

After returning from the forest of Katyn, the Americans and British visited an 'improved farming village' according to German plans and, for comparison, a run-down kolkhoz in the region of Smolensk. The officers stayed in Berlin for another week, they were even allowed to walk several times in a large park under guard. Goebbels' propaganda officers tried in vain to persuade them to make statements for the press and radio.[50]

Hitler's opponent Gersdorff, who said he spoke to almost all foreign visitors, later summarised the situation: 'I have not met anyone who was not convinced of the Soviet guilt for this crime.'[51]

But neither the American nor the British public learned about it, even from their own officers who were in Katyn. Stevenson was finally brought to Portugal, as he had hoped, and came there in the care of the British Embassy, but only in the spring of 1945.[52] The other participants of the officer's journey to Katyn, however, remained in their camps in the German Reich until the end of the war.

Van Vliet later reported that he had led several escape attempts from his oflag. A tunnel was dug and American airplanes should have taken in the escaped officers. But all escape plans failed; Van Vliet was not released until May 1945 with the German surrender.[53]

Chapter 9

Isolation of the
Polish Government in Exile

Shortly after the break between the Kremlin and the Polish government in exile, the American special envoy Joseph E. Davies arrived in Moscow in May 1943 on a secret mission. Davies had been one of Roosevelt's closest friends for three decades. His mission was so delicate that not even US Ambassador William H. Standley, not to mention the British allies, should know about its objective.[1]

The two US diplomats did not get along and disliked each other: Davies had been Washington's representative at the Moskva from 1936 to 1938 and raved about the American–Soviet friendship, while Admiral Standley was extremely sceptical. Moreover, Davies did not hide the fact that he could visit Roosevelt at any time. The gnarled admiral later called him in his memoirs an 'oily self-promoter'.

A few weeks earlier Standley had confused the White House and the State Department. He had complained at a briefing with American correspondents that Moscow was thwarting the agreed exchange of military information and, moreover, that the Soviet press did not report on the enormous supplies of military equipment and food under the Land Lease Act.

Davies was angry with Standley; he wanted to avoid any quarrel with the Kremlin. Molotov also expressed his anger in a conversation with Standley. But when soon after Soviet newspapers brought first reports about the Land Lease Act, the admiral could feel he was the winner in the conflict. He later wrote that the Kremlin apparently assumed that he had criticised the Soviet press with the backing of the White House.[2]

A little later the German Katyn campaign reached its climax. Roosevelt himself never made a public statement, Davies did so for him: before his departure for Moscow he declared that there could be no doubt about the German perpetrators in Katyn. He claimed that Roosevelt was of the same opinion.[3] He thus gave an important signal to the Kremlin: no problems are to be expected from the White House in the Katyn case.

Davies thus thwarted Standley's reports, which he disagreed with. The admiral was by no means the only one who wanted to convince the president

Joseph E. Davies, a great admirer of Stalin and Roosevelt's special ambassador for the Soviet Union, called Katyn a German crime.

of the Soviet perpetrators. This included Roosevelt's influential advisor Franklin Jay Carter. The latter referred to Ernst Hanfstaengl, the former head of the NSDAP press department responsible for contacts abroad, who had been in American custody since 1942. Hanfstaengl worked for a research and evaluation group that Carter had set up with Roosevelt's approval.[4] Carter had worked for several years for the magazines *Liberty* and *Vanity Fair*. In 1932 he had sought an interview with Adolf Hitler in Berlin, but the NSDAP press office only arranged him a meeting with Hermann Göring, who led the party's Berlin organisation.

From 1936 he wrote columns on White House internals under the name Jay Franklin. However, the readers did not learn that the articles were agreed with the Roosevelt staff. Carter enjoyed the confidence of the president; he offered to provide him regularly with background information from the milieu of journalists, politicians and diplomats. Roosevelt accepted the offer; his style of government included maintaining other information channels besides the official governmental bureaucracy. So Carter became a kind of a private spy who regularly came to the Oval Office to report personally without the media branch knowing about it. He was generously paid for it and also got the means to recruit a small circle of employees.

For the White House, Carter compiled a list of the names of the most important heads of the Nazi regime.[5] In the summer of 1942 he had a spectacular success: he was the first to report to the White House about the extermination camp Bełżec, in occupied Poland; his men had interviewed refugees from Eastern Europe in the port of New York. Carter's top secret operating group thus preceded the Office of Strategic Services (OSS), the military intelligence service.

At that time Carter also learned that Hitler's former press chief Hanfstaengl was in an internment camp for German citizens in Canada. They knew each other. It was Hanfstaengl who had arranged the interview with Göring ten years earlier. The almost two-metre tall German had an American mother, he had studied at Harvard before the First World War, cultivated contacts with journalists in the

USA and also made a name for himself as a pianist at private concerts for the elite in Washington. In New York he ran an art salon that his parents had founded. In his circle of friends, the tall man was nicknamed 'Putzi'.[6]

But after the First World War he was expropriated as a member of an 'enemy nation'. He moved to the German Reich, where he met Hitler. He was enthusiastic about him, he supported the Nazi newspaper *Völkischer Beobachter* financially and was also looking for supporters of the NSDAP in the upper class of Munich. He taught Hitler manners for a better society and introduced him there as well.

His wife even tried, but without success, to teach Hitler how to dance. Since 'Putzi' continued to give private concerts, he was called 'Hitler's piano player'. From 1931 he was responsible for contacts with foreign journalists in the NSDAP press staff. His statements in which he promoted Hitler were often printed in the American and British press so his name was known to newspaper readers.[7]

The BBC correspondent Alexander Werth, who later also played a role in the debates about Katyn, met Hanfstaengl in Berlin. The latter had raved about Hitler: 'The man has an artistic temperament, and a deep emotional strain. A wonderful man – so human.' Werth wrote about Hanfstaengl: 'His joviality had a slightly threatening intonation.'[8]

After Hitler seized power in 1933, however, the relationship between the two men deteriorated, although Hanfstaengl had initially caused a sensation when he had composed a 'Hitler Suite' in 'military tempo'. Even *The New York Times* reported about it.[9]

But the sophisticated, polyglot, rich bourgeois, who had also written a dissertation on Bavarian history in the eighteenth century, expressed himself disdainfully about the primitivities of leading Nazi politicians. He had also repeatedly urged the Führer to be moderate in his dealings with political opponents and sharply criticised the Nazi excesses of violence and their anti-Semitism. In any case, Hanfstaengl reported it in his memoirs.

Moreover, great tensions arose between him and Goebbels, who demanded that all contacts with the foreign press should pass through his ministry. Since Hanfstaengl feared that he would be liquidated as a confidant of dark chapters about the financing of the NSDAP, he fled to Great Britain via Switzerland in 1937. The case caused a sensation, above all in the USA; *The New York Times* reported on Hanfstaengl's flight from Nazi Germany.[10]

According to Goebbels' diaries, Hitler and SS leader Himmler urged him to bring Hanfstaengl back to the German Reich to 'silence him'. Goebbels was worried that Hanfstaengl ('a first-class pig') could pass on his knowledge of NSDAP internal affairs to the British press: 'If he unpacked, that would put all other emigrants far in the shade.' He therefore made Hanfstaengl an offer: he should participate in the composition of a film score.[11]

But Hanfstaengl ignored Goebbels' advances and stayed in London. At the beginning of the war he was arrested there as a German and taken to the internment camp in Canada.[12] When his old acquaintance John Franklin Carter learned of Hanfstaengl's internment, he suggested to Roosevelt that he use his intimate knowledge of the Nazi elite: the German should create psychological profiles of Hitler and other Nazi leaders. Roosevelt agreed, stating he knew Hanfstaengl from events for Harvard graduates.

The president personally supported the transfer of Hanfstaengl to the US authorities, but the latter retained the status of a British prisoner of war. His tasks now included listening to speeches by Nazi greats on German radio and writing dossiers about them.[13] The reports of 'Putzi', as he was also loosely called by the American intelligence experts, were sent not only to the White House, but also to the FBI, the OSS and the Office of War Information (OWI).

In his dossiers, Hanfstaengl proposed, among other things, to broadcast the speech of an American general in the territories occupied by the Germans. In the speech, the officers of the Wehrmacht were to be promised cooperation and fair treatment if they overthrew Hitler. This was best done by Dwight D. Eisenhower; the Germans knew his name because the troops he commanded had defeated them in North Africa. But Roosevelt did not accept this idea. In his eyes, Prussian Junkers set the tone in the officers' corps of the Wehrmacht, with whom he ruled out any kind of alliance.[14]

Katynisation of the elite

Carter later reported on Hanfstaengl's reactions when he read the first reports about the mass graves in Katyn Forest in mid-April 1943:

> He became extremely excited. He said it was the most important political event of the Second World War. He said also that he knew Goebbels well enough to know that at that time Goebbels was telling the truth. He hated and distrusted Goebbels as a politician.[15]

Hanfstaengl wrote two analyses on Katyn, which Carter passed on to Roosevelt. The president had read with great interest his psychological studies about the Nazi leaders. But it had annoyed him that the dazzling German expressed criticism of the war goal formulated by Roosevelt: the unconditional surrender of the Third Reich. This goal weakens only Hitler's opponents in the Wehrmacht, because now the Germans would fight to the end, argued Hanfstaengl.

In earlier dossiers he had also predicted a rebellion of the Wehrmacht and an uprising of the population against Hitler because of the Allied bomb war. But neither of these things had happened, so that he was no longer taken very seriously in the White House to the great sorrow of his patron Carter.[16]

So the two Katyn reports by Hanfstaengl were ignored. He predicted that the Katyn case would lead to a split in the cabinet of the Poles in London and that one of Sikorski's ministers would resign in order to make himself available to Hitler as head of a Polish collaboration government. It was another miscalculation.[17]

In the covering letter to the second Katyn analysis, Carter pointed out that the discovery of the mass graves had met with a strong response 'not only among the Slavs but in European Catholic circles'. Hanfstaengl asked the question: 'If the Soviet Government were able to face an international investigation commission on the mass-graves in Katyn Forest, why then did they shirk from this superb chance to expose Goebbels & Company while exonerating themselves?'

Ernst Hanfstaengl, 'Hitler's piano player', wrote two analyses about Katyn for the White House.

The upheaval caused by the reports about Katyn in the 'non-Bolshevik world' created new perspectives in Europe for Hitler, Hanfstaengl wrote. The Germans succeeded in spreading the terms 'katynisation' and 'katynise' as a synonym for the extermination of the elite by the Bolsheviks. As a result, many Europeans now feared an Allied invasion of Western Europe, for this would inevitably lead to the threat of katynisation of a large part of the 'Old World'.[18] Hanfstaengl alluded to the scenario that in the case of a second front formed by the Western Allies, the Germans would have to thin out the Eastern Front and thus the Red Army could advance faster to Central Europe.

But Carter had to accept that Roosevelt did not agree with Hanfstaengl's premise, that in the case of Katyn the propaganda of Goebbels was true. The president also rejected the suggestion that the German should report to him personally: 'I don't think I should see Putzi.'[19]

The president's scepticism regarding Hanfstaengl was reinforced by the secret service OSS, whose experts tended to believe that the Germans were the perpetrators. The OSS office set up in London with the permission of the British evaluated the materials of the Polish government in exile and the German press releases. In the analysis sent to the OSS chief in Washington, General William J. Donovan ('Wild Bill'), the words 'evidence' and 'massacres' were written in quotation marks, as if the authors ironically wanted to distance themselves from it.[20]

The *Völkischer Beobachter (People's Observer)*, the organ of the Nazi party, took up the term 'katynising' and published a cartoon about a dialogue between two NKVD men under the heading 'Bolshevik Future Dreams' (17 April 1943):

- *With the help of our English-American friends, we will get the whole of Germany and Europe into our hands.*
- *And what will we do with it, comrade?*
- *Katynise of course, you sheepheads!*

However, it cannot be ruled out that the OSS had already learned of the Katyn massacre a year earlier, in 1942. At least this was later claimed by the secret service colonel John V. Grombach. The graduate of the officers' academy Westpoint, formerly a member of the American national fencing team and also a successful amateur boxer, had founded a top secret spy cell code-named 'Pond' – in competition with the OSS. Formally, it was a private detective agency, but was paid for by the Military Intelligence Service (MIS); yet Grombach remained an officer in the US Army and was directly subordinate to the MIS chief. One of the tasks of 'Pond' was to recruit informants in the European countries occupied by the Germans, the agents Grombach operated from Berne and Madrid.[21]

In Paris, Grombach had recruited the doctor Marcel Petiot, who, as it turned out later, also worked for the Gestapo, but above all was a serial killer: Petiot pretended to allow Nazi opponents to flee the German occupation zone for money, but then murdered and robbed about two dozen people who wanted to flee.

Grombach published a book about Petiot in 1980 under the title *The Great Liquidator*. In it, he briefly described that in 1942 the Paris doctor had reported about a Polish patient. The Pole told him about the massacre of several thousand Polish officers in Katyn Forest. The former intelligence officer stated in the book that he had informed the Washington authorities, but his report of Petiot's testimony had obviously been suppressed and had not been sent to the White House.[22]

In any case, in the spring of 1943, President Roosevelt saw no reason to change his policy of American–Soviet partnership in the fight against Nazi Germany and never even spoke publicly about Katyn. He left this to his trusted friend Joseph E. Davies, his former Moscow ambassador, whose belief in Stalin remained unbroken. When the American press published the first reports about Katyn, it was immediately clear to Davies that this was a propaganda campaign by Goebbels. He urged the Polish government in exile 'to do well with the Soviet Union', as Goebbels noted in his diary after reading the summaries of the American press reports.[23]

A German fabrication

Davies was by no means alone in this assessment. Most American newspapers thought Goebbels' campaign was a complete lie. The tone was set by the influential liberal journalist Dorothy Thompson, who had been the correspondent in Berlin for ten years, from 1924 to 1934. In 1932, she conducted an interview with Hitler and published a small booklet of thirty-six pages entitled *I Saw Hitler*. The first sentences were:

> When I walked into Adolph Hitler's room, I was convinced that I was meeting the future dictator of Germany. In something less than fifty seconds I was quite sure that I was not. It took just about that time to measure the

startling insignificance of this man who had sat the world agog ... He is the prototype of the Little Man ... Involuntarily I smiled: Oh Adolph, Adolph! You will be out of luck![24]

It was a blatant error: just one year later Hitler was the sole ruler in Germany, and another year later Dorothy Thompson was expelled as the first foreign correspondent from Nazi Germany. It was again Ernst Hanfstaengl who told her that she had to leave the country within twenty-four hours. After her return she described Hanfstaengl as an 'urban gentleman', but she accused him of serving a regime that brutally persecuted political opponents such as socialists and liberals, but, above all, the Jews.[25]

Through her expulsion from the Third Reich she became known in the USA. The wife of the president, Eleanor Roosevelt, met her and the two women befriended each other, both united in their commitment to women's rights. Dorothy Thompson had often been a White House guest. She had learned from her miscalculation of Hitler: she analysed German domestic politics very carefully and was thus one of the fiercest critics of the Nazi regime in the entire international press, constantly condemning racism and the human rights violations of the Nazis. Her columns were reprinted in newspapers. *Time* magazine even featured her on its front page as the most influential woman in the American press.[26]

In spite of all her criticism of the Nazis, however, unlike many other journalists, she did not close her eyes to developments in the Soviet Union. She

sharply criticised the Ribbentrop–Molotov Pact and called on the US government to stand up for occupied Poland. The Polish embassy in Washington, which was under the exile government, gave a dinner for her.

Goebbels was informed about Dorothy Thompson's publications; he had met her personally during her time as foreign correspondent in Berlin. Thus he wrote angrily on 5 April 1942 in his diary: 'Dorothy Thompson makes an absolutely crazy speech against Hitler. It is shameful and provocative that

Dorothy Thompson during her time as correspondent in Berlin.

such stupid women, whose brains can only consist of straw, have the right to speak out against a historical figure like the Führer.'[27]

When the news about the mass graves of Katyn went around the world, it was clear to Dorothy Thompson right from the start: 'Katyn is a German fabrication.' In her opinion it was impossible to identify corpses after three years, so they must have been in the ground for a shorter time. Also, if the Russians had been the murderers, they would have buried the dead further inland. Since she was also known as a critic of the Soviet Union under Stalin, her assessment was particularly important.[28]

The accentuation of alleged Jewish perpetrators by the German newspapers strengthened the American press in the view that Katyn was nothing more than another propaganda action by Goebbels to distract attention from Nazi crimes. After all, *The New York Times* admitted to him that this propaganda had been quite successful. The newspaper found that the London Poles had fallen into a 'Nazi trap'. But the German version is 'beyond the bounds of credulity'.[29]

The Washington Post went one step further by accusing the 'predominantly reactionary and feudal' government in exile of 'deliberately playing into the hands of Nazi propaganda'. The newspaper's commentator demanded: 'The assumption of all loyal members of the united nations must be that the Poles were killed by the Germans.'[30]

Together with the influential Dorothy Thompson, the two most important political newspapers in the USA set the tone for almost the entire American press. An exception was the conservative *Chicago Tribune*. In an editorial it was said:

> As the Bolsheviks have murdered millions of their own people, including many hundreds of revolutionary comrades, there is no inherent reason to believe that the man who ordered all these executions would hesitate on humanitarian grounds to kill a relatively small number of Polish leaders.

The Soviet explanations 'spring from a sense of guilt'.[31]

Goebbels studied intensively the translations from the American press, which he received daily. He followed the activities of Roosevelt's special ambassador Joseph E. Davies. He noted about him in his diaries:

> Davies gives a declaration about the Soviet Union. Stalin is described as a good-hearted, nice daddy, who has no bad thoughts in his heart. I think this propaganda is extremely dangerous in the Anglo-Saxon countries, especially if it is carried out by eyewitnesses who can be trusted to judge the situation in the Soviet Union.[32]

The *Völkischer Beobachter*, Goebbels' mouthpiece, attacked Davies repeatedly. Commenting on the turmoil caused by the reports from Katyn among

London Poles, the newspaper wrote: 'With great zeal Davies, a Jew, took it for granted that the Soviet government would maintain silence on all issues raised by Sikorski.'[33] The Nazi organ also quoted Davies with the words 'We can trust the Soviet Union' and called him an 'American bourgeois' and 'thug'.[34] Other German newspapers quoted Davies as saying: 'If I had been born in the Soviet Union and not in America, I would probably be a Bolshevik today.'[35]

Davies was accompanied on his trip to Moscow in May 1943 by a servant and a personal physician; the crew of the plane consisted of nine persons.[36] Because of the war, it was not possible to take the direct route via Europe. Rather, the American delegation first flew to Brazil, from there across the Atlantic to Dakar, the seat of the administration of French West Africa, now the capital of Senegal, further via Luxor in Egypt, Baghdad, Tehran and Kuibyshev to Stalingrad, where he visited a destroyed quarter.[37] When he learned that German planes were still being sighted over Stalingrad, he asked for escorts by Russian combat aircraft to continue his journey.[38]

After his arrival in Moscow, Davies briefly informed Ambassador Standley that he should hand over a sealed letter from Roosevelt to Stalin; but he was not allowed to inform the ambassador about the contents, nor should the latter be present at the meeting with Stalin. Standley understood that Roosevelt distrusted him, and in his memoirs he wrote: 'I felt as if I had been kicked to the stomach.'[39]

As became known later, Roosevelt proposed in the letter to Stalin a meeting in a very small circle: only the two heads of state who had not yet met, interpreters and secretaries, but without their staffs and ministers. The meeting could take place in a place west or east of the Bering Strait, at the far end of the Soviet Union or in Alaska. Africa was out of the question because of the summer, as well as Iceland, which was the closest country for both of them, but then they should also have to invite Churchill. But Roosevelt wanted to avoid this; he was obviously disturbed by the fact that the British prime minister mistrusted Stalin.[40]

Roosevelt had written to Churchill a few months before Davies' mission to Moscow: 'I think I can personally handle Stalin better than either your Foreign Office or my State Department. Stalin hates the guts of all your top people. He thinks he likes me better.'[41] But Roosevelt had not informed Churchill of his plan to meet Stalin alone.

Davies was a great admirer of Stalin, as were many left-wing liberals between the two world wars. He began his career as a young lawyer in the management of the Federal Trade Commission, an authority that was supposed to break up the big trade monopolies in the interest of consumer protection. However, Davies was reproached that his management had led only to the strengthening and not to the weakening of the large corporations.[42] In any case, he made many contacts with the economic elite at his post; as a lawyer he repeatedly represented large companies and thus became a dollar millionaire.

When he had headed the US representation in Moscow from 1936 to 1938 as Roosevelt's confidant, he had met Stalin repeatedly. Davies sent enthusiastic reports on industrialisation and the legal system in the Soviet Union to Washington, from which he gained personal impressions: he sat in the VIP tribune at one of the grand show trials and witnessed Prosecutor General Andrey Vyshinsky insulting the accused. Davies, who did not speak Russian, then declared that the trial had been conducted in accordance with the best constitutional principles, and that the accused deserved the death penalty because they had formed a Fifth Column for Hitler's Germany.[43]

Davies' enthusiasm for Stalin, however, met with contradiction in his own embassy, not least from the young diplomat George F. Kennan, who studied Russian history in Berlin and obtained a translation diploma for Russian. Kennan had previously been vice consul in Tallinn and embassy counsellor in Riga, where he had maintained contacts with emigrants from Russia. He later wrote about Davies: 'A politically ambitious man who knew nothing about Russia and had no serious interest in it.'[44]

Davies made sure that Kennan, who annoyed him, was officially recalled from Moscow 'for health reasons', and also had to leave the Soviet Union department in the State Department.[45] Kennan later became one of Davies' opponents in the department and also in the disputes over Katyn.

When Davies left Moscow a little later, he was able to take along numerous icons and paintings as well as a large collection of Russian porcelain with the permission of the Soviet authorities.[46] After returning to the USA, Davies wrote an enthusiastic book about his three years as an ambassador. It was published in 1941 under the title *Mission to Moscow*, received excellent reviews and sold 700,000 copies. In it, he reaffirmed his praise for the Moscow show trials: he described Prosecutor General Vyshinsky as a 'calm, dispassionate, intellectual, able and wise person', for whom he felt 'respect and admiration as a lawyer'. Davies justified the verdicts in the show trials: the defendants had confessed their great guilt, namely high treason and espionage for a foreign power. Marshal Tukhachevsky was rightly condemned to death, and he was also doomed for being too garrulous towards a woman who was probably a German spy.

Davies wrote about Stalin: 'His brown eye is exceedingly wise and gentle. A child would like to sit on his lap and a dog would sidle up to him.' He found also words of praise for other members of the Moscow leadership: Molotov was full of wisdom, in army chief Voroshilov, whom contemporaries described as primitive and violent, he even identified 'intellectual power'. He called the Armenian Mikoyan, who supervised the show trials on behalf of the Politburo, a Georgian.[47] On many occasions Davies defended the Ribbentrop–Molotov Pact, the annexation of Eastern Poland by the Soviet Union and the Red Army attack on Finland in 1940. Energetically, he ensured that Stalin critics were removed from the State Department.[48]

Totalitarian propaganda for mass consumption

One year after its publication, the book was filmed in Hollywood – subsidised with public money on instructions from Roosevelt. The subtitle was: 'One American's Journey into the Truth.' Famous actors took the leading roles, Stalin was portrayed as a strict, but just and wise president of a thoroughly democratic country in which social differences were largely overcome. Roosevelt congratulated Davies on this success.[49] The film was nominated for the Academy Award for the best interior design of a black and white film, but did not receive the award.

But among American intellectuals, the film aroused a fierce controversy. The liberal philosopher John Dewey and the feminist publicist Suzanne La Follette accused Davies in a joint analysis published in *The New York Times* of serious historical falsification and 'totalitarian propaganda for mass consumption'. Davies' meetings with members of the Moscow party leadership, which the film shows, had never actually taken place because these men had long since been imprisoned or even executed as opponents of Stalin. Likewise, the scenes of a trial in which Marshal Tukhachevsky was proven to have conspired against the leadership were simply invented; in reality, Tukhachevsky was shot without trial. Moreover, the film is anti-British; it claims that London, together with the French, drove Stalin into Hitler's arms through their policies in 1939; but the film does not even suggest that the two dictators attacked and shared Poland together.

According to his critics, the film was characterised by obvious twists in the style of Nazi propaganda, which only gave the viewer a feeling of 'moral callousness'. Dewey and La Follette did not exempt Roosevelt

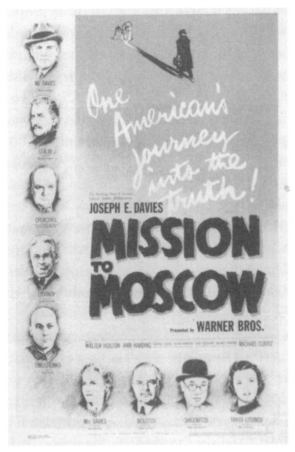

The movie Mission to Moscow provoked controversy among American intellectuals because it praised Stalin as a great democratic leader.

from their criticism, because the president had given it a 'semi-official' seal by his support for the film.[50] Dorothy Thompson also criticised the film sharply.[51]

Davies ignored the criticism. He had the title of the book and the film painted in capital letters on his aircraft: Mission to Moscow. Roosevelt had actually intended to send Davies back to the Moskva as permanent ambassador to replace the annoying admonisher Standley. But Davies' doctors strongly advised against it.[52]

Shortly after his arrival in the Russian capital, Davies invited the American correspondents to a briefing at the embassy. He raved about the excellent relations between the USA and the USSR. He warned the journalists: 'You can do tremendous harm to our country by criticising the Soviet Union in your articles.' But some of the correspondents strongly contradicted him: they were severely hindered in their daily work by the Soviet authorities, their articles were censored. They demanded that Davies bring these problems to Stalin's attention. But when he claimed that these could only be isolated cases by subaltern officials, a storm of protest broke out – Standley closed the meeting to avoid a scandal.[53]

The American president and his special ambassador were not alone in their passion for Stalin and the Soviet Union. Rather, it corresponded to a widespread mood in the USA. After the German defeat at Stalingrad, the magazine *Life* published a special issue with Stalin on its cover. The revolutionary Vladimir Lenin was called 'perhaps the greatest man of modern times'; the 'red terror' against political opponents, ordered by Lenin, was not mentioned. One of the texts said that the NKVD was a 'national police similar to the FBI'.[54] The major daily newspapers, above all *The New York Times*, were also full of Stalin's praises.

Davies brought a copy of the film about his 'Mission to Moscow' to the dinner in the Kremlin to which Stalin invited him. Some of the highest dignitaries participated, including Kalinin, Mikoyan, Molotov and Voroshilov, all of whom had signed the secret execution orders for Katyn, Kharkov and Kalinin.[55] They undoubtedly noted with satisfaction that Davies, with whom they toasted the Soviet–American friendship, had accused the Germans of being the perpetrators.

The press was not informed of the content of the Kremlin talks, although *The New York Times* reported on the menu at the feast, the main course was sturgeon ridge in sauce.[56] Admiral Standley described the evening in his memoirs: Stalin made a toast to his guest. Davies answered, but not briefly and concisely, as would have been the tradition, but began a quarter-hour speech, which was then translated into Russian for another fifteen minutes, while society stared hungrily at the empty plates.[57]

After dinner, the two-hour film was shown. One of the diplomats noted that the hosts had looked at him 'with glum curiosity'. Stalin took it rather indifferently: 'He kept a straight face throughout the showing. He never laughed once.' The admiral himself found the film 'nauseating and darned mad'. In it the Davies actor gave about the same speech as the original at the beginning of the dinner. After the end of the film Stalin withdrew without comment, but visibly tired.[58]

When Davies had finished his talks in Moscow after a few days, he was given a Soviet sub-machine gun and a captured German carabine as a farewell present from Stalin. Then he returned to Washington via Siberia and Alaska.[59]

However, Davies' secret mission was not successful: the meeting between Stalin and Roosevelt did not take place. But the American's visit to the Kremlin was an important signal for Stalin: he understood that Roosevelt had no particular sympathy for Churchill and also had other political goals. When Churchill learned of Roosevelt's plan to meet Stalin alone, he was deeply upset. Roosevelt then falsely informed him that Stalin had taken the initiative.[60]

The contents of Davies' talks with Stalin were also withheld from Ambassador William H. Standley. It was the occasion for the admiral to ask for his discharge from diplomatic service; he had realised that Roosevelt no longer trusted him. The president agreed, Standley had increasingly irritated him with his critical reports about the Soviet leadership and especially about Katyn.[61]

Davies had assured Stalin that the White House would support the Kremlin's demand for the future Soviet–Polish border on the Curzon Line, so that Moscow could keep Eastern Poland annexed in autumn 1939. But Davies asked the Kremlin chief not to go public with this information. He did not bring up the subject of Katyn. When Davies returned to the White House, Roosevelt told him: 'Why of course we will not fight Russia for Poland.' But the plan to force Poland to renounce its eastern territories must be implemented 'without offending democratic public opinion'.[62]

Conspiracy theories about the death of Sikorski

Stalin was also very popular in Great Britain in 1943 after the victory of Stalingrad. Churchill, however, did not allow himself to be carried away by this wave of enthusiasm; he remained extremely sceptical of the Soviet autocrat. This was helped by Sir Owen O'Malley's report on the Katyn massacre. O'Malley was British ambassador to the Polish government in exile in London and studied very carefully all materials about Katyn. His conclusion was clear: The perpetrators were among the Russians and not among the Germans.[63] The British secret service SOE, which also evaluated the publications of the Germans, came to the same conclusion: 'The summary of the evidence gathered shows that the report submitted by the Germans seems to be well-founded.'[64]

But not all Foreign Office experts saw things like O'Malley and the SOE. Secretary of State Alexander Cadogan's report to Churchill reflected the uncertainty of the experts. In it, Cadogan wrote about O'Malley's analysis:

> There may be evidence, we do not know of, that may point another direction. But on the evidence we have, it is difficult to escape the presumption of Russian guilt. ... But we have perforce welcomed the Russians as Allies and have set ourselves to work with them in war and peace. ...

How, if Russian crime is established, can we expect Poles to live amicably, side by side with the Russians for generations to come?[65]

Cadogan wrote in his diary:

> Years before Katyn the Soviet Government made a habit of butchering their own citizens by the 10,000s, and if we could fling ourselves into their arms in 1941, I don't know that Katyn makes our position more delicate. The blood of Russians cries as loud to heaven as that of Poles. But it's very nasty. How can Poles ever live amicably alongside Russians, and how can we discuss with Russians execution of German 'war criminals', when we have condoned this?[66]

But O'Malley's report was classified, only members of the cabinet and King George VI got a copy.[67] Churchill also had it sent to Roosevelt. In his covering letter he made an ambiguous comment: 'It is a grim, well-written story, but perhaps, too well written.'[68]

In public, Eden repeatedly called the German reports about Katyn a Nazi propaganda campaign, giving the British press the impression that he thought Moscow's version was right. Goebbels also understood it this way, noting in his diary: 'Eden makes the downright grotesque attempt to blame us for Katyn.'[69]

O'Malley saw perfectly the dilemma of the British leadership, which wanted to avoid a break with Stalin. But he questioned whether London's dealings with Katyn could also be morally justified towards the Poles, for whose freedom the British had gone to war. He wrote:

> In handling the publicity side of the Katyn affair we have been constrained by the urgent need for cordial relations with the Soviet government to appear to appraise the evidence with more hesitation and lenience than we should do in forming a common sense judgment on events occurring in normal times or in the ordinary course of our private lives; we have been obliged to appear to distort the normal and healthy operation of intellectual and moral judgments; we have been obliged to give undue prominence to the tactlessness or impulsiveness of Poles, to restrain the Poles from putting their case clearly before the public, to discourage any attempt by the public and the press to probe the ugly story to the bottom. ... We have in fact perforce used the good name of England like the murderers used the little conifers to cover up a massacre.[70]

Churchill tried to put pressure on the Polish exile press in Britain, which openly accused the Soviet leadership of Katyn's mass murder. This is exactly what he had promised both Stalin and Roosevelt in secret telegrams.[71]

But Churchill knew he could not keep that promise. Although the war restricted the freedom of the press, the measures and possibilities of the government were far from comprehensive censorship. Churchill also wanted to avoid an open confrontation with the Polish government in exile. On the one hand, he was well informed about the performances of the Polish pilots who fought against the Luftwaffe in the service of the Air Force and achieved the best shooting quotas. On the other hand, he did not want to weaken Sikorski, who was already accused by members of his cabinet of being too submissive towards London and, above all, towards Moscow.

Churchill and Eden had long recognised that Stalin did not want to give up the Polish eastern territories that the Soviet Union had annexed in October 1939. Both had a great understanding of Stalin's position that the Polish claims to areas in which the Poles had made up only a small part of the population were doubtful, just as the Foreign Minister George Curzon had already stated almost a quarter of a century earlier. Churchill believed that among all Polish exile politicians only Sikorski had the assertiveness to make concessions on this point.

The British press was divided in its attitude to the London Poles. Catholic papers, which had repeatedly reported about the persecution of Christians by the Bolsheviks in Soviet Russia, stood unreservedly behind them, defended Poland's demands for the pre-war borders and demanded an explanation about Katyn. But most national newspapers, from left to right, were traditionally critical of and negative towards the Poles.

Editorialists accused the government in exile of endangering the alliance against Hitler because of its demands for the pre-war borders. Goebbels wrote in his diary: 'The Poles are bawled out as if they belonged to the enemy camp.'[72] *The Times* even went so far as to praise Stalin as a guarantor of the future peace order in Central Eastern Europe, therefore the Soviet Union should be allowed a zone of influence there. The newspaper justified its position with Stalin's assurance that he wanted a 'strong and independent Poland after the war'.

These words were in an interview Stalin gave to the Moscow correspondent of *The Times*, Ralph Parker. It was not a classic interview; Parker, who also worked in the Moscow office of *The New York Times*, had submitted his questions to the government press office and they were answered in writing. Parker had previously vigorously defended the Soviet position in his coverage of Katyn. As became known many years later, he had been a sympathiser of the Soviet regime since his years at Cambridge, as had the famous spy Kim Philby, who had studied there at the same time.[73] Pro-Soviet Ralph Parker would still play a role in the controversies surrounding Katyn. The position of *The Times*' editorial staff on the news from Katyn was clear: it was a German propaganda lie.[74]

The left-leaning press, which traditionally reported positively on the 'workers' paradise' of the Soviet Union, called on the government to cancel the newspapers

1,5 MILLIONEN POLEN

JOHN BULL: „Meine lieben Polen, mehr kann ich für euch nicht tun. Ihr müßt euch mit dem Bär nun selbst verständigen!"

The Nazi press stressed that the British government was betraying the Poles who were deported by the Soviets. The cartoon of the weekly Das Reich shows how John Bull throws 1.5 million Poles to the Russian bear for food. He says: 'My dear Poles! That's all I can do for you. You must now make yourselves understood with the bear.' (16 May 1943)

of the Poles in exile. The communist *Daily Worker* stood out in particular. The paper named the reports in the Polish exile press about the evidence of Soviet perpetrators in Katyn 'fascist, anti-Soviet and anti-Semitic agitation of the Polish Junkers'.[75] Leading trade unionists called the demands of the Poles for an investigation of the Katyn graves an attempt to engage in 'fascist propaganda' in Great Britain. The Foreign Office received numerous telegrams and letters demanding that Poles should no longer receive asylum or financial support.[76]

George Orwell was one of the few journalists who opposed the attacks on London's Poles. He saw himself as a leftist and sharply criticised the British left for closing its eyes to the obvious shortcomings and crimes of Stalin's regime. He saw very clearly that Poland had become the victim not only of German, but also of Soviet aggression.[77]

The Poles in London fell into an almost hopeless situation after 4 July 1943. Władysław Sikorski, their prime minister and commander-in-chief, died in an air accident late that evening. Sikorski had inspected the Polish troops in the Middle East under Anders' command, and on the way back from Cairo the Liberator bomber, which had been provided to him by the British Air Force, landed in Gibraltar. He was received by the British governor, General Noel Mason-MacFarlane, who had previously been a military attaché in Moscow and was well informed about the search for the missing Polish officers. Sikorski undoubtedly explained to him the arguments in favour of the Soviet perpetration in Katyn.

Mason-MacFarlane accompanied the Polish delegation to the small airport of Gibraltar late in the evening. At 11.06p.m. the plane took off for to London, but only sixteen seconds after take-off it crashed into the sea. All sixteen persons in the passenger cabin, to which the cargo hold on the underside had been converted, were killed, but five bodies were not found. Only the pilot, an Czech emigrant, could save himself.

The British government published the navy's investigation report, according to which it had been an accident: the elevator was blocked. But since then, many conspiracy theories have focused on the death of Sikorski. Essentially, three possible groups of perpetrators were identified who would have had a motive to eliminate him. Even an exhumation and examination of the mortal remains in 2008 did not provide any clarity, the forensics simply confirmed that Sikorski had neither been shot nor beaten to death. The murder hypotheses assume, however, that he drowned because water could enter the passenger cabin too quickly.

According to the 'British hypothesis' Churchill increasingly saw Sikorski as a risk factor, the government in exile had endangered the alliance with the Soviet Union by demanding that the Katyn crime be solved. Against this version, however, it is argued that Churchill regarded Sikorski as the only politician among the exiled Poles willing to compromise. Besdies, high-ranking British officials were among the passengers. However, the files will remain under lock and key until 2041.

The 'Soviet hypothesis' locates the perpetrators in Stalin's secret services. These had either tampered with the aircraft mechanics or induced the pilot to carry out ditching. The fact that he started with a life jacket, contrary to his other habits, speaks in favour of a fake accident. The NKVD either blackmailed or bribed him. On the day of Sikorski's stopover, the Soviet Ambassador Ivan Maisky had also made a stop in Gibraltar, and agents must have been among his escorts. In addition, British double agent Kim Philby was on the peninsula, supervising every step taken by the Polish prime minister. He headed the MI6 Spain department and spied for Moscow at the same time.

Finally, the 'Polish hypothesis' refers to the numerous enemies Sikorski made among the exiled Poles. On the one hand, these included the Piłsudski supporters, whom he and his followers had removed from all leadership positions, and on the other, the uncompromising defenders of the pre-war borders, who accused Sikorski of leadership weakness and retreating from Churchill and Stalin.

Churchill participated in the Requiem for Sikorski in the cathedral of Westminster. His successor as head of the government in exile was the former member of parliament Stanisław Mikołajczyk of the Peasants' Party. He had only once appeared nationwide before the war, when in 1937 he organised a farmers' strike with road blockades, but which was crushed by the Polish army and police after ten days. He was considered a political lightweight and had no international contacts. It took him five months to get an appointment for his inaugural visit to Roosevelt in Washington.

Nazi propaganda proclaimed that the British and Soviets had jointly planned Sikorski's assassination. In the cartoon of the satirical magazine Kladderradatsch an English lord offers Sikorski's head to the fat Bolshevik and says: 'Order executed!' (25 July 1943)

The German resistance and photos from Katyn

The German opposition against Hitler also wanted to make contact with the White House, and Katyn played a role in this. At least this was described by the Russian princess Maria Vassiltchikova, who lived in Berlin at the time, in her diary published half a century later. Maria Vassiltchikova was a friend of the Gersdorff family; she found shelter in their Berlin house when her own apartment was bombed out. The 23-year-old emigrant, whose family had fled the Bolsheviks, first worked for the German radio, then in the Ministry of Foreign Affairs.

Her immediate superior was Adam von Trott, an opponent of Hitler. Since his studies in Oxford and a longer stay in the USA, Trott had cultivated various contacts in both countries. In the summer of 1939 he travelled to London to inform leading British politicians of the German preparations for war. But he was just as unheard as the lawyer Fabian von Schlabrendorff, who had also come to London at the same time with the same concern.[78]

According to the testimony of the Russian emigrant, middlemen were to take photos of the mass graves from Katyn to Washington. she wrote in her diary on 24 October 1943: 'I have a new urgent assignment: the translation of the captions for a large number of photographs of the remains of some 4,000 Polish officers found murdered by the Soviets in Katyn Forest near Smolensk. The mind boggles.' Vassiltchikova added that the pictures should be 'on President Roosevelt's desk' within a week.[79]

According to the report, the pictures should first be sent to the German ambassador in Turkey, Franz von Papen. The conservative Catholic was the penultimate Chancellor of the Reich before the National Socialists came to power in 1933. Originally, he had supported Hitler's appointment as Reich Chancellor in the naive belief that the latter could thus be better controlled and civilised by the conservative government apparatus. Though he rejected the Nazi policy of violence and his relationship with Foreign Minister Ribbentrop was extremely tense, he was seen abroad as a follower of Hitler: his name is on the list of leading Nazis that Roosevelt's advisor John Franklin Carter had compiled.[80] In Ankara in 1942 Papen had barely escaped an assassination attempt by the NKVD. Trott came from Berlin to gain him as a permanent liaison for the secret opposition against the Führer.[81]

Hitler's opponents had learned that Papen had secret contacts with an important American diplomat in Istanbul. It was George H. Earle, who was an old friend of Roosevelt. Trott and his fellow combatants hoped that information about Katyn would reach the president via Papen's contact in Istanbul.

Earle was a special envoy from the White House to the Balkans. He was the son of a rich sugar merchant from Philadelphia, and during the First World War he had been the commander of a submarine fighter. He owned a private plane and was considered a womaniser. In the years before the war he had been governor of

Pennsylvania, thus a political heavyweight, and had supported Roosevelt's policy of the New Deal. He had previously gained diplomatic experience at the US Embassy in Austria and as US envoy in Bulgaria. In the Bulgarian capital, Sofia, he had caused a small scandal because he had hit a champagne bottle on the head of a Nazi official in a bar.[82]

In Istanbul, at that time a hub for agents and spies, he was officially naval attaché. But his main task was to maintain contact with Hitler opponents in the occupied countries. He himself described his task as an 'undercover agent'.[83]

In the spring of 1943 he received an unannounced visit to his hotel. To Earle's great surprise, the visitor introduced himself as Admiral Wilhelm Canaris, head of the German military espionage. In excellent English, Canaris had explained that a group of officers in the Wehrmacht wanted to kill Hitler, Earle reported after the meeting to the White House. After the conspirators had taken power, the German units in the West were to surrender to the Americans and the British, but at the same time the Eastern Front was to be held, for Bolshevism was the real enemy of Western civilisation. Earle was to ask Roosevelt whether the US wanted to support the German resistance in these plans and, above all, whether the White House could thus move away from an unconditional surrender of the German Reich as a war target. This goal was announced by Churchill and Roosevelt at the conference in Casablanca in January 1943, when Earle was part of the American delegation. Canaris announced that he would contact Earle in two months' time.

In his report to Roosevelt, Earle also informed him that an envoy from Ribbentrop approached him independently of Canaris to explore the prospects for a ceasefire in the West.[84] But he did not get an answer. The White House obviously wanted to stick to the Casablanca decisions and, by no means, even after Hitler's fall or death, to make a separate peace with the Germans that would exclude the Soviet Union.

When Canaris called Earle in Istanbul two months later, the latter told him that the White House had not responded.[85] These contacts escaped the security service (SD) controlled

The special envoy George H. Earle tried in vain to convince Roosevelt of the Soviet perpetration in Katyn.

by SS leader Heinrich Himmler. Earle caught the SD's eye just for his personal life: A 'Jewish cabaret dancer' was supposedly his mistress.[86]

Canaris was not satisfied with Earle's decision: With the help of the co-conspirator Adam von Trott from the Ministry of Foreign Affairs in Berlin, he succeeded in making contact with General William J. Donovan, chief of the American secret service OSS. Donovan was a conservative Catholic of Irish descent. During the First World War, as commander of a regiment, he received high orders for bravery. As Roosevelt's confidant he was sent to Churchill in the summer of 1940 to talk about covert military aid from the officially still neutral USA.[87] Adam von Trott had met Donovan three years earlier when he spent several months in the USA for study purposes. The two met again in 1941, when Washington was not yet officially in war.[88]

Former defence agents reported many years after the war that Canaris had even met Donovan once in 1943 to raise the same concern with him: the White House should signal that it would accept a ceasefire on the Western Front if Hitler's opponents liquidate it. In this case, the Wehrmacht would immediately leave the occupied territories in the West, according to Canaris' proposal. The meeting was supposed to have taken place under strictly conspiratorial circumstances in the Spanish port city of Santander.[89] Canaris also spoke Spanish very well; he was a German agent in Spain during the First World War. However, so far no documents have been found in American and Spanish archives that would confirm this encounter between Canaris and Donovan. Later, Donovan played a central role in the Katyn controversies.

Via middlemen, Trott also informed the OSS resident in Switzerland, Allen W. Dulles, about the plans of the German resistance to overthrow Hitler. Dulles sent details about the German opposition to Donovan in Washington. He had informants in Ribbentrop's ministry who sent him eminently important messages, including the deciphering of American secret codes, the morale of the troops on the Eastern Front, German preparations for D-Day and the situation of Wolf's Lair, Hitler's headquarter in Eastern Prussia, which had previously been completely unknown to the Allies.[90]

Dulles, a declared anti-communist, who also spoke out against effective aid measures for the Jews threatened in occupied Europe, learned of the plan to eliminate Hitler during a visit to the Eastern Front. For security reasons, however, he did not know the location or the names of the assassins. It was the officers Tresckow, Gersdorff and Schlabbrendorff who were able to place a bomb package in Hitler's plane after his visit to the Army Group Centre in Smolensk.[91]

Probably Moscow learned of the contacts between the OSS and the German resistance, because the Soviet intelligence service NKGB had a number of agents in the OSS. Donovan had no illusions about this, but he tried to control the situation by proposing to Roosevelt official cooperation between OSS and the NKGB, which had been spun off from the NKVD in 1943. It was headed by Vsevolod

Merkulov, the organiser of the mass murders of Katyn, Kalinin and Kharkov. Moscow's informants in the OSS told Merkulov that Donovan had praised Stalin: he was 'the most intelligent person among all those heading today's governments'.

Donovan argued to Roosevelt that the OSS could also officially station its people in Moscow, which was impossible so far. The president initially had no objections to close cooperation between the secret services. He had already warned Donovan before: 'You must treat the Russians with the same trust you do the British.'[92] However, FBI chief J. Edgar Hoover, an enemy of Donovan, opposed official cooperation. Hoover argued that it would be easy for the Russians in Moscow to control the OSS people deployed there, although he could not guarantee this. Rather he saw the great danger that even more attempts would be made than before to infiltrate the structures of the US government. Roosevelt accepted Hoover's line.[93]

Donovan would not admit defeat. As a first step, he envisaged an exchange of information between American and Soviet agents who were in contact with the occupied countries in the Balkans from Istanbul. But for the time being he had to limit himself to supplying the Russians with special weapons, mini cameras and the equipment to develop microfilms.[94]

At this time further contacts between the Hitler opponents and the OSS ran via Istanbul, probably Donovan acted on his own initiative behind Roosevelt's back. The German Ambassador von Papen appealed to his American contacts to assure the German resistance that Washington would no longer insist on unconditional surrender in the case of Hitler's removal of power. Otherwise, forces in the resistance sympathising with socialism could seek a separate peace with Stalin.[95]

Special Envoy George H. Earle, official naval attaché, also continued his efforts to help establish links between the German opposition and Washington. In the meantime, he had received the Katyn reports of two members of the International Medical Commission, the Romanian Alexandru Birkle and the Bulgarian Marko Markov. Both left no doubt about the Soviet perpetrators. He informed the White House about Birkle's and Markov's reports.

Obviously, the Hitler opponents in Berlin learned that Earle was well informed about Katyn. This was the reason why the diplomat Trott wanted to send him the Katyn pictures via ambassador Papen. But it remained unknown whether Earle had received them. The pictures whose description had been translated by Maria Vassiltchikova, Trott's secretary, were intended to convince Roosevelt that Stalin, so courted by him, was also at the head of a murderous regime.

However, in his memoirs Rudolf-Christoph von Gersdorff made no mention of Maria Vassiltchikova. Franz von Papen later wrote about Earle's attempts to persuade Roosevelt to support the German resistance, but not about photographs from Katyn. Earle later reported that he had submitted such pictures to Roosevelt and that he had received them from Russian emigrants.[96] But it is unlikely he meant Maria Vassiltchikova.

Information about Katyn also came to Washington from a completely different, surprising source: an anonymous letter written in Russian was received in the office of FBI chief J. Edgar Hoover at the beginning of August 1943. The author listed the names of diplomats from the Soviet representations in Washington, New York and San Francisco, who were, in fact, officers of the NKVD, and also gave their American contact persons. The letter revealed internal details: 'Zubilin and Mironov hate each other.' It was said about the two of them:

> In the NKVD line they directed the occupation of Poland. Zubilin interrogated and shot Poles in Kozelsk, Mironov in Starobelsk. All the Poles who were saved know these butchers by sight. 10,000 Poles shot near Molensk was the work of both of them.

The letter was obviously written in a great hurry; it contained many typos. Thus, by 'Molensk', the author undoubtedly meant the city of Smolensk.

The letter writer also gave the real names of the two allegedly hostile NKVD officers: Mironov is actually Vasily Markov; Zubilin was the code name for the NKVD colonel Vasily Zarubin. The latter also worked for the Germans and the Japanese.[97] It was Vasily Zarubin who had led the questioning of Polish officers in the Kozelsk camp and decided on their selection for the shooting in Katyn. Before he was sent to Washington as a resident, Stalin personally outlined his most important task to him: to do everything to prevent a rapprochement between the USA and the Third Reich; there should under no circumstances be a separate peace in the West. At the same time, Zarubin was to gain informants in the American arms industry, especially in the atomic bomb project.[98]

The FBI was already observing Zarubin at the time because he had contacts with American communists and apparently financed them.[99] At first, the FBI was of the opinion that the anonymous letter was intended to put them on the wrong track.[100] Finally, Hoover wrote a report on it to the White House. NKVD learned about this from its informants in Roosevelt's staff. Zarubin now expected that he would have to leave the country as an exposed spy.[101]

But the White House confined itself to informing the Soviet embassy in Washington that one of their people was uncovered as an agent. In view of this restrained reaction, Zarubin remained in the country for the time being and continued to expand his network of informants in war-important industry.[102]

The anonymous reference to the murder of Polish POWs by the NKVD near Smolensk was apparently not followed up in the US authorities; at any rate, there is no record about this in the files of the White House or Donovan's OSS. Only later did the Signals Intelligence Service (SIS) decipher coded reports, which Zarubin had sent from Washington to Moscow. In one of the messages, he expressed fears that he was being spied on and that his role in Kozelsk had become known.[103]

The rise of Berling

While the Kremlin's spies in Washington felt growing pressure, Stalin established a pro-Soviet Polish leadership in Moscow, setting up the Union of Polish Patriots (ZPP). Zygmunt Berling, who had left the Anders Army a few months earlier, was appointed to the presidium. He had declared to Stalin his willingness to take over the leadership of Polish units, which were to be under Soviet supreme command.

In May 1943, immediately after the break with the London Poles, Stalin set up the first Polish infantry division under the command of Berling, who was promoted to brigadier general. Most of the soldiers had previously been drafted into the Red Army.[104] The name patron of the division was the freedom hero Tadeusz Kościuszko. Apparently, the idea came from Stalin, who loved macabre jokes: Kościuszko had led an uprising against Russian invasion troops at the end of the eighteenth century and then spent two years in imprisonment in Russia.

In October 1943, Berling's division faced its first test: integrated into Soviet units, it was to break through a German defence line some 80 kilometres southwest of Smolensk. But the Wehrmacht repulsed the Soviet and Polish attackers. The Polish division suffered considerable losses, around 1,600 men, a quarter of its manpower.

The communist functionaries in the Union of Polish Patriots oversaw the further expansion of the armed forces: over the next few months they grew to more than 100,000 men, their commander-in-chief remained Berling. Wojciech Jaruzelski, 20 years old, joined the armed forces in autumn 1943 as an officer candidate. Four years earlier, at the beginning of the war, he was deported with his relatives to Siberia, where his father died. However, since Jaruzelski achieved poor results in the officers' course, he was only promoted to ensign.

The government in exile closely observed the formation of Polish units in the Soviet Union. The new prime minister, Mikołajczyk, made moves to resume diplomatic relations with Moscow. He ordered the underground forces in occupied Poland not to fight against the Red Army if it was to advance into Polish territory. The officers of the Anders Army in the Middle East were also ordered not to speak out negatively about the Soviet Union.[105] Stalin, however, ignored all efforts of Mikołajczyk.

The Poles of London also had to take note of further unfavourable developments in the West. Special Envoy Joseph E. Davies and other advisers to Roosevelt described them in their statements for the White House as reactionary and russophobic. The Office of War Information (OWI) and the OSS were ordered to ignore them.[106] The authorities took no steps to correct a campaign of communist organisations in the USA against 'the fascist Polish government in London'.[107]

The New York Times also propagated the Soviet version of the German perpetrators in Katyn. An alleged former prisoner of the Sachsenhausen concentration camp named Victor von Tohathy was cited as a witness. He told that he had been released from prison because the German merchant navy needed personnel. He was among the rescued sailors of a German freighter sunk by the US Navy off the coast of Ecuador. According to *The New York Times*, Tohathy testified that he had talked to Russian prisoners in Sachsenhausen. They had told how they had to bury 10,000 Polish officers shot by the Germans in Katyn Forest. The report said he was also an eyewitness to how SS guards beat the son of former Austrian chancellor Kurt Schuschnigg to death.[108]

It was precisely the fate of Schuschnigg's son, one of Hitler's most prominent opponents, that moved the American public. Only after the war did the Americans learn that the story was wrong. Schuschnigg's father and son had actually survived the concentration camp. Tohathy was an activist of the Communist International, probably spreading the Katyn story on behalf of Moscow. However, in the late summer of 1943, it met with a broad response in the USA and was also adopted by other newspapers.

When Mikołajcyzk learned that the big three – Churchill, Roosevelt and Stalin – wanted to meet in Tehran in late November 1943 to negotiate the post-war order. He asked for a meeting with the British prime minister. But he didn't get an appointment.[109]

In Tehran, the leaders of the Western powers did not want to endanger the alliance with Moscow under any circumstances: Churchill still feared that Stalin could make a special peace with the Germans. To please him, the British delegation presented Stalin with a gift from King George VI: a sabre of honour with a golden handle. Roosevelt was hoping for help in the war against the Japanese.

Churchill campaigned for a relaunch of diplomatic relations between the Kremlin and the Polish government in exile, stressing that Britain had gone to war because of Hitler's attack on Poland. But Stalin fought back abruptly. According to the protocol of the Foreign Office that was published sixty years later, he repeated the statements that Moscow's propaganda apparatus had already spread many times in the previous months: 'They have joined forces with Hitler in their slanderous propaganda against Russia.'

Suddenly, Stalin called for recognition of the connection of Eastern Poland to the Soviet Union. The British Foreign Minister Eden asked pointedly: 'Do you mean the Molotov–Ribbentrop Line?' Stalin replied gruffly: 'Call it whatever you like.' Churchill now approached Stalin, explaining that his government understood Moscow's territorial demands. But Britain wanted a strong and independent Poland, which was, of course, friendly towards the Soviet Union.

Churchill proposed shifting Poland from East to West at the expense of the German Reich, so that Stalin would retain the territory that had been granted to him by the Ribbentrop–Molotov Pact. Poland should be compensated with East Prussia, Pomerania and Silesia. These regions were to become the new home of around two million inhabitants of the former eastern Poland, who were forced to relocate to the west. Churchill illustrated his plan with three matches: he moved the right one to the far left, from east to west. He added that the Poles could be quite satisfied with the areas given to them if they were compared with the ceded territory: 'The value of this land is much greater than the Pripet marshes.'[110]

After Tehran, Roosevelt praised Stalin as a reliable, honest partner and from then on called him 'Uncle Joe'. He told his advisers: 'He won't try to annex anything and will work with me for a world of democracy and peace.'[111]

At the banquet, Stalin spoke of Katyn, reporting on the documents allegedly found among Polish officers, which proved the perpetrators to be the Germans. He proposed to have 40,000 to 50,000 German officers shot in retaliation for this mass murder. After a short break he added that this proposal was meant as a joke.[112]

When some weeks later Mikołajczyk came to the White House for his inaugural visit, Roosevelt told him about Stalin's joke.[113] However, the Polish premier was not informed that a decision was taken in Tehran to shift Poland westwards. For Roosevelt lied to his guest when he was asked about rumours about the plans for the restructuring of Eastern Europe, on which the Big Three are said to have reached an agreement in Tehran.

Mikołajczyk only learned about the decision on Poland's eastern border ten months after Tehran when he attended a conference in Moscow. Molotov informed him, whilst Churchill, Eden and US Ambassador Harriman were present but remained silent.[114]

The expert on Russia, George F. Kennan, who was a member of the American delegation, wrote, depressed, in his diary: 'We can only bow our heads in silence before the tragedy of a people who have been our allies, whom we have saved from our enemies, and whom we cannot save from our friends.'[115]

Stalin was encouraged by the attitude of the Western Allies to prepare the takeover of control of Poland. Officially, he emphasised the national Polish character of the Berling army. Thus, it was given military chaplains, and the pledge of allegiance to the Soviet Union was removed from the flag oath. But Soviet officers, now in Polish uniforms, occupied two-thirds of the staff and command posts.[116]

Chapter 10

Burdenko's Report

After the termination of the exhumation work in June 1943, Goebbels confidently entered in his diary: 'In autumn I will continue the excavations.' But the Wehrmacht had to withdraw from the Smolensk region at the beginning of autumn. In the months before, the Kremlin had noticed very carefully that Berlin's Katyn campaign was largely ineffective on the Western Allies. But Stalin was not satisfied with that: the secret services and the censorship were given the task of consistently rewriting history in the Katyn case.

In September 1943, shortly after the reconquest of Smolensk, the Red Army closed the cemetery in Katyn Forest and prevented the inhabitants from leaving the village. The NKVD took over the rest. Beria commissioned the most suitable man at his disposal for the Katyn project: his former deputy Vsevolod Merkulov, who in the meantime headed the People's Commissariat for State Security NKGB, spun off from the NKVD. Merkulov had already planned in detail the murder of the Polish officers in spring of 1940.

At the end of September 1943 Merkulov arrived in Katyn at the head of a larger group of experts of the NKVD, the NKGB and the military secret service Smersh (abbreviation for 'Death to Spies').[1] German aerial photographs, which were found decades later in American archives, clearly prove that excavators and bulldozers were used for extensive earthworks on the cemetery from October to December 1943. A part of the mass graves, which the Germans had closed again in June, was reopened.[2] The forgery workshops of the Soviet secret services were ordered by Merkulov to produce documents dated between autumn 1940 and summer 1941. They were to prove that the Polish POWs were still safe in Soviet camps during this period. The documents were attached to some of the bodies.[3]

The NKVD found seventeen witnesses who the Germans had mentioned in the *Official Material* or who were involved in the exhumation work, including local workers, cooks and cleaners of the German signal regiment 537 stationed there. Interrogation officers threatened them that they would be hanged as collaborators if they did not accuse the Germans in their statements. Several of them died in prison, which Russian historians later concluded was from torture.

From Merkulov's point of view, the most important witness was Boris Bazilevsky, the head of Smolensk's observatory, whom the German occupiers had appointed as deputy mayor. Merkulov, known for his violence, took the reticent, small astronomy professor aside personally on several occasions while he was in NKVD custody.[4] Bazilevsky had to neutralise the testimony of Mayor Boris Menshagin, who had fled West with the Wehrmacht. Also, an alleged notebook of Menshagin was prepared, in which he described the Germans as perpetrators.[5]

In order to make the production perfect, Merkulov had many other people prepared as witnesses. According to the files of the NKVD department of Smolensk, it was a total of ninety-five persons.[6]

The Soviet press, which was completely subject to party censorship, reported extensively on the work of the 'Special Commission to Determine and Investigate the Circumstances of the Execution of Polish POWs by the German-Fascist Conquerors in Katyn Forest'.

The commission was headed by Nikolai Burdenko, professor of medicine, who was regarded as the founder of modern accident surgery in Russia and held the post of chief surgeon of the Red Army in the rank of lieutenant general. On 19 January 1944, the Special Commission arrived in Katyn. In addition to top officials of the state apparatus, including the Military Medical Service and the People's Commissioner for Education, Vladimir Potemkin, it also included the chairman of the Soviet Red Cross and Red Crescent. The specialist in ancient Hebrew, who had also published a multi-volume *History of Diplomacy*, depicted as a consequence of class struggles, could refer to his experience with Polish affairs: as Deputy Foreign Minister, he announced the break-off of diplomatic relations to the Polish Ambassador to Moscow, Wacław Grzybowski, immediately before the Red Army invaded Eastern Poland on 17 September 1939.

Two prominent figures, the Russian Orthodox Metropolitan of Kiev and Halich Nicholas and the former chairman of the USSR Writers' Union Alexey Tolstoy, were also members of the commission. Tolstoy was one of

It is still unclear whether the professor of medicine Nikolai Burdenko was actively involved in the manipulations of the NKVD or whether the NKVD also wanted to mislead the members of the commission.

the most popular writers in the Soviet Union. His fairy tale 'Buratino', the Russian version of the Pinocchio theme, was an extremely popular children's book. His novel biography *Peter the Great* had pleased Stalin and had been printed in huge editions.

Professor Viktor Prozorovsky, Director of the Research Institute of Forensic Medicine of the People's Commissariat for Health Care, was appointed secretary of the commission. Burdenko was assigned a group of seventy-five medical staff, including five professors. Foreign experts were not invited.

Winter clothing in summer

Burdenko presented the final report on 24 January and, two days later, *Pravda* published it in full. The short distance between the Commission's meeting and the publication of its report suggests, according to historians, that it, too, was largely prepared. Half a century later it became known that the report had been written by NKVD experts under the auspices of Merkulov.

The document described in detail that the Polish officers had been taken to three camps near Smolensk in the spring of 1940. There they were used in road construction. After the German invasion of the Soviet Union on 22 June 1941, it was not possible to evacuate these three camps in time due to a lack of transport capacity. While the Soviet guards had to withdraw, the Poles had fallen into the hands of the advancing Germans.

The report listed the names of the camp commanders and cited several witnesses for the account. However, it only indicated the abbreviations 1-ON, 2-ON and 3-ON for the camps, but not their exact geographical location.

According to several witnesses, the mass executions were carried out by the Wehrmacht Pioneer Battalion 537. When the front approached Smolensk again in the spring of 1943, the Germans panicked. In order to anticipate the discovery of the mass murder by the Soviets, they themselves had opened the graves. Their propaganda show had served the purpose of slandering the Soviet side. They threatened the inhabitants of Katyn with death if they did not testify that the Russians had shot the Polish prisoners in the spring of 1940.

According to the Burdenko Commission, 500 Soviet prisoners of war were deployed to prepare the graves. They had to remove the documents proving the German guilt from the clothes of the dead Poles; cut or torn pockets of the uniform jackets proved this. Moreover, they had to bring bodies from 'peaceful Soviet citizens' and put on these Polish uniforms.

According to the report, numerous documents were overlooked during these manipulations. These can be dated to the period between 12 November 1940 and 20 June 1941, in which, according to German accounts, the Polish officers no longer lived. The report contained detailed descriptions of these documents, including letters, postcards, a handwritten picture of a saint in a Catholic prayer book, and a receipt from the Soviet state jewellery trade for the purchase of a gold watch – the POWs were allowed to sell their jewellery to it.[7]

Burdenko said that his forensic doctors autopsied a total of 925 corpses in the third week of January 1944. However, this figure meant that each of the experts must have examined an average of more than twenty corpses per day. In reality, it appears that no autopsies were carried out at all because of the heavy frost.

The Soviet forensics found that the Poles were murdered in August and September 1941. However, the authors of the report made another mistake here: they correctly stated in other places that a large number of the Poles wore winter clothes with long underpants. At no point, however, did they mention the wounds on the corpses, which were inflicted by square-shaped bayonets – such bayonets were only used by the Red Army and the NKVD. They also did not publish a list of names, nor a list of objects found with the dead.[8]

The Burdenko Commission concluded that the Poles were shot by the 'German fascists' in the same way as many other 'peaceful Soviet citizens'. The 500 Soviet POWs who had been used to prepare the Katyn graves had also died in this way. Lieutenant Colonel Arnes, commander of the Wehrmacht Pioneer Battalion 537, was responsible for this.

The new US ambassador, W. Averell Harriman, who was already well known in Moscow as the White House representative for the Land Lease Act, sent a dispatch to Washington on the report of the Burdenko Commission. He saw the German perpetrators in Katyn proven: 'As a result of materials in the possession of the Special Commission, including testimony of over a hundred witnesses and medical and other data, the base sequence of German Fascist provocations, murders and falsifications has been revealed.'[9]

Unlike the Germans, the Kremlin propagandists did not invite foreign medical examiners to Katyn, but journalists were very welcome. However, these were selected very carefully: The invitation to participate in the trip from Moscow to Smolensk was sent only to correspondents of influential Western media.

Most of them had already participated in organised trips to destroyed cities that the Red Army had liberated. They had seen traces of German crimes, including the mass graves in the gorge of Babi Jar near Kiev, where the Germans had murdered around 50,000 Jews. Some members of the group made no secret of their admiration for Stalin and the Soviet Union, first of all the Americans Jerome Davis, Richard Lauterbach and Edmund Stevens and the Britons John Gibbons, Ralph Parker and Alexander Werth. Their articles had a great influence on the debates about Katyn in the USA and Great Britain.

- Jerome Davis (*Toronto Star*), son of a missionary who founded the first Christian university in Japan, was during the First World War a member of the YMCA staff in a program to care for POWs in camps in the Asian part of the Tsarist Empire and in the early 1920s in a program to help with the famine in Soviet Russia. In 1926 he conducted the first interview with Stalin for the American press. Since then, he had been fascinated by the Soviet leader. Davis wrote that his favourite hobby was reading poems. Under him, democracy was developing more and more, and he understood the needs of the people: 'Everything he does reflects the ideas and desires and hopes of the masses at a large degree.'[10]

Davis became professor of sociology at Yale University and toured the Soviet Union repeatedly. In several books and numerous articles he defended collectivisation, the show trials in the Soviet Union and the Ribbentrop-Molotov Pact. It was wrong to accuse Moscow of an aggressive foreign policy: 'Stalin does not consider it wise, or even possible, to impose Communism to any country.'[11]

• John Gibbons (*Daily Worker*) was enthusiastic about the ideas of communism already as a young man; the British Communist Party sent him to the International Lenin School in Moscow, where he was trained as an agitator of the Comintern. His three brothers fought against Franco's troops in the Spanish Civil War in the International Brigades. At first, he worked in Moscow as a translator of propaganda literature. In 1938, the year of terror, he made a career jump: he became head of the English programme of *Radio Moscow*.

However, after the Molotov–Ribbentrop Pact was signed, he was caught up in a major conflict of loyalty, as British colleagues later reported: for the Soviet Union was now, in fact, allied with Nazi Germany, and the Germans bombed English cities. Gibbons is also said to have privately criticised the weakness of the Red Army, which at that time could not defeat Finland.[12]

But with the German attack on the Soviet Union in June 1941, Gibbons' doubts vanished. Several months later he took over the Moscow office of the *Daily Worker*. Many of his colleagues mistrusted him, he was suspected of reporting to the NKVD about the talks among the journalists. As news of the mass graves of Katyn went through the international press, Gibbons made it clear that the Germans were the perpetrators: He had seen Stalingrad destroyed, and he had written a brochure about the mass graves of Babi Jar, 'the most terrible place in the world'.[13]

• Richard Lauterbach (*Time Magazine*) had also created an extremely likeable picture of Stalin: humorous and hard-working, the people loved his works, they were bestsellers in the Soviet bookstores. Stalin was highly educated; he certainly knew more about English classical literature than an Oxford don. He could drink thirty vodkas in a row without anyone noticing it. Among the members of the Politburo there was an atmosphere of friendship – Beria was a solid police chief. The reports of purges were exaggerated, politicians who violated the rules of party democracy were given other tasks.[14]

Because of his pro-Soviet articles, the NKGB was interested in Lauterbach, as the files evaluated half a century later showed. It was considered to recruit him as an informant. But in Lubyanka there were also concerns about him: it was not ruled out that he was an American spy, his publications were supposed to distract from it.[15]

- Ralph Parker (*The Times*, London) had studied Russian literature at Cambridge. Even as a student, he was enthusiastic about the Soviet regime, from which he hoped to build a just social order. In the spring of 1939 he witnessed the German invasion of Prague as a freelance journalist, and he sent reports to the editorial office of *The Times*. Later, it became known that he also worked closely with the British MI6. He maintained contacts with the Czech underground and smuggled plans of the arms industry out of the country after the Germans occupied it. The American diplomat George F. Kennan, with whom he had made friends, helped Parker escape from the Germans. Kennan had been transferred to Prague the year before.

  After returning to London, Parker got a contract as a *Times* correspondent in Belgrade, where he also worked for MI6. Together with several British diplomats he was expelled from Yugoslavia in 1940, allegedly under pressure from the Germans. As he spoke Russian well, his editorial staff sent him to Moscow two years later.[16] In his coverage of the Katyn controversy, he defended the Soviet version. He also attacked the Polish government in exile in London.[17]

- Homer Smith (*Associated Negro Press*), the only African American in the group, had lived in Moscow since 1932. He had come with a group of compatriots to participate in a feature film sponsored by the Comintern entitled *Black & White*. The fable: when the police of the US state of Alabama brutally crack down on a black steel worker strike, they are rescued by a Red Army command and led to victory. The film project did not come about, but Smith remained in Moscow enthusiastic about the Soviet system. As he had worked in the administration of the US mail, he was assigned to the build-up of the Soviet State Post. He also attended secret courses for training as a Comintern propagandist.

  Under the pseudonym of 'Chatwood Hall', Homer Smith began to send press releases from Moscow to the USA, especially for the *Associated Negro Press* (ANP) and the *Baltimore Afro-American*.[18] In his articles he praised Stalin's constitution of 1936, as it codified 'equality of races and nations'.[19]

Smith married a 20-year-old Russian woman from a working class family. She was under strict control of the NKVD, probably even an informant. But obviously she played a double game: secretly, she was very religious and she opened his eyes to the hard everyday life of the people. Above all, Smith noted that the rumours of mass arrests were not unfounded: first his former boss in the State Post disappeared, then his friend Lovett Forte-Whiteman, an African American communist and trade unionist from Chicago, who was also trained secretly in Moscow as a Comintern agitator. Forte-Whiteman had been given the nick name 'red uncle Tom'.[20]

Increasingly, Homer Smith distanced himself from the Soviet system. During the war he was the only African American correspondent on the Eastern Front. He noticed during his visit to the battle zones, that the Germans set up military cemeteries everywhere for their fallen, but the Red Army did not: 'I always suspected the Russians burned their corpses.'[21] Smith later confessed what interested him most about the trip to Katyn: he secretly searched for African American victims of the NKVD and hoped to find any clues at the mass graves.[22]

- Edmund Stevens (*Christian Science Monitor*) had also defended the Ribbentrop–Molotov Pact. Just 24 years old, he came to the Russian capital in 1934 because he was convinced that 'a brave new world' would emerge in the Soviet Union. He first worked for the shipping company Cunard, then as a translator for the Soviet foreign publishing house, before reporting for several British regional newspapers. He was married to a Russian woman and was friends with US Ambassador Joseph E. Davies. Later, Stevens also enjoyed the special trust of Ambassador W. Averell Harriman, who took him to a meeting of Stalin and Churchill in the Kremlin as advisor to the US delegation. Stevens called the writer Alexey Tolstoy 'my old friend'. [23] He was one of the correspondents invited to the war crimes trial in Kharkov one month before the trip to Katyn; officers and soldiers of the Wehrmacht were sentenced to death for mass executions.[24]

- Alexander Werth (BBC, *Sunday Times*) was considered an aesthete: he had 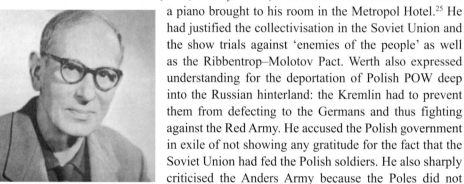 a piano brought to his room in the Metropol Hotel.[25] He had justified the collectivisation in the Soviet Union and the show trials against 'enemies of the people' as well as the Ribbentrop–Molotov Pact. Werth also expressed understanding for the deportation of Polish POW deep into the Russian hinterland: the Kremlin had to prevent them from defecting to the Germans and thus fighting against the Red Army. He accused the Polish government in exile of not showing any gratitude for the fact that the Soviet Union had fed the Polish soldiers. He also sharply criticised the Anders Army because the Poles did not want to fight on the Eastern Front under Soviet command; the citizens of the Soviet Union had the feeling that the Poles had left the country 'like rats leaving a ship they thought was sinking'.[26]

The American news agency *United Press* (UP) was represented by Harrison Salisbury, who had just ten days earlier been sent to Moscow. In his diary he recorded his first impressions of his colleagues, almost all of whom lived in the Metropol Hotel opposite the Bolshoi Theatre and often spent their evenings playing cards and drinking vodka: 'A tiny little circle of correspondents being more interested in their petty feuds than trying to get out and seeing Moscow and the Russians.' He was bewildered to learn that most of them did not speak Russian, even if they had been living in Moscow for several years: 'That is ridiculous.' Not without arrogance Salisbury stated: 'Many of them are stupid. Others are just afraid of their jobs.'[27]

The head of the Moscow office of the influential agency *Associated Press* (AP), Henry C. Cassidy, also took part in the trip. He had the year before published a book entitled *Moscow Dateline* about the alliance between Anglo-Americans and Soviets against Hitler. The sceptical former ambassador William H. Standley, who knew Cassidy well, called the book 'over-enthusiastic'.[28] The AP correspondent also described the exodus of the Anders Army from the Soviet Union, but did not mention the search for the missing officers.

Cassidy had become known in press circles because he had been temporarily arrested by the Germans in occupied Paris in 1940.[29] In autumn 1942 he had submitted questions for an interview with Stalin in the Kremlin, and, to his great surprise, *Pravda* published this brief 'interview' on 6 October, in which Stalin called for increased support from the Western Allies.[30]

The British press agency *Reuters* was represented by Duncan Hooper (see photo), who had reported on the German attacks on the British Isles at the beginning of the war. *Reuters* was the largest press service in the world and extremely influential, with more than 4,000 newspapers worldwide printing the dispatches with the abbreviation rtr. Hooper,

then 31 years old, did not speak Russian. Like most correspondents, he lived under constant observation by the NKVD in the Metropol Hotel. In letters to his wife he complained about the bad food and insufficient heating in winter. With a group of correspondents he had visited a unit of the Berling army.[31]

The youngest in the group was William H. Lawrence (*The New York Times*), the trip taking place a week before his 28th birthday. He did not speak Russian, but had made a name for himself as an fearless war reporter and merciless interviewer. Together with Salisbury, Lawrence repeatedly fought persistently with Soviet officials and censors.[32]

Originally, the journalists had been told that they should take food for two days, and that the approximately 400-kilometre route from Moscow to Katyn would be covered by car. But then two other participants joined the group: Kathleen Harriman, the 25-year-old indulged daughter of the US Ambassador, and John Melby, Third Secretary of the US Embassy, as her guardian.

W. Averell Harriman, a political companion of President Roosevelt, was a multimillionaire, his father had been one of the great shipping and railway magnates on the American west coast and owned the Union Pacific Railroad. Among his countrymen, Harriman campaigned for a government bond to support Stalin in the war against the Germans, and he organised the supply of armaments to the Red Army, both of which made him particularly valuable to Moscow. Harriman had a positive attitude towards the Soviet Union, complaining about the FBI, which looked everywhere for communists. In their coded correspondence, in which no clear names were allowed to be used, the Soviet agents gave him the pseudonym 'Capitalist'.[33]

Harriman assertively explained to his predecessor at the head of the embassy in Moscow, Admiral William H. Standley: 'Stalin can be handled.' In his memoirs, Standley called him a 'bravado' who is at the same time 'arrogant and obsequious'.[34] Harriman was divorced; his ex-wife had died, so that his attractive and sporty daughter, Kathleen, of whom he was visibly proud, lived with him. She had gone with him to Moscow and often accompanied him to official meetings. She had learned a little Russian so she could have simple conversations. Her participation in the journalist trip to Katyn was justified by her occasional involvement in the Office of War Information (OWI).

Like her father, Kathleen Harriman was given special care by the Soviet authorities. She was invited to participate in equestrian competitions. As a hobby skier she was allowed to participate in the Moscow slalom championship as a foreign guest, the Soviet organisers gave her third place after two army athletes. The Soviet newspapers also reported about her frequently, so she was known throughout the country.

The NKVD shaded and protected her on her excursions to the city. Young NKVD officer Pavel Sudoplatov, later chief of NKGB operations abroad, was responsible for this. In his memoirs he described that as alleged representative of the Ministry of Foreign Affairs he cautiously warned her father that something could happen to his daughter during her 'excursions to the city with young people', because unfortunately there was still a lot of 'hooliganism'.[35] Kathleen Harriman saw little of the everyday life of Soviet citizens, so she came to a euphoric judgement about the Soviet Union in a letter: 'By comparison to what critics painted it to be, it's damn near paradise.'[36]

Since Harriman was extremely important for Soviet warfare and was to be kept in a good mood, the Kremlin decided to provide a special train for the trip to Katyn. It consisted of two sleeping cars and the former saloon car of the Tsar. Edmund Stevens described it: 'The dining car was one of those early twentieth-century dreams of richly carved and polished black walnut and shiny brasswork, reflected in a profusion of mirrors.'[37]

On the trip the guests of the Soviet government were well served, there was caviar, the Crimean champagne flowed in streams.[38] Lauterbach wrote in his report for *Time* magazine that some of the correspondents spent their time playing cards on the journey to the mass graves. The ambassador's daughter was in a good mood: 'Kathy had a plaid skirt, an orange pullover sweater and garnet nail polish.'[39]

She had her own sleeping car compartment and also participated for several rounds in the card game, in which small sums of money were invested, as Salisbury noted in his diary. The UP correspondent described the 400-kilometre train journey, which lasted eighteen hours, over several pages. The toilets were clean, there was toilet paper, which was 'a great event in Russia'. The train had priority over troop transports and hospital trains. When the train stood at a station, he observed soldiers being taken to the front, young people no older than 15 or 16 years of age. While the correspondents dined like princes, the young Russians spooned cabbage soup. The route led past burnt villages, but work was being done everywhere on the rebuilding. The railway bridges destroyed by the Germans had been replaced by wooden constructions.

Kathleen Harriman led a privileged life in Moscow and had an unrealistically positive image of the everyday life of the Russian population.

Salisbury noted that Cassidy, Lauterbach and Lawrence had got drunk in the course of the evening. They made 'nasty and insulting remarks' to the accompanying Soviet officials. After a short night's rest, some of the correspondents woke up with a thick head in the morning.[40]

Tolstoy and the Ambassador's daughter

The group from Smolensk drove to Katyn Forest in American jeeps that had been delivered on the basis of the Land Lease Agreement; the cameramen from the newsreel accompanied the delegation.[41] In the snow-covered forest, the guests from Moscow were able to take a closer look at several of the mass graves from which a strong stench emerged. Homer Smith tried to conduct a short interview with Professor Burdenko, whom he knew from an earlier meeting, but the latter declined abruptly.[42]

Salisbury noted that the fresh pine smoke from the campfires only covered the stench from the graves to a small extent. The sight of the corpses, he admitted in surprise, touched him far less than he had expected: 'Ten thousand bodies are not the wrench on your emotions that one bleeding wounded man is.'[43]

After visiting the cemetery, the journalists were taken to a heated military tent. Professor Viktor Prozorovsky of the People's Commissariat for Health, who had put red rubber gloves on, showed them parts of tissue, including strips of brains and livers, from whose state of decomposition the time of death in late summer 1941 could be deduced. Edmund Stevens of the *Christian Science Monitor* did not lose sight of the ambassador's daughter:

> She got herself a front row position alongside one of the dissecting tables where a rubbergloved Commission member with a scalpel was slicing the corpse as zestfully as though he were carving a Thanksgiving turkey. He held up chunks of the putrefied flesh for our inspection triumphantly exclaiming how 'fresh' the tissue was, thus proving that the body couldn't possibly have been there nearly four years as the Germans had asserted, but dated from 1941 at the earliest. Holding our noses, we politely assented.[44]

After Prozorovsky's demonstration, the journalists were taken to their train, where they had lunch in several courses, as described in detail in Salisbury's diary. They had a total of five opulent meals in the former salon car of the Tsar.

The group then went on to a heated wooden house for a press conference. the meeting was chaired by Education Minister Vladimir Potemkin, who since his time as Soviet ambassador to several western capitals has been regarded as a hard-nosed tactician. Five locals entered the room. They were presented as important eyewitnesses and reported in turn on the events that are said to have taken place at that time.

The first witness, 73-year-old Parfen Kiselev, spoke for exactly seven minutes, as William H. Lawrence noted for *The New York Times*. He seemed to be intimidated – he was only released from NKVD custody immediately before the recordings. The files evaluated five decades later permit the conclusion that the NKVD officers had broken his arm in prison, and he had also become deaf in one ear – but he had to attribute these tortures to the Germans in front of the Western journalists. Kiselev told them the story of how he was pressured by the Gestapo to sign a testimony, according to which it was the Soviets who shot the Poles in spring 1940.[45]

After Kiselev, the 27-year-old villager Anna Alexeyeva hastily described the events that allegedly took place in Katyn in the late summer of 1941. The young woman had worked in the kitchen of the Dnieper Manor. According to her, the Wehrmacht Pioneer Battalion 537 was there under the command of Lieutenant Colonel Arnes. Lawrence described her in *The New York Times*: 'A tall, sharp-featured brunette with boyish bob, a rapid-speaking witness.' Lawrence summarised her story: 'On one occasion she had hidden in the bushes beside the road and watched Polish soldiers drive into Katyn Forest. Soon she heard a number of individual revolver shots at frequent individuals.' According to Alexeyeva, German officers came out of the forest, 'their sleeves were spotted with blood'.[46]

The third witness also accused the Germans; it was the former Deputy Mayor of Smolensk, professor of astronomy Boris Bazilevsky. Edmund Stevens described his performance: 'A frightened wisp of a little old man, limp and faded as an old rag doll who spoke in a tired broken voice'.[47] Bazilevsky reported how he had talked to Mayor Boris Menshagin about the camp for Soviet POWs near Smolensk and the Polish officers. Menshagin had explained to him what the Germans had decided: 'The Russians can at least be left to die off, but as to the Polish war prisoners, the orders say that they are to be simply exterminated.'[48]

After Bazilevsky, a medical examiner gave his expertise on the state of decomposition: The bodies could not have been in the ground for much longer than two years, so they were buried by the Germans. Finally, a railwayman from the Gnezdovo station explained that during the German advance in the summer of 1941 there were not enough trains available to evacuate the camps with the Polish POWs in time. Thus the Polish officers stayed behind and fell into the hands of the Germans.

Since not all participants of the press conference had a good knowledge of Russian, Alexey Tolstoy repeatedly intervened as an interpreter.[49] The nobleman spoke very good English; during the First World War he had temporarily reported from Great Britain as a correspondent for the Russian press.

Ambassador Harriman and his daughter, Kathleen, had been invited to Tolstoy's country estate several times. The American diplomat remembered the opulent food, vast amounts of exquisite wines and cognac – at a time when the overwhelming majority of Soviet citizens suffered from the war-related shortages.[50]

Seventy years after his appearance for the Burdenko Commission, his grandson Ivan Tolstoy, editor at *Radio Liberty* in Prague, published an article about what Alexey Tolstoy had entrusted to his son about the work of the 'Commission for the Investigation of German atrocities':

> In the conditions of an uninterrupted exchange of opinions, often lasting for days, over breakfast, lunch and especially dinner, around midnight – with a large quantity of vodka – people became more and more used to each other. And some day, after drinking a lot, the conversations became more and more confidential. … He and some other members of the Commission had become absolutely clear that a whole series of crimes had not been committed by the Hitlerists, but by the people of the NKVD. Anyway, this was clear about the executions of Katyn.[51]

This version sounds quite plausible. Already two years earlier Tolstoy had been informed by the Polish painter and poet Jozef Czapski, officer of the Anders Army, about the search for the missing officers when they met in Tashkent. Being well informed about the omnipotence of the NKVD, Tolstoy knew that he had to keep his doubts to himself.

From the point of view of Merkulov and his patrons in the Kremlin, the journalists' trip was a success: Alexander Werth made the NKVD version his own in his reports for both the BBC and the British press. He wrote: 'The Russians conducted their publicity round the case (including the visit of the Western press to Katyn) with the utmost clumsiness and crudeness.' But he had no doubts: 'The technique of those murders was German, rather than Russian.'[52]

Richard Lauterbach also concluded in his report for *Time* magazine: 'The Germans had slaughtered the Poles.' He quoted the eyewitness Anna Alexeyeva with the words: 'Then the men would come in with blood on their tunics and get drunk.' He summed up: 'Nobody ever doubted that the Germans had done it.'[53] Things were also clear for Jerome Davis from *Toronto Star*: 'Every correspondent who visited Katyn Forest came away convinced that it was another Nazi atrocity.'[54]

Edmund Stevens wrote on the demonstration of the execution technique by the Burdenko Commission: 'This provided a striking parallel with the method used by the Germans in similar mass executions else.' In his book *Russia is no Riddle*, published in the last year of the war, in which he praised Stalin as a wise leader, he closed the Katyn chapter with the comment that he feared he had caught bedbugs on the journey, as had happened to Kathleen Harriman: 'As soon as I got back to Moscow, I took several hot baths and sent everything I had worn on the trip to be laundered or dry-cleaned.'[55]

The statements of Anna Alexeyeva and Professor Prozorovsky were also cited by John Gibbons of the communist *Daily Worker* as striking evidence of the German guilt. He called Katyn 'German's biggest hoax of the war'.[56] He echoed the answer of a woman from Smolensk to the question of the perpetrators:

> If you had lived through what we experienced during these two years you wouldn't ask questions like this. In and around Smolensk there are 80 or more pits like those you saw at Katyn and altogether they hold well over 120,000 people who died at the hand of the Germans. Do you think that the murderers of 120,000 Russians would show pity for Polish officers?'[57]

But some of the correspondents had expressed doubts about the presentation of the Burdenko Commission already on their way back to Moscow. In their opinion, the Commission had not provided a convincing explanation for the fact that the majority of the killed officers wore winter clothes in the summer. In any case, several of the journalists concluded that the Soviet side had staged a show. Henry C. Cassidy of the Associated Press later reported: 'We were not convinced by what the Russians showed us that the Germans had done it.'[58]

On their way back, the sceptics agreed that they would not answer the crucial question in their reports on the Burdenko Commission: Was Katyn a German or a Soviet crime? Later, Cassidy described the discussion among the correspondents: 'On the way back, on the train, we discussed what had been presented to us very frankly with the Russian censors and conducting officers, and told them that we had not been convinced by the case they presented.'[59]

The mood on the way back became more and more cheerful. Until four o'clock in the morning, the correspondents sang songs and drank plenty again. Salisbury noted: 'The Russians joined us and it was all very gay.' Then he added: 'We wished we knew who killed them.'[60]

But Salisbury sent a telex to the UP editorial office, in which he presented some of the information from the Burdenko Commission report as fact: at the time of the German attack on the Soviet Union in June 1941, the Polish officers were still seen working on the roads near Smolensk.[61] UP spread the message based on this: 'The Germans were responsible for the death of 11,000 Polish war prisoners.'[62]

Reuters' Duncan Hooper, on the other hand, followed the line recommended by Cassidy not to answer the question of perpetrators in the reports. Unlike some of his colleagues, Hooper had no illusions about the Soviet regime; every day he was confronted with censorship. He kept his distance from the loudest Stalin apologist among Western correspondents, the American Jerome Davis. In a letter to his wife, he drew up an unpleasant picture of Davis: he was stingy and unpopular with his colleagues.[63]

Hooper's report was factual and dry. The *Daily Mirror* and *The Times* printed excerpts of it. Hooper wrote of the corpses, which lay in a can like 'oil sardines', and added another picture: 'We saw several layers of bodies, just as though a section of a football crowd had been lifted up bodily and pressed in the earth … The shrunken figures look like rag dolls.'[64] In addition, *The Times* printed excerpts from the official report of the Commission under the heading 'German Guilt'.[65] A commentary referred to the 'eminent authority' of the members of the Commission, including Metropolitan Bishop Nicholas.[66]

British diplomats interviewed several of their compatriots who had taken part in the trip, including Hooper. The report summarises the correspondents' impressions: 'Although they were not really inclined to reject the Soviet version, they were not fully satisfied with what they were told.' The embassy expressed fear, 'if anti-Soviet criticism is reflected in the editorials of British newspapers, a storm may break out in the Soviet press'.[67] Obviously, some of the correspondents had doubts. For in only one British newspaper appeared a report from Katyn: that of Gibbons in the communist *Daily Worker*.

The dilemma was particularly deep for Homer Smith, because his Russian wife had to expect reprisals if his publications did not meet with the approval of the Soviet authorities. So he decided not to write anything about the trip to Katyn for the time being. He was also very familiar with the mechanisms of censorship. Later, he explained: 'To file a story that the Russians had done it would have been an out and out provocation.'[68]

On the other hand, the young William H. Lawrence of *The New York Times* dared to express his doubts about the version of the Burdenko Commission in his article – and outsmarted the censorship. In addition to the reference to the winter clothes that the murdered Poles allegedly wore in the summer, he made another remark in his report, referring to the more experienced colleagues: 'The reporters said that the experiences of German atrocity investigation in Kiev and Kharkov had showed that mass executions had been carried out with machine guns.'[69]

But most readers obviously couldn't read between the lines. Instead, the accounts of Jerome Davis, Richard Lauterbach, Edmund Stevens and Alexander Werth shaped the opinion of the Anglo-American public. The Katyn reports of the four pro-Soviet correspondents were later reprinted by the press in the USSR and the People's Republic of Poland.

At the time, the public learned nothing of the report by US diplomat John Melby, who had accompanied the ambassador's daughter, Kathleen Harriman, to Katyn. He wrote of a 'show' that the Burdenko Commission had staged for the correspondents. Their witnesses would have given a weak performance: 'All the statements were glibly given as though by rote. Under questioning the witnesses became hesitant and stumbled.' Despite these doubts, the diplomat came to the conclusion that the Germans were the perpetrators of Katyn:

It is apparent that the evidence in the Russian case is incomplete in several respects, that it is badly put together, and that the show was put on for the benefit of the correspondents without opportunity for independent investigation or verification. On balance, however, and despite loopholes the Russian case is convincing.[70]

From Moscow's point of view, the success was completed by Kathleen Harriman's nine-page report, which John Melby had helped with. She said that the evidence was 'petty' according to American standards. But the 'methodical manner in which the job was done' is an argument for the German perpetration of the crime.[71] The ambassador's daughter was particularly impressed by the documents proving that the Polish officers were still alive until the advance of the Wehrmacht into the Smolensk area. In a private letter she wrote: 'They found a letter dated the summer of 1941, which is damned good evidence.'[72]

Complemented by a cover letter from her father on the official letterhead of the US embassy, Kathleen Harriman's report was forwarded to Washington. Harriman wrote, addressed directly to Roosevelt, that the participants of the journey had come to the conclusion: 'In all probability the massacre was perpetrated by the Germans.'[73]

Obviously, as a reward for his reporting, the *Time* correspondent Richard Lauterbach was invited to a reception in the Kremlin a few days later on the twenty-sixth anniversary of the founding of the Red Army given by Molotov. He recorded his observations in his book *These Are the Russians*: 'Ambassador Averell Harriman looked like a nervous young curate at a national Episcopal Convention. He seemed out of place in his too-long double-breasted business suit which he tried to formalise with a stiff collar. But it only served to make him look uncomfortable.' On the other hand, 'his skinny daughter' Kathleen shone in an elegant blue evening dress.

Politburo member Anastas Mikoyan tried to get Harriman drunk with many toasts in a row. Molotov had previously exposed the US ambassador by stating loudly that he only drank mineral water. With Mikoyan there was no escape for Harriman, as Lauterbach noted in ironic allusion to the railway company owned by the Harrimans: 'The Union's Pacific headlines were gradually dimming in the Russian fog.'

No less drunk was Marshal Kliment Voroshilov. When he, 'the face beet-red', wanted to get too close to the Russian wife of an American correspondent, whose name Lauterbach did not mention, his aides pulled him away and took him out of the room.

The Polish general Zygmunt Berling also had his performance at the reception. He toasted with Molotov to the good health of the Red Army, but then he avoided the American Ambassador Harriman and British diplomats, because their countries continued to recognise the Polish government in exile in London.[74]

Berling's appeal and descent

Only a few days before the reception in the Kremlin, Berling had been at the head of a delegation of 600 of his soldiers in Katyn Forest. In his speech he said about the murdered officers: 'The Germans shot them like wild animals, shot them with their hands tied together. ... We now have a weapon in our hands which our friendly ally, the Soviet Union, has given us, on which the Germans wanted to shift their own guilt.' Berling announced that a tank unit of Polish units under Soviet supreme command would be named 'Katyn's avengers'.[75]

A former press officer of the Berling Army who fled to the West reported in 1948 to the American military intelligence service CIC that anyone who doubted the version by the German perpetrators had been transferred to a punishment company. This company had been almost completely destroyed in battles at the front. He saw a report by a Polish politruk that several drunken soldiers accused the Soviets. This 'enemy propaganda' must be counteracted and all debates about Katyn must be stopped, said the report.[76]

The day after Berling's speeches, a Catholic requiem took place in the cemetery, and in the sermon the Polish chaplain also accused the Germans of mass murder.[77] After the mass, some of the Berling Army officers wanted to talk to villagers, but NKVD soldiers had blocked off the way. After all, they learned that none of Katyn's former inhabitants could still be found there, the population of the village had been completely exchanged.[78]

As only became known decades later, the witnesses presented by the Burdenko Commission also had to leave their home village. Some of them were imprisoned for collaborating with the Germans; it was only in 1956, during the first wave of amnesties three years after Stalin's death, that they were released. The traces of the farmer Parfen Kiselev and some others were completely lost.[79] In the early 1990s, former police General Dmitry Tokarev, who was involved in the mass execution of Poles in Kalinin, reported that Moscow had given the order 'not to let any of the witnesses alive'.[80]

The Burdenko Commission also attracted a lot of attention in London. The British Embassy in Moscow reported that the correspondents were not very impressed with the presentation in Katyn. However, the diplomats warned against criticism, as this could lead to 'explosions' by the Soviets.[81] The British ambassador to the Polish government in exile, Owen O'Malley, referred to numerous inconsistencies in the report. He saw it as an indirect admission of guilt that the Soviets had not invited American or British specialists to Katyn.[82]

Some experts in the Foreign Office, on the other hand, considered the Soviet report more plausible than the *Official Material* of the Germans, for the very reason that the latter had been commissioned by Goebbels.[83] The experts also pointed out that the speaker of the International Medical Commission in Katyn, the Hungarian Ferenc Orsós, could not be considered objective because he was known as an anti-Semitic sympathiser of the Nazi regime.[84] Churchill finally ordered: 'We should none of us never speak a word about it.'[85]

O'Malley was suspected of being under the influence of the London Poles and of not keeping a proper distance from them. His 'final ghoulish vision of Stalin condemning the Poles to a knacker's yard' should evoke only 'anti-Soviet passions', an analysis in undiplomatic language said.[86]

In view of the unclear situation, Foreign Minister Eden and his Secretary of State Alexander Cadogan gave a clear instruction: 'The truth may never come out. So far, however, it seems that the available evidence tells us to refrain from any assessment.' Cadogan added his personal comment on the contradictory Katyn reports of the Germans and Soviets: 'Lies and propaganda came out of both the Russian and the German sides.' According to him, the Soviet experts were faced with the alternative: 'To participate in the manipulation or find themselves in another mass grave.'[87] Churchill finally decided: 'We should none of us never speak a word about it.'[88]

O'Malley's analyses therefore went into the archives, while Burdenko's report was translated into English for King George VI and the British authorities. But O'Malley continued his investigations on his own. He received analyses of the materials from British medical examiners. He also asked them to contact Orsós, but this request was not fulfilled. After all, the British experts certified that they had met the Italian Palmieri and the Croatian Miloslavich as serious scientists.[89]

Senior officials of the Foreign Office appealed to the London Poles to accept the Burdenko Commission's version and to overcome its reservations about the Soviet Union.[90] Goebbels wrote in his diary: 'The English are shameless enough to adopt the Soviet representation and persuade the Poles to also adopt it. How low England intends to sink in this war!'[91]

The German press once again wrote of 'Bolshevik lies'. The Polish newspapers controlled by the Germans published a statement by former Prime Minister Leon Kozłowski who lived in Berlin under control of the Gestapo:

> I had the opportunity to take a look at the circumstances in Katyn that leave no doubt about the murder of Polish officers by the Soviets. The report from the Soviet Special Commission sent to me has not changed the conclusions I have drawn from my close inspection. This whole thing reminds me of a very bad movie.[92]

Two months later, Kozłowski suffered fatal injuries in an air raid on Berlin.

At that time, Roosevelt's advisor John Franklin Carter, who provided him with confidential information from the press and political circles in Washington, campaigned for a swift end to the war through negotiations. Carter was still convinced that his colleague Ernst Hanfstaengl ('Putzi'), Hitler's former

EN ZIJ WEENDEN BITTERE TRANEN...

(Stalin heeft onlangs bij de graven van Katyn een mis laten lezen en het Poolsche communistenlegioen laten paradeeren.)

(Overgenomen uit de Brüsseler Zeitung.)

The newspaper Storm, published in occupied Belgium, printed a cartoon under the heading 'And they shed bitter tears', which shows the metropolitan Nicholas, Stalin and Molotov at a funeral service for '11,000 brave Polish officers' (2 February 1944).

'piano player' and foreign press chief of the NSDAP, was right in his assessment that the Russians and not the Germans were the perpetrators of Katyn. Carter questioned diplomats from the Polish embassy in Washington, who were still under the government in exile. He wrote a new Katyn Memorandum himself, based on the materials received from the Poles, and presented it to Roosevelt. But the president refused to deal with it.[93]

In the early summer of 1944, Carter made another attempt to dissuade Roosevelt from the goal of forcing the Wehrmacht into an unconditional surrender, as this would continue to demand enormous sacrifices. He reported to the president of Hanfstaengl's proposal to broadcast a fake speech by Hitler over occupied France, read out by a voice imitator. In it, the false Hitler was to announce that the Third Reich had concluded a ceasefire with the Western Allies in order to concentrate fully on the fight against the 'Jewish hordes of Asiatic Bolsheviks'. This speech should be broadcast on the eve of the planned invasion of Normandy to confuse the German troops stationed there and get them to welcome the Americans with open arms. But the suggestion came too late: Carter's letter arrived at the White House on 7 June 1944, three days after the invasion of Normandy (D-Day).[94]

The State Department, which was opposed to the 'Putzi Project' from the very beginning, pointed out Hanfstaengl's misjudgements to date. He had enervated the officials with his demands for payment, a Steinway grand piano, better food and the restoration of his teeth.[95] Roosevelt told Carter to stop the cooperation with Hanfstaengl. The latter was returned to the internment camp in Canada. His predictions about Hitler's next steps were no longer in demand in view of the military success of the Allies.[96]

Hitler had given the order to put down mercilessly any resistance in the occupied territories. He had a fierce confrontation with Mussolini, during which Katyn also came up for discussion. At least this was reported by the Turin newspaper *La Stampa* after the war. In autumn 1944 the SS had shot several hundred Italians who allegedly supported partisans, including many children from the village of Marzabotto, not far from Bologna. Mussolini had been overthrown and imprisoned in July 1943 after the Allies landed in southern Italy, but then a German command liberated him. Hitler reinstated him as head of government, but he only controlled the north of Italy. Mussolini saw his regime completely discredited by the Marzabotto massacre and complained about it in a telephone call later confirmed by several witnesses. According to *La Stampa* he said: 'You can't protest over the mass graves of Katyn when there is Marzabotto here in Italy.'[97]

Exactly two years after the publication of the report of the Katyn Commission headed by him, Burdenko received his old acquaintance Boris Olshansky, a mathematics teacher, in his Moscow apartment. At least Olshansky later described it in a letter to the journal *Sotsialistichesky Vestnik* published by Stalin opponents in Paris. According to Olshansky, Burdenko had explained to him that the report did not correspond to the actual results of the investigation. Rather, the murdered Polish officers had already been in the mass graves since 1940. But he was unable to tell the truth: 'We were instructed to refute the version propagated by the Germans. By Stalin's personal order.'[98]

A short time later Olshansky was transferred to the Soviet administration in East Berlin, he worked as a supervisor for German schools and was provided accommodation with a German woman. In 1947 the couple fled together to West Berlin. He married the woman and moved with her to Bavaria. There, he began working for Russian exile magazines financed by the Americans.[99]

By this time Berling had long since disappeared into political oblivion. Western diplomats had initially regarded him as Poland's future strong leader. But Berling was suspected of removing the military from control by the Communist Party. Thus, after only one year, he lost his post at the head of the Polish armed forces under Soviet supreme command. He no longer played a role in Stalin's policy.

Nor did his name appear in the propaganda brochures of the Union of Polish Patriots printed in Moscow. The Polish communists published a summary of the Burdenko Commission report entitled 'The Truth about Katyn', supplemented by reports by Jerome Davis, Edmund Stevens and Alexander Werth. [100]

These three Moscow correspondents played a role in the controversy surrounding the book *Report on the Russians* by William Lindsay White, which appeared in early 1945. White had come to the Soviet Union in the summer of 1944 with a delegation from the US Chamber of Commerce invited by Foreign Trade Commissioner Anastas Mikoyan. The small delegation completed the last stage of the long journey from Tehran to Moscow on the plane of US Ambassador Harriman, who, as so often, was accompanied by his daughter. There were also two armed Soviet air traffic controllers on board. [101]

Karykatura *Oskarżyciel* Z. Wasilewskiego. „Wolna Polska" nr 5/1944

Cartoon of the magazine Wolna Polska (Free Poland), published under Soviet control in Moscow, the title is: The accuser (5/1944).

Meanwhile, Harriman had a more sober relationship with the Soviet Union than at the beginning of his time in Moscow. This was due in no small measure to his deputy George F. Kennan, whom, previously, Ambassador Joseph E. Davies did not want in Moscow. Kennan, however, unlike Harriman, had no doubts about the Soviet perpetrators in Katyn. But the conflict had long since ceased to play a political role. He noted later: 'The tacit rule of silence which was being applied at that time to the unpleasant subject in question.' [102]

With his scepticism towards the Soviet regime, Kennan found the open ears of William Lindsay White, who took part in several organised trips to the Russian province.

White described with compassion the people in the towns and villages who were marked by the war. Without naming his informants, he reported on the omnipresent control of society by the NKVD and labour camps for critics of the Soviet regime. Later, he explained why he wrote the book: 'Most Americans pictured Stalin as a big, lovable, fun-loving Santa Claus to whom we were deeply in debt because he had been obliging enough to get a lot of Russians killed at Stalingrad to make it a comfortable war for us.'[103]

In Moscow, White lived in the Metropol Hotel, where some of the foreign correspondents stayed. He had long talks with some of them, including Henry C. Cassidy (AP), Richard Lauterbach (*Time*) and William H. Lawrence (*The New York Times*). One of White's topics of conversation was Katyn. In his book, he did not answer the question of whether the perpetrators were Germans or Soviets, but he reported: 'Moscow correspondents say the most severe political censorship was imposed on their stories of the Katyn Forest Massacre.'[104]

White's book was on the bestseller list in the USA for several weeks in 1945, but most reviews were negative. The Soviet press reacted sharply, William H. Lawrence quoted from the *Pravda* in his report for *The New York Times*: 'The usual stew from the Fascist kitchen with all its smells, calumny, unpardonable ignorance and ill-conceived fury, written by an obscure American newspaperman of doubtful reputation.'[105] It was therefore no surprise that the National Council of Soviet-American Friendship attacked White, even publishing a brochure entitled *The Truth about the Book the Nazis Like.*

Sixteen journalists signed a statement that White strongly criticised, including Jerome Davis, John Gibbons, Richard Lauterbach, Ralph Parker, Edmund Stevens and Alexander Werth.[106] The text said: 'White's book must rank as a highly biased and misleading report, calculated to prolong the oldest myths and prejudices against a great ally, whose sacrifice in this war has saved us incalculable bloodshed and destruction.'[107]

Edmund Stevens criticised White in his own book *Russia is no Riddle*, in which he praised the Soviet system: 'The abuse of Soviet hospitality is the shabbiest aspect of the White episode.'[108] Henry C. Cassidy (AP), on the other hand, praised the book, not publicly, but in a private letter to the author. In it he stated that the protests made the book a bestseller.[109] Harrison Salisbury of UP also wrote a letter to White, but he did not praise the book, rather he implied that some episodes were distorted or even invented.[110]

Duncan Hooper (*Reuters*) and William H. Lawrence, both of whom had also taken part in the correspondents' trip to Katyn, did not participate in the attacks on White. Lawrence had already argued with the pro-Soviet Ralph Parker before this controversy and ensured that he could no longer publish in *The New York Times.*[111]

Similarly Homer Smith, who still lived in Moscow, refrained from commenting on White, just as he kept to himself his doubts about the Burdenko Commission's demonstration and his concerns about the fate of his African American compatriots who went to the Soviet Union. Smith had no doubt that the Soviet regime was as criminal as the National Socialist regime with its racial ideology. He had been part of the delegation of journalists who had visited the liberated Majdanek concentration camp in August 1944 at the invitation of the Soviet Foreign Ministry. The group included four other journalists who had also travelled to Katyn in January: Jerome Davis, Richard Lauterbach, Ralph Parker and Alexander Werth. They felt strengthened by their impressions in Majdanek in their view that the Germans were also the murderers of Katyn.

It was exactly twenty years after his visit to Katyn Forest that Homer Smith published his memories of his return to the USA. He gave his book, a bitter reckoning with the Soviet system, the title *Black Man in Red Russia*, in which he also memorialised his friend Lovett Forte-Whiteman, the 'red uncle Tom', who died in the Gulag.

He did not directly answer the question about the perpetrators in Katyn, but he pointed out the numerous inconsistencies of the Burdenko Commission:

> Why had no foreign newsman been invited to be present when the opening of the graves began? Why had we not been permitted to be present when the first autopsies were being performed. Why had Stalin not invited any Allied or neutral experts to join the Soviet investigation team? Why had the spruce saplings that had been removed from on top of the grave grown to a height indicating that they had been planted three or four years ago?'

However, he concluded his remarks on the Burdenko Commission with the sentence: 'But I did not ask these questions.'[112]

Chapter 11

Persecution of Annoying Witnesses

The work of the Burdenko Commission was only a first step in the Kremlin's attempt to completely rewrite the history of the Katyn massacre. The next step was to ensure that none of the witnesses could uncover the manipulations of Merkulov and his collaborators. For this reason, Moscow's secret services were ordered to neutralise all witnesses – by defamation, intimidation or liquidation. There were three groups: residents of Smolensk and Katyn; Poles who participated in the exhumations or examined them; the members of the International Medical Commission, who in their report for the German government had compiled all the evidence for the Soviet perpetrators.

The actions against witnesses who could confirm Soviet guilt began in Smolensk and the surrounding area. There, after the Germans withdrew, numerous executions of alleged collaborators took place under the command of the NKVD hangman Ivan Stelmakh, who was already involved in the mass murders of 1940.[1] After his work was done, Stelmakh received the Lenin Order, the highest award of the Soviet Union.[2]

The next chapter took place in Moscow, focusing on the two NKVD officers Vasily Zarubin and Vasily Markov, who had led the interrogations of Polish officers in Kozelsk and Starobelsk in 1940 and later were based in the Soviet embassy in Washington. Both had been denounced as Soviet agents with diplomatic passports in 1943 in an anonymous letter to FBI chief Hoover. As later became known, in 1944 Markov accused his superior Zarubin of cooperating with the FBI in a letter addressed to Stalin personally. Both were then ordered back to Lubyanka for an internal investigation. However, since Markov was unable to produce any evidence, he was removed from the service for defamation. The doctors in the service of the NKVD also came to the conclusion that he was schizophrenic. He was sentenced to five years in the camp.[3]

While still in Moscow prison, Vasily Markov secretly wrote down information about Katyn and tried to have the cashier smuggled out. It was supposed to get to the US Embassy. But this plan came to light, and the details have not been known to this day. Markov was sentenced to death in a second secret trial and shot shortly afterwards. In Lubyanka it was also concluded that he was the author of the anonymous letter to Hoover, which had long been known from informants in the FBI.[4]

Boris Menshagin, the former mayor of Smolensk, was at the top of the search list of Moscow's secret services. Before the war, as a lawyer he had got to know the Soviet administration from inside; he was well informed about the role of the almighty NKVD, which permanently broke Soviet law. In his post as mayor, he had received several medals from the German occupiers.

Menshagin and his family reached the Czech city of Karlovy Vary, which was liberated by the US Army shortly before the German surrender. He was interned by the Americans. While he was in an American camp, the US units withdrew and left Karlovy Vary to the Red Army as agreed previously. When Menshagin was released after several days, he found his apartment in the city devastated, the door had been broken open. He supposed his wife had been arrested by the Soviet secret police. To spare her interrogation and torture, he surrendered himself to the Soviet authorities. He was immediately taken to Lubyanka in Moscow.[5]

However, the news of his wife's arrest was false. She had fled with the children from Karlovy Vary to Bavaria; later, they found asylum in the USA.[6] But they never saw their husband and father again, they only learned about his whereabouts after decades.

On the Moscow search list was also the railway fitter Ivan Krivozertsev, who had given the Germans his detailed observations about the arrival of Polish officers at Gnezdovo railway station. As he later reported, he received a group of visitors one night in late summer 1943, shortly before the Wehrmacht withdrew from the Smolensk region: they were Soviet partisans, asking him to seek protection 'in the forest' until the Germans withdrew. But Krivozertsev, a bachelor, was suspicious; he feared that a field tribunal and a firing squad were waiting for him with the partisans. So he hid. When the first Germans left, he, his mother and his 6-year-old niece were allowed to join them.[7]

In the turmoil of the last weeks of the war, his mother and the child were killed, the exact circumstances were not known. After the end of the war, Krivozertsev contacted a US unit in Bremen as a refugee from the Soviet Union. But for lack of interpreters, the US officers did not understand his request and wanted to transfer him to the Soviet occupation zone, later East Germany. When Krivozertsev realised this, he withdrew. He learned that units of the Polish government in exile were stationed under British supreme command in the northwest German town of Meppen, and made his way there.

As the Polish command in Meppen understood that Krivozertsev could make statements about Katyn, he was immediately taken to the staff of the Anders Army, which was located in the North of Italy in the region of Ancona. He got a room in a villa where officers of the staff were accommodated. One of them was the writer Ferdynand Goetel, who had meanwhile become a press officer in the Anders Army. Goetel was ordered to question Krivozertsev in detail about Katyn. The publicist Józef Mackiewicz, who like Goetel had visited the cemetery in Katyn

The Russian railway locksmith Ivan Krivozertsev became an important witness for the Poles. In Katyn Forest he had told the Belgian medicine professor Speleers and the Hungarian Orsós (both with notepads) about the discovery of the mass graves.

Forest at the invitation of the Germans, also came to Ancona to learn more from the Russian refugee.

Krivozertsev also commented on the Burdenko report: He contradicted the version that the Germans had shot the Russian villagers and POWs, a total of 500 people, after the exhumation work had been completed. According to him, only one was executed as a marauder because he took coins and medallions from the dead.[8]

The staff of the Anders Army had no doubt that Krivozertsev was highly endangered as an inconvenient witness for Moscow. He received Polish identity papers with the name Michał Łoboda. With the majority of the soldiers of the Polish units, who did not want to return to their communist homeland, he moved to Great Britain. He was assigned a village in the southwest of England as a safe place to live.

There he was found dead in 1947, hanged from a tree. British police concluded it was suicide. Mackiewicz, who had maintained contact with Krivozertsev, doubted this version: he had not been depressed. However, the organisations of the exiled Poles were strongly infiltrated by the communist secret services after the war, so that the whereabouts of the Katyn witness could probably be easily found out.[9]

The feature film *Katyn – The Last Witness*, a Polish–British co-production from 2018, focuses on the fate of Krivozertsev. In the film he is murdered by the Soviet secret service. An English reporter, a fictitious person invented by the scriptwriter, had recorded Krivozertsev's account of Katyn's events in the film – and was shot by the British secret service because Her Majesty's government wanted to suppress the truth about Katyn. The film thus confirmed the very popular version of events in Poland that the British had deliberately lied and manipulated in the Katyn case. But in reality there is not the slightest evidence in the archive material of a British secret service attack on Krivozertsev. In the film, the fiancée of the murdered reporter published under his name a report on Katyn based on Krivozertsev's statements. But in reality there was no such article, it was also the result of the scriptwriters' fantasy.

Mackiewicz, who had analysed the Krivozertsev case in more detail, had fled west in time before the advance of the Red Army and was able to make his way to Italy. Goetel, on the other hand, had remained in Poland for the moment.

After the withdrawal in January 1945, a government coalition was formed in Warsaw, including the former premier in exile Stanisław Mikołajczyk. But almost all key positions in the army, police and judiciary were occupied by communists who had been trained for it during the war in the Soviet Union.

In Poland, civil war prevailed at that time between AK units, which returned to the underground on one side, and the communist-controlled army units and state security bodies on the other. Communist propaganda accused the anti-Soviet AK of having made common cause with the 'Hitler fascists', although they had carried the main burden of the partisan struggle against the German occupiers. AK officers were sentenced to long prison terms. The secret police UB, dominated by cadres loyal to Moscow, committed a large number of political murders, and in many cases the Soviet secret services were directly involved in the operations.

With the agreement of the Soviets, the office of Minister of Justice was taken over by the Socialist Henryk Świątkowski, who spoke out in favour of an alliance with the communists. At the beginning of the war he was deported by the Germans to the Auschwitz I labour camp, but was released after one year. This unusual release led to suspicions that he had served as an informant to the Germans.

Among Świątkowski's tasks was the preparation of a Polish show trial for the mass murder of Katyn. The Poles who were brought to Katyn in 1943 by the Germans were to be accused of being collaborators. They were almost all representatives of the pre-war bourgeois elite who were to be affected by this process.

Hiding places in monasteries and railway depots
In Krakow, the prosecutor Roman Martini led the investigation. He had survived the years of occupation in a German officers' camp. Martini was a harsh prosecutor. During the interrogation he strongly questioned the prelate Stanisław Jasiński. The old priest buckled under this pressure and signed a declaration according to which he had already been 'of the inner conviction that everything was the work of the Germans', when he blessed the dead in the mass graves of Katyn.[10]

Martini also examined 78-year-old Archbishop Sapieha, who had sent his confidante Jasiński to Katyn. The prosecutor apparently saw this as an act of collaboration, but the Archbishop stated: 'The only motive of my decision was that it was inevitable to send a clergyman to the place where so many tragically murdered compatriots lie, who would do them the last service required by religion.'[11] Sapieha had no doubt, however, who the killers of Katyn were. He had carefully studied the materials of the Technical Commission, which the young priest Stefan Niedzielak had smuggled from Warsaw to Krakow during the war.[12]

Martini also persuaded other participants of the trips to Katyn to accuse the Germans of mass murder in their statements. When he also invited Ferdynand Goetel, the latter disappeared: he was hiding in a Krakow monastery.[13] Goetel understood that he had to leave Poland because of his knowledge of Katyn. Middlemen got him a forged Dutch passport; in the summer of 1946 he could travel via Czechoslovakia, Bavaria and Austria to Italy.[14] His books have been removed from all libraries in Poland.

Kazimierz Skarżyński, the head of the Red Cross delegation that had visited Katyn, also fled persecution by the communist authorities. He first hid after the prosecutors had asked him for an explanation of the German perpetrators. He had also enraged the communist leadership by saying that the Poles did not blame the Russian people but the Bolshevik regime for Katyn.

Skarżyński also fled via Czechoslovakia to West Germany, from where he could travel on to London.[15] In exile in Britain, he wrote another report on his findings about Katyn and handed it over to the Foreign Office, which classified it as 'secret' and put it in the archives. A top diplomat, who had no illusions about the Soviet regime, commented on his report: 'If it were known that Mr Skarzynski had given us a copy, his life would be in danger.'[16]

Dr Marian Wodziński, who led the exhumations in Katyn, also found asylum in England. He had been interrogated by the NKVD. When he was released after a few days, he hid. Martini searched for him and the official law gazette published the warrant of arrest. Wodziński therefore fled Poland. In exile in Britain, he wrote another report on the investigations.[17]

In Krakow, Prosecutor Martini also focused on the Institute of Forensic Medicine, after the NKVD had discovered twenty-two notebooks in a monastery wall containing files on the AK as well as notes on investigations into Katyn. The secret police found out that the chemist Jan Zygmunt Robel from the institute was the author of the notes; he was immediately arrested by the NKVD and interrogated by Martini.[18]

In the institute, German experts, assisted by Polish lecturers who had to work as assistants during the occupation, had once again examined the materials found in the mass graves of Katyn, especially the documents, but also uniform parts, watches, wedding rings, medals, coins and banknotes. Thanks to the chemical treatment of the documents, the names of other victims became visible; the institute notified the relatives if they could be located.[19] Robel was one of these Polish experts. After the German invasion of Poland, he had been taken to the Mauthausen concentration camp, but after a few months he could return to Krakow.[20]

As the front approached, on Robel's initiative the Poles working in the institute secretly copied the investigation reports as well as the contents of the documents. Then they packed the evidence in tin boxes. The plan was to solder the boxes watertight and sink them at the bottom of a pond. But the Germans found out about the project and brought the boxes with a military truck to the Institute of Forensic Medicine in Breslau (now: Wrocław).[21] However, its director Gerhard Buhtz, who had led the investigation in Katyn, had just died in an accident near Minsk: while preparing to withdraw his unit, he was run over by a locomotive.

Shortly before the Red Army closed the ring around Breslau, a Wehrmacht transporter, again accompanied by Beck, brought the boxes to Dresden in January 1945, where their traces were lost. They were probably burned in the bombing of the city. But the documents about Katyn were not lost. Indeed, the NKVD had confiscated Robel's copies of the original documents, which Beck brought to Dresden. But as a precaution, Robel had copied his own notes and hid the second set of notebooks in a box in the attic of the Collegium Medicum. He only informed one employee of the institute about this secret, who passed it on to his daughter. After the fall of the party regime in 1991, she gave the decisive clues that led to the discovery of Robel's materials.[22]

Robel was released in autumn 1945 after three months in custody. The reason was the suspension of preparations for a Polish show trial around Katyn as a result of a visit to Moscow by the Minister of Justice Świątkowski. He had informed Deputy Foreign Minister Vyshinsky, the former Prosecutor General of the USSR, that the Polish authorities were preparing to interrogate the members of the International Medical Commission prior to the opening of the planned trial. They should confirm that the Germans had forced them to sign the final report. Świątkowski stated that he would send his most eager investigator, Prosecutor Martini, to Geneva, Brussels,

Andrey Vyshinsky, who was first Soviet General Prosecutor, then Foreign Minister, became a key figure in the manipulations concerning the mass murders of Katyn.

The Hague, Prague and Sofia for this purpose. But Vyshinsky ordered the Polish minister to refrain from a Katyn trial in Warsaw without giving any explanation.[23]

Soon after Świątkowski's return from Moscow, the Katyn propaganda of the Germans as perpetrators was stopped in Poland. It was a topic that was to disappear from the public debate as it was too dangerous because the communists had not yet finally consolidated their power and also had not yet brought the press completely under control.[24]

Prosecutor Martini was found beaten to death in his apartment in March 1946. The crime gave rise to numerous speculations, which culminated two years later, on 13 February 1948, in a sensational article in the Stockholm daily *Dagens Nyheter*: referring to witnesses not mentioned by name, it stated that Martini had inspected NKVD files during an official trip to the Soviet Union and found contradictions to the Burdenko report. The questioning of Soviet witnesses had increased his doubts; after all, he had come to the conclusion that the Germans had by no means committed this crime.

The Swedish newspaper even mentioned the names of six NKVD officers who allegedly led the executions, among them Chaim Feinberg and Abram Borisovich; these two names had already appeared in the Nazi press in 1943. Two communist agents were ordered to kill the annoying Martini, the crime was disguised as robbery. The NKVD then liquidated the two perpetrators, a young woman and a student, in order to cover up the evidence. The reports in which Martini expressed his doubts had disappeared from his safe deposit box.

This version of events published by the Swedish newspaper was echoed in the British and German press and it also went down as proven fact in books about Katyn. But Polish emigrants who knew the situation in Krakow described the version of *Dagens Nyheter* as grotesque. As a source for the report they cited a friend of Martini who had emigrated to the West. His name was Mieczysław Gorączko; he was known for his imposture. He occasionally appeared as an ex-general and sold invented sensational stories from the countries behind the Iron Curtain to Western newspapers.[25]

Gorączko was also suspected to be behind a series of sensational articles about Katyn, with which the German magazine *7 Tage* (7 Days) made headlines in July 1957: reports of an NKVD commander named Tartakov from 1940 had appeared in the West. The articles mentioned the execution of Polish officers, not only in Katyn, but also in two other places: the inmates of the Starobelsk camp were shot and buried in Dergachi near Kharkov, those from Ostashkov near the small town of Bologoye in the Kalinin district. In the first case, the invented report was not far off: Dergachi is only 12 kilometres away from the mass graves of Pyatikhatki. In the second case, however, the location was a long way from the facts: from Bologoye, it is 180 kilometres to Mednoye, the actual burial site.

While the Tartakov report finally turned out to be a fake with the publication of Soviet archive materials in the early 1990s, the Martini version still has supporters. Today, however, Polish historians assume that Martini's death was unrelated to his Katyn investigations. It is not ruled out that the perpetrators came from the anti-communist underground, which regarded him as a servant of the Soviets. His personnel file, however, suggests quite different motives for murder: Martini was involved in black market transactions, in addition, he had stalked a 17-year-old girl and had apparently therefore got into a fierce quarrel with her boyfriend. But neither Polish nor Soviet archives found the slightest indication that he was allowed to evaluate original NKVD documents or question Soviet witnesses, let alone travel to the Soviet Union in his investigations.[26]

Repression and press campaigns
Under no circumstances should the Soviet secret services lose control of these investigations. They also took care of the members of the International Medical Commission, to which the Polish Minister of Justice Świątkowski would have liked to send his eager investigator Martini. Throughout Eastern Europe, cadre communists trained in Moscow occupied key positions in the police and judiciary, and death sentences against political opponents were the order of the day. In this way, the Croatian doctor Eduard Miloslavich, member of the International Medical Commission in Katyn, was to be liquidated. But Miloslavich, who was also a US citizen, had fled in time and was sentenced to death by a Yugoslavian court in absentia.[27]

At the end of 1944, Professor Marko Markov, a member of the Medical Commission, was arrested in the Bulgarian capital, Sofia. He was threatened with the death penalty for collaborating with the Germans. After he had declared after three months in prison that the Germans had forced him to sign the report of the Commission, the People's Court acquitted him in February 1945.[28] A brochure was published under his name in Bulgarian and German, entitled *Neck Shot*, which confirmed the version of the Burdenko Commission.[29]

His Prague colleague František Hájek was also unable to escape Moscow's secret services. In June 1945 he was arrested, and after three weeks he signed the desired declaration: the Germans had murdered the Polish officers in Katyn, but while visiting the mass graves he was forced by them to claim the opposite. Hájek was released; he gave a radio lecture about Katyn, in which he accused the Germans of being the perpetrators, and took over the chair of forensic medicine in Prague again.

He published a twenty-two-page report on the Medical Commission that had visited Katyn Forest at Goebbels' instigation. It said that the members of the Commission had been put under pressure to sign the protocol of the Germans. The communist-controlled judicial authorities commissioned Hájek to investigate several spectacular deaths in the ranks of the opposition, which was still permitted at the time. As desired, Hájek always recognised accidental death or suicide.[30]

Italian professor of medicine Vincenzo Palmieri commented on the news saying that his Czech colleague Hájek and Bulgarian Markov distanced themselves from the 1943 report of the Medical Commission: 'I would probably have done the same if Naples had been liberated by the Red Army.' Because of such statements Palmieri, a practising Catholic, was subjected to fierce attacks by the Italian communists, who were firmly behind Stalin at the time. Communist students with Stalin posters systematically interrupted his lectures at the University of Naples, and the party paper *L'Unità* led a campaign against him. He also received death threats, so that he preferred to be in public only accompanied by his assistant as personal guard. As a precaution, he buried his large photo documentation from Katyn in his garden and spread among his acquaintances that it had unfortunately been destroyed in a house fire.[31]

Palmieri's Romanian colleague Alexandru Birkle was also on the NKVD list because of Katyn. He was warned in time and found a hiding place with friends in Bucharest; in case of danger he had to crawl into a niche, which was camouflaged by a wardrobe in front of it. For months he hid in this way, lost more than 20 kilograms and suffered skin problems because he couldn't get into the sunlight.

In 1946, a military court sentenced him in absentia 'for collaboration' to twenty years in a labour camp. The Romanian secret police took his wife and daughter into custody for a month, but they did not reveal the hiding place. After she was released the daughter managed to go to the American and then British embassies to ask for help for her father. But the diplomats of both states saw no reason to do anything for a man who had made himself available for Goebbels' propaganda action. Finally, his relatives bought a forged passport for ten gold coins, allowing Professor Birkle to leave for Austria. Via France he reached Argentina, from where he moved on to Peru. He worked as a doctor and lecturer at the University of Lima.[32]

František Šubík, the former rector of the University of Bratislava, a Catholic Modernism poet and translator of Polish poetry, also managed to escape via Austria with his pregnant wife. There, his first son was born. But the American occupation authorities handed him over to Czechoslovakia. He was taken with his family in a US Army truck directly to Prague, where he was immediately sent to prison.

During the interrogations he was threatened with death if he did not withdraw his signature from the report of the Medical Commission: 'Not even a dog will know where you disappeared to.'[33] The officers of the communist-dominated secret police accused him of collaborating with the Germans, accusing him of having enforced the provision on the removal of 'non-Aryan doctors' from the health service. But a group of professors relieved him of this accusation: he had indeed helped several Jewish doctors. His wife collected money from friends to bribe the judges. So he was released after two and a half years without signing a confession.[34]

However, Šubík was deprived of the title of professor and had to work as a doctor in a rural area. He was under the control of the secret police, who detained him from time to time for several days or even several weeks and tried to recruit him. He was repeatedly accused of causing more damage to the 'glorious Red Army' with his lectures on Katyn than the loss of two divisions on the battlefield meant. He was also no longer allowed to publish, and his works were removed from public libraries.[35]

His Hungarian colleague Ferenc Orsós had fled the Red Army from Budapest in time. He was in Halle in Eastern Germany at the end of the war. From there he made his way to West Germany and hid.

Fearing extradition to the Soviet Union, Arno Saxén in Helsinki burned his materials about Katyn shortly before the end of the war and fled his Finnish homeland to Sweden. After six months he returned and was summoned by a 'control commission', in which representatives of the Soviet embassy set the tone. They urged Saxén to withdraw his signature from the Katyn report of the medical commission. But he resisted and several professors defended him. The trial against him was finally closed; the Soviets gave in as they did not want an open confrontation with the Finns.[36]

His Danish colleague Helge Tramsen was also accused of participating in the trip to Katyn. The Danish communists wanted to have him tried for collaboration with the Germans, but failed. Tramsen had been a member of the resistance against the Germans.[37]

Belgian Professor Reimund Speleers, on the other hand, was arrested for collaborating with the German occupiers.[38] In his house, members of a communist group found his Katyn documentary and burned it immediately. A court sentenced him to twenty-five years' imprisonment; his property was confiscated.

His Dutch colleague Herman Maximilien de Burlet was to go to prison for four years and lose his civil rights for ten years. But the trial took place without him; he had fled to neutral Switzerland in time. De Burlet's son had fought in a Dutch volunteer unit on the side of the Germans on the Eastern front and was considered missing.[39]

The consequences of his trip to Katyn were much milder for François Naville, Ordinarius of Geneva University. In his hometown, the Stalinist communists, who then occupied 36 out of 100 seats in the cantonal parliament, demanded his expulsion from the university because he had collaborated with the Germans in Katyn. They also accused him of taking money from the German government. However, Naville rejected this in a report for the Swiss authorities. He denied that the members of the International Medical Commission in Katyn had been put under pressure by the Gestapo.

His appearance met with a considerable response in the press. The daily *La Tribune de Genève* even printed excerpts from Naville's report. The Soviet embassy in Bern protested against this, but the Swiss Foreign Ministry rejected the accusation that the Geneva debate had had an anti-Soviet character. The attacks by the communists and Soviet diplomats on Naville were extremely counterproductive because the Swiss press once again used them as an opportunity to report in detail on Katyn.[40]

Even for some of the foreign writers, participation in the trip to Katyn as part of Goebbels' propaganda campaign did not remain without consequences. For example, the three Belgians who had been part of the writers' delegation had to go to prison after the war for collaborating. However, Katyn was not mentioned in any of the judgments. Flemish Hitler admirer Ferdinand Vercnocke was sentenced to life imprisonment, later reduced to sixteen years. But he was released after six years, found a job in a Brussels film studio and remained an activist of the Flemish movement. Filip De Pillecyn was sentenced to ten years' imprisonment by the judges, but was released after half the time; he regretted his collaboration with the German occupying forces. Today, an academic journal is dedicated to the life and work of the Flemish Catholic.[41] The Walloon Pierre Hubermont was sentenced to sixteen years, six of which he served. Under a pseudonym he later wrote articles against Walloon chauvinism.[42]

The two Frenchmen Fernand de Brinon and Robert Brasillach who had travelled to Katyn were hit harder: they were sentenced to death for collaborating with the Germans. In view of the American advance on Paris in late summer 1944, Count de Brinon left for Sigmaringen in southern Germany with several hundred high dignitaries of the Vichy regime. De Brinon became president of the Vichy

The Swiss François Naville (center) and the Italian Vincenzo Palmieri, here examining a skull with a German secretary in Katyn, were attacked by communist groups as collaborators of the Nazis.

government in exile. When the US Army approached Sigmaringen, he tried to flee to Switzerland, but was arrested at the border and extradited to the French authorities. The Supreme Court sentenced him to death for collaboration and 'national dishonour', and he was executed on 15 April 1947.

At that time, the writer Brasillach had been dead for more than two years. After the Wehrmacht withdrew, he initially hid in Paris. But when the French authorities arrested his mother, he turned himself in. At his trial, the public prosecutor accused him of spreading Goebbels' propaganda, naming his reports about Katyn. Brasillach wrote in a statement: 'We wanted to see Katyn, we saw it and said what we saw.'[43]

In a trial lasting only six hours, he was sentenced to death for treason and espionage. His defence attorney complained that a law passed in 1944 had been applied retroactively. Although many prominent French writers, who were not burdened by collaboration, stood up for him, the sentence was executed by shooting on 6 February 1945. Today, Brasillach is honoured by the nationalist right in France. On the anniversary of his death, Spanish Falangists laid flowers on his grave in a Parisian cemetery because he had praised the dictator Franco in his books.

The Spaniard among the writers in Katyn, Ernesto Giménez Caballero, however, continued his career after the war: he joined Franco's diplomatic service, and after several years at the Spanish Embassy in Brazil, he became ambassador in Paraguay. He also made a name for himself as a documentary filmmaker, focusing on Latin America and the Spanish cultural heritage.

He worked on the subject of Katyn once again in his memoirs, but he did not change his initial assessment, which was reflected in a brochure immediately after returning from the trip. But his report contained an unsavoury episode about an 'unforgettable lunch', which he had left out in his 1943 brochure:

> In the large luxurious manor house in the forest of Katyn, where the NKVD, the People's Commissariat, once the GPU, had its seat, we have a frugal lunch, it consisted of sakuski and tea. Dr. Buhtz came, his sleeves rolled up without washing his hands that were covered in cadaveric poison. He sat down, took a bread roll and pressed a kind of pus, allegedly salmon pate. He held the roll in his hand for a while so that it would take on the smell of the corpse and offered it to me in a challenging way. I took it. And even bit into it. Bravo, bravo, always the proud Spaniard!

The smell followed Giménez Caballero as far as Spain: 'When I opened the suitcase in my hotel in Barcelona, the smell of Katyn rose again, meandering through the room, and since I was alone, I dropped dizzy on the bed, disgusted, puking on Katyn!'[44]

Chapter 12

Defeat of the Kremlin in Nuremberg

A verdict of the Nuremberg War Crimes Tribunal would crown the efforts of the Soviet leadership to enforce its version of the events of Katyn: the judges, including those from Western states, were to certify it by convicting German perpetrators. So it was important that the lawyers of the Western Allies should have no doubts about this.

The conditions were favourable: there was no one who could credibly represent the version of the Soviets as perpetrators in the media. Thus the members of the International Medical Commission were neutralised: the Czech Hájek and the Bulgarian Markov had been forced into custody to dissociate themselves from their signatures under the German report; the Slovak Šubík and the Belgian Speleers were imprisoned; the Dutchman de Brunet, the Croat Milosevich, the Hungarian Orsós and the Romanian Birkle had gone into hiding; the Finn Saxén, the Dane Tramsen, the Italian Palmieri and the Swiss Naville saw themselves put under pressure by organised attacks of communist groups and therefore did not want to express themselves publicly on Katyn.

In France, the court that had sentenced the writer Robert Brasillach to death as a Nazi collaborator had classified his texts about Katyn as Goebbels' propaganda; thus the Soviet version was officially sanctioned. The newly founded daily newspaper *Le Monde* described Katyn as the 'game of German propaganda'.[1]

Katyn, on the other hand, was not mentioned in the sensational trial of the doctor Marcel Petiot in Paris. He had been convicted of murdering and robbing a total of twenty-seven people during the war, people who wanted to flee from the German occupying forces. He had injected cyanide into his victims on the pretext that they had to be vaccinated for the allegedly arranged crossing to South America. Petiot had also been an informant of the American intelligence cell 'Pond'. The head of 'Pond', Colonel John V. Grombach, claimed in a book published in 1980 that his contacts had already received information about Katyn from Petiot in 1942. The French authorities did not learn at the time that Petiot had worked for the Americans during the war. However, it became known that he had served the Gestapo. Petiot was sentenced to death in 1946 and was sent to the guillotine.[2]

In London, Foreign Office experts analysed all available reports on Katyn, including the *Official Material* of the Germans, the depictions of the Polish

Red Cross and the Burdenko Commission as well as the detailed dispatches of Ambassador Owen O'Malley. However, they came to no clear conclusion: 'There is some ground for suspicion against the Germans.' But: 'Possibly, the Polish story, related by Sir O. O'Malley, is true.'[3]

The Foreign Office was dominated by experts who were sceptical of the Soviet Union. Members of the British delegation in Nuremberg also had doubts about the Soviet version of the mass murder of Polish officers. One of them told US Brigadier General Telford Taylor, assistant to the chief prosecutor Robert H. Jackson, that he saw a big problem in the charges relating to Katyn. In his opinion it would be hard to imagine punishing German war crimes given the fact that the Western Allies had allowed the Soviets to include Katyn in the lawsuit: 'How can we discuss with Russians the execution of German war criminals when we have condoned this?'[4]

But in Washington, the report of Lieutenant Colonel John H. Van Vliet, who had been brought to Katyn by the Germans as a POW, disappeared in the archives; the press learned nothing of its existence. A few days after his release from a German Oflag at the end of the war, Van Vliet had reached an American troop command in Leipzig. There he briefly reported about his trip to Katyn, concluding that in his opinion the Soviets, thus the allies of the USA, were the perpetrators. He was taken to the US headquarters in Europe, in Reims, France, where he wrote his first brief report on his Katyn trip. From Paris he took a plane to Washington for further questioning at the Pentagon. There he wrote his official report about his observations in Katyn.[5] His superiors classified the report as secret. Van Vliet received the official order to maintain silence because of the 'possible political implications'.[6]

The American poet Ezra Pound, who in the first years of the war had worked as a Mussolini follower in Rome for the English-language programme of Italian radio, remained cut off from the public. In this programme he had accused the Soviets of perpetration at Katyn. In May 1945 he was arrested by American troops in Italy. He was put into solitary confinement, including three weeks in an open-air iron cage. Psychiatrists found him mentally disturbed, partly because he equated Hitler with Joan of Arc.

In prison he continued to write his main work, *The Cantos*, in which he cited the 'mass graves of Katin' (sic) as example of the cruelty and dishonesty of mankind. Finally, Pound was brought to the USA. Before the trip he read to his guards from the bestseller *Mission to Moscow* by Stalin worshipper Joseph E. Davies and commented loudly on some passages that seemed particularly grotesque to him.[7] He was sent to a closed psychiatric institution in the USA, which he could leave only after twelve years.

In the summer of 1945, on the other hand, a press campaign via Scandinavia obviously steered by Moscow met with a great response from the Western media.

The campaign was intended to get the American and British public in the mood to accept the Soviet Katyn version at the Nuremberg trials. Several sensational reports were launched in the Scandinavian countries.

It all started with the left-leaning Swedish newspaper *Trots Allt*. Referring to alleged sources in the Netherlands, it reported that during the war German policemen had taken their holidays in Holland and bragged that they had killed Jews and put them into Polish uniforms for the mass graves of Katyn.[8]

The New York Times reported from Stockholm about a former Norwegian concentration camp inmate. He testified that Jewish prisoners in the Gestapo counterfeiting workshop in the concentration camp of Sachsenhausen had produced the Polish documents that had been added to the bodies in the mass graves in Katyn. In addition, the correspondent reported, citing alleged information from former SS officers, that Ribbentrop and Goebbels had jointly arranged the 'fraud of Katyn'. The bodies of 12,000 murdered concentration camp prisoners were put into Polish uniforms and buried in Katyn Forest.[9]

The Swedish daily *Stockholms Tidningen* published a report on 10,000 bodies of victims of Nazi terror, citing former concentration camp prisoners, who had been presented to visitors from abroad in Katyn Forest as Polish officers. Two years earlier, the newspaper's Berlin correspondent, Christer Jäderlund, was firmly convinced of the Soviets as perpetrators after his visit to Katyn; now he did not write about it. The reports obviously launched by Moscow's influential agents in the Scandinavian press were circulated in Western Europe and the USA through the major press agencies.

In this climate, legal experts from the victorious powers met in London to prepare the Nuremberg trials. In the London Charter, they agreed that each side could submit a list of issues that were not to be the subject of court hearings. The Ribbentrop–Molotov Pact, the three Baltic States and Polish–Soviet relations were listed on the Moscow ban list. Katyn, on the other hand, was on Moscow's wish list – as a crime committed by Germans.

In order to shorten the procedure, the legal experts agreed on a provision that was entirely in the Kremlin's interest: the final reports of war crimes already investigated by the victorious powers should be admitted as evidence. Article 21 of the Charter read:

> The Tribunal shall not require proof of facts of common knowledge but shall take judicial notice thereof. It shall also take judicial notice of official governmental documents and reports of the United Nations, including the acts and documents of the committees set up in the various allied countries for the investigation of war crimes, and of records and findings of military or other Tribunals of any of the United Nations.

Moscow scripts for the Tribunal

The Soviet delegation used this passage to introduce the Burdenko Commission report into the trial as 'irrefutable evidence' under the document number USSR-54. The American Chief Prosecutor Robert H. Jackson later admitted that the US Department of Justice had instructed him to keep the Katyn case 'as small as possible'. British lawyers had even been instructed by their government to leave the issue entirely to the Soviet side without intervening. A senior Foreign Office official noted that the delegation sent to Nuremberg had 'instructions to take no part in this business … and the British judges are aware of the snags. With luck we shall avoid trouble'.[10]

The new British prime minister, Clement Attlee of the Labour Party, propagated the slogan of the unbreakable British–Soviet friendship. His party and the trade unions still believed that Stalin was on the way to building socialism. Moscow agents in London, such as Kim Philby, helped create the pro-Soviet mood.[11] Philby received important information about the FBI's actions against Soviet agents as part of the cooperation of the Western Allies' secret services.

Attlee had cooperation with the Polish government in exile in London completely suspended. The Poles were not invited to the victory celebration

Above left: *The American chief prosecutor Robert H. Jackson withheld from the public that he played an important role in the Katyn case in Nuremberg.*

Above right: *The Soviet chief prosecutor Roman Rudenko tried to stage a show trial based on the Moscow model, but met with American and British resistance.*

on the first anniversary of the end of the war, although more than a hundred thousand had fought under British supreme command.[12] Some left-leaning press and above all leaders of trade unions heavily infiltrated by communism attacked the Poles as 'neo-fascists' because they denounced Katyn as a Soviet crime and did not want to return to their homeland because of the Stalinist terror.

However, British lawyers in Nuremberg did not consistently follow the Labour government's line. Several of them analysed the Katyn materials that the Polish government in exile sent them unofficially. The Americans also ignored the recommendations of their government: Telford Taylor, Jackson's assistant, even met with former officers of the Anders Army on the fringes of the trial.[13]

Behind the scenes, several members of the British and American delegations tried to convince the Soviet Chief Prosecutor, Lieutenant General Roman Rudenko, that the Katyn charge had to be dropped. Diplomatically, they said it was unclear who the perpetrators were. But Rudenko insisted on his position.[14]

In Moscow, a group of experts had been set up to prepare the Nuremberg trials, headed by no less than Deputy Foreign Minister Andrey Vyshinsky. He had great experience in the preparation of large-scale trials, because the scripts for the Moscow show trials during the Stalin purges had been written under his direction. The Chief Prosecutor Rudenko had been one of the executors of the Great Terror under Stalin in the Soviet Republic of Ukraine, working closely with Nikita Khrushchev, the party leader there.

Rudenko had already had experience with Poland. In June 1945, he had been the prosecutor in the Moscow 'Trial of the 16'. Here, too, Vyshinsky himself had written the script; Stalin had it accepted.[15] In this show trial, Polish politicians and military leaders who opposed their country's affiliation to the Soviet bloc were sentenced to long prison terms. Stalin obviously wanted to demonstrate with this process that the pro-Western politicians of Poland did not have to count on any support from the West. The Soviet NKGB had lured them into a trap in Poland and then kidnapped them to Moscow.

Among them was Leopold Okulicki, chief of staff of the Anders Army, who had his teeth knocked out in Soviet custody at the beginning of the war. He had returned to occupied Poland and had become one of the leaders of the AK underground army. After the withdrawal of the Wehrmacht at the beginning of 1945, he wanted to continue the fight against the new occupiers, the Red Army. Once again Okulicki, whom the prosecutors called 'ally of the German fascists', because of his rejection of the Soviet system, was severely tortured in Moscow. Obviously, he had also not fallen into oblivion as he, a companion of General Anders during a visit to the Kremlin, had vigorously contradicted Stalin when the latter had claimed that the disappeared Polish officers had fled to the General Government.

The Moscow *Times* correspondent Ralph Parker, who took part in the presentation of the Burdenko Commission, had submitted questions to the Kremlin for a written interview on the situation in Poland. Stalin's answer to the 'Trial of the 16' was:

> The arrest of the 16 Poles in Poland, headed by the notorious diversionist General Okulicki, is in no way connected with the question of reconstruction of the Polish Provisional Government. These gentlemen were arrested by the virtue of the law dealing with the safeguarding of the rear of the Red Army from diversionists, analogous to the British law of the Defense of the Realm.[16]

Parker was released by *The Times* a little later. A senior British diplomat had complained about him in a letter to the editor-in-chief. Parker had praised the Soviet Union for wanting to establish a genuine democratic order in Czechoslovakia. In the Foreign Office, however, it was found that Parker's reporting consisted of 'perversions of essential facts'. It was also alleged that he was completely influenced by his wife, a Russian who, according to British diplomats, worked for the Soviet secret service.[17]

Parker had already irritated his editor-in-chief in the last months of the war. In a letter to him, he explained why he did not want to report the rape of women by Red Army troops in Poland, Czechoslovakia and eastern Germany: this would damage the reputation of the Soviet Union. Soon after his release, he found a new employer: he succeeded Comintern agitator John Gibbons as Moscow correspondent for the *Daily Worker*.[18] Gibbons became head of an English-language propaganda magazine of the pro-communist peace movement controlled by the Kremlin.

The *Daily Worker* praised the 'Trial of the 16'. Okulicki and the other accused were insulted as 'reactionaries, fascists and enemies of the Polish people'. The Western media largely ignored the background to the process. George Orwell blamed the British press for uncritically repeating the Soviet version that the Poles were 'somehow guilty'. He tried in vain to draw the public's attention to the fact that this was a crime of justice; but his articles on the matter were not published.[19] Okulicki died in the Lubyanka, presumably from the effects of torture.

The Kremlin was apparently counting on the smooth running of the scripts for Nuremberg, drafted in Moscow, the last chapter of which was the execution of the accused. The Chief Prosecutor Rudenko confidently announced at the start of the trial on 20 November 1945, that he would demand the death penalty for all defendants, since Soviet investigations had proven their guilt.

However, Rudenko had obviously expected the trial to be conducted according to a previously agreed script without a real defence, a process he was used to in the Soviet Union. It was a gross misjudgement, because the American and British judges did not see it that way.

So Rudenko had to accept, helplessly, that against the protests of the Moscow delegation German witnesses could raise the Secret Additional Protocol to the German–Soviet non-aggression pact. Rudenko had tried to block their statements and hastily wrote a secret letter to the representatives of the Western Allies in which he pointed out the 'political damage' that such a discussion could do. But the recipients ignored it. So Rudenko had nothing else to say but that the document was a forgery. However, the accused secretary of state and SS brigade leader Ernst von Weizsäcker, father of the later German president, confirmed its authenticity.

The British and American press then published longer articles on the division of Eastern Europe into a German and a Soviet sphere of interest, on the division of Poland by Hitler and Stalin and on the annexation of the Baltic states by Moscow.

These publications were probably the cause of the death of the Soviet Major General of the Judiciary Nikolai Zorya. He was one of Rudenko's assistants; he had to make sure that none of the German accused spoke about the Secret Additional Protocol negotiated with Molotow. A few days after Weizsäcker's appearance, the major general was found dead in his room in Nuremberg.

Officially, the Soviet delegation announced that it was an accident while cleaning his pistol. However, half a century later, members of the delegation expressed the view that Zorya had committed suicide. He had been held responsible for the public discussion of the Ribbentrop–Molotov Pact. He feared torture in the Gulag. Rumours spread that Stalin had a fit of rage after the news of his death and shouted: 'Bury him like a dog!' Without the usual military ceremony he was buried in the Soviet military cemetery in Leipzig.[20]

However, Russian historians today do not rule out the possibility that he was murdered in connection with the Katyn indictment, because here too the Soviet delegation had lost control of the proceedings. Zorya's superior Rudenko had the passage included in the indictment: 'In September 1941, 925 Polish POW officers were killed in the Katyn forest.' The number corresponded to the report of the Burdenko Commission, which allegedly exhumed 925 bodies. Several days later, the Soviet delegation corrected this passage, and now, as previously in the Soviet press, there was talk of 11,000 murdered.

Zorya had also worked out the Soviet process strategy for the Katyn case. He was considered particularly suitable for the task because before his delegation to Rudenko he had been legal advisor and also supervisor of the Polish Committee of National Liberation. The committee was founded in Moscow on Stalin's orders, and the post-war communist leadership in Warsaw emerged from its ranks. According to Russian historians, Zorya had expressed doubts about the Burdenko report after talks with Polish politicians in exile in Moscow and the analysis of documents.

He had wanted to inform Vyshinsky of this without knowing that the latter had played a leading role in the manipulations. As a security risk to the Soviets, Zorya was removed by Beria's agents.[21]

In parallel to the Nuremberg Tribunal, the Soviet authorities organised half a dozen show trials for German war crimes. According to the files evaluated half a century later, the sentences were not only passed before the trials began, they had also been personally approved by Stalin and Molotov.[22]

Thus, at the turn of the year 1945/46, a general of the Wehrmacht, seven officers and corporals as well as three soldiers were tried for war crimes by a military tribunal in Leningrad. A group of foreign correspondents was among the several hundred spectators.

Soldier Arno Dürre was accused not only of involvement in the shooting of Russian civilians and the burning of Russian villages, but also in the Katyn massacre. The news agency TASS, for which the Russian war reporter and writer Pavel Luknitsky reported about the trial, announced that Dürre's interrogation had revealed 'new details about the terrible misdeeds of the fascists in Katyn Forest'. He said that 15,000–20,000 Polish officers, Russians and Jews had been shot there.[23]

Arno Dürre (in Russian documents wrongly written only with one R: Дюре) had volunteered for the Wehrmacht at the beginning of the war at the age of 19. He rose to the rank of sergeant in anti-aircraft defence, but was demoted to a simple soldier after a military criminal case and was assigned to a penal battalion on the Eastern front after several months in prison. He was wounded and taken into Soviet captivity in July 1944.[24]

In his front diary published later, Luknitsky went into the Dürre case in more detail than in the TASS reports: the latter did not participate directly in the executions in Katyn, because this was a matter for the SS. But he belonged to the command that dug the mass graves: 'With others who, like him, had been brought

into this forest, they dug huge trenches for the mass graves at night. The SS people threw corpses, tens of thousands: Polish officers, Russians, Jews, into these trenches. And Dürre had a hand in burying them.'[25]

However, the protocols of the Leningrad trial, which were evaluated by Russian historians half a century later, also record that Dürre gave absurd answers at the court hearing.

The German prisoner of war Arno Dürre testified in the Leningrad show trial that the SS had shot the Poles in Katyn.

For example, he stated that Katyn was in Poland, the mass graves had a depth of 15 to 20 metres and were covered on the sides with tree trunks.[26]

However, Katyn was no longer mentioned in further reporting on the trial, not even in the prosecutor's charge. Eight of the accused were sentenced to death for their alleged involvement in war crimes, the remaining three were sentenced to forced labour, including Dürre, who received fifteen years.[27] In the justification of the sentences there was general talk of 'mass executions, bestialities, acts of violence against the peaceful Soviet population, burning down and plundering of towns and villages and deportation of Soviet citizens into German slavery'.

The execution of those sentenced to death took place on 6 January 1946 in front of thousands of onlookers in a square in Leningrad. Four military trucks, each with two death candidates on the loading platforms, drove under the gallows. They got the rope around their necks, then the four trucks drove away at the same time, eight bodies dangling from the gallows and reportedly remained there for several weeks. The Soviet newsreel filmed the execution, the scene can be seen on the Internet today.[28]

The hour of the resistance fighters

A short time later the Soviet delegation in Nuremberg approached the subject of Katyn. Since the International Military Tribunal had only to decide on the individual guilt of leading heads of the Nazi regime, Rudenko had to appoint a person responsible for the mass murder. He chose Reichsmarschall Hermann Göring.

According to Rudenko, Göring personally issued the order that 'a German military formation' under the codename 'Staff 537, Pioneer Battalion' commanded by Lieutenant Colonel Arnes, had executed the Poles in the summer of 1941. Rudenko, however, could not have known that this officer would come forward and thwart his entire plan. The family name was not Arnes, but Ahrens, and his first name Friedrich. He was the man who discovered a birch cross over a soldier's grave in the snow-covered forest of Katyn while tracking a wolf.

It was a fortuitous event: one of Ahrens' former subordinates, Lieutenant Reinhart von Eichborn, who had been the head of the switchboard of the Central Army Group in Smolensk, read in a newspaper about the Soviet indictment. However, important facts were not correct in the report. Ahrens was not the commander of a pioneer battalion, but of the Signal Regiment 537. He had only taken it over at the end of 1941, months after the time when, according to Rudenko, the Katyn murder had taken place.

Eichborn now investigated the whereabouts of Ahrens. Furthermore, he made a declaration on oath to a notary that, to his knowledge, the Signal Regiment 537 commanded by Ahrens was in no way involved in the mass murder of Katyn. He himself belonged to the regiment.[29]

After locating Ahrens, he contacted the member of the German resistance, Fabian von Schlabrendorff, who also had been stationed in Smolensk. Both knew each other from studying law in Halle/Saale. Eichborn had understood that Ahrens was in mortal danger.[30] The German press had reported about the Leningrad show trial in which the soldier Arno Dürre had been sentenced to fifteen years in the Gulag for alleged aiding and abetting the murders at Katyn. Should the Nuremberg court confirm the charge, Ahrens, as the alleged commander of the executions, would be threatened with extradition to the Soviet Union and the gallows there.

Eichborn himself had belonged to the resistance group that had planned attacks on Hitler; he knew that Schlabrendorff, a former concentration camp prisoner, had a very good reputation with the Americans. Schlabrendorff had been arrested after the failed assassination by Colonel Claus von Stauffenberg against Hitler in his headquarters 'Wolf's Lair' on 20 July 1944; he had been one of Stauffenberg's contacts. In Berlin's Gestapo prison, however, even under torture he did not reveal the names of his fellow conspirators, thus saving his friend Rudolf-Christoph von Gersdorff, who had supervised the exhumations at Katyn.[31]

The co-conspirator, Henning von Tresckow, who had meanwhile become general, had committed suicide after Stauffenberg's failed coup because he feared not being able to resist torture by the Gestapo and betraying co-conspirators. Also, he had repeatedly pleaded for a strengthening of Stalin's opponents in Russia and demanded an end of the German occupation of terror.[32]

In the last months of the war, Schlabrendorff passed through the concentration camps in Sachsenhausen, Flossenbürg and Dachau. Two weeks before the German surrender on 8 May 1945, he was brought to South Tyrol together with other prominent prisoners, including former Austrian Chancellor Kurt Schuschnigg, closely guarded by the SS. In South Tyrol, a unit of the Wehrmacht liberated the prisoners from the hands of the SS – it was a unique event in the war. Shortly afterwards American troops arrived – the German soldiers surrendered without a fight.

Schlabrendorff's name was already known to the American secret service OSS. The OSS resident in Bern, Allen W. Dulles, had been reported by his informant in Berlin, a German businessman who regularly travelled to Switzerland, about the investigations after Stauffenberg's assassination attempt. Dulles was very interested in the history of Hitler's opponents in the Wehrmacht; he was already working on a book about it. Schlabrendorff was questioned and protected by the OSS. When he expressed the desire to meet his family in Bavaria, which he had not seen since his arrest by the Gestapo, heavily armed US soldiers took him there in their jeep. He was considered endangered because he cooperated with the Americans. He wore an American uniform for reasons of camouflage.[33]

The OSS chief himself, General William J. Donovan, also questioned Schlabrendorff. He, too, was well informed about the German resistance against Hitler. Donovan had met the diplomat Adam von Trott before the war when the latter came to the USA for a study visit. Former German intelligence officers reported that in 1943 Donovan also met the head of the German counter espionage, Admiral Wilhelm Canaris, under the utmost secrecy in the Spanish port of Santander, to talk to him about the German resistance.[34] However, this encounter is not documented. In order to better understand the psychology of the enemy, Donovan even learned his language and made so much progress in it that he was soon able to conduct conversations in German.[35]

The OSS was dissolved in September 1945 by the new American President Harry S. Truman, but Donovan became chief advisor to the American chief prosecutor Robert H. Jackson in Nuremberg, and he was thus closely involved in the preparations for the trial of the 'major war criminals', as it was officially called.[36]

Donovan was under great political pressure: shortly before, a woman who was an informant for the Soviet NKGB had revealed herself to the FBI. Her report showed how strongly the OSS was penetrated by informants from Moscow. Donovan was accused by his enemy, Hoover, the FBI chief, of uncritically accepting sympathisers with the communist regime into his service.[37] Some of the informants had been led by NKGB resident Zarubin, the former NKVD interrogator in the Kozelsk camp, the same Zarubin, who had been accused of participating in the Katyn massacre by an anonymous letter to FBI chief Hoover.[38]

When Donavon noticed after the first questionings of Schlabrendorff how well the German knew about the Wehrmacht leadership, he accepted him into his advisory staff.[39] The Hitler opponent wrote a series of analyses for him, including on the attitude of the most important generals of the Wehrmacht towards Hitler; he divided them into three groups: the war criminals devoted to Hitler, doubters who did not have the courage to confront him, as well as active opponents who should under no circumstances be treated as war criminals in Nuremberg. In the last group he named Rudolf-Christoph von Gersdorff, who had been promoted to major general two months before the end of the war.[40]

Schlabrendorff, who was a lawyer, also wrote a memoir for Donovan in which he pointed out a fundamental construction error in the Nuremberg trials: the victorious powers were both accusers and judges. He urged the American side to drop the charges on Katyn. He wrote about the Burdenko report:

> This is not true. I was myself, at this time, in Katyn and I was an eyewitness of the discovery of the Polish officers' graves. According to this, there is no doubt that the Polish officers had been captured and shot by the Russians. This undeniable fact is known not only by thousands of ex-German soldiers and officers, but also by Polish priests, English officers and non-German physicians of European nations. The democracies would very much jeopardise their good cause in advertising a provable untrue confirmation.[41]

His memorandum was classified as 'secret'.

Schlabrendorff later described Donovan's reaction to the passage on Katyn: 'His face turned red because he realised in a flash that it was impossible to put the blame on the Germans, as the Russians wanted. Had it been done, the perpetrators would have acted as accusers.'[42]

Donovan understood that the Katyn case threatened the credibility of the Western powers. He forwarded the translation of Schlabrendorffs' memoir to his superior Jackson, whom he called 'Dear Bob'.[43] In a brief note he informed Jackson that Göring's lawyers could insist on an interrogation of witnesses about Katyn, 'who will testify that this murder was done by the Russians'.[44] The former OSS chief also saw an obvious chance of defeating the Soviet side; unlike many State Department top people, he no longer believed Stalin's promises, but had a clear understanding of his political goals and the methods of Soviet diplomats and agents.[45]

Donovan managed to get Jackson to meet Schlabrendorff and other Hitler opponents. They reported orders from the Nazi leadership in violation of international law, including instructions not to capture American pilots and paratroopers who had been shot down, but to shoot them. Jackson wrote in his diary after the meeting: 'All these men were Anti-Nazi, but not Anti-German.'[46]

Only more than 60 years after the Nuremberg Trial did it became known that Fabian von Schlabrendorff and William J. Donovan had thwarted Soviet strategy in the Katyn case.

In this way Schlabrendorff played a decisive role in convincing the initially hesitant Jackson of the necessity of questioning witnesses. Jackson's assistant Telford Taylor noted that the chief prosecutor was now convinced that he had to offer 'strong opposition' to the Soviet Katyn charge.[47]

Change of tactics of the defenders

The Americans now supported the German defence's request to question witnesses about Katyn. That Schlabrendorff had tuned them in behind the scenes did not become known. It was a serious affront to the Soviet delegation. Rudenko protested, citing the agreement that evidence from completed proceedings should not be questioned. The American judge Francis Biddle contradicted him: the defence generally has the right to question the evidence. Rudenko received instructions from Moscow to insist on his position, accusing the judges of violating their duties and making a 'gross error'.

As Telford Taylor noted, Biddle now took drastic action, threatening in a sharp tone behind closed doors: 'Rudenko's position was so slanderous and arrogant that in the U.S. he would be cited for contempt, and he would be sent to prison immediately.' Biddle proposed to read an appropriate statement in open court, 'before General Rudenko is arrested'. As a result, the Soviet delegation in Nuremberg gave in and no longer resisted a questioning of witnesses.[48]

But the angry Russians demanded the admission of an unlimited number of prosecution witnesses; they pointed out that the Burdenko Commission had documented 120 statements about German guilt. Göring's defence attorney Otto Stahmer, who had been an opponent of Hitler, should be allowed only two witnesses. After fierce discussions behind the scenes, however, the representatives of the Western powers prevailed with the proposal that each side should limit itself to three witnesses.[49]

Both sides were now feverishly trying to win high-profile witnesses for the Katyn indictment. Stahmer sent a letter to Władysław Anders in exile in London; but the Polish general categorically refused to testify in favour of a high-ranking Nazi like Göring.[50] Anders had previously protested in vain that only representatives of the communist leadership in Warsaw were admitted to the trial, but not what he called the only legitimate Polish government in London.[51]

Finally, he proposed to make his documentation available to the Nuremberg Court, but did not receive an answer to his letter. Anders' opposition to the Nazi regime did not prevent the communist press in Western Europe from insulting him as a fascist, as he equally firmly rejected the Soviet system.[52]

But Anders had materials sent to Stahmer about Katyn and suggested Józef Czapski, the head of the search office of his army, as a witness for Nuremberg.[53] Czapski had met George Orwell after the war and explained the political background of the mass murder at Katyn to him. Orwell tried to find a British publisher for Czapski's book *Inhuman Land* about the fate of Polish POWs in the Soviet Union, but was ultimately unsuccessful.[54] Orwell also appealed in vain to the British press not to bring the Poles in exile close to fascists.[55]

Swiss professor François Naville also wrote to Stahmer that he saw no reason to come to Nuremberg for Göring: he had nothing to add to the 1943 report of the International Medical Commission.[56]

In one of his reports to Donovan, Schlabrendorff recommended his friend Gersdorff, who had supervised the opening of the mass graves, as a witness to the Katyn case. At that time Gersdorff was in American captivity as a POW, but in a privileged position: he belonged to the small group of former General Staff officers who were to provide military historians from Washington with information for a chronicle of events on the European theatre of war.[57]

On 6 March 1946, more than three months after the trial began in Nuremberg, Gersdorff wrote a report entitled *The Truth about Katyn* for the Americans.[58] However, the report was not forwarded to Jackson, but was translated only four years later for the Historical Division of the US Army Headquarters for Europe. The eight-page translation, however, disappeared in the archives for seven decades before it was rediscovered there. At the beginning of the text he stated: 'I do not intend to cast doubt upon, or to weaken, the abundance of accusations against the Nazi terror which were laid bare during the action, for I was always convinced of the guilt of the National Socialist government.'

In his concluding remark, Gersdorff summed up his position in the conflict: 'This crime in Katyn is surpassed in great measure by the murdering of Jews and other Nazi-crimes, especially in the concentration camps. But also, I know for sure that those Polish officers were not killed by Germans and especially not by the members of the Army.'[59]

Defence attorney Stahmer applied to the Military Tribunal to allow a statement by Gersdorff on Katyn.[60] In fact, the Americans brought him to Nuremberg. But to his own surprise, Gersdorff was not called as a witness to Katyn at all, nor was any explanation read out by him in court. Instead, outside the main trial, he was questioned about a report he had written to the German Supreme Command in which he had protested against the massacres of Jews committed by the SS in Russia. The prosecutors classified this report as incriminating of the German General Staff.[61]

Since the court did not put Gersdorff on the witness list, Stahmer relied on Ahrens and Eichborn. Officers of the American military intelligence service CIC contacted the two former Wehrmacht officers and advised them to keep their plans as secret as possible, as Bavaria was overrun with Soviet agents. Later, Eichborn reported: 'The Americans even warned me that one day I might be picked up by a fake jeep.' The Americans also brought Ahrens' family members living in the Soviet zone to safety in West Berlin.[62]

A similarly intoned warning was given by General Donovan to Schlabrendorff: he should leave Nuremberg as soon as possible! The reason given was that Donovan himself would leave and he could not foresee what his opponents would do if he could no longer protect uncomfortable co-workers and witnesses. Donovan gave up his post as advisor to the chief prosecutor, Jackson, because he had quarrelled with him thoroughly.

The general had fundamental reservations about the 'show trial' because the new law was applied retroactively – moreover, by the victors against the defeated. A small but influential group of journalists in the American press shared this view, above all Dorothy Thompson, who made a name for herself with sharp analyses of the criminal character of the Nazi regime.[63]

Donovan had also pondered Schlabrendorff's argument, warning that the trial of the Germans could be considered a victors' justice. Because of this legal uncertainty, Donovan had suggested to Jackson to limit the trial to Göring. He himself had offered to convince Göring in a private conversation to take the main blame. The other defendants should be tried by German judges. Donovan justified his proposal with the international situation, as Schlabrendorff noted:

> From the point of view of foreign policy, America must rely above all on Germany as its ally and thus on the whole of Western Europe. With a trial lasting for months, yes, years, the whole of Germany will be put to shame. …
> The aim is to prevent Germany being driven into the arms of Russia.[64]

But Jackson was not convinced of this concept, on the contrary: he forbade all delegation members to contact the accused directly.[65]

Vyshinsky's new manipulations
At the same time that Donovan was instructed by Schlabrendorff, the Soviet commission for the Nuremberg Trial met in Moscow under the leadership of Vyshinsky. Among the participants was Vsevolod Merkulov, who now headed the new Ministry of State Security (MGB).[66]

The protocol, discovered in the 1990s, listed six measures to prepare the Katyn indictment:

- preparation of the Bulgarian witnesses
- preparing between three and five of our witnesses and two medical experts
- preparation of Polish witnesses
- preparation of original documents found on the corpses and autopsy protocols
- preparation of a documentary film about Katyn
- preparation of a German witness who participated in the provocation of Katyn.[67]

There were no problems with the preparation of the Russian witnesses, Merkulov's men had great experience in it. Among them were relatives of the railway fitter Ivan Krivozertsev, who was one of the most important witnesses in spring 1943 and fled to the West with the Wehrmacht. His relatives were supposed to refute his testimony.[68] Vyshinsky quickly backed away from the plan to have Polish witnesses at Nuremberg, who were supposed to incriminate the Germans; the motto for Poland was no longer to touch the subject.[69]

So it was all the more important to find German witnesses. The choice fell on Arno Dürre, who had already accused the SS of the mass murder in Katyn in the Leningrad Trial of January 1946. But in the end, the Soviet side renounced this witness.[70] The British diplomats who analysed all information about Soviet war trials called it an 'interesting field of speculations' as to why Dürre had not been used by Rudenko despite his 'striking testimony'.[71]

Dürre was no longer useful to the Soviet experts who prepared the Soviet indictment for Nuremberg.[72] He was deported to a camp in the Sverdlovsk district east of the Urals and had to work in a diamond mine. He was 25 years old at the time. The prisoner mortality rate was very high.[73]

In Moscow it finally became clear that the subject of Katyn could only cause unwanted debates among the Germans because too many soldiers of the Wehrmacht had taken part in the organised tours through Katyn Forest.

Finally, the Bulgarian medical examiner Marko Markov, his Soviet colleague Viktor Prozorovsky, who had been a member of the Burdenko Commission, and Boris Bazilevsky, the former deputy mayor of Smolensk, witnessed the charges. MGB agents did not let the three out of sight for a moment in Nuremberg.

The Military Tribunal first called the defence witnesses in the Katyn case: Ahrens, whom the Soviet accusers wanted to brand as the murderer of the Polish officers; Eichborn, who wanted to save him, and Lieutenant General Eugen Oberhäuser, in Smolensk, the superior of both.

Ahrens was the first to take the stand. He reported how the mass graves were found in early 1943 and also described his conversation with a Russian couple who were engaged in beekeeping at the edge of the forest. They observed the arrival of the Poles in spring 1940 and later heard screams and shots from the forest. Ahrens clarified that there was neither a pioneer battalion 537 nor that he had been in Katyn in the summer of 1941, according to Soviet accounts, the time of the crime.[74]

Eichborn was asked about the communication structures in the Army Group Centre in Smolensk. He explained that all the secret messages from Berlin had passed over his desk before they were forwarded to the General Staff. He had not received any reports of Polish prisoners of war. The Soviet prosecutor, however, asked him about the SS units that committed mass murders behind the front; Eichborn could not give any information.[75]

Lieutenant General Oberhäuser was the last to be called. A few days earlier, he was still in an American officer's camp and he was brought to Nuremberg in a US jeep. He confirmed that Ahrens was a lecturer at the army communication academy in Halle/Saale, 1,200 kilometres from Katyn, at the time when, according to the Soviets, the mass murder had taken place. No Poles were in the Smolensk district throughout 1941. But he had to admit that there were about 150 Walther pistols in his regiment of the type with which the executions of Katyn were carried out.[76]

Gersdorff wrote in his memoirs:

> Certainly the prosecutors knew that nobody could give better information than I could. The Western accusers apparently suspected that I could prove the guilt of the Soviets in this case. ... Instead of me, witnesses were summoned who, with the best will in the world, could not provide any substantial information.[77]

Then the witnesses on the Soviet side were questioned. However, Boris Bazilevsky from Smolensk and Marko Markov from Sofia were unable to meet the expectations placed upon them by Vyshinsky and Rudenko, although MGB chief Merkulov had had them intensively prepared for their Nuremberg role by detention and at least psychological torture.

Bazilevsky had been threatened with the gallows if he did not make the desired statements in Nuremberg. He first repeated his accounts, which he had already delivered to the Burdenko Commission in 1944: Mayor Boris Menshagin had told him that the Germans had shot the Poles. When asked what he knew about the whereabouts of Menshagin, he explained that he had vanished without a trace in the chaos of war.[78]

However, this information did not correspond to the facts. At the time, Menshagin was in a single cell in Lubyanka. He had previously withstood the torture and pressure of the endless interrogations with which he was to be prepared as a witness for Nuremberg. In a secret trial he was sentenced to twenty-five years in prison for collaborating with the Germans. He spent nineteen years in solitary confinement without the right to visits, correspondence and parcels, but he was not broken.[79] Officers of the American military intelligence service CIC, who evaluated the Nuremberg Protocols, suspected that Menshagin was a fictitious person who had never existed.[80]

Immediately after Bazilevsky, the Bulgarian Markov took the stand. He explained that the Germans had forced him to sign the report of the Medical Commission they had formulated. During the cross-examination, however, he fell into the trap of Göring's defence attorney Stahmer: he admitted that the dead he had seen were wearing winter clothes.[81] However, this contradicted the Soviet statement of claim, which dated the crime to the summer of 1941.

A small victory for the German defence

The third witness for the Soviets, Viktor Prozorovsky, did nothing to change the unfavourable impression Markov and Bazilevsky left during the Nuremberg cross-examination. He was the chief medical examiner of the Burdenko Commission. Prozorovsky focused on the German ammunition in the graves and described in detail the letters and other documents dated 1941 that had allegedly been found near the bodies, but which had, in fact, been produced at the counterfeiting workshop of the NKVD on Merkulov's precise instructions.

Although Markov had not fulfilled the expectations of the Moscow organisers of the trial, the Bulgarian judiciary dropped the case against him on his return from Nuremberg.[82] Bazilevsky, however, was not allowed to return to his hometown Smolensk, but was banished to Novosibirsk and shielded from any contact with foreigners. He was, however, allowed to work at scientific institutes.[83]

After the questioning of the witnesses, defence attorney Stahmer presented a 50-page documentary by the Polish government in exile about the Katyn massacre. He had received the English documentation from a former Polish officer who had travelled to Nuremberg on behalf of General Anders. Rudenko tried to defame the documentary as a 'fascist pamphlet' and demanded its confiscation by the court. But the judges included it in the official documentation of the trial. One of the American prosecutors read the documentation carefully and took detailed notes.[84]

The questioning of witnesses and presumably also the Polish documentation finally led the American delegation to the conviction that the Soviet version could not be maintained. They got the court to drop the charges on Katyn. Rudenko had no arguments to counter this and had to accept defeat.

Churchill wrote ambiguously in his great work about the Second World War: 'The Soviet Government did not take the opportunity of clearing themselves of the horrible and widely believed accusations against them.' He added that obviously 'belief seems an act of faith'.[85]

However, finding the perpetrators of Katyn was not the task of the court. It simply did not refer to the matter any more; it was not mentioned in the 209-page verdict read out on 30 September and 1 October 1946. Even without the charge of Katyn, the judges found Göring and nine other defendants, including Ribbentrop and former Governor General Hans Frank, guilty of the most serious war crimes and sentenced them to death by hanging.

Göring filed a motion to be shot, but the court rejected it. On the night before the execution date, 16 October 1946, Göring himself put an end to his life with a cyanide capsule. Former health minister Leonardo Conti, who had received the Katyn report of the International Medical Commission in 1943, also committed suicide: he hanged himself in his cell in Nuremberg. Seven defendants were sentenced to long prison terms, but three were acquitted. Among the latter was the former Reich Chancellor Franz von Papen, who was to pass on Gersdorff's Katyn pictures to the American diplomat George H. Earle.

Stalin told the group of lawyers sent from Moscow to Nuremberg that he was 'not satisfied' with the outcome of the trial.[86] The Kremlin waived participation in further international trials. A Soviet edition of the Nuremberg protocols did not appear, Soviet publications did not include Katyn.

Rudenko's career had not been harmed by this failure. He returned to his post as Prosecutor General of the Ukrainian Soviet Republic. The communist leadership in Warsaw awarded him a high order.

Schlabrendorff, who contributed significantly to the failure of Rudenko's Katyn case, made a career in the judiciary of the Federal Republic of Germany: he was appointed judge of the Federal Constitutional Court. He did not talk about his role at Nuremberg, probably because he did not want to expose himself to the accusation of having cooperated with the Americans. He also rejected the Americans' offer to promote him in Bonn as president of the Federal Office for the Protection of the Constitution (BfV), the West German domestic secret service.[87] His Nuremberg memoranda for General Donovan only became known seven decades later, as did Gersdorff's Katyn report.

Gersdorff provided an explanation in his memoirs as to why Schlabrendorff and he did not publicly report on their cooperation with the Americans: most of the former Wehrmacht officers would have viewed this as treason, as were the attacks on Hitler. Only two decades after the war did it become clear in Germany that Count Stauffenberg and his comrades-in-arms acted like heroes.

Reinhart von Eichborn, who also played a significant role in the Soviet defeat at Nuremberg, first worked as a lawyer after the war, taking on management positions in the private sector. After his retirement, he devoted himself to his life's work, a German–English business dictionary that is now regarded as a standard work under the name *The Big Eichborn* (*Der große Eichborn*).

Chapter 13

Cold War and Realpolitik in the West

The dispute over the Katyn case was in the background of the Nuremberg Trials and did not reach the public. The Labour government in London, which sympathised with Stalin, suppressed any information about it. In the White House and the State Department in Washington, many advisers to the late Roosevelt, who were also largely positive towards Stalin, still had an influence on the foreign policy guidelines. In the last years of his life, Roosevelt himself harshly rejected any criticism of Stalin. FBI chief J. Edgar Hoover had written in vain letters to the White House about the infiltration of the administration by Soviet agents and informants.

In the same way, Roosevelt's old political companion George H. Earle, his special representative for the Balkans, met with a lack of understanding from him, when they met in early 1945. When Earle asked him whether the Soviet Union would not become a great threat after the expected German defeat, the president replied: 'These Russians, they are 180 million people, speaking 120 different dialects. When this war is over they are going to fly to pieces like a centrifugal machine cracked through and through, traveling at high speed.'[1]

However, Roosevelt was of the opinion that the war with Japan could last another fifty years if the Soviet Union did not build up a second front in Asia. That is why the USA continued to support Stalin's troops on a large scale with weapons and supplies. Meanwhile, the US president was in office for over a decade. His illness had progressed further and further, and it was increasingly difficult for his closest associates to talk to him about current problems. Numerous testimonies about Roosevelt's mental state in his last phase of life have become known. Churchill wrote in his memoirs about his role at the Big Three conferences: 'He had a slender contact with life.' Vice President Harry S. Truman observed at the time: 'The President seemed feeble and when he tried to pour cream into his tea more went into his saucer than the cup. He is just going to pieces.'[2]

Roosevelt's biographers later found that he had succumbed to the palace syndrome: he tolerated only yes-men around him; he reacted allergically and vindictively to criticism. Thus, at the time of the Katyn conflict, the inner circle of the White House was made up exclusively of advocates of a close

American–Soviet alliance. The same mood dominated a large part of the American press: journalists Jerome Davis, Moscow correspondent not only of the Canadian *Toronto Star*, but also of American newspapers, Richard Lauterbach (*Time*) and Edmund Stevens (*The Christian Science Monitor*), who had confirmed the version of the Burdenko Commission in their reports, played a significant role in this.

As a result, reports about Katyn, sent by American services to the White House, did not even get to the presidential office or were not taken seriously there. During the Second World War, eight reports from official sources stating that Katyn probably was a Soviet crime were sent to Washington:

1) The US diplomats accredited to the Polish government in exile repeatedly reported on the search for missing officers, whose traces were lost in the spring of 1940 after being removed from the Kozelsk, Ostashkov and Starobelsk camps, and also on the investigation of the mass graves.

2) The US ambassador to Moscow, William H. Standley, analysed Moscow's reactions to the first reports from Katyn and saw strong evidence of Soviet guilt.

3) The military secret service CIC sent its analyses according to which Goebbels' version of Katyn was probably correct.

4) The British forwarded their reports of the Katyn interviews to Washington, including the analysis of the ambassador to the Polish government in exile, Owen O'Malley, but other experts of the Foreign Office in London disagreed.

5) Lieutenant Colonel Henry J. Szymanski, the US liaison officer with the Anders Army in the Middle East, questioned Polish officers who were interned in the Soviet Union, including Józef Czapski, who had gathered all the evidence. The Polish-born West Point graduate compiled a documentation. But he was severely reprimanded by his military superiors: His reports were 'biased', he did not have to interfere in politics.

6) The Balkan envoy George H. Earle wrote messages about the Katyn reports of Romanian Alexandru Birkle and Bulgarian Marko Markov, who had been members of the International Medical Commission, and about other materials he had received from Polish diplomats.

   At a meeting with Roosevelt in May 1944, he wanted to bring up Katyn; he also had photos of the mass graves, perhaps from Gersdorff's collection, which should have come to him via the German ambassador in Turkey, Franz von Papen. But the night before, Earle was warned by an editor of *The New York Times* that the White House was completely under the control of Stalin worshippers: 'If you go over and report against Russia, you would be finished.' The warnings were well founded, because Roosevelt interrupted Earle: 'This is entirely German propaganda and a German plot.'

Earle reported later: 'To my horror, when I got here I found the President really believed that the massacre of those 10,000 Polish officers was done by the Germans.'[3]

7) In May 1945 Lieutenant Colonel John H. Van Vliet dictated his report on the visit of the American and British POWs to Katyn. The military leadership classified the report as secret. Van Vliet was ordered not to talk to anyone about his observations in Katyn.

8) Roosevelt's advisor John Franklin Carter drafted a memorandum based on the analyses of the Polish government in exile and the assessments of Ernst Hanfstaengl ('Putzi'), the former foreign press chief of the NSDAP.

These eight dossiers remained under lock and key for the next few years; their results were not included in the White House strategy papers – they were not even mentioned. Instead, top officials were given background information about Katyn by Kathleen Harriman, the daughter of US Ambassador W. Averell Harriman, who had uncritically adopted the results of the Burdenko Commission.

Arthur Bliss Lane, the new ambassador designated for Warsaw, also received only Kathleen Harriman's paper in preparation for the post. At a brief meeting with Roosevelt, he described the danger that Stalin would establish communist puppet regimes in the countries where the Red Army was standing. Roosevelt only told him that he would not fight a war over it. Rather, he wanted to accept a Soviet zone of influence. But in ten to fifteen years the White House should press for a referendum in which the Poles should vote on whether they really wanted socialism. Lane wrote in retrospect: 'I expressed doubt whether such a project would be practicable.'[4]

Lane was extremely surprised when he learned after taking up his duties on the Vistula in the summer of 1945 that many of his interlocutors did not blame the Wehrmacht but the NKVD for the mass murder of Katyn.[5]

According to his biographers, Roosevelt believed until the end in Stalin's sincerity and did not understand that for the Soviet leader democracy meant something completely different. He intended to work with the Soviet Union in the United Nations to guarantee peace in the world.

For this reason, his reaction was extremely brusque when his friend George H. Earle announced in a letter at the end of March 1945 that he wanted to go to the press with his Katyn report. Roosevelt wrote him that he could not allow the spread of 'an unfavorable opinion' about an ally and thus inflict 'irreparable harm' on the joint war effort. He formally forbade him to address the public about Katyn. Since Earle was still in diplomatic service, he was subject to White House staffing policy. Roosevelt gave instructions to transfer Earle to the staff of the Governor of American Samoa in the South Pacific, as far away from Washington as possible.[6] It was one of Roosevelt's last decisions; two weeks later, on 12 April 1945, he died.

His successor, Harry S. Truman, initially also had a very positive opinion of Stalin. Unfamiliar with foreign policy himself, he left the State Department's top officials in office. At the beginning of July 1945, both Washington and London broke off diplomatic relations with the Polish government in exile. The isolation of London's Poles was formally justified by the formation of the new government in Warsaw, which included the former exiled prime minister Mikołajczyk as deputy prime minister and minister of agriculture. Thus, from the point of view of the Western powers, legal continuity was assured. The former Polish ambassador to Moscow Stanisław Kot, who had repeatedly asked Stalin, Molotov and Vyshinsky about the missing officers, also placed himself at the service of the new leadership: he became ambassador in Rome.

The inexperienced Truman had little to oppose Stalin at the Potsdam Conference in Summer 1945, especially since his advisers included the special envoy Joseph E. Davies, the Stalin admirer and bestselling author, who was taken over from Roosevelt. Davies had recently been awarded the Lenin Order, the highest Soviet Order of Merit, which only rarely went to foreigners. In his acceptance speech he paid special tribute to Stalin's commitment to peace in the world.

According to the memoirs of an American diplomat, Truman asked Stalin about the missing Polish officers at the Potsdam conference. Stalin answered frostily: 'They went away.' Truman was satisfied with that answer. Later he told his staff about his first impressions of him: 'Stalin was a fine man who wanted to do the right thing.'[7]

Churchill was far more sceptical when he travelled to Potsdam. He had instructed the General Staff to draw up a concept for the further advance of the Western Allies towards the East under the code word 'Unthinkable' in order to secure Poland's independence. But Churchill remained alone with his ideas, he did not inform the White House, knowing full well that Stalin was still trusted there.[8]

In addition, he had to give way to the new Prime Minister Clement Attlee in the middle of the Potsdam conference after the Conservatives surprisingly lost the general election to the Labour Party. Attlee was even more inexperienced than Truman, so that neither blocked the Soviet leader from installing communist puppet governments in all countries occupied by the Red Army.

In Warsaw, conflicts soon became apparent within the coalition government, in which the former exiled prime minister Stanisław Mikołajczyk headed the agricultural office. Outraged, he had to take note of the fact that Justice Minister Henryk Świątkowski prepared a trial for Katyn as a German war crime. When Mikołajczyk realised that the communists systematically faked all elections and did not shy away from political murders, he fled Poland and found asylum in the USA. Stanisław Kot also resigned as ambassador in Rome; he remained in exile.

Anti-communist counter-offensive

Truman initially concentrated on domestic and economic policy, while the pro-Soviet Joseph E. Davies and his followers continued to have a major influence on foreign policy. Thus, even in the first post-war years, the State Department watched over the fact that the broadcaster *Voice of America* did not report about Katyn in its Polish-language program. For example, several chapters from Mikołajczyks' book *The Rape of Poland* about communist rule were read out, but without the passages about Katyn. The painter and writer Józef Czapski was invited to report on his experiences as an officer of the Polish troops under Allied supreme command, but only on condition that he did not mention Katyn.[9]

The situation was similar for journalist Julius Epstein, who also had a clash with *Voice of America*, which, however, was to have far-reaching consequences. Epstein came from a Jewish family in Vienna. In 1933 he published an anthology on the growing anti-Semitism in Central Europe under the title *World Court on Hatred of the Jews*. Originally, he was a communist, but reports about everyday life in the Soviet Union and his experiences with dogmatic party officials had dissuaded him.

Immediately after the Nazis seized power in the German Reich, he moved to Prague, and in 1938 he fled with his family to the USA. There he worked as a correspondent for Swiss newspapers as well as publications of German Hitler opponents in exile. During the war he got a job as an evaluator and author of German-language news in the Office of War Information (OWI), but had problems because of his former membership in the Communist Party.[10] He learned about the secret reports about Katyn during his work, but the topic was taboo for the OWI.

Epstein had a great talent for languages and soon also worked for American newspapers. The topic of Katyn continued to occupy him and he asked representatives of Polish associations in the USA about it. When he suggested the subject to the *Voice of America* for a program in Polish, it was decided that there was 'no green light' for it: 'It would create too much hatred against Stalin!'[11] In 1949 he wrote articles for the *Herald Tribune* and the German weekly *Die Zeit* about the mass murder in which he accused the US authorities of a 'conspiracy of silence'.[12]

Epstein contacted Arthur Bliss Lane. The former American ambassador to Warsaw was well aware of the Stalinist terror in Poland. When he had served in Warsaw, he had a good relationship with the vice-premier Mikołajczyk, whose closest associates had been arrested, murdered by allegedly unknown persons or simply disappeared. He also had an overview of the merciless persecution of the Social Democrats by the communists, who relied on the Red Army and Moscow's secret services. William T. Lawrence, who had been sent to Warsaw by *The New York Times*, reported on the merciless struggle of Polish communists against the other political parties. He called Poland an 'unhappy country'.[13]

Together with British diplomats, the US Embassy under Lane's leadership had assembled sixteen groups of observers who recorded the systematic manipulations during the parliamentary elections in Poland in 1947. He left the country after the communists took full power following the rigged elections. Lane wrote a book about his experiences on the Vistula under the title *I saw Poland Betrayed*, in which he also accused the White House of naivety and ignorance towards the Stalinists. He wrote about Katyn in it: 'Not only were the Nazis and Soviets in agreement on the annihilation of the Polish state, but they employed similar police-state measures to snuff out the spirit of Polish independence.'[14] Soon after Lane left Warsaw, the new strong leader on the Vistula, President Bolesław Bierut, who was a NKVD agent, had show trials staged against opponents and introduced the Stalin cult in Poland. The establishment of Stalinist regimes throughout Eastern Europe and the attempt by communist units to seize power in Greece with armed force led to a change in the political mood in the USA. Truman had also long since given up all illusions about Stalin.

He proclaimed the foreign policy principle that went down in the history books as 'Truman Doctrine': the US would help all 'free peoples' to resist subjugation by armed minorities or external pressure. It was a profound break with Roosevelt's illusion that the USA and the Soviet Union could jointly guarantee world peace. This political turn also ended Joseph E. Davies' diplomatic career; Truman had realised that the former ambassador had a completely illusionary attitude towards the Soviet Union and said about him that he should join the 'American Crackpots Association'.[15]

Together with Epstein, Lane founded the American Committee for the Investigation of the Katyn Massacre and also took over the chairmanship.[16] Several politicians joined the committee, including the later CIA chief Allen W. Dulles. William J. Donovan, former head of the military intelligence service OSS, dismissed by Truman, also acceded to it. The prominent publicist Dorothy Thompson was elected deputy chairman. She had thus corrected herself for the second time after her legendary misjudgement of Hitler as 'little man of startling insignificance'. Immediately after the discovery of the mass graves she had claimed: 'Katyn is a German fabrication.'

Epstein looked for witnesses. He found the medical professor Eduard Miloslavich, member of the International Medical Commission, who agreed to a meeting after some hesitation. Lane wrote a letter to Andrey Vyshinsky, now Soviet Foreign Minister, asking questions about Katyn and the missing officers from the Ostashkov and Starobelsk camps. He didn't get an answer. However, the US government also ignored the committee's requests for file inspection. At the beginning the major media also took no notice of the committee.

Unnoticed by the American public, however, the military secret service CIC had begun to collect information about Katyn from Russian and Polish refugees and former soldiers of the Wehrmacht in occupied West Germany. The task was to answer the basic question: 'Responsibility German or Soviet?'[17] However, some of the data were contradictory and in most cases could not be verified. The CIC agents also questioned German generals, including the famous tank general Heinz Guderian, whose troops had conquered Smolensk in 1941. But he could not make any statements about Katyn.[18] In 1948, the CIC compiled a first Katyn dossier.[19]

But the American press discovered the subject only after the USA entered the Korean War on behalf of the United Nations in 1950. Stalin had given the green light for the attack by the North Korean terror regime armed by Moscow on the southern part of the country. The vote at the UN had been scheduled when Moscow boycotted the meetings of the Security Council and was therefore unable to veto the issue. The UN boycott was one of many cardinal errors in the last years of Stalin's life, when he suffered increasingly from paranoia and ordered new purges not only in the Soviet Union but also in the occupied countries of Eastern Europe.

In the USA, reports of the killing of American prisoners of war by North Korean and Chinese troops made headlines. The columnists of the major newspapers asked why the White House had allowed the whole of Asia to be threatened by the yoke of communism. The year before, after their victory in the civil war, the Chinese communists had established a terror regime to which, as before in the Soviet Union, millions of 'class enemies' fell victim. American war reporters reported from Korea that Soviet pilots were sitting in shot down planes with Chinese emblems. This proved that the Soviet Union was also a warring force in the conflict.

The news of the Korean War finally changed the political mood in the USA: 'Uncle Joe', treated with great indulgence by Roosevelt and a large part of the American media, had now become an enemy to the general public. The former ally, who had been armed and alimented during the war, was now regarded as a threat, especially since the first Soviet nuclear bomb had been detonated in 1949. According to a part of the US media, the Russians had been able to build the bomb because their agents had spied on the American nuclear secrets.

Wisconsin's Republican Senator Joseph McCarthy led the movement to protect the country from the Soviet threat. He claimed that the State Department had been infiltrated by Soviet influence agents. The House Committee on Un-American Activities, which was originally founded to ward off the infiltration of American politics by Nazi sympathisers, took up the subject.

The Committee focused on Roosevelt's special ambassador Joseph E. Davies for his naive Stalin worship. It found that the film *Mission to Moscow*, based on Davies' book of the same name, was pro-Soviet propaganda. Davies was also reproached for not having understood Stalin's intentions.

Davies had written a euphoric preface to the Soviet Union book by former Moscow correspondent Jerome Davis, which appeared in 1949 under the title

Behind Soviet Power. In this book Davis repeated the accusation that the Polish government in exile had willingly adopted the Katyn version of Goebbels. He also praised the Polish Stalinist Bolesław Bierut as a wise leader. He explained in detail that the Soviet Union grants absolute religious freedom, also to the Catholic Church. Stalin was ready to work for world peace together with Pope Pius XII.

Davis claimed that all US diplomats who warned of Stalin's aggressive foreign policy 'are really Nazis at heart and are working for economic imperialism'. He vigorously contradicted the view that the Soviet Union wanted to dominate its neighbours. As a counterargument he cited a quote from Soviet Deputy Foreign Minister Andrey Gromyko: 'Moscow respects principles of equality and mutual recognition of their interests.'[20] So Davis concluded: 'Stalin does not consider it wise, or even possible, to impose Communism to any country.' Davis had returned from Moscow to become a lecturer in sociology and at the same time became involved in the pro-communist peace movement. The report of the Commission for Non-American Activities mentioned him eight times.[21]

The work of his British colleague John Gibbons, who, like Davis, had taken part in the press conference of the Burdenko Commission in Katyn, was also discussed before the Committee. Former communist activists who were disappointed by Stalin had testified that the party newspaper *Daily Worker* was subsidised by Moscow. Gibbons had therefore repeatedly sent secret messages from Moscow for the guidelines of communist propaganda in the USA.[22]

The former Moscow correspondent of *Time*, Richard Lauterbach, who had similarly confirmed Burdenko's version in his articles, also came into the sights of the investigators who were looking for Soviet sympathisers. His enthusiasm for the Soviet Union had diminished somewhat in the early post-war years. In his book about a trip on the Trans-Siberian Railway from Vladivostik to Moscow, he also mentioned 'concentration camps for political prisoners' fenced in barbed wire.[23] These undertones, however, reinforced the NKGB's mistrust of Lauterbach, as the Soviet files show.[24]

However, Lauterbach by no means questioned the Soviet social order; he still thought the concept was great. He came into conflict with the editor-in-chief of *Time* when he reproached him for publishing more and more anti-Soviet articles. As a result, Lauterbach was dismissed.[25] He died unexpectedly of polio in 1950; he was just 36 years old.[26]

The Madden Committee

The Korean War and the Iron Curtain in Europe were portrayed in the American press as a result of a misguided policy by Roosevelt and his advisers. Against this background, Epstein tried to take the subject of Katyn to the media. He pointed out that American prisoners of war were murdered in the Korean War in the same way as the Poles in Katyn: by shooting them in the back of the neck.

Meanwhile, Epstein had learned that US Lieutenant Colonel John H. Van Vliet and other American and British officers had been taken to Katyn by the Germans as witnesses. However, Van Vliet's report had not been entered in any official register; it had apparently disappeared without a trace.

Epstein came to the conclusion that information about Katyn should systematically be withheld from the American public. He wrote a fifteen-page brochure about his research, which was published by a Catholic publishing house under the title *The Mysteries of the Van Vliet Report*. In it, Epstein accused Roosevelt's top officials and advisers that in their fight against Hitler, they had closed their eyes to Stalin's criminal nature.

Democratic Congressman Ray J. Madden from Indiana, where many Polish emigrants lived, became interested in the case. Madden, a moderate rather than a radical, got a majority in the House of Representatives to set up a committee of inquiry. It was to clear up the blockade of information about Katyn by the American authorities. The circumstances of the mass murder were also to be reconstructed. Madden himself became the head of the 'Committee to Conduct an Investigation and Study of the Facts, Evidence, and Circumstance of the Katyn Forest Massacre'. The Madden Committee, as the media called it, included four congressmen from the ruling Democratic Party and three Republicans. Two of them came from Polish immigrant families and spoke Polish.

Between 1 October 1951 and 14 November 1952 the Committee questioned a total of eighty-one witnesses and travelled from Washington to Chicago, London,

Berlin, Frankfurt and Naples. It included 181 pieces of evidence in its documentation, mainly copies of documents, but also photographs, and it evaluated more than 100 written statements. Madden also asked the governments in Warsaw and Moscow for materials and answers to questions about Katyn.

The Foreign Ministry of the People's Republic of Poland briefly informed Madden that they had no intention of coming back to the matter, which had already been finally resolved. In Moscow, Deputy Foreign Minister Andrey Gromyko, previously Ambassador in Washington, recommended to the Politburo that the letters of the Madden Committee be left unanswered. But ultimately the Soviet

Democratic Congressman Ray J. Madden led an investigation, the results of which were sharply critical of the Democratic administration.

Embassy in Washington sent the report of the Burdenko Commission without further explanation.[27]

In this situation White House officials suggested that Truman should underline Washington's position in the conflict: he should receive the former Polish foreign minister Tadeusz Romer – 'it would have a very fine effect on the Kremlin'.[28] Romer was the Moscow ambassador of the Polish Government in Exile, to whom in April 1943 Molotov had brusquely announced the break off of diplomatic relations because of the controversy over Katyn.

The Kremlin was well informed about the White House's strategy towards the Soviet Union. Meanwhile, Kim Philby had become the head of the representation office of Britain's secret service SIS. He also met with FBI chief J. Edgar Hoover and CIA director Allen W. Dulles to exchange information and learned details of their 'fight against the communist threat'. Philby also received information about the deciphering of Soviet dispatches as well as about contacts of the Americans in the People's Republic of Poland. Reports of internal investigations into Katyn also went through his desk.

The very first witness the Madden Committee heard was US Lieutenant Colonel Donald B. Stewart, who had been brought to Katyn Forest in May 1943 together with John H. Van Vliet in a group of Western POWs. Stewart confirmed his earlier statement: his American and British comrades had come to the conclusion that the clothes of the murdered Poles were in good condition and that they could only have been in the camp for a short time. If they had really been used in road construction for more than a year, as the Soviet side claimed, uniforms and boots would have been worn down.[29]

Van Vliet also confirmed his report, which he had written immediately after the war: in his opinion, the perpetrators came from the ranks of the NKVD. At the time the Madden Committee was established, Van Vliet was involved in the Korean War. When he received the summons to the Committee, he was immediately recalled from the war zone: under no circumstances did the leadership of the US Army want to take the risk that he was taken prisoner by the communists as an important witness. The Committee also questioned military intelligence officers to whom Van Vliet had submitted his first report, but allegedly none of them could remember exactly. The whereabouts of the document could not be determined.

Lieutenant Colonel Henry Szymanski, the Polish-born US liaison officer with the Anders Army, explained to the Committee how his superiors disqualified his Katyn dossier as 'biased' and forbade him to investigate further.

George H. Earle, the former Governor of Pennsylvania and Special Envoy for the Balkans, told the amazed Committee members how Roosevelt had sent him to American Samoa for his criticism of the White House's pro-Soviet policies. According to Earle, the former ambassador Joseph E. Davies was guilty of turning Stalin into 'Santa Claus'. He added that Roosevelt had made the cardinal mistake of ignoring German resistance against Hitler. Admiral Canaris, the head of the German counter espionage, had helped the Western Allies with his information and even saved Churchill from assassination. Canaris had described to him the attitude of important generals of the Wehrmacht: 'They dislike Himmler; they hate Ribbentrop, and the whole crowd.'[30]

In press articles, Earle later accused the late US president of unnecessarily prolonging the war because of his refusal to support the fight of German resistance against Hitler and thus to have the lives of hundreds of thousands of American soldiers on his conscience. Roosevelt was also to blame when the Red Army had penetrated Central Europe and Moscow was subjugating the occupied countries.[31]

Roosevelt's former advisor John Franklin Carter, who had spied on the Washington journalism and political scene for him and had since become Truman's speechwriter, reported how the White House had ignored his analyses of Katyn. From the beginning, he was convinced that his collaborator Ernst Hanfstaengl, who created psychological profiles of the Nazi leaders for the Americans, was right in his assessment that Goebbels had not lied in the case of Katyn.

Carter told the Committee about the reactions of Roosevelt and his closest associates to the analyses, which pointed to Soviet perpetrators: 'They didn't want to believe it, and that if they had believed it they would have pretended not to. I assume that it was because of the desire to retain the wartime alliance with Russia.'[32]

Before the end of the war, Hanfstaengl, Hitler's former piano player, had been taken from the internment camp in Canada to England. He was released after the war, after he had been classified by a verification commission merely as a former follower of the Nazis, who, moreover, had credibly turned away from Hitler. He returned to Munich, where he took over the art publishing house founded by his grandparents.

No less harsh than John Franklin Carter was the criticism of former US Ambassador William H. Standley: in the Katyn case Roosevelt and his White House advisers never tried to find out 'which side is telling the truth'. The retired admiral, now almost 80 years old, was an active member of the Council against Communist Aggression (CACA), which included arch-conservative military, politicians and publicists, but also activists of socialist groups who saw Stalin as a traitor to the workers' movement. In his memoirs, Standley dedicated a chapter to the diplomatic entanglements surrounding Katyn.[33]

The Committee put pressure on Standley's successor in Moscow, V. Averell Harriman. In the meantime, he had lost all those illusions about Stalin that he still had during his time in Moscow in 1943. At the Yalta Conference in February 1945, to which his daughter Kathleen accompanied him, he was still one of the proponents of a Soviet zone of influence that was to encompass Poland. On his departure from Moscow a year later, Stalin gave him and his daughter two precious show horses for his services to the Soviet Union.[34] But soon after his return to Washington, Harriman joined the advocates of the 'policy of containment' defined in the 'Truman Doctrine', who saw Stalin's expansionism as a great danger to the democratic states.

The Madden Committee confronted Harriman with the statements of several American correspondents who, together with his daughter, took part in the presentation of the Burdenko Commission in Katyn in January 1944, but considered it a fake. Harriman was criticised for not mentioning the doubts of the correspondents in his report to the White House. But he claimed that he could not remember.

Kathleen Harriman, the diplomat's daughter, made an even worse impression before the Committee. She also pretended not to remember most of the controversial points. She had to admit meekly that she lacked any competence to give a verdict on the Soviet presentation of Katyn. In her 1944 report, she had claimed that the evidence of German guilt was overwhelming. The Committee found that her amateurish report was the only Katyn dossier forwarded by the State Department to other US departments, while all the expert analyses that had come to the opposite conclusion were not circulated to the authorities.[35]

Arthur Bliss Lane confirmed that he had only received the paper by Harriman's daughter in preparation for his new post in Poland. Nuremberg's chief prosecutor Robert H. Jackson also had to admit before the Committee that he had not been provided by the State Department with suitable materials on Katyn and had not learned of the existence of analyses that underlined the Soviet perpetrators.[36] However, Jackson did not say a word about Schlabrendorffs' memorandum passed on to him by General Donovan in Nuremberg. Their names do not appear anywhere in the minutes of the Committee.

John Melby, the diplomat who accompanied Kathleen Harriman on her trip to Katyn, also appeared before the Committee. He could not give a clear answer to the question why he came to the conclusion in his report that Katyn was a German crime, although he listed 'to 95 percent' indications that 'the Russians are lying', as the Committee reproached him. Melby had to admit that he was now convinced that the Soviets were the perpetrators.[37]

Only one of the American correspondents who attended the press conference in Katyn was questioned by the Madden Committee: Henry C. Cassidy, then head of the AP office. His statement about the Burdenko Commission was clear: 'The performance was entirely staged.' He explained the dilemma: 'As practical reporters we knew what could go through Soviet censorship and what could not, so we did not write anything that we knew would not go through.'[38]

This was Cassidy's key word for the members of the Committee: they cited as evidence the book by William Lindsay White, *Report on the Russians*, which pro-Soviet journalists, including Jerome Davis, John Gibbons, Richard Lauterbach, Ralph Parker, Edmund Stevens and Alexander Werth, had sharply criticised. White had described the mechanism of censorship in the Soviet Union using the example of reporting on Katyn.[39]

The Katyn report in *The New York Times*, in which William H. Lawrence had tried to undermine censorship, was also discussed. He had no illusions about developments in the Eastern bloc; he had just been expelled by the communist authorities in Sofia for his critical reporting. He had written that Bulgaria was now 'wedded to the Soviet Union'.[40] Lawrence also quoted a sentence about the political attitude of the late Richard Lauterbach: 'He jumped the fence and was very pro-Soviet-minded at that time.' Cassidy confirmed this conclusion.[41] Admiral Standley maliciously added that Lauterbach 'had received quite a few favours from the communistic government'.[42]

The Committee did not invite Harrison Salisbury, who had reported on the journalists' trip to Katyn for UP agency. In the meantime, he had become a correspondent for *The New York Times* in Moscow – and had also learned Russian. It was clear to the Committee that Salisbury would have problems with the Soviet authorities if he appeared as a witness.

On the other hand, there were also doubts about his political position. He had written that the Soviets were not involved in the Korean War; ordinary Soviet citizens also saw the Americans as aggressors in the war. However, Salisbury later reported that Soviet censorship had falsified his texts. He had asked his editors to add the word 'Censored' to his reports, but the publishers had refused.[43] When Salisbury returned to New York from Moscow in 1954, he quickly dispelled doubts about his attitude towards the Soviet Union. In an article he wrote about 'the horrors on life in the world's greatest police state'.[44]

The Committee also refrained from questioning Jerome Davis about his visit to Katyn; his position was well known. Edmund Stevens was also not summoned. After the war he became a correspondent in Rome, where he found the time to write another book about the Soviet Union: *This Is Russia – Un-Censored*. In it he describes the frustrated and exhausted post-war society that was still subject to severe repression; as the first American author, he depicts the anti-Semitic campaigns of the late Stalin era. He received the Pulitzer Prize for the book, proof of the change in political mood in the USA. However, in the book he did not correct his earlier account that the Germans were the perpetrators of Katyn, and did not say a single word about the controversy.

Similarly, the Committee made no effort to interview the British correspondents who had taken part in the press conference of the Burdenko Commission and described Katyn as a German crime. Alexander Werth (BBC) remained in Moscow as a correspondent until 1948. Stalin had done him the honour of answering his questions about American nuclear armament in writing: 'The monopoly on the possession of the atom bomb cannot last long.'

Werth's name appears on a list of sympathisers of the Soviet regime compiled by George Orwell in 1949.[45] He did this privately for a friend who worked for the Information Research Department of the Foreign Office, but the latter passed the list, which only became known in 2002, on to her superiors. The list was used for training British diplomats to fend off Soviet propaganda during the Cold War. Orwell had made it clear in his publications, however, that he was only interested in the intellectual confrontation with the Stalin worshippers, who had betrayed the ideals of the left. He clearly spoke out against investigations or even reprisals, as Senator McCarthy did in the USA.[46]

Orwell had also put the former *Times* correspondent Ralph Parker, who was likewise in Katyn, on the list. Parker had returned to Moscow, attacking the governments in London and Washington as 'enemies of world peace' in articles for the *Daily Worker*. He also wrote books in which he raved about the Soviet social order. In a book with the simple title *Moscow Correspondent* he said: 'The Communist party keeps its ear to the ground and as the Soviet Union is not riven by class differences, its leaders have exceptional facilities for knowing and understanding the desires of the masses.'[47] In contrast to his colleagues Jerome Davis and Richard Lauterbach, Parker refrained from hagiographic praises of Stalin in the book as if he wanted to distance himself from the cult of personality. The topic of Katyn is not in the book.

The Stalinist John Gibbons, who had been Parker's predecessor in the *Daily Worker* and a participant on the trip to Katyn, had also remained in Moscow. He took over a leading position in the English-language propaganda programs of the Kremlin. In 1948, when the 'anti-cosmopolitanism campaign' against alleged foreign spies began, Gibbons was suspected of being a British agent.[48] However, he survived this purge unscathed. His children adopted Soviet citizenship, his son became a Komsomol official, and his daughter became a lecturer at Lumumba University, where under the supervision of the KGB, students from the Third World were trained to build socialism in their home countries.

The Madden Committee did not consider questioning *Reuters* correspondent Duncan Hooper, whose report on the Burdenko Commission had been published in excerpts by several British newspapers. Hooper had become known to journalists shortly before the end of the war because he was the first to report on Hitler's and Goebbels' suicide in the Western media. He had heard it from a Soviet press officer. Meanwhile, he was a correspondent in India. He later became the head of the newly founded Australia Associated Press and one of Australia's most influential journalists. He never spoke publicly about Katyn again.

The Committee could not reach Homer Smith, who had hoped in vain that on his trip to Katyn he would receive information about the whereabouts of his missing African American compatriots. He had managed to leave Moscow a year after the end of the war: He accepted the offer to move to Addis Ababa.

Ethiopian diplomats, whom he had met in Moscow, had offered to set up the English-speaking department of the government press service.

The NKVD leadership let him go because they still considered Smith a loyal communist. They hoped he would spy on the leadership in Addis Ababa for Lubyanka. After one year, his Russian wife was also allowed to join him. Two children of the couple were born in Ethiopia.

But Smith contacted the US embassy in Addis Ababa. He did it secretly and very carefully, knowing that the secret services of Moscow were liquidating defectors and traitors. He also had to reckon with the American diplomats seeing him as a double agent; he was registered with them as a communist. But he was able to convince the CIA people in the US embassy that he had become an anti-communist.

In 1962, after thirty years, he returned to the USA, accompanied by his family. He explained that enormous progress had been made in the fight against racial discrimination in his home country. He also made it clear that the Soviet regime was extremely repressive and exploits the population, and he also wrote about anti-Semitism among Russians.[49] Smith found a leading position with a textbook publisher and wrote political commentaries for *Ebony*, the African American magazine.

Two years after his return he published his memoirs *Black Man in Red Russia*, which contained the chapter 'Murder in the Katyn Forest'. His statements on Soviet censorship were consistent with those of his colleague Henry C. Cassidy, who had accepted him as correspondent in the Moscow AP office in the last year of the war. Smith's descriptions were absolutely credible in the eyes of his reviewers, as he also impressively described crimes committed by Germans during the Second World War.

For the Madden Committee, not only Soviet censorship was an issue, but also American censorship. The former head of the Office of War Information (OWI), the well-known radio journalist Elmer Davis, was questioned. Davis, a declared liberal who was regarded as Roosevelt's close confidant, had sharply attacked Senator McCarthy in his comments because, in his opinion, the hunt for communist sympathisers had in many cases violated fundamental civil rights.[50]

Elmer Davis told the Madden Committee that, according to the information he received in the spring of 1943, he had no doubt that Katyn was a propaganda campaign by Goebbels to distract attention from the German crimes in occupied Poland. He called Goebbels 'a man whose reputation of veracity was extremely low'. But in the meantime it has also become clear to him that Katyn was probably 'the only time he was right'.

Sensational confessions by the hooded man

The second large group of witnesses were the Poles, starting with Władysław Anders. The general provided information on the Kremlin talks with Stalin and Molotov; the former ambassador Stanisław Kot confirmed the statements.

The writers Ferdynand Goetel and Józef Mackiewicz described their observations during the examination of the mass graves. Kazimierz Skarżyński, the former secretary general of the Polish Red Cross, confirmed that the mayor of Smolensk, Boris Menshagin, had indeed accused the NKVD.

The painter and writer Józef Czapski explained how he systematically collected information about the missing officers. Stanisław Mikołajczyk, who being vice-premier had fled Poland, reported on the communists' attempt to organise a show trial in Warsaw in which the guilt of the Germans was to be established.

The performance of an alleged eyewitness was spectacular: he stated that he could only appear in disguise, otherwise he would have to fear for the lives of his relatives in the People's Republic of Poland. The witness, who was given the pseudonym 'John Doe', was thus allowed to testify with a bag of white cloth pulled over his head, into which holes for the eyes and mouth were cut. Photos of it appeared in the entire international press.

John Doe explained that he fled a Soviet camp with two other Polish soldiers in mid-October 1940. On the run to the west, the group came through Katyn Forest one night. When the refugees heard engine noise, they climbed a tree to hide. From the tree, they watched NKVD officers shoot 200 Polish officers in the light of previously installed spotlights. John Doe also showed the members of the Committee how exactly the pistols were set for execution.[51] However, the Polish exile press classified him as an untrustworthy impostor.[52]

Another Pole appeared with a mask. Chairman Madden told the press that this was done with regard to relatives of the witness in Poland, who was called Mr B. It was the economics professor Stanisław Swianiewicz, who once again described how his comrades were taken from Gnezdovo railway station to Katyn Forest.[53]

The American congressmen attributed particular importance to the members of the International Medical Commission. After all, their two members left behind in Soviet power, the Czech František Hájek and the Bulgarian Marko Markov, had distanced themselves from the German Katyn report of 1943. The Madden Committee invited both to the hearing by mail, but the letters were intercepted by the secret police in both Prague and Sofia.

In addition to these two, four of the twelve physicians did not appear before the Madden Committee: the Slovak František Šubík, who was still under the supervision of the communist authorities of Czechoslovakia; the Dutchman Herman Maximilien de Burlet, who meanwhile lived in West Germany, but as a former activist of a Nazi group was not invited by the Madden Committee; the Belgian Reimond Speleers had died in prison shortly before the establishment of the Committee in 1951; the Finn Arno Saxén had died of a heart attack at a conference in Zurich shortly before the date on which he should make his statement, although he had been considered to be in perfect health.[54]

Swiss forensic expert François Naville, on the other hand, travelled to Frankfurt. He thus ignored a recommendation from the Swiss authorities, which had indicated to him that they had objections. But they had not stopped him.[55] The Hungarian Ferenc Orsós, the Dane Helge Tramsen, the Italian Vicenzo Palmieri, the Croatian-born US citizen Eduard Miloslavich and the Romanian Alexandru Birkle also appeared before the Committee. Without exception, they confirmed that their final report had come about without interference and pressure from the Germans.[56] Miloslavich caused a sensation during his questioning when he demonstrated the execution technique of the NKVD to a committee member, similar to one that John Doe had done before him.[57]

Birkle, however, had testified anonymously and not at the public hearing. His family was still in Romania. Nevertheless, the Romanian secret service learned of this. A court in Bucharest sentenced his wife and daughter to five years of forced labour for 'collaboration with the enemy of the state'. After Stalin's death, the sentence was reduced by half.[58]

The fact that the Bulgarian Marko Markov expressed no doubts about the Soviet perpetrators in Katyn was confirmed by Rudolf-Christoph von Gersdorff, who had meanwhile founded 'St. John's Ambulance' (Johanniter-Unfall-Hilfe), which helps victims of traffic accidents. As the responsible staff officer of the Central Army Group in Smolensk, Gersdorff had given a meal for the medical commission and sat next to the Bulgarian.

Gersdorff also explained that he was informed about all events with prisoners of war in the Smolensk area and that there were no Poles in the area of the Central Army Group during this period. It would also have been impossible for the SS to shoot more than 4,000 Poles unnoticed near Wehrmacht sites.[59] The former major general had a high degree of credibility with the Americans, for it had become known that he was involved in two attempts on Hitler's life.

In the USA the book by Allen W. Dulles about Hitler's opponents in the Wehrmacht had meanwhile been published.[60] Dulles had learned a lot from a description of the prehistory of the failed Stauffenberg coup on 20 July 1944, which Schlabrendorff had written for OSS chief Donovan.[61] In a text for the American press, Dulles called Schlabrendorff 'one of the boldest and bravest of the Anti-Nazis'.[62]

Schlabrendorff's comrade-in-arms, former Lieutenant Reinhart von Eichborn, as well as his former supervisors Lieutenant Colonel Friedrich Ahrens and Lieutenant General Eugen Oberhäuser, also testified before the Madden Committee. As in the Nuremberg Tribunal, they contradicted the Soviet version that Ahrens led the execution of the Poles, and that he was not stationed in Russia at all during the period in question.

Responsibility at Marx and Lenin

The Committee made great efforts to refute key points of the Burdenko report in detail. For example, it specifically analysed the weather forecast for the Smolensk region of July and August 1941: temperatures were between 65 and 75 degrees

Fahrenheit (18 to 24 degrees Celsius) throughout. Most of the Poles who died in these two months, according to Burdenko, wore winter clothes.

Madden and his colleagues also worked out contradictions: according to the Burdenko Commission, the peasant Parfen Kiselev was tortured by the Germans until he confirmed that he was an eyewitness to the shooting of the Poles by the Russians. The *Official Material* of the Germans, however, did not mention eyewitnesses of the executions. The Commission also interviewed Boris Olshansky, a Russian mathematics teacher who had fled to the West and who had reported in a sensational letter about a conversation with Burdenko, a friend of his family. According to Olshansky's letter, published in a magazine, Burdenko had asserted privately that the bodies had been in the ground for about four years when his commission was investigating the mass graves in 1944.

Speaking to the Committee, Olshansky who had just moved to the USA with his German wife, quoted Burdenko as saying: 'Our NKVD friends made a mistake.'[63] He further reported that he had not asked the Moscow professor why he had nevertheless put his name under the Soviet investigation report: 'For every Soviet citizen it was obvious – he had to lose his head if he would not have signed it.'[64]

The Madden Committee found the Burdenko Commission's statement that shots in the back of the neck were common practice during executions by Wehrmacht soldiers to be incorrect. Instead, the American congressmen stated: 'Typical German methods of mass murder were the 'factory of death', the gas chamber, machine gun shooting, etc., and not the more 'primitive' method of individual revolver shots.'[65]

The poet Ezra Pound, who had been sent to a psychiatric clinic, closely followed the reports about the Madden Committee, as he was allowed to read newspapers. He sent a letter with newspaper clippings to an acquaintance. He also wrote verses himself again, in which he dealt with Katyn:

> Greasy hypocrisy today re/ atrocities in Korea, 'surprise' AFTER Katyn.
> And no wops / making esprit re/ Churchill /// Note evidently started last
> August / lost in turmoil [66]

Pound was able to leave the clinic in 1958 at the instigation of American intellectuals. He returned to Italy. There he again contacted Gotthardt Maucksch, the German agent for literature, who now ran a large bookstore in Florence.[67] In 1943, Maucksch had prepared Pound's trip to Katyn as an employee of the cultural department of the German embassy in Rome. Maucksch, who was later honoured for his contribution to German–Italian cultural relations, did not leave any records. The files of the German Foreign Ministry on the plan to bring Pound to Katyn were burned during the bombing of Berlin.

The British Parliament and the government in London refused any cooperation with the Madden Committee. The Conservatives had returned to power in 1951;

Churchill and Eden had resumed their former positions as Prime Minister and Foreign Minister. Although both had no illusions about the character of Stalin's regime, they maintained their policy of silence on Katyn. Eden wrote in an internal memo: 'I dislike all this very much. The effect on Anglo-American relations may be bad.' The British were also displeased by the fact that the Madden Committee swore in the witnesses on United Kingdom soil.[68] Foreign Office officials told the Americans that a successful investigation would only be possible with the cooperation of the Soviets. They warned: 'As a propaganda stunt Katyn is too closely identified with Dr Goebbels.'[69]

The British authorities did not hide their displeasure at the questioning of a total of 32 witnesses, mainly from Polish emigration circles, by the Madden Committee at London's Kensington Palace Hotel. They even attempted to prevent a press conference by Madden and his colleagues, who did not get insight into British documents.

The Foreign Office had also blocked the former military doctor Stanley Gilder and South African reserve Colonel Frank Stevensen from testifying before the Committee; the Germans had them brought to Katyn together with the two US officers Donald B. Stewart and John H. Van Vliet. The invitations sent to them from Washington via diplomatic channels did not reach them until the interrogations had already been completed. The Madden Committee also did not learn of Stevenson's detailed Katyn report, which the British kept under lock and key. It was discovered in an archive only in 2010.[70]

The British press, in which the war generation still set the tone, including Alexander Werth, reported distantly or ironically on the American investigation. Especially the appearance of John Doe, the 'hooded man', provoked mocking comments.[71]

However, a documentary released by the British Foreign Office in 2003 on the sixtieth anniversary of the discovery of the mass graves proves that Churchill and Eden were by no means silent on Katyn out of political opportunism, as the Polish exiled press, in particular, insinuated. Rather, the experts of the British government did not unanimously evaluate the materials, so Eden declared internally: 'The evidence is conflicting.'[72]

The Foreign Office therefore rejected an application from General Władysław Anders, who had remained in exile in London, to appoint a British commission of inquiry. Internally it was argued that in this case one would run the risk of justifying Goebbels' propaganda.[73] When Churchill gave a press conference during a visit to Washington in 1952, he ignored a question from Julius Epstein about Katyn. When Epstein inquired at the British Embassy, he got the answer: 'Mr Churchill does not want to answer to this question.'[74]

The final report of the Madden Committee contained a total of 2,363 pages in seven volumes. It concluded that the Poles were murdered by the NKVD in the spring of 1940. Its authors saw the deeper reason in the teachings of Karl Marx, who described violence as a means of politics, and in the Bolshevik ideology as represented by the revolutionary leader Vladimir Lenin: 'That the victorious proletariat should completely destroy the whole apparatus of the bourgeois state, leaving not one stone upon another.' The US deputies concluded from Lenin's doctrines: 'If we take into account this doctrinaire basis of Soviet policy, it becomes clear that, it would, from the Communistic point of view, be quite reasonable to exterminate systematically the leaders of the armed forces of the State which it was intended should be destroyed.'[75]

The report sharply criticises Roosevelt and his foreign policy advisors:

> It becomes apparent to this committee that the president and the State Department ignored numerous documents, which strongly pointed to Soviet perfidy. It is equally obvious that this desire for mutual cooperation completely overshadowed the dictates of justice and equity to our loyal but weaker ally, Poland.

In the highest government and military circles, a 'strange psychosis' prevailed in the final phase of the war; the Soviet Union could seek a separate peace with Nazi Germany. In a few sentences, the Committee drew a picture of Soviet and American politics in the Second World War:

> The Soviets had plotted to take over Poland as early as 1939. Their massacre of these Polish officers was designed to eliminate the intellectual leadership which subsequently would have attempted to block Russia's ultimate designs for complete communisation of Poland. This was but a step of the Soviets toward the complete communisation of Europe and eventually the entire world, including the United States.
>
> The record of this committee shows that the United States had been forewarned of Soviet Russia's treacherous designs on Poland and the rest of Europe. Whatever the justification may be, this committee is convinced the United States in its relations with the Soviets found itself in the tragic position of winning the war but losing the peace.

Finally, the Committee formulated a resolution for the House of Representatives: the government should be asked to hand over the Katyn documentation to the UN in order to present it to the Plenary Assembly. The government should apply to the UN for the Soviet Union to appear before the International World Court of Justice.[76] The House of Representatives approved the resolution by a large majority. But British Foreign Secretary Eden wrote to the UN General Secretariat that Her Majesty's government was against putting Katyn on the UN agenda. The Foreign Office remained in its previous position: 'Although there is strong circumstantial evidence against the Soviet Government, there is no conclusive proof.'[77]

The former US Chief Prosecutor of Nuremberg, Robert H. Jackson, caused a sensation when he was questioned by the press about the prospects of international criminal proceedings against the Soviet leadership. Jackson said the chances of that were slim. But if Stalin was caught he would be ready to stand against him in a trial. [78]

After the Committee's report was published, many American newspapers accused the Washington authorities of withholding basic information about Katyn from the public. But only a few of them were as self-critical as *The Washington Post*, which wrote in retrospect of the spring of 1943: 'It is now painfully plain that the suspicion of the western governments and press concerning the Russian version of the Katyn story ... should have been aroused when the Kremlin refused to permit an investigation by the International Red Cross, as was requested by the Polish government-in-exile.'[79]

Renouncement of political campaign in the USA
There was speculation that three members of the International Medical Commission did not survive the years 1951/52, when the confrontation between Washington and Moscow over Katyn reached a new climax. The Belgian Reimond Speleers and the Finn Arno Saxén died shortly before the establishment of the Madden Committee, the US Croate Eduard Miloslavich succumbed to a heart attack a few months later at a symposium in Madrid.[80]

In the same year, the Romanian Alexandru Birkle was seriously injured in a traffic accident in the USA and the cause could not be clarified. He died in New York in 1987 without seeing his family again. He never spoke publicly about Katyn after his appearance before the Madden Committee. After his death, an employee of the Securitate, Romania's communist secret service, who posed as his daughter, exploited his legacy in the USA. The real daughter learned about this when she was able to view her Securitate files after the end of the communist system in Romania.[81]

The Committee's report was led by the Republicans against the then ruling Democrats in the 1952 presidential campaign. In front of Polish immigrant organisations ex-ambassador Arthur Bliss Lane, who acted as an election speaker for the Republicans, accused the government of Democrat Truman of withholding documents about Katyn.[82]

In 1953, the US Mission to the UN submitted the report of the Madden Committee to the UN Secretary-General[83] – but there it was put in the archives. After the American presidential elections, the Republican winner, General Dwight D. Eisenhower, took no steps to bring Katyn to the UN. Six weeks after

Eisenhower took office, Stalin died on 5 March 1953. Eisenhower believed that the new Moscow leadership was interested in ending the Korean War and avoided all steps that the Kremlin could take as provocation.

Allen W. Dulles, one of the initiators of the Katyn investigation, also accepted this line. Under Eisenhower he became head of the CIA, his older brother John Foster Dulles became foreign minister. The subject of Katyn was thus settled for American politics. The media were no longer interested in it either.

Unnoticed by the American press, a Russian witness of the Madden Committee, former mathematics teacher Boris Olshansky, returned to the Soviet Union in 1956, leaving his German wife with two young children. He had not gained a foothold in the USA, had no fixed income, was in debt and had become an alcoholic, according to reports by his acquaintances. They suspected that he had been recruited by the KGB in a Russian emigrant bookshop in Washington, where he worked.[84]

The media also completely missed the return of the former soldier Arno Dürre from the Gulag to Germany in 1956. During the amnesty for political prisoners after Stalin's death in 1953, Dürre revoked his statements in the Leningrad war crimes trial. He had declared at the trial that he had participated in the Katyn massacre and was sentenced to fifteen years of forced labour. Dürre stated that he had been blackmailed into testifying at the time.[85]

The Soviet authorities shortened his detention period and gave him the choice whether he wanted to leave for West or for East Germany. In January 1956, after a total of eleven and a half years in Soviet captivity, he arrived in the Rhineland. He worked in a steel factory for a low wage, but became disabled after a serious industrial accident. Arno Dürre died in 1975 in Leverkusen near Cologne, he was only 54 years old.[86]

None of the Polish witnesses of the Madden Committee who saw the mass graves of Katyn with their own eyes ever returned to their homeland. Kazimierz Skarżyński, General Secretary of the Red Cross, remained in Calgary, Canada, for the rest of his life; writer Ferdynand Goetel died forgotten in London; his colleague Józef Mackiewicz spent his retirement in very modest circumstances in Munich, where he worked for *Radio Liberty*, financed by the US Congress.

The Hungarian forensic scientist Ferenc Orsós could not return to his communist homeland either; in the last years of his life he worked as a teacher of anatomy at the Art Academy in the city of Mainz in West Germany.

His Slovak colleague František Šubík, also a member of the International Medical Commission, who was extradited to the Czechoslovak authorities from Austria by the Americans in 1945, managed to flee to the West with his family seven years later on a second attempt. Shortly before, the Madden Committee in a letter to him had asked if he wanted to make his statement. The letter from the USA was addressed to the University of Bratislava. There someone had put it in a new envelope and sent it to the hospital in the province, where Šubík worked as a simple doctor after his title 'professor' was revoked.

In this way, the unknown sender saved him from the Stalinist secret police.[87] Since Šubík feared that Moscow would hold another Katyn tribunal in response to the Madden Committee, he fled with his wife and six-year-old son to Austria. The escape through the border fence took place under dramatic circumstances, as his son got caught in barbed wire; the fugitives were discovered by a patrol of Czechoslovak border troops that opened fire. At the last moment they reached Austrian territory. Šubík contacted the US authorities in Salzburg. There he made his first statements about Katyn. Afterwards he got a US visa; he found a job as a doctor in the USA.[88]

Italian medical professor Vincenzo Palmieri also reiterated his assessment that the perpetrators were to be found in the NKVD, despite continuing attacks by the communists in his hometown Naples. Palmieri made a career in politics: in 1962 the Christian Democrat became mayor of Naples, but had to resign after just ten months.

Although his Danish colleague Helge Tramsen stayed away from politics, the shadows of Katyn caught up with him: his daughter had fallen in love with a Polish musician and had moved to Warsaw. One morning she was found dead in the apartment in the old building; the prosecutor gave gas poisoning as cause of death, the gas heating had been defective. Tramsen doubted this version; he wanted to examine his dead daughter himself. But the authorities of the People's Republic of Poland refused him a visa. For the rest of his life he was firmly convinced that the KGB had murdered his daughter in revenge for his participation in the Katyn mission ordered by Goebbels.[89]

Only six decades after the Madden Committee, in 2013 and 2014, the National Declassification Center in Washington released large files about Katyn. These included the dispatches of liaison officer to the Anders Army, Lieutenant Colonel Henry Szymanski. Many of the documents revolve around the search for the missing report of Lieutenant Colonel John H. Van Vliet. They prove that in the American administration it was considered inappropriate to let the Katyn case be discussed publicly.[90] The original report of Van Vliet, which for so long was considered to have disappeared, was found by chance: it was in the files of the American embassy in Paris. Van Vliet had written it in 1945 in the US Army office in the French city of Reims.[91]

The US Department of Defense had also registered Rudolf-Christoph von Gersdorff's eight-page report 'The Truth about Katyn', which he put on paper in Nuremberg during the trial, but which had not reached the Military Tribunal.[92] Gersdorff had written a second report on Katyn in 1948 at the request of the CIC. The CIC officers classified him as a Category B witness: usually reliable.[93] Once again, he underlined that most of the visitors had come to Katyn very sceptically, but then without exception were convinced of the Soviets as perpetrators. This also applies to the Bulgarian professor Markov and the Polish prelate Jasiński, both of whom had described the Germans as murderers at Katyn under pressure from the communist secret police after the war.[94]

The files of the secret spy cell 'Pond' were also released. According to their head, John V. Grombach, one of its informants in Paris, the doctor and serial killer Marcel Petiot, had already told them about the Katyn massacre in 1942, months before the Germans discovered it. But in the released files for 'Pond' there is not a single reference to Katyn. The former fencer and boxer Grombach, a dazzling figure, had made a name for himself after the end of his career in the secret service as an author of spy novels and books on sports, especially boxing, and also tried to become a manager of artists.

His book about Petiot, published in 1980 under the title *The Great Liquidator*, is considered unreliable by historians. It is also not ruled out that he was wrong about the date, i.e. that only after 1943, when Katyn was already a topic of the international press, did he receive this information from Petiot and not, as he claimed, as early as 1942, when the name of this Russian village was still completely unknown to the public.

The files also show that the expert at the State Department believed the Swedish publication on the assassination of the Krakow prosecutor Roman Martini because of his alleged Katyn researches. On the other hand, the statements of the hooded man John Doe were seen as 'conflicting'.[95]

Chapter 14

Fakery and Oppression in the Eastern Bloc

As expected, the Madden Committee's report provoked fierce attacks on the US by the Soviet press. The Soviet Foreign Ministry set up a working group to develop a counter-campaign. The Ministry was now headed by former Prosecutor General Andrey Vyshinsky. The group included Professor Viktor Prozorovsky, director of the Forensic Medical Institute in Moscow, who had already been a member of the Burdenko Commission and witnessed the Soviet prosecution in Nuremberg.[1]

The Soviet press started a campaign against Washington. George F. Kennan, now US ambassador to Moscow, cabled the State Department: 'I have never seen anything to equal in viciousness, shamelessness, mendacity and intensity what is now being done in this country to arouse hatred, revulsion and indignation with regard to Americans in general and our armed forces in particular.'[2] When a high Soviet diplomat in Washington was confronted with protests against the campaign, he replied to his American interlocutors: 'The Soviet press is a free press and confines itself to factual reporting.'[3]

The party paper *Pravda* printed an 'appeal to all scientists in the world' to protest against the 'defamations' of the Madden Committee. Among the signatories were, not surprisingly, the members of the International Medical Commission who remained in the Soviet bloc: the Czech František Hájek and the Bulgarian Marko Markov, both of whom had been temporarily imprisoned in order to bring them into line. The *Pravda* printed a long report about Hájek, who praised the version of the Burdenko Commission as the only real one.[4]

The leaders of the People's Republic of Poland also abandoned their policy of silence about Katyn. In Warsaw, the Stalinist Bolesław Bierut, with the help of Moscow's secret services, had eliminated all internal party rivals, first and foremost the former party leader Władysław Gomułka, who was imprisoned. The Soviet Marshal Konstantin Rokossovsky, who was born and educated in Warsaw but had lived in Russia since his youth, took over the Polish Ministry of Defence and more and more Soviet officers occupied key positions in the Polish armed forces.

The Polish secret police UB relentlessly intervened against 'slanderers of Soviet power'. For example, a student at the Lodz Film School was sentenced to one year in prison for accusing the NKVD of murdering her father and uncle in Starobelsk and Kozelsk in conversation with fellow students.[5]

Bierut and Rokossovsky had a group of senior Polish officers tried in 1951, because they had criticised the sovietisation of their army. One of them was Division General Stefan Mossor, whom the Germans had brought to Katyn eight years earlier with a small group of Polish prisoners of war. He told German officers at the time that he was convinced that 'the Bolsheviks' had murdered his comrades.[6] After the war, the communist regime had given him

The profile of Stalin on Polish stamps symbolised the subjugation of the country by the Soviet Union.

the choice either to be convicted as a collaborator or, if he branded the Germans as the murderers of Katyn, to be rewarded with a post on the General Staff. Mossor chose the second variant.

With his knowledge of Katyn, however, Mossor was an ideal candidate for a show trial to break resistance to the sovietisation of the army in the Polish officer corps. While preparing four arrested generals for trial, military intelligence officers tortured them. The Warsaw military court sentenced them to life imprisonment for an alleged conspiracy in the army. Mossor was also accused of collaborating with the Germans on the trip to Katyn.[7]

The Polish Minister of Justice Henryk Świątkowski had a plan drawn up for

The Polish General Stefan Mossor, who had been taken to Katyn as a prisoner of war by the Germans in 1943, became a victim of the Stalinist purges in the Polish People's Republic.

Warsaw to go on the offensive against the international public. From Joseph Goebbels' and Hans Frank's diaries, which had fallen into the hands of the Soviets in 1945, fragments about Katyn were to be taken out of context and published as evidence of the Germans as perpetrators. Western lawyers and physicians sympathetic to Stalinism were to publish corresponding essays and articles. The association of former concentration camp prisoners should attack the Germans as murderers at Katyn.

The authorities in the other communist states should also find witnesses who should be handled accordingly. The Hungarian forensic physician Ferenc Orsós and his German colleague Gerhard Buhtz were named in Świątkowski's draft.[8] However, this plan failed: Orsós lived in West Germany and Buhtz had died in the war.

Warsaw's measures were limited to Poland, in the first place this involved a press campaign. The party paper *Trybuna Ludu* set the tone: 'The Polish people condemn with indignation the cynical provocations of the American imperialists who want to exploit the tragic death of Polish citizens.'[9] The satirical magazine *Szpilki* published an anti-American caricature about the appearance of hooded man John Doe. The Iron Cross of the Wehrmacht is emblazoned on his uniform, the frame of his lectern consists of dollar signs.[10]

The Americans as successors of the German Nazis became the central topic of the campaign, which was closely observed by the State Department in Washington. So again and again the assertion was made that the US troops did in the Korean War exactly the same thing as the Germans did in Katyn.[11] On the same lines

were reports that the German tank general Heinz Guderian was preparing another war against the Soviet Union under American leadership.[12] Poland had applied in vain to the Americans for Guderian's extradition as a war criminal.[13] Also, demonstrations against the USA were organised in numerous factories.[14]

The book *The Truth about Katyn* by the communist journalist Bolesław Wójcicki was published in two editions. He had lost his parents and two brothers in the war: the German

Cartoon in the satirical magazine Szpilki (Pins), which was controlled by the Polish Communist Party (11/1952)

The daily Życie Warszawy attacked the 'Voice of America': The caricature shows the channel as Goebbels' megaphone (56/1952).

occupiers had murdered them.[15] The author, who praises the Soviet Union extensively, refers to the Burdenko Commission. According to his account, the days of the German execution squad always ended the same way after work was done: 'Then they ate. Then they drank. They drank a lot. Then they went to bed.'

Wójcicki repeated the version that the documents found among the dead were produced on behalf of the Gestapo in the Sachsenhausen concentration camp, a version that *The New York Times* had also uncritically spread. Some of the dead were murdered prisoners who had been taken to Katyn. Congressman Ray J. Madden was attacked as a fascist, journalist Julius Epstein as a Trotskyist.

The main part of the book consists of attacks on the Americans, who now allegedly did the same thing with the Korean freedom fighters as the Germans did in Katyn. It contains photos of the Ku Klux Klan and of canisters allegedly containing cholera and plague bacteria sprayed by the Americans in Korea.[16] The appendix contains articles from the *Pravda* about Katyn as well as a report by the prominent BBC correspondent Alexander Werth, who maintained the Germans were perpetrators.

Polish newspapers also quoted from Richard Lauterbach's *Time* report, which spoke of the binge drinking of the German execution squad. They also cited the 1943 articles by publicist Dorothy Thompson, in which she had described Katyn as a 'fabrication of the Germans'. But the Polish press was silent about the

George F. Kennan was the first US ambassador to the Soviet Union who was well prepared for the post: he spoke Russian very well and had no illusions about Stalin's regime.

fact that Dorothy Thompson had long since changed her mind and was even vice president of the Katyn Committee, which Julius Epstein and the former ambassador Arthur Bliss Lane had founded.[17]

In view of the strong reactions provoked by the Madden Committee, George F. Kennan, the US ambassador to Moscow, asked whether it would make sense to provoke Stalin in this way. He wrote in his diary: 'If we keep cool and use our heads, we will manage to subdue him in such a way that he will cause us less trouble.'[18] His caution did not pay off. In October 1952 he was declared '*persona non grata*' by Foreign Minister Andrey Vyshinsky. In a briefing for American journalists, Kennan had compared his everyday life in the Soviet Union with his experiences in Berlin at the beginning of the war: 'Had the Nazis permitted us to walk the streets without having the right to talk to any Germans, that would be exactly how we have to live in Moscow today.'[19]

From afar, from Ethiopia, Homer Smith, who had visited Katyn Forest as Moscow correspondent, followed the work of the Madden Committee. He attentively read all the reports about it in the American newspapers that reached Addis Ababa. In his memoirs, *Black Man in Red Russia*, he wrote about the Soviet counteroffensive against the Madden Commission: 'The Kremlin bungled an excellent opportunity of producing, if it could, convincing proof of German guilt.'[20]

Struggle for Power in Moscow

Stalin's death on 5 March 1953, exactly thirteen years to the day after the murder orders were signed, pushed all other topics into the background. In the power struggle for the succession, the Ukrainian Nikita Khrushchev, who had been underestimated by all, joined forces with Molotov and Voroshilov against Beria. Molotov returned to the head of the Foreign Ministry, the former cavalry general Voroshilov even became head of state as chairman of the presidium of the Supreme Soviet.

Khrushchev made his Ukrainian comrade-in-arms Roman Rudenko, one of the chief prosecutors of Nuremberg, prosecutor general of the USSR. One of

Rudenko's first tasks was the trial of Beria, who was now imprisoned as an 'enemy of the people'. Beria's chief sidekick, Merkulov, was also arrested.

Referring to the report of the Madden Committee, Rudenko accused Merkulov of treason: he had told a group of Polish officers headed by Zygmunt Berling, that the NKVD had made 'a big mistake' with their missing comrades. According to the protocol, however, Merkulov denied ever having made this statement: 'It would be ridiculous to even talk about the possibility of such an answer. Of course, I did not give such an answer.' According to him, Beria also had not expressed himself in this way.[21]

Khrushchev and Molotov proposed to the Politburo that Beria and Merkulov be shot. It was another serious breach of the law, because it was not the political leadership but a court that had formally to decide on it. The two former NKVD chiefs were executed on 23 December 1953.

Beria's elimination also meant two years in prison for the former Soviet ambassador to London, Ivan Maisky, the negotiating partner of the exiled premier Władysław Sikorski. He had come to Lubyanka on charges of being a British spy during the last anti-Semitic purges a few weeks before Stalin's death. The accusation was that he had passed on secret materials to Churchill via his wife, whom Foreign Minister Eden himself had recruited Maisky for the British secret service. His interest in English culture and Anglophile lifestyle was also cited as evidence of his guilt. Beria personally beat him during the interrogation, Maisky later reported in a private circle. But it was Beria who shortly after Stalin's death offered him high positions and released him. But after Beria's fall, Maisky had to return to Lubyanka as his alleged political fellow. His petitions to Khrushchev, Voroshilov and Rudenko remained unanswered.[22]

One of Rudenko's predecessors as prosecutor general of the USSR, Andrey Vyshinsky, whom Stalin had promoted to foreign minister, survived the top secret service agents for only eleven months: Molotov, his predecessor and successor at the head of the Foreign Ministry, transferred him to the post of Soviet Representative at the UN in New York. Vyshinsky died there on 22 November 1954, and the official cause of death today is suicide. But Russian historians see evidence that an agent from Moscow had poisoned Vyshinsky in order to eliminate him in the power struggle.

On 3 February 1955, Vasily Blokhin, the mass murderer in the service of the NKVD, took his own life in Moscow. At least this was what the former NKVD commander of Kalinin Dmitry Tokarev later claimed.[23] Blokhin's personnel files, on the other hand, report a heart attack as the cause of death. After evaluating his personnel file and execution records, Russian historians have come to the conclusion that he personally shot at least 15,000 people in three decades as the executor of the secret police. He had received the highest awards from Stalin: the Lenin Order and the Red Banner Order three times.

But after the execution of his patrons Beria and Merkulov, Blokhin first had to accept his reduction in rank, then his release from the secret police. Already an alcoholic, he surrendered completely to the drink. He was buried with all honours in the cemetery of the Donskoy Monastery in Moscow, where many of his victims were buried anonymously in a mass grave, including Marshal Mikhail Tukhachevsky, the popular writer Isaac Babel and the famous theatre director Vsevolod Meyerhold.[24] In Russian tradition, the tombstone also shows the image of his wife – the mass murderer had a family.

In Poland, party leader Bierut had the general terror intensified after Stalin's death. A broad campaign against the Catholic Church began, and many priests were arrested. Khrushchev also ordered reprisals against the Orthodox Church. Thousands of Christians had to go to prison and endure banishment in Khrushchev's church struggle.

At the same time, he tried to consolidate his position of power with a campaign against Stalinism, although earlier, as party leader of the Ukrainian Soviet Republic, he himself had been one of the agitators in the Great Purges.

Vasily Blokhin, the executioner of the NKVD, and his wife were given a gravestone with an orthodox cross.

Hundreds of thousands were released from the camps and prisons, including former ambassador Ivan Maisky.

At the CPSU's XX party conference in February 1956, Khrushchev gave a speech behind closed doors in which he settled accounts with the 'crimes of Stalin' committed against party members. He did not mention the millions of victims who did not belong to the party, nor did he mention the crimes committed by the Red Army and the NKVD against citizens of other states. The Polish Stalinist Bierut present at the speech was so upset about its contents that he suffered a heart attack, a few days later he died in a Moscow clinic.

The text of the secret speech reached the West, where it generated a tremendous media response. Ralph Parker, a participant in the correspondents' trip to Katyn, was the first to quote extensively from the text in his reports. In addition to his work for the *Daily Worker*, Parker was working on translations, including fiction on the development of socialism and the war memoirs of Red Army generals.

Originally an ardent Stalinist, Parker had felt growing doubts about the Soviet regime in Stalin's latest years. Khrushchev's speech confirmed his doubts. As a consequence, he translated Russian authors who criticised Stalinism and even came through censorship, at least in the first years under Khrushchev, including Alexander Solzhenitsyn's first work 'One Day in the Life of Ivan Denisovich'.

Parker even gained a certain popularity in the Soviet Union during this time: he took on supporting roles in two Soviet movies, both times portraying Englishmen.[25] He also re-established contact with the British Embassy. When he died of heart disease in 1964, British diplomats attended the funeral service. He was only 56 years old.[26]

Khrushchev's secret speech, which Parker was the first to spread, prompted Julius Epstein and several members of the Madden Committee to send letters to the Kremlin. They encouraged Khrushchev to further investigate Stalin's crimes and asked explicitly about the missing Polish prisoners from the camps of Ostashkov and Starobelsk. They never received an answer.[27]

The reports of Khrushchev's secret speech left the former Moscow correspondent Jerome Davis unimpressed. He had vigorously defended the Soviet

The British–Soviet double agent Ralph Parker in the Russian feature film Memory of the Heart *(Pamyat sertsa)*

version of Katyn: he continued to celebrate the Soviet regime as an exemplary social order, praised Khrushchev as the keeper of Stalin's message of peace, held seminars on the successes of the Soviet Union and continued to travel to Moscow at the head of groups of American pacifists.[28]

Radio Liberty in Munich, financed by the US Congress, devoted many hours to Khrushchev's speech in its programs for the Eastern Bloc countries. In Poland, many people saw their rejection of the regime confirmed, and the first strikes took place. In June 1956, workers at repair facilities of the State Railways in Poznan demanded a fair wage system and an end to political repression by the secret police UB. The riot expanded into an uprising during which workers stormed the headquarters of the Polish Workers' Party in Poznan. The army defeated the unrest by force of arms and at least fifty-seven strikers were killed. However, the situation was not stabilised, the Polish party leadership had to resign under pressure from Moscow.

The new leader of the Polish Workers' Party was Gomułka, who had been imprisoned under Bierut for four years. Under him, the domestic political situation initially eased. In this short thaw, which lasted only one year, the wife of the economics professor Stanisław Swaniewicz, the witness to the transportation of the prisoners into Katyn Forest, received permission to leave Poland. She hadn't seen her husband, who lived in Great Britain and had teaching posts in North America and Indonesia, for seventeen years.[29]

The sentence against Stefan Mossor and the other defendants in the 'trial of the generals' was also reversed. But a few months after his release, Mossor died of the late effects of the torture he had suffered in prison. At the funeral, Wojciech Jaruzelski, the youngest Polish general at 33, represented the army supreme command. Jaruzelski had been especially promoted in his career by Marshal Rokossovsky. According to Polish historians, he owed his rise to the fact that he had committed himself as an informant for the military secret service, which was under strict Moscow control, and spied on his comrades.

From Khrushchev to Brezhnev

Gomułka was celebrated by tens of thousands during his first public speech in the centre of Warsaw, when he promised a 'Polish way' to socialism. But he rejected the demands that the mass murder of Katyn be investigated. His statements are recorded at a meeting with representatives of the Polish communist youth organisation a few weeks after he took power:

> If I had any hard facts, I would not hesitate to turn to the Soviet Union and say: 'Stalin committed so many crimes, now confess them too!' ... But do we really need this for ourselves and for our relationships? Do we really need another thorn in our crown of thorns? ... No, it's not necessary and it's not appropriate.[30]

Information spread in the West that Khrushchev had suggested at that time that Gomułka should publicly blame Stalin and Beria for Katyn. However, there is not the slightest indication in Polish and Soviet archives that both party leaders had exchanged views on Katyn.[31] The issue remained taboo for the Polish media, not even the version of the Burdenko Commission was mentioned.

After Stalin's death, the Polish and Soviet encyclopaedias no longer contained the keyword 'Katyn', although they devoted a large amount of space to German war crimes. In the same manner Katyn is not mentioned in Khrushchev's memoirs, the manuscript of which was smuggled to the USA after he fell from power and printed in an English translation.

Gomułka negotiated the 'repatriation' of the Poles still held in the Soviet

The new Polish party leader Władysław Gomułka did not take the opportunity to proclaim the truth about Katyn in the political thaw following Stalin's death.

Union, who had become Soviet citizens in the war after the Kremlin annexed the Eastern regions of Poland. However, the agreement, which came into force in 1957, dashed the hopes of many Poles that prisoners from the Ostashkov and Starobelsk camps may have survived. There was still no trace of them.[32]

However, the limited de-Stalinisation under Khrushchev went too far for Molotov. In 1957, together with other members of the Politburo, including Kaganovich and Voroshilov, he wanted to overthrow him. But Khrushchev was able to fend off the attempt, not least because Voroshilov changed sides at the last moment. He was therefore allowed to remain in his post as head of state until 1960, when Leonid Brezhnev replaced him. However, Khrushchev took revenge on the two main conspirators, but no longer using Stalin's methods: they were not liquidated, but merely removed. Molotov became ambassador in Mongolia. Kaganovich ran an asbestos factory in the small town of Asbest on the edge of the Ural Mountains.

Khrushchev appointed the 39-year-old Alexander Shelepin, leader of the Komsomol, as the new head of the secret service, now called the KGB. Shelepin looked through the documents on the murder of Polish POWs in 1940. In order not to let any subordinate employees know of this, a note was handwritten for Khrushchev on 3 March 1959. Whether Shelepin himself drew up the document in calligraphy, his wife or another person of trust is not known. In it he took stock of the NKVD's action against the Polish prisoners of war in spring 1940: '21,857 were shot.'

In breaking down this number, however, he mixed camps and places of execution: Katyn 4,431, Starobelsk 3,820, Ostashkov 6,311, in other camps and prisons in Western Belarus and Western Ukraine 7,305. In his letter Shelepin proposed the destruction of documents on the mass murder, with the exception of the minutes of NKVD troika meetings, which passed the death sentences.

Indeed, most of the documents were destroyed, but by no means all. Beria's letter of 5 March 1940, in which he proposed the shooting of the Poles and which Stalin and other members of the Politburo signed, made its way with Shelepin's handwritten draft into the safe-deposit box of Khrushchev. It already contained the original of the Secret Additional Protocol to the Ribbentrop–Molotov Pact. The reasons why the documents proving the criminal actions of the Soviet leadership were not destroyed remain unknown to this day.

When Shelepin got the information that playing children had found bones and Polish uniform buttons on the grounds of the mass graves near Kharkov, he gave the order to pour concrete over them.[33] In Mednoje near Kalinin, a layer of concrete also covered the mass graves. In the late 1960s Yuri Andropov, Shelepin's successor at the head of the KGB, gave the order to fence in and guard the cemeteries, which were next to the dachas for secret service officers.[34]

In Warsaw, Gomułka publicly avoided the topic, but at closed party meetings, contrary to his better knowledge, he maintained that Katyn was a 'Goebbels provocation'.[35] This was also in line with Brezhnev's policy, who overthrew Khrushchev as party leader in 1964: the Stalin era was largely taboo. One of the first steps was that diplomats of the Polish Embassy in Moscow laid a wreath 'for the victims of fascism' for the first time on All Saints' Day 1967 in Katyn. This was to confirm the Soviet version of the mass murder.[36]

The controlled media in the Eastern bloc did not disclose the fact that eight months earlier an important witness had begun to reveal secrets about Stalin and his satellites. It was none other than Stalin's daughter, Svetlana Alliluyeva. The Soviet leadership under Brezhnev had allowed her a three-month trip to India. This was preceded by a conflict over her plan to marry a much older Indian communist who had come to Moscow for medical treatment and whom she had met in the sanatorium. But the party leaders forbade her to marry. As her Indian friend's health deteriorated and he finally died, she was allowed to travel to his relatives. In India, she was closely monitored by the Soviet Embassy in Delhi at the behest of Foreign Minister Andrey Gromyko.

Two days before the planned return flight, the 41-year-old woman managed to escape from her KGB guards. She went to the US Embassy in Delhi and asked for asylum. The American diplomats were completely surprised – her name was

In American exile Stalin's daughter Svetlana Alliluyeva accused her father of the massacre of Katyn.

alien to them. But when her identity was established, she was put on the first plane to a NATO state, it was a flight to Rome. From there she was first brought to Switzerland under the strictest secrecy.

Svetlana Alliluyeva spoke excellent English; she had seen many Hollywood films on her father's dacha that never came to Soviet cinemas. She also read original works by American and British writers blacklisted by the Soviet censors. In addition, she had been particularly interested in the USA during her history studies; she wrote a seminar paper on Roosevelt's New Deal.

In her Swiss hiding place she showed the American diplomats a manuscript she wanted to publish in the West. This was the *Twenty Letters to a Friend*, in which she described the dark side of her life in the Soviet Union. The State Department asked former ambassador George F. Kennan, now Professor of Contemporary History at Princeton University, to review the text. Kennan found the script excellent; he flew to Switzerland and persuaded Svetlana Alliluyeva to move to the USA.

After continuing her journey to the USA, now in public, she first lived in Kennan's country house, which reminded her of a Russian mansion from the time before the revolution. She made friends with him and his family. Kennan arranged the publication of the *Twenty Letters to a Friend*; the book became an international bestseller and secured the author's financial future.[37]

Kennan also helped her with her autobiographical notes under the title *Only One Year*, in which she described how her decision to flee matured. She was tired of being constantly patronised and treated as 'state property' in Moscow.[38] It was in this book that she gave her father the responsibility for the mass murder of Katyn. Kennan was of the same opinion; he could explain to her the conflict among the great powers over Katyn.

Moscow's reaction did not take long. The *Pravda* called her 'a hysterical and sick woman with a sexually troubled face'.[39] Former *New York Times* correspondent Harrison Salisbury, well known to Kennan since the Moscow days, commented that Stalin's daughter's escape had hit the Kremlin particularly hard, as the 50th anniversary of the Bolsheviks' seizure of power in the 'October Revolution' was to be celebrated with great pomp in the same year.[40] Salisbury had, meanwhile, become an influential authority among the American experts for the Soviet Union. Despite his criticism of the Kremlin's policy, he spoke out in favour of an intensified dialogue between Washington and Moscow.

Fight against dissidents and emigrants

In 1970, three years after the sensational escape of Svetlana Alliluyeva, the former mayor of Smolensk, Boris Menshagin, was released from prison after a total of twenty-five years. He had spent the last nineteen years in solitary confinement in the infamous Vladimir prison 200 kilometres east of Moscow, which was particularly feared for its harsh conditions. He was assigned a remote village in the Arkhangelsk district on the White Sea as his residence.

In a modest wooden house Menshagin secretly dictated his memories to an acquaintance on tape. The recordings were smuggled out of the country and edited as a book by an emigrant publishing house in Paris. In it he contradicted the statements of his former deputy in Smolensk, Boris Bazilevsky, who had been a witness of the Burdenko Commission and the Nuremberg Trial. According to Bazilevsky, Menshagin had assured him that the Germans were the murderers of Katyn.[41] Menshagin died in 1984 in the wilderness of cold northern Russia, four years before his memories appeared in the West.

Secret criminal proceedings such as the Menshagin Trial seemed to the Kremlin's propagandists to be far from sufficient to suppress information about the mass murder. The authorities also sentenced residents from the Katyn area to prison or labour camps for accusing the NKVD of the crime in private talks.[42]

In order to mislead their own compatriots, but also the international public, at the beginning of the seventies a gigantic memorial with huge sculptures for the victims of the German occupation terror was erected on 50 hectares in the Belarusian village Khatyn near Minsk. In Khatyn in March 1943, a command of the Waffen SS had shot several dozen villagers because German soldiers had been attacked by partisans in the area. Twenty-eight houses of the village were set on fire by the Germans, just as it happened in dozens of other places in the region.

The place was not mentioned in the *Great Soviet Encyclopaedia* before the erection of the huge monuments, nor was it marked in atlases. The choice had obviously fallen on the village Khatyn (in Russian: Хатынь) because of its name: it is easily confused with Katyn (Катынь), 300 kilometres to the northeast.

From now on visitors to the Soviet Union were regularly guided to Khatyn. US President Richard Nixon laid a wreath in front of the monument during his state visit in 1974. But in this case, only half of the propaganda goal was achieved: *The Washington Post* did not mention Katyn in its report, but *The New York Times* did, even in the headline: 'Nixon sees Khatyn, a Soviet Memorial, not Katyn Forest'.[43]

Under the title 'Khatyn is not Katyn' (*Khatyn ce n'est pas Katyn*), Belgian author Pierre Hubermont, who visited the mass graves with the writers' delegations in 1943, made a clear statement. Hubermont, who was in prison for six years after the war for collaboration with the Germans, explained in the introduction that he had long hesitated to write this text: 'It cannot be overlooked that the number of ten to fifteen thousand Polish officers does not count against the incomprehensible mass of victims of the Nazi camps.'[44]

Hubermont describes his journey to Katyn in 111 pages and also tries to refute the reports of the BBC reporter Alexander Werth about the German perpetrators. But he could not find a publisher for his text. The manuscript was never edited, it is located in the 'Centre for the Study and Documentation of War and Contemporary Society' (CEGES) in Brussels.

At the very time when the controversies surrounding Khatyn were taking place, Polish emigrants in London, with the support of the still existing government in exile, were fighting to erect a monument to the victims of Katyn. The city council initially rejected the application on the grounds that the large memorial in the Soviet village of Khatyn already existed. However, this decision provoked strong opposition from several Conservative MEPs, including Winston Spencer-Churchill, a grandson of the former prime minister.

His parliamentary colleague Nicholas Bethell, a prominent publicist and historian, accused Churchill, Eden and their Secretary of State Cadogan of 'covering up a crime'.[45] The Labour government tried in vain to silence the critics. Most daily newspapers took up the topic in background reports.

The BBC broadcasted a documentary about Katyn and the responses of all governments since 1940. There was no criticism of the press, because there was no one left at the major daily newspapers who sympathised with the Soviet Union. BBC reporter Alexander Werth had finally lost his faith in the human development of the Soviet system because of the tanks with the red star suppressing the 'Prague Spring' in 1968. Already seriously ill, a few months later he committed suicide. He transferred his late doubts to his son Nicolas Werth, who later became a history professor specialising in crimes of the Soviet regime and one of the authors of the *Black Book of Communism*.

Former ambassador to the exiled government, Owen O'Malley, publicly called on former foreign minister and prime minister Anthony Eden to finally take a stand in the Katyn issue. He had written memoirs under the title *The Phantom Caravan* after leaving the diplomatic service, but had not received permission from the Foreign Office to mention Katyn in them. In his analysis, O'Malley accused former governments of serious misconduct, negligence and ignorance on twenty-four points. Lord Bethell also demanded that Eden finally 'cleanse himself of the old swamp'. But Eden only explained that he did not want to 'tear open old wounds'.[46]

In the face of this public pressure, a spokesman from the Foreign Office reaffirmed before the parliament: 'Her Majesty's Government have absolutely no standing in this matter.' In response, several Conservative MPs put a parliamentary question to the government. The historian Rohan D'Olier Butler, who officially acted as an advisor to the Foreign Ministry, was therefore commissioned to prepare an internal dossier on London's position on Katyn.

The Butler Memorandum stated that the officials of the ministry and the diplomats directly involved with Katyn had no doubt about the Soviet perpetrators. However, there were 'some uncertainties' at the top level in the Foreign Office, mainly because of the strong echo of the Burdenko report. Butler made the recommendation, which was considered cynical: 'We see no advantage in breaking the silence that we have preserved for nearly 30 years.' A secretary of state was of the same opinion: London should avoid 'unproductive anti-Soviet propaganda'.[47] The Butler Memorandum was not published until 2003 on the occasion of the sixtieth anniversary of the discovery of the mass graves in Katyn Forest.

It explains in detail how in the early 1970s the British government joined forces with the leaders in Moscow and Warsaw to prevent the planned monument in London. The case was considered so serious that the Politburo in Moscow dealt with it. The party leaders instructed Foreign Minister Andrey Gromyko to formally protest against the project through the Soviet Embassy in London. Moscow's diplomats should warn that the use of 'anti-Soviet forgeries' would worsen the 'international situation'. The KGB should also exert pressure on political decision-makers through its 'unofficial channels' in the press, social organisations and the churches in Britain. The Soviet Embassy in the UK was pleased to report to Moscow that the Anglican diocese had spoken out against a monument in central London, as this would run counter to the 'principle of reconciliation'.[48]

The government of the Polish People's Republic warned London of disadvantages for British investors if the monument was erected. The British Embassy in Warsaw concluded that the dispute over the monument had cost its own economy at least three major contracts.[49]

But despite all warnings and threats, the dispute over the London monument ended in a defeat for Moscow and Warsaw: in 1976 it was inaugurated, albeit not in the centre of the British capital, but at the Gunnersbury cemetery in a suburb. The obelisk bore the inscription 'Katyn 1940', a Polish eagle bound with barbed wire symbolised the lot of the victims. While the Labour government had banned British uniform wearers from attending the ceremony, several Conservative MEPs, including Winston Spencer-Churchill and Nicholas Bethell, attended. The US Embassy in London also sent one of their diplomats; the Russian Orthodox Church in Exile and the Association of Jewish Communities of Great Britain sent greetings.[50]

The British press reported extensively on it. *The Economist* wrote sarcastically about London's official position: 'The Foreign Office made a diplomatic but ill-judged and unsuccessful attempt to protect the reputation of Joseph Stalin.'[51] The Governor of California, Ronald Reagan, also took up the topic in one of his weekly radio broadcasts.[52] Later, as US president, he had American documents on Katyn released for the first time.

Summer of Solidarity and Ice Age in Poland

KGB leader Andropov, who had dissidents sent to psychiatric hospitals as allegedly insane, where their will was to be broken, was extremely dissatisfied with this development: he demanded that Moscow's and Warsaw's diplomats better coordinate their measures against propaganda of 'anti-Soviet content'.[53]

The London controversy was echoed in Polish society via the Western short-wave stations. The illegal democracy movement took up the issue of Katyn. Underground publishers printed documents about the massacre. Jan Abramski and Ryszard Żywiecki – the first and last name on Katyn's death list – were listed as authors. Typewritten and hand-made copies also appeared under the editors' names – Ribbentrop and Molotov.[54]

After a Polish censor fled to Sweden in 1977, it became clear how hard the Warsaw leadership tried to stick to the line set by Moscow. A Polish publisher in exile published a book with excerpts from the guidelines of press censorship, and shortly afterwards a reprint appeared in the Polish underground. The Main Office for Press Control, Publications and Theatre Plays, as the censorship authority was officially called, laid down rules for dealing with Katyn:

1) Any attempt to blame the Soviet Union for the death of Polish officers in Katyn Forest is inadmissible.
2) In scientific works, memoirs and biographies, formulations of this kind are permissible: shot by the Hitlerists in Katyn, died in Katyn, perished in Katyn. If a date of death is indicated for the use of the phrase 'perished in Katyn', it must be after July 1941.
3) The term 'prisoners of war' must be eliminated in relation to the Polish soldiers and officers interned by the Red Army in September 1939.

The correct term is 'internee'. The names of the Kozelsk, Starobelsk and Ostashkov camps in which the Polish officers shot by the Hitlerists in Katyn Forest were interned are free for use.

4) Obituaries, announcements of church services for the victims of Katyn and all other ways of commemorating them may only be released with the permission of the authorities.[55]

A debate about Katyn began in circles of the democratic opposition and of the Catholic Church, but the issue remained taboo for the media. The secret police SB tried to suppress this debate. Thus it searched for the producers of the *Katyn Bulletin* (Biuletyn katyński), whose texts appeared in small print because of the paper deficit. The runs ranged between 100 and 1,500 copies.[56]

The *Bulletin* reported on the suicide of 76-year-old Walenty Badylak in the middle of the main market in Krakow. The former soldier of the anti-communist underground army AK had chained himself to a historical fountain on 21 March 1980, poured gasoline over his body and set fire to himself. The emergency doctor couldn't save him. He carried a tin plate with him on which he had written that he wanted to signal a 'protest against the murderers of Katyn and their paid renegades in the country'.[57]

Badylak was by no means the only Pole who wanted to remember the murder of the Poles in Katyn Forest exactly forty years earlier in the spring of 1980. In all major Polish cities, the SB observed Katyn actions, often starting from Catholic churches. A particularly large number of young people took part.

In the churches people prayed for the victims of Katyn. The SB archive contains the names of the priests who had thus 'shown their negative attitude towards the USSR and the so-called Katyn affair'.

In Warsaw, the SB secured around 100 black armbands with the words 'Katyń 1940' embroidered on them. Several dozen people were imprisoned throughout the country, leaflets printed underground about the 'Katyn lie' were distributed, and several thousand sheets were confiscated.[58]

In 1981 the first congress of the independent trade union Solidarność took place in Gdansk to the great annoyance of the communist leadership. The Solidarity programme called for the Katyn crime to be investigated and a monument to the victims to be erected. The communist leadership had to allow the trade union in August 1980, the 'Summer of Solidarity', after a wave of strikes. The country was in a deep economic crisis. The electrician Lech Wałęsa, who was elected chairman of Solidarity, succeeded in recruiting numerous intellectuals from the illegal democracy movement as advisors. These included the Catholic publicist Tadeusz Mazowiecki and the two lawyers Jarosław and Lech Kaczyński.

In 1981, the Powązki cemetery in Warsaw became the focus of the small war over Katyn as part of the power struggle between the communist leadership and the democracy movement. Warsaw citizens repeatedly laid flowers on a symbolic grave for the victims of Katyn and lit grave candles in their memory. Only a few steps away was the burial mound for the Stalinist party leader Bolesław Bierut, who had everyone doubting the Soviet Katyn version persecuted, and the grave of Justice Minister Henryk Świątkowski, who wanted to organise a Polish show trial.

The priest responsible for the cemetery, Stefan Niedzielak, suggested that a Katyn monument be erected. As a young priest in the war, Niedzielak had smuggled documents about Katyn for the Polish underground from Warsaw to Krakow to Archbishop Sapieha. In his sermons he repeatedly demanded the 'truth about Katyn'.[59] A Warsaw sculptor created a four and a half metre high cross of rusty iron struts, with only the words 'Katyn 1940' on a panel. It was set up at the end of July 1981 by a total of thirty Solidarity activists. They were filmed by SB agents. But the next morning the cross had disappeared without a trace.[60]

Solidarity grew to almost ten million members. In the Kremlin it was seen as a threat to the communist power. General Jaruzelski, who had taken over the leadership of the Polish Workers' Party, therefore committed himself to breaking up the democracy movement. The imposition of martial law on 13 December 1981, an ice-cold winter day, was accompanied by the most serious human rights violations, political murders, the boldest propaganda lies and the most blatant lack of provision. The leaders of the democracy movement around Lech Wałęsa were arrested.

When the communists, led by General Jaruzelski, saw their power secured again and considered Solidarity to be destroyed, a new cross was erected on the Powązki cemetery in 1985. The inscription read: 'To the Polish soldier resting in the earth of Katyn, victims of Hitler fascism – 1941.'

Father Stefan Niedzielak, who preached against these 'historical lies', received anonymous death threats by telephone. Twice, attempts to kidnap him in Warsaw failed. Once, he was attacked and beaten down by unknown people in the Powązki cemetery.[61]

Chapter 15

Gorbachev's Errors and Tricks

While in Poland, the political ice age continued, in 1985, drastic changes began in the Soviet Union. On 11 March, 54-year-old Mikhail Gorbachev was elected the new secretary general of the CPSU. Shortly after taking office, he surprised his compatriots with an anti-alcohol campaign, which made him unpopular among large sections of the population. His advisor Alexander Yakovlev, who had intensively studied the mechanism of the social market economy in his former position as ambassador to Canada, was able to convince him of the need for far-reaching reforms after this first failure. Gorbachev attempted to modernise the encrusted Soviet system under the keyword 'perestroika' (reconstruction).

In Warsaw, the head of state and party, Wojciech Jaruzelski, understood at this time that he could not bring Poland out of its deep crisis with hard repression. He saw the opportunity to strengthen his own position of power by approaching the reformer Gorbachev; he initiated the first cautious and very limited economic reforms. However, he suppressed any attempts to shake the communist power monopoly, the secret police SB remained an important instrument of his policy.

Jaruzelski had no illusions that the vast majority of his compatriots had an extremely negative attitude towards the Soviet Union. As a condition for a change of mood he saw the working-up of the historical ballast between both countries. While so far he had vehemently defended the communist versions of history, he made a U turn and tried to get on the offensive: at a meeting with Gorbachev in 1987, he convinced him to set up a joint commission of historians in order to come to terms with the 'white spots' in historiography. The Soviet side sent professors selected by the Central Committee to the Commission; activists of the Polish Workers' Party also dominated the Warsaw delegation. Neither party leadership wanted to lose control of the historical discourse.

The Poles presented their list of topics at the first meeting: the Ribbentrop–Molotov Pact and deportations from Poland to the Soviet Union 1939–1941; Katyn was soon added to the list. When the Poles asked at one of the meetings in Moscow for access to the original documents on the disputes, the Russian hosts had to admit meekly that they themselves had not received permission to see them.[1]

Jaruzelski intervened personally. He saw in the settlement of the Katyn question one of the last opportunities for the Communist Workers' Party to regain recognition in society. Gorbachev's visit to the Vistula in July 1988 was supposed to bring a breakthrough. But the Soviet leader communicated to Jaruzelski that there were no documents in the archives disproving the version of the Burdenko Commission of the German perpetrators.[2]

Consequently, the Kremlin chief in Warsaw did not comment on Katyn. Members of the Soviet delegation later reported that Gorbachev misinterpreted the warm reception that had been prepared for him in Warsaw. As the first Soviet party leader he had walked among the crowd, shaken hands and had been celebrated by the carefully controlled audience. He had hoped that these declarations of sympathy would relieve him of the obligation to have the disputes from history resolved.[3] It was a blatant miscalculation, for Polish intellectuals were deeply disappointed in him.

To settle the conflict concerning Katyn, he promised to erect a memorial in Katyn for the coming USSR five-year plan. In the instruction for the Ministry of Culture, however, a monument to the 'Soviet prisoners of war destroyed by the Germans' is also listed. This referred to the 500 captured Red Army soldiers who, according to the Burdenko report, were deployed by the Germans during the exhumation of Polish officers and subsequently shot; it was one of many false statements therein. But the message was clear: it should be conveyed that Russians and Poles alike had become victims of the Germans in Katyn.

A few weeks later, the first official travel group drove from Warsaw to Katyn, including widows and children of officers shot there. This was the first time that an association of relatives was established, the 'Families of Katyn'. Among the founders was Prelate Stefan Niedzielak, courier of Archbishop Sapieha during the war and initiator of the Katyn Cross at the Powązki cemetery in Warsaw. However, at their destination, where an honorary guard of the Soviet army was posted, the Polish group was irritated by the plaque with the inscription 'The victims of fascism who were shot by Hitler fascists in 1941'. A Polish military priest celebrated a mass, the first since the memorial service in January 1944, at which General Zygmunt Berling had accused the Germans of the crime and sworn revenge.[4]

The Polish party leader and head of state General Wojciech Jaruzelski, successfully exerted pressure on the Soviet leadership in the controversy over the Katyn massacre.

The topic became even more explosive with the violent death of the prelate Stefan Niedzialak, co-founder of the 'Families of Katyn': unknown perpetrators killed him in his apartment on the night of 21 January 1989. The coroners found a karate blow to the larynx as the cause of death. The suspicion fell on forces in the SB or KGB, who wanted to provoke a hardening of domestic politics.[5]

In view of the obvious delay in the Soviet authorities' handling of the Katyn case, General Jaruzelski tried to put Gorbachev under pressure via the Polish public: in the spring of 1989, the Polish press, which was still controlled by censorship, published the first articles in which Katyn was described as a crime by the NKVD. The newspapers also quoted new witnesses.

The Polish offensive was closely observed from the Kremlin. Valentin Falin, the new head of the International Department of the Central Committee, recognised its explosive power for Soviet–Polish relations. In an analysis for the Politburo, he referred to the publications of the Warsaw media. Falin warned that the Polish opposition could instrumentalise the issue in the power struggle on the Vistula.

Indeed, the power of the Polish communists was threatened: after another wave of strikes, the government had to legalise the Solidarity trade union again. From February to April 1989, the Round Table negotiated the democratic movement's participation in power. The Workers' Party and the opposition also agreed on new elections.

The lists of the railroaders

Falin wanted to solve the Katyn problem as quickly as possible. The directors of the 'Special Archives' in Moscow, where the most important state documents were kept and which were directly subordinate to the party leader, continued to claim that there were no documents on Katyn. Falin, however, learned about the work of two historians who, independently of each other, had found important traces by chance: Natalia Lebedeva and Yuri Zorya.

Natalia Lebedeva worked on a book about the Nuremberg Trials. A journalist of the reformist *Literaturnaya Gazeta* who had reported on crimes committed by the NKVD contacted her. He had received a letter from a former officer of the NKVD transport troops from the Smolensk region. The man was outraged and rejected the accusation that his units had been involved in the shooting of the Poles. According to him, his men accompanied the transport from the Kozelsk camp, but did not harm the POWs. He indicated the number of his unit, it was NKVD Transport Battalion 136.

Lebedeva pursued this trace. In this way she found the files of the NKVD transport troops and finally the lists of the Poles who had been brought from Kozelsk to the railway station Gnezdovo near Smolensk.[6] But since the Special Archives remained closed to her, she could not get any further at this point until she had consulted with the military lawyer Yuri Zorya.

Zorya also dealt with the Nuremberg Trials. His starting point was the questioning of the so far officially denied Secret Additional Protocol of the Ribbentrop–Molotov Pact, which had also become an issue in Moscow: MPs in the Supreme Soviet demanded the disclosure of all documents. Zorya was also interested for personal reasons: he was the son of the general in the judicial service Nikolai Zorya, the assistant to the Chief Prosecutor Roman Rudenko, who died in a mysterious manner in Nuremberg. So the son also looked in the files for clues. He knew the rumour that the NKVD had liquidated his father because he had discovered the truth about Katyn.

Zorya received a copy of the *Official Material* of the Germans from 1943. The book deepened his doubts about the version of the Burdenko Commission. Together with Lebedeva, he compared the list of names in the book with the NKVD files on the prisoner transports from the Kozelsk camp – they were the same people. In addition, the two historians learned that the Smolensk department of the NKVD destroyed the personnel files of the Poles in 1940. The reason was obvious for them: the files were no longer needed because the Poles were dead.

However, the archive directors repeatedly tried to obstruct Lebedeva's and Zorya's investigations. But Falin, with the support of Gorbachev advisor Yakovlev, who was now a member of the Politburo, ensured they could continue working.[7] Yakovlev was regarded as the brain behind 'perestroika'; he imposed a relaxation of censorship, thus he promoted the reporting of mistakes and shortcomings in the Soviet system – and made a large part of the party apparatus his enemy.

Falin summarised all the information about Katyn in several letters to Gorbachev. Since he did not receive an answer, however, he turned to Foreign Minister Eduard Shevardnadze and KGB leader Vladimir Kryuchkov. In April 1989, in a joint letter, they proposed the Politburo should admit the actions of the NKVD in Katyn.

Gorbachev did not answer this either. Shortly afterwards, Falin and Yakovlev informed him personally that they had given the order to search in the archives for the execution orders and the Secret Additional Protocol. Yakovlev noted that Gorbachev had replied rather indifferently: 'Search!' The head of his office, Valery Boldin, had added 'with a slight smile' that such documents did not exist.[8]

That was a lie. Shortly before this, Boldin had brought to Gorbachev 'Folder No. 1', stamped 'top secret', from the Special Archives. It contained one of the two originals of the Secret Additional Protocol, Beria's draft on the execution of the captured Poles with the signatures of Stalin and other members of the Politburo, and other secret documents. During Stalin's lifetime they were kept in his apartment in special containers that guaranteed a constant temperature and humidity. As Boldin later reported, Gorbachev had examined the documents for the first time in 1987; otherwise, only former Foreign Minister Gromyko, who had risen to head of state, knew their contents.

In fact, the date notes of the archive administration on the cover confirm Boldin's version. Gorbachev's predecessors, Andropov and Brezhnev, were also aware of its contents according to the paraphs on the cover. As Boldin described it, the Kremlin chief read it carefully a second time on 18 April 1989, after which he sealed the envelope again. He commented on the content with the words: 'Can you imagine what these documents mean?' Boldin had received the strict instruction: 'No one should be told anything about this! I decide who may know.'[9]

Against better knowledge, Gorbachev repeated to Jaruzelski that there were no documents about Katyn. Jaruzelski had come under increasing political pressure, because in the election campaign before the first partially free elections on 4 June 1989, some Solidarity candidates demanded Poland's withdrawal from the Soviet bloc. The Workers' Party wanted to secure its power through the electoral code: two thirds of the seats of the Sejm, the House of Commons, should be reserved for the communists and their allies, only one third and the Senate, the Upper House, should be freely elected. However, the elections ended in a fiasco for the Workers' Party: Solidarity headed by Wałęsa won all but one of the mandates available for free election.[10]

Although the new Sejm, in which only a third of the members of parliament had democratic legitimacy, still elected Jaruzelski as president, there was no majority for a head of government from the ranks of the Workers' Party. Finally, Jaruzelski had to accept the Catholic publicist Tadeusz Mazowiecki as the new prime minister; he was the first non-communist head of government in the Eastern bloc. In his speeches, Mazowiecki avoided any criticism of the Kremlin – there were still 400,000 Soviet soldiers in the country.

While the party regime collapsed in Warsaw in the summer of 1989, historians in Moscow uncovered further archive material, and in Smolensk Russian journalists spoke to former NKVD men involved in the shooting of the Poles. But none of this information was allowed to be published. The Polish side did not learn anything about this either, just as it did not know anything about Lebedeva's and Zorya's research.

Zorya had come across materials from the Central Administration of Prisoners of War from 1940, from which the fate of Polish officers could be reconstructed. The archive also contained documents on the transport of the prisoners of the Ostashkov and Starobelsk camps to Kalinin and Kharkov, of which the historians were previously unaware. Yakovlev asked Zorya to summarise the new information in a 'Documentary Katyn Chronicle'. In it he took stock: the shooting of 14,000 Polish prisoners of war by the NKVD was proven, about 4,500 of them were in Katyn Forest. But Zorya was instructed not to publish this information.[11]

Difficult breakthrough in Moscow

At this time, the newspaper *Moskovskie Novosti*, which had focused on coming to terms with the Stalin era, undertook its first investigations into Smolensk and Katyn. In its report, much room was given to the shooting of Soviet citizens in the 1930s. The mass graves of the Poles were also mentioned the report, but without naming the perpetrators.

According to the report, relatives of witnesses, namely of the peasant Kiselev and the railway locksmith Krivozertsev, still lived in the vicinity. However, all Katyn inhabitants who were interviewed by the journalists stated that they knew nothing about the events of the war. The same information was given to the reporter in the Smolensk department of the KGB: there were no documents, nor was anything known about witnesses.[12]

But that, too, was a lie. For KGB Major Oleg Zakirov, an Uzbek whose grandfather had himself fallen victim to Stalin's repression, had long since begun investigations, albeit without the permission of his superiors: he had found documents in the archive containing the names of the NKVD officials involved in the shooting of the Poles. Some of them were still alive. Among them was Ivan Titkov who brought the Poles shot in the basement of the NKVD building in Smolensk to Katyn Forest. He was encouraged by his relatives to lighten his heart and reveal all his knowledge; he also showed Zakirov the exact locations of the mass graves.

The prison guard Pyotr Klimov described the execution process. He lived alone at his former workplace, he had furnished a prison cell, the washbasin was in the corridor. The former NKVD guard Kirill Borodenkov, who lived alone and desolate in a completely run-down, urine-smelling hut, even wrote a report about the firing squad to which he himself had belonged.[13] Zakirov also found evidence in the files that witnesses of the Burdenko Commission received a reward from the NKVD. Later, the KGB arrested people in Smolensk who accused the NKVD of being the perpetrators in Katyn.

Behind the backs of his superiors, Zakirov sent a brief report on his findings to the editors of *Moskovskie Novosti*. Two reporters arrived. Zakirov led them to the Goat Hills in Katyn Forest. The area was surrounded by a fence, with additional patrols of shepherd dogs.

Behind the back of his superiors, KGB officer Oleg Zakirov informed the press about his research on Katyn.

Behind a high wall was a holiday residence for the KGB leaders, in which high-ranking guests from Moscow were occasionally accommodated, among them Gorbachev.[14] A television team from Moscow also came.

But the newspaper report was not allowed to appear; as the author later learned, Gorbachev himself intervened with the editor-in-chief.[15] The television documentary did not come about either because the Smolensk KGB confiscated the video cassettes. On the way between two locations the reporters' car was forced off the road by a truck and landed in a ditch.

The two former NKVD men Borodenkov and Titkov were pressured to withdraw their statements about Katyn. But they both showed stubbornness and did not give in to the pressure. Zakirov received anonymous threatening calls, his colleagues shunned him. Two KGB leaders came from Moscow to warn him of his insubordination.[16]

The research in Smolensk remained unknown in Poland at first. But the new leadership in Warsaw irritated Moscow considerably when on 12 October 1989 the Polish Attorney General asked his Soviet counterpart to initiate criminal proceedings 'for the murder of Polish officers in Katyn and other unidentified places'. In the reply from Moscow, however, it was pointed out that there was no new evidence that called into question the results of the Burdenko Commission of 1944.

Two weeks after the fall of the Berlin Wall on 9 November 1989, the new Polish Prime Minister Tadeusz Mazowiecki travelled to Moscow on his inaugural visit, where Gorbachev received him in the Kremlin. Two and a half months had already passed since his election; his first trip abroad had led him to the Vatican to Pope John Paul II.

The Polish delegation flew from Moscow to Smolensk and from there took a bus to Katyn. There was biting frost, the forest was deep in snow. As a greeting, a military band played first the Polish, then the Soviet national anthem. Although the year 1941 was removed from the monument, the dedication to the 'victims of fascism' could still be read. A priest, who was a member of the delegation, celebrated a Catholic mass.

The trip of the Polish government delegation to Katyn prompted the American correspondent Edmund Stevens, who still lived in Moscow, to report for the first time after 45 years on his own trip to the press conference of the Burdenko Commission, but this time with a different accent. Stevens had returned to Moscow at the beginning of the short thaw under Khrushchev in 1956 and worked there for several American magazines. He maintained contact with writers and artists, and his daughter was accepted into the ballet troupe of the Bolshoi Theatre.[17] Since he and his Russian wife were allowed to export icons and paintings, especially from the avant-garde of the 1920s, and sell them through galleries in New York, his Western colleagues suspected that he had very good contacts with the KGB.[18]

Stevens wrote about the correspondents' trip to Katyn in January 1944, saying that he and his colleagues noticed the dead Poles wearing coats despite allegedly being shot in the summer. Burdenko's statements were not convincing. Stevens also told a Russian journalist that the testimonies of the alleged witnesses who claimed that the Germans shot the Poles sounded rehearsed.[19] Stevens hadn't written of all this, however, in 1944; rather, immediately after the trip, he had uncritically repeated the official version of the Burdenko Commission.

On the occasion of Mazowiecki's visit, the local radio station in Smolensk broadcast a programme based on the results of Zakirov's research, in which one of the former NKVD men also had his say. The chiefs of the KGB in Smolensk became very angry.

In March 1990, members of the Moscow human rights organisation 'Memorial', dedicated to the investigation of Stalinist crimes, demonstrated together with a group of locals in the centre of Smolensk, asking for the recognition of the mass murder at Katyn. On banners was the slogan: 'Poles, forgive us for Katyn!' Afterwards, the demonstrators visited the cemetery. In Moscow, 'Memorial' organised a scientific conference and exhibition entitled 'Katyn 1940–1990'.[20]

Meanwhile, the Moscow historian Natalia Lebedeva had found new archive material from 1940 that proved that Beria and Merkulov were aware of the murder of the Poles. She informed Falin, who informed the Politburo.

However, the majority of the latter, under Gorbachev's leadership, decided that the contents of these documents should not become known. But the editors of *Moskovskie Novosti* bypassed this ban and printed an interview with Lebedeva under the headline 'The Tragedy of Katyn'.[21] It was the first publication in the Soviet Union to refute the official version after Burdenko.

Years later, the editor-in-chief of *Moskovskie Novosti* described that Gorbachev had called him after the publication and shouted at him again: 'So far the Poles could not find the real perpetrators, and now they are served to them by a petty article writer on a tray.'[22] Officially, however, the Kremlin chief remained silent, and Lebedeva received the backing of Politburo member Yakovlev.

After this publication, Yakovlev finally convinced Gorbachev that another blockade of information about Katyn would place him completely on the defensive. On the other hand, admitting the truth would earn him respect abroad. In the spring of 1990, the Kremlin chief was under the greatest pressure: his attempts to keep the German Democratic Republic alive even after the fall of the Berlin Wall had been sabotaged by the East Germans. In the first free elections in the GDR in March 1990, they elected a parliament whose overwhelming majority voted for German reunification.

In Poland, Gorbachev's ally Jaruzelski was in trouble: the Workers' Party had been dissolved, and the chairman of Solidarity, Wałęsa, demanded the withdrawal of Soviet troops from Poland and the resignation of Jaruzelski from the presidency because the latter was not democratically legitimised.

A state visit by Jaruzelski to Moscow was planned during this time. Gorbachev wanted to anchor Poland more firmly in the Soviet bloc to prevent it from drifting away. But the Polish president made the visit conditional on a breakthrough on the Katyn issue. So the Moscow leaders decided to support him by officially acknowledging the actions of the NKVD in Katyn. Falin formulated the line of argument: Beria and Merkulov were the culprits, but the case was legally closed because both had been executed for their crimes.[23] When Jaruzelski arrived in Moscow on 13 April 1990 for a state visit, the official news agency TASS published a communiqué:

> Recently, Soviet archivists and historians have found documents about the Polish prisoners of war held in the NKVD camps of Kozelsk, Starobelsk and Ostashkov. They show that in April and May 1940, 394 of the approximately 15,000 Polish officers held in these three camps were taken to the Gryazovets camp. The others were transferred to the district administrations of the NKVD of Smolensk, Voroshilograd and Kalinin and never again mentioned in the statistics of the NKVD.
>
> All the archival material discovered suggests that Beria, Merkulov and their subordinates were responsible for the atrocities in Katyn Forest. The Soviet side expresses its deepest condolences for the tragedy of Katyn and declares that it is one of the most serious crimes of Stalinism.

Gorbachev handed Jaruzelski copies of the documents on the camp at Kozelsk and the transport of the Poles to Katyn. The Polish president, whose father had not survived deportation by the NKVD to Siberia, drove from Moscow to Katyn, where the false memorial had been removed in the meantime. After the military ceremony, he kneeled in front of the monument. In the memorial book he wrote: 'For the victims of a cruel Stalinist crime.'

In Poland, a number of books were published on the crime, including the memoirs of the witness Stanisław Swianiewicz. Now 91 years old, he returned to his homeland for the first time since the beginning of the Second World War, reporting on television and in press interviews on his observations at the Gnezdovo railway station near Smolensk.[24]

Wałęsa called for the punishment of the perpetrators still alive. A few months later, Jaruzelski agreed to clear the way for new presidential elections in December 1990. Wałęsa won by a big margin. He set an example for his inauguration: he did not invite Jaruzelski, but Ryszard Kaczorowski, the president of the still existing government in exile in London. Kaczorowski gave him the official seals of the head of state rescued from the Germans in 1939 and declared the government in exile dissolved. It was a symbolic link to the time before the German and Soviet occupations.

Stubborn old communists

Under file number 159/1990, the military prosecutor in Moscow initiated proceedings to identify the perpetrators of the unlawful shooting of the 14,700 Poles mentioned in the NKVD documents. Shortly before, the location of the mass graves of Pyatikhatki on the outskirts of Kharkov and in Mednoye near Tver, the former Kalinin, had been disclosed. The authorities quickly managed to identify eyewitnesses from the NKVD for each of the three places of execution and the first interviews began.

The prosecutors also interviewed a witness whose name had even been in the international press: Anna Alexeyeva, the kitchen maid at the Dnieper Manor, who at the conference of the Burdenko Commission, had impressed some of the American correspondents and above all the ambassador's daughter, Kathleen Harriman. Already during the first questioning, the now 74-year-old woman declared that she had never heard any shots in Katyn Forest and had never seen any German soldiers in bloodstained uniforms. She accepted the work for the Wehrmacht in Katyn because she was afraid that otherwise she would be deported to the German Reich for forced labour. But in a second interview six weeks later, she revoked her statement and repeated the version of the Burdenko Commission. One of the Russian prosecutors later expressed the suspicion that Anna Alexeyeva had in the meantime been put under pressure by old KGB cadres.[25]

The pressure on Gorbachev did not ease. In May 1991, the Prosecutor General's Office asked him to search the Special Archives for a decision by the Politburo on the shooting of the Poles, which Stalin himself had signed. Former NKVD officers had spoken of such a document in the interviews. But Gorbachev did not respond to this question either.

The Kremlin chief was obviously aware that the publication of this document would render obsolete the previous line of defence according to which the heads of the NKVD Beria and Merkulov had acted on their own. Alarmed, he therefore asked Boldin, the head of his office, whether he had destroyed the documents from 'Folder No. 1', including the Secret Additional Protocol and Beria's draft signed by the Politburo on the shooting of the Poles. At least that's how Boldin described it in his memoirs. He denied this and explained that the system of multiple registration of documents would immediately attract attention if they were destroyed.[26]

On 25 July 1991 the last of the six signatories of the murder plan for Katyn died in Moscow: Lazar Kaganovich. He was 97 years old, and until shortly before his death he had enjoyed excellent health. Even during 'perestroika' he defended the shooting of the Poles in an interview: they were 'rapists, bandits, murderers'. According to him, they were guilty of the deaths of Red Army prisoners of war in the early 1920s and of the hunt for communists in Poland. However, the interview, in which Kaganovich vulgarly attacked Yakovlev as a 'shithead', was not allowed to appear, as allegedly the KGB prevented this.

Five years before Kaganovich, Vyacheslav Molotov had died at 96. Until the end, he, too, had defended the liquidation of political opponents as necessary for the construction of the Soviet Union. In a telephone conversation a few months before his death, he admitted the shooting of the Poles by the NKVD, but put the number of victims at 3,000.[27] Kaganovich and Molotov had never been called to account for their involvement in countless political murders.

Gorbachev did not realise until it was too late that the centralist system built up by Stalin could no longer be maintained. In order to reduce political pressure, he pushed ahead with the federalisation of the Soviet Union. But on 19 August 1991, several members of the Politburo, among them KGB leader Vladimir Kryuchkov, staged a putsch against Gorbachev. Kryuchkov first had advocated the investigation of Katyn, but then in a turnaround had tried to block the topic. A short time before the coup against Gorbachev Kryuchkov had ensured that the annoying Major Zakirov of the KGB department in Smolensk had to leave the service 'because of schizophrenia'.[28]

However, the poorly prepared coup failed after three days due to the mass demonstrations in Moscow and the resistance of the recently elected Russian President Boris Yeltsin, who was still healthy and powerful at the time.

During the trial against the members of the Politburo, it turned out that Gorbachev's office chief Boldin had also sided with them. In his memoirs, Boldin portrayed his patron as a waverer who had neither a concept for a new political order nor for economic reforms. Gorbachev acted like Khrushchev in coming to terms with the crimes of the Stalin era, Boldin wrote: first he pushed them forward, but then he stopped halfway and began to 'trick and lie'.[29]

Similar, though not with such harsh words, was the reaction of Gorbachev's long-time confidant Alexander Yakovlev, who was later denounced by both the communists and anti-Semitic right-wing extremists as one of the main culprits behind the disintegration of the Soviet Union. In December 1991, Yeltsin and the leaders of the Soviet republics Ukraine and Belarus agreed to dissolve the Soviet Union. Thus, Gorbachev had lost his office; he had to make room in the Kremlin for Yeltsin, whom he personally hated. Both agreed to ask Yakovlev for the handover of the offices as witnesses. As the latter later described, the conversation lasted eight hours, both had treated each other with respect, Gorbachev had not shown his bitterness, Yeltsin had suppressed his feelings of triumph.

Gorbachev took two sealed envelopes from the safe and handed them over to Yeltsin. They were now opened. These were the codes for the nuclear weapons and the 'Folder No. 1' with the Secret Additional Protocol, the four-page paper on the execution of the captured Poles of 5 March 1940, the handwritten report of Shelepin and other documents. Gorbachev said: 'I fear they cause international complications.' Yeltsin took a look inside, started to read and said briefly: 'We must think about it seriously.'[30]

Yakovlev continued: 'I looked Gorbachev in the eye. He understood immediately what I meant. After all, I asked him a hundred times about these documents … He looked at me and his expression clearly said that he thought I was a newbie who didn't understand anything about big politics.'[31]

Chapter 16

From Cooperation Back to Confrontation

After the failed August coup in 1991, Boris Yeltsin, the president of the Russian Federation, banned the Communist Party. But numerous party members complained about this presidential decree, and the case was brought before the Constitutional Court. In support of his lawyers, Yeltsin had a group of historians compile documents to support the argument that the Communist Party was a criminal organisation. However, the Constitutional Court, consisting exclusively of former members of the Communist Party, allowed the party to return with restrictions. During the preparations for the trial, the historians had, for the first time, seen the contents of 'Folder No. 1'. However, the lawyers of the presidential office refrained from including the Katyn paper of 5 March 1940 in their arguments. The Kremlin lawyers feared Polish claims for damages if it became known.[1]

But Polish historians had come to the conclusion that the murder of their compatriots must have been ordered or at least approved by Stalin. The new Polish President Lech Wałęsa, like his predecessor Jaruzelski two years before him, made a state visit dependent on the publication of the presumed documents.

Yeltsin now accepted the publication of the murder order and other Katyn materials. He was interested in rapprochement with Poland and democratic Western Europe, and needed support for reforms in the economically hard-hit country. It was also an opportunity to discredit his predecessor in the Kremlin, Gorbachev, who was still respected in the West. Gorbachev had always denied the existence of such documents. A messenger from Moscow brought Wałęsa copies of them. In response, Wałęsa promised to waive an action against Russia as the legal successor of the Soviet Union before an international court.

The former head of the Solidarity trade union arrived in Moscow shortly afterwards for his first state visit. On 14 October 1992, Yeltsin presented him with a facsimile of Beria's four pages signed by Stalin and his closest followers. This was tantamount to a public admission that the executions of Katyn, Kalinin and Kharkov were mass murders ordered by the state. Yeltsin also had copies of forty-one other documents handed over to the Polish delegation.[2]

In August 1993 Yeltsin came to Warsaw for a return visit. He laid a wreath at the monument to the Katyn victims in the Powązki cemetery, then kneeled down for a moment and said: 'Forgive us!' In a public statement, Yeltsin promised to press ahead with the prosecution of those responsible.

Indeed, the Russian military prosecutors made great progress in preparing criminal proceedings for the 1940 mass murders, also interviewing former KGB leader Shelepin. But he only explained that all documents had been destroyed.

Several young prosecutors interrogated the surviving perpetrators. In this way they were able to precisely reconstruct the course of the executions; they could also work out the forgeries by Merkulov's secret command in Katyn at the end of 1943 and by the Burdenko Commission at the beginning of 1944.

Among the accused was the 83-year-old former NKVD general Pyotr Soprunenko, who had headed the Main Administration for prisoners of war. However, he wasn't very talkative, and several times he denied that signatures on the documents came from him. He only gave information about the camps' daily routine, but emphasised that he had not been involved in the executions. Soprunenko, who was almost completely blind, died during the investigation in 1992.

Former driver Ivan Titkov willingly gave information about the murders in the basement of the NKVD building in Smolensk. Former NKVD guard Kirill Borodenkov, who had even written a short report on Katyn's firing squad, had died in the meantime.[3] The investigators also learned that the NKVD officer Ivan Stelmakh, who had led the executions in Katyn Forest, died exactly two decades later 'under the most horrible physical torments', presumably from cancer. One member of the execution squad slit his throat with a razor in the attic of the NKVD building, a second member also committed suicide.[4]

In Kharkov, the former prison guard Mitrofan Syromiatnikov, who drove bodies to the mass graves, reported in five long sessions on the execution of the Poles. When asked if he thought the Poles were guilty, he replied: 'They rebelled against our power.' According to him, in the annexed eastern Poland representatives of the Soviet power were attacked, their bodies thrown into wells. The members of the NKVD firing squad received a monthly bonus that almost doubled their usual salary.[5]

The most productive were the interviews of the former head of the NKVD district Kalinin, Dmitry Tokarev, who in the post-war years was Minister of State Security in the rank of Major General first in the Tajik Soviet Republic and then in the oil-rich Autonomous Republic of Tatarstan. According to the prosecutors, the 89-year-old man wanted to get rid of a great burden.[6] He reported that three members of the firing squad, including its leader Vasily Blokhin, had committed suicide. Another had 'gone mad':

> He had disturbed his consciousness because of his alcohol consumption and began to pour out his heart to others. He said, everyone told him he

was a drunk, but nobody asked why he drank. And then he added: 'Do you know how many people have passed through my hands, among them so many Poles?'[7]

An anthology about the Soviet secret service in the Autonomous Republic of Tatarstan, headed by Tokarev in the last years of Stalinism, depicted the fate of a witness of the Madden Commission: Boris Olshansky, who had caused a stir with his story that Nikolai Burdenko had described the report of the Soviet Katyn Commission as fake. After his surprising return to the Soviet Union in 1956, Olshansky came under the supervision of the KGB. One of the officers responsible for him wrote the biographical profile of him. Soviet propaganda, however, did not take advantage of his return, the subject of Katyn had long since become taboo.

The returned emigrant settled in Kazan, Tatarstan, where his first wife lived. According to the report, he died of kidney failure two years after returning. However, acquaintances reported that he had been an alcoholic and died from cirrhosis of the liver. It also became known that Professor Burdenko was seriously ill and completely deaf in his last year; his relatives stated that a man named Olshansky certainly had not been one of his friends. Former acquaintances among Russian emigrants described Olshansky as an unreliable person with a tendency to confabulate and lie. Historians deduce from this that the former mathematics teacher invented the information about his conversation with Burdenko in order to get an American visa as an alleged witness threatened by the NKGB in the Katyn case.[8]

In 1994, the military prosecutors in Moscow stopped proceedings for the executions of the Poles. Citing the Nuremberg Statute, they qualified them as 'crimes against peace, against humanity', thus as war crimes. But the case had to be suspended because the persons who had given the orders had long since died and no direct identified perpetrators were still alive. It cannot be ruled out that the eyewitnesses questioned by the prosecutors had assisted in the crimes, but that offence had already become time-barred.

However, this decision, which was obviously in line with the facts, met with strong protests in Poland. Dozens of books and thousands of articles about Katyn had been published since the collapse of the communist regimes. The Poles were also not satisfied that the next proceeding annulled this decision; it was by no means to continue the investigation, but because the legal qualification was apparently regarded as a risk, it could be the basis for claims for compensation. It was therefore rejected as 'inappropriate'.

As a result, Russian historians complained that they were hindered in their research into the fate of Polish prisoners. The publication of the Russian version of the four-volume document collection, published by the Polish Academy of Sciences (PAN), was also made more difficult. After all, the Polish side had to bear most of the costs. Only two volumes were published in Russian.[9]

In 1995, the US National Security Agency (NSA) published more than 3,000 documents from the Venona project. The project, in which American and British services worked together, primarily deciphered German and Soviet secret messages from the Second World War. Some of the documents indirectly concerned Katyn: the list of NKVD informants included the two journalists Richard Lauterbach and Edmund Stevens, who took part in the presentation of the Burdenko Commission in 1944 and then praised it. Both were also secret members of the Communist Party of the USA. In Lauterbach's case, the documents indicate that he did not consciously cooperate with the NKVD and the NKGB. Rather, he was definitely not trusted in Lubyanka. In any case, no documents were found to prove that he was committed to cooperation or even took money from the Soviet side.[10]

On the other hand, the documents on Stevens were clear, at least at first glance: he was registered as a secret collaborator of the Comintern in the 1930s.[11] However, after the Second World War he distanced himself from Stalin's regime. But after his return to Moscow three years after Stalin's death, he obviously maintained close contacts with the KGB. Stevens started to write memoirs at the end of his life, but did not complete them. However, he did not say a single word about his connections to the NKVD and later to the KGB, and his journey to Katyn is not mentioned either.[12] Stevens died in Moscow in 1992, and *The New York Times* dedicated an extensive obituary to him.[13]

But it also became known in 1995 that former OSS chief William Donovan had stood up for Stevens four decades earlier when the journalist was threatened with trial for defaming a CIA officer. Donovan got the CIA man to withdraw his case. Intelligence experts concluded from this information that Stevens had always maintained good contacts with the OSS.[14]

An even more important role than that of Stevens for the Soviet secret services was played by another participant in the journalist's trip to Katyn: the former correspondent of the London *Times*, Ralph Parker, who remained in Moscow after the war, translated Soviet literature into English and even took on supporting roles in two feature films. According to Russian sources, Parker was recruited by the Soviets on the eve of the Second World War, when *The Times* sent him to Belgrade as a correspondent. He was already working for British MI6 at the time, so he became a double agent. He was reportedly as valuable as Kim Philby as an informant for Soviet intelligence.[15] But the Soviets never fully trusted Parker. In Khrushchev's time, the KGB assumed that he had re-established contact with British services.[16]

Another participant of the correspondents' trip, sociology professor Jerome Davis, whom the American authorities suspected of being Moscow's spy because of his pro-Soviet attitude, was not found in the Venona papers. He was apparently an idealist who closed his eyes to the reality of the Soviet Union.

Termination of the investigations

Despite the problems between Moscow and Warsaw, the exhumation work on the cemeteries continued. In the second half of the 1990s, other mass graves of Poles were discovered near Kharkov and not far from the small town of Tavda in the Ural region.

The governments in Moscow and Warsaw agreed to jointly finance a memorial in Mednoye and the redesign in Katyn. At the laying of the foundation stone in Katyn, a message was read from Yeltsin who had not come to the ceremony. He explained that around 10,000 people from other nations, especially Russians, were also killed in this forest. All had become victims of totalitarianism.[17] In Poland, however, this address was understood as an attempt to negate Russia's responsibility as the legal successor of the Soviet Union by constructing a Polish-Russian community of victims.

Finally, the Polish side took over the largest part of the costs of the memorials.[18] They were completed in 2000. Contrary to expectations, the new Russian president, Vladimir Putin, did not come to Katyn for the inauguration. Representatives of the Russian leadership repeated Yeltsin's argument that there are Russians and Poles side by side, who together have become victims of totalitarianism.

Russian President Boris Yeltsin (right) and his successor Vladimir Putin.

From then on, speeches by Russian politicians no longer spoke of the guilt of the Soviet perpetrators, but of Russian victims. Poland reacted with irritation to this shift of accent, which, however, corresponded to a general mood in Russia: the accusations and self-recriminations of the Russian people must come to an end.

Putin also followed this line. He called it his goal to bring together 'the best traditions' of the Tsarist Empire and the Soviet Union. Putin had a plaque put up at the Lubyanka, still secret service headquarters, to commemorate the late KGB chairman Yuri Andropov, the inventor of psychiatric compulsory treatment for dissidents.

In addition, the general political situation further clouded relations between Moscow and Warsaw: the German–Russian project of a gas pipeline through the Baltic Sea was immediately understood by Poles as an instrument of the Kremlin's neo-imperial politics. As a reaction, the Poles followed Washington closely; in 2003, under American command, they even became an occupying power in Iraq. At the same time Putin strengthened his ties to Berlin. The clashes of interests in geopolitics also became apparent when Warsaw supported the 'Orange Revolution' in Kiev in 2004, whose goals included the political emancipation of Ukraine from Moscow.

In the same year, the Polish State Prosecutor officially asked about the status of the Moscow proceedings concerning the mass executions of 1940, but the request from Warsaw prompted the military prosecutors in Moscow to finally close the case. A spokesman explained that the acts of 1940 were to be regarded as an 'abuse of power with serious consequences' that had long since become time-barred, but 'neither in the legal nor in the state sense' as genocide does not become time-barred. In addition, Beria's assessment that among the executed Poles there had been 'spies, diversants and terrorists' had not been refuted. Moreover, only the death of 1,803 Poles from the three special camps had been officially established, and only 22 had been officially identified.

The written justification for the decision was never made public; according to the authorities, 116 of the 183 volumes on which the decision was based were still subject to the secret clauses.[19] Polish historians suspect that these files also contain information about the Polish officers recruited by the NKVD in 1940.

The Moscow human rights organisation 'Memorial' officially filed a complaint against the termination of the trial. Neither the legal qualification of the crime nor the stated number of deaths, which constitutes only 12 per cent of the victims identified so far by historians, had been justified. The authorities would also have a duty to identify deceased perpetrators. Above all, the continued use of the secret clauses was illegal.[20]

In May 2005, the Russian Orthodox metropolitan of Smolensk Kirill stated his own position in the debates over Katyn. He consecrated the foundation stone for an Orthodox church not far from the cemetery. Kirill had been bishop in Smolensk

The Metropolitan of Smolensk Kirill accused Stalin of the crimes of Katyn and prayed for the Polish victims.

since 1984; he had followed the debates about Katyn very closely and also supported the search by 'Memorial' for victims of the terror under Stalin. In his sermon and prayer in Katyn Forest, he paid special tribute to the Polish victims who had been murdered on Stalin's orders. He also recalled that all the Orthodox clergy from the Smolensk region who were murdered under Stalin had been buried in Katyn Forest. He explained how, from a theological point of view, Poles and Russians should deal with the crime: 'If the Russian people should repent of their sins, then before God, but not before other peoples. You can apologise to the others. It's a very good thing to ask forgiveness.'

After the service Kirill condemned with sharp words the fact that holiday houses and even villas were built in the immediate vicinity of the graves. He added: 'I can't imagine how to live quietly on these bones.'[21]

Political relations between Warsaw and Moscow deteriorated further in the autumn of 2005 when the national conservative party 'Law and Justice' (PiS), led by Jarosław Kaczyński, won the parliamentary elections and shortly thereafter his twin brother, Lech, won the presidential elections. Both placed the demands for apology and compensation for war crimes at the centre of their policy.

On the sixty-sixth anniversary of the Katyn massacre in April 2006, Lech Kaczyński visited the memorial. However, the fact that he chose Katyn as the destination of his first trip to Russia and did not pay his respects to his Kremlin counterpart, Vladimir Putin, as would have been the case with diplomatic traditions, was seen there as an affront. The two heads of state would never meet.

One year later, Andrzej Wajda's film *Katyn* was released in Polish cinemas. Wajda had thought about the project for many years; since his father Jakub had been one of the victims of Starobelsk, other directors let him take the lead on the subject. Wajda showed the tragedy from the perspective of the mothers, wives and daughters of the victims. He had the executions staged precisely according to the descriptions of the NKVD men involved.

President Lech Kaczyński had the world premiere celebrated as a state act: it took place in the Warsaw Opera House, attended by the entire political leadership, the Armed Forces High Command, bishops, prominent artists and diplomats. The Ministry of Defence made going to the cinema a must for all officers and soldiers. But the Poles did not succeed in bringing the film to the cinemas of Russia.

The Katyn revisionists

In view of the tense political relations, the judicial authorities of the two countries no longer cooperated. The military prosecutor in Moscow considered that the descendants had no right to a legal rehabilitation of the victims, which would only be available to the 'injured persons'. But these were dead.

In Poland, this justification was perceived as extremely cynical. Seven families of Katyn victims asked 'Memorial' for help in their dispute with the Russian justice system. The aim was to rehabilitate the victims, and a second procedure was to achieve the release of the 116 volumes of files that were still blocked. The families concerned expressly stated that they did not want to claim any material compensation. In both proceedings, which lasted several years and each went through three instances, 'Memorial' was defeated.

The decisions of the Moscow judicial authorities reflected Putin's political line: the Soviet past was increasingly glorified, Stalin was once again celebrated as a military commander who led the country to victory in the Great Patriotic War. The textbooks marginalised the crimes of the Stalin era; but they praised the Chekists, the secret services, who had protected the country from saboteurs and spies. The secret services of the Russian Federation emphasised that they saw themselves as direct heirs of Cheka, GPU, NKVD and KGB.

More and more publications on Katyn appeared that accused the German occupiers of being the perpetrators of the Katyn massacre. Most of the authors were close to the Communist Party or came from military circles. Even in academic journals, articles appeared that branded the results of historians Natalia Lebedeva and Yuri Zorya as unproven allegations or even counterfeits.[22]

The books *Katyn Detective Fiction* and *Anti-Russian Shabbiness* by the amateur historian Yuri Mukhin were a great sales success. He vehemently defended the Burdenko report in them.[23] Mukhin, a metallurgical engineer, has described many conspiracies in his books: Khrushchev murdered Stalin because the latter had planned far-reaching reforms, the Americans had never landed on the moon, Yeltsin had already died in 1996, and a double had replaced him during the last four years of his term of office. Some of his publications, including *The Secret of Jewish Racism*, have been criticised as anti-Semitic.

Mukhin claims that the NATO states have pushed the conflict over Katyn because they wanted to destroy the Soviet Union and drag Moscow's allies into their alliance. In the Second World War the Poles had been a 'fifth column' in the Soviet Union, leaving the Kremlin no choice but to fight them. The Polish government in exile was a 'Goebbels' brigade'. As proof of the German perpetrators in Katyn, he cites figures: 98.5 per cent of the victims were shot directly in the head, which was the typical method of execution used by the Germans, while the NKVD shot in the neck. However, Mukhin did not state where these figures and information came from.[24]

Katyn revisionist Yuri Mukhin justifies the crimes of Stalin in his bestsellers.

Half a dozen other books appeared with similar theses, including *Katyn – A Lie Becomes History* with a portrait of Goebbels on the cover.[25] The supporters of the version 'Katyn 1941' who propagandized the German perpetration accused Gorbachev and his closest advisor Yakovlev of systematically causing the downfall of the Soviet Union in the service of a 'bourgeois-bureaucratic counterrevolution'.[26] They alleged that the Poles wanted to obtain billions of euros in compensation and that they were extremely ungrateful: they had forgotten that the Red Army had freed them from Hitler fascism.

According to some of these publications, which have been widely echoed in the press and on the Internet, the Germans dug up dead bodies in the Smolensk cemetery and placed them in the mass graves of Katyn. They would also have put Soviet prisoners of war into Polish uniforms and then shot them. The authors of these books considered it proven that the documents of the Politburo released by Yeltsin were forgeries. They referred to different typewriter fonts as well as different hooks in signatures. As proof of the NKVD's innocence, an instruction is also cited according to which it was forbidden to 'insult and rudely deal with POWs'.[27]

But apart from the Burdenko report, Mukhin and his comrades-in-arms could not cite a single Soviet document or witness that the Polish officers were still alive when the Wehrmacht moved into the Smolensk area. However, the version that the Poles were murdered by the NKVD in 1940 was confirmed not only by former KGB generals Soprunenko and Tokarev, but even by KGB directors Shelepin and Kryuchkov in their official correspondence. Shelepin has never denied that the handwritten report for Khrushchev in 'Folder No. 1' came from him. Likewise, Kryuchkov has never distanced himself from the letter to Gorbachev written jointly with the high party official Falin and Foreign Minister Shevardnadze in which the authors confirmed the guilt of the NKVD.

Above all, the four Kremlin leaders Gorbachev, Yeltsin, Putin and Medvedev accused the NKVD of being the perpetrators. They relied on the findings of the secret services, the military prosecutors and the direction of the State Archives of the Russian Federation. The State Duma has also expressed its regret at the mass murders committed by the NKVD.

In the same way the Russian Orthodox Church had no doubt that Stalin gave the murder order, as the Smolensk metropolitan Kirill repeatedly underlined. But Mukhin and his comrades-in-arms continue to claim that the Polish government has bribed all these Soviet and Russian officials, politicians and clergymen – but they have neither documents nor witnesses.

The defenders of the 'Soviet honour' around Mukhin also attacked the Russian actors, who took over the role of NKVD henchmen in Andrzej Wajda's Katyn film, as 'traitors'.[28]

Similarly, former KGB Major Oleg Zakirov, who questioned former NKVD men in Smolensk about the murder of the Poles, became the target of attacks. Finally he emigrated to Poland at the invitation of the 'Families of Katyn'. But his struggle with the Warsaw authorities for residence and work permits lasted several years. During his unemployment Zakirov received hardly any financial support; his wife, a teacher, had to earn money as a cleaning woman.[29] In the end, he received a high Polish Order of Merit and citizenship for his contributions to solving the mass murder of Katyn.[30] However, he was unable to gain a foothold in his professional life due to a lack of support from official bodies. Bitter and impoverished, Oleg Zakirov died in 2017. In obituaries it was lamented that the Republic of Poland did not manage to give this courageous and sincere man a worthy life.

Russian nationalists also defamed historians such as Lebedeva and Zorya as 'paid influential agents' of the Poles and as propagandists of the 'Goebbels thesis'. Moreover, Lebedeva had to defend herself against a libel action by Yevgeny Jughashvili, one of Stalin's grandchildren. Because of the defilement of his grandfather's reputation, Jughashvili also demanded 9.5 million roubles (210,000 euros) from the liberal newspaper *Novaya Gazeta* and the secret service FSB. The newspaper had printed a supplement by 'Memorial' about Stalin's crimes, including the 1940 murder order, which the FSB, according to Jughashvili, forged. The action was dismissed in 2009.[31]

Crash of the president's plane near Smolensk

The legal representatives of thirteen family members of Polish victims brought an action before the European Court of Human Rights in Strasbourg against the closure of the two Moscow proceedings. The Republic of Poland joined the proceedings as a third party plaintiff. The Court asked Moscow to provide evidence by 19 March 2010 that the plaintiffs had access to the files and demanded the written justification for the closure of the proceedings.

The statement from Moscow was received in Strasbourg one day before the deadline. It said again that rehabilitation requires a previous sentence on the basis of the penal code, but that was not the case. The death of the victims by shooting had also never been officially established. The justification for the closure of the proceedings must remain secret, since it is based on secret documents. Moreover, the crime has become time-barred.[32]

Despite this evasive decision, a breakthrough in the controversy seemed to be imminent. On 7 April 2010, Polish Prime Minister Donald Tusk and his Russian counterpart, Vladimir Putin, who had transferred his post as head of state to his former right-hand man Dmitry Medvedev, met on the occasion of the 70th anniversary of the massacre at the Katyn Memorial. On the Vistula, Tusk's journey had been preceded by a fierce political controversy. President Lech Kaczyński claimed to lead the Polish delegation. Tusk's followers argued that in this case the Moscow leadership would not participate in the celebration.

The dispute could not be resolved. Kaczyński decided to fly to Katyn three days after Tusk at the head of the military leadership and the delegation of the 'Families of Katyn'.

Tusk was accompanied by Lech Wałęsa, Andrzej Wajda and former prime minister Tadeusz Mazowiecki. Five days before their trip to Katyn, a Moscow television channel had broadcast Wajda's film for the first time; it was Good Friday. However, the programme was only available in Moscow.

It was the first time a Russian head of government had been to Katyn. Tusk included in his speech the memory of the Soviet citizens also murdered in Katyn. But Putin generally spoke of victims of a 'totalitarian regime'; Russian Cossacks, officers of the Tsar's army, orthodox priests, professors and simple peasants also lie in Katyn. He added: 'For decades, attempts were made to conceal the truth about the executions of Katyn with cynical lies, but it would be just as much a lie to blame the Russian people for it.'[33]

Afterwards, both heads of government laid the foundation stone for a Russian Orthodox church. Putin's speech, however, met with criticism in Poland because it contained neither an admission of the guilt of the then Moscow leadership nor a request for forgiveness. A headline in the influential tabloid *Fakt* read: 'New lies of Prime Minister Putin.'[34]

Three days later, on 10 April, the Polish president's plane crashed into a wood on its approach to Smolensk in dense fog. All ninety-six people on board died, including Lech Kaczyński and his wife, three vice-presidents of parliament, the five highest Polish generals, three vice ministers and eighteen members of parliament. Among the dead were children and grandchildren of officers murdered in Katyn and the 90-year-old Ryszard Kaczorowski, the last president of the Polish government in exile in London.

The shock of the plane crash led to a wave of sympathy in Russia. The state television broadcast Wajda's film during prime time, so millions of Russian citizens learned about the real course of events for the first time. Numerous newspapers printed articles about Katyn. Russian President Medvedev flew to Krakow for the funeral of Lech Kaczyński. In his short speech he called Katyn the 'criminal work of Stalin'. Patriarch Kirill also left no doubt about this. The new head of the Russian Orthodox Church, who had previously been a Metropolitan of Smolensk, travelled to the crash site and prayed for the victims. He called Katyn 'the site of a massacre committed on Stalin's orders against a total of 22,000 Poles'.[35]

A month after the death of his Polish counterpart, whom he had never met, Medvedev had sixty-seven volumes on the 1940 mass murders handed over to Warsaw, but they did not contain any significant new information. Moreover, none of the documents classified as secret was among the released papers. The State archives in Moscow also posted Beria's murder warrant and five other basic documents on the Internet. Within just one week, they were clicked on more than two million times.

On 26 November 2010, the State Duma adopted a declaration 'On the tragedy of Katyn and its victims', which continued the Kremlin's line in the Katyn case describing a community of Polish and Russian totalitarian victims:

> The massive extermination of Polish citizens on USSR territory was an arbitrary act of a totalitarian state that has also subjected hundreds of thousands of Soviet citizens to reprisals on the basis of their political or religious beliefs, according to social and other criteria.

The Duma declared its 'deep condolences' to all members of the families of the victims and expressed the hope that common remembrance would contribute to reconciliation between the two peoples as well as the memory of the 'Red Army fighters who gave their lives for the liberation of Poland from Hitler fascism'. In Poland, the resolution was largely seen as a sign of good will, but many commentators were again irritated by the lack of any commitment to Russia's obligations as the legal successor of the Soviet Union in dealing with the crime.

However, the cautious rapprochement between Warsaw and Moscow broke off abruptly when the Russian Commission of Investigation into the Smolensk air crash presented its first interim report in January 2011. It blamed only the pilots and an allegedly drunken Polish Air Force general who forced them to land in the thick fog. The report completely omitted the serious mistakes made by air traffic controllers in Smolensk and the confusion of commands on the Russian side. Moreover, the Russian officers involved were not allowed to be questioned by Polish investigators.

The new Polish President Bronisław Komorowski and Kremlin Chief Dmitry Medvedev tried to give new impetus to the dialogue at their meeting in Katyn on the first anniversary of the air disaster. The two presidents were supported by Patriarch Kirill I, who travelled to Poland in 2012 as the first head of the Russian Orthodox Church. In his sermons and speeches he emphasised that reconciliation between Russians and Poles was particularly important to him. He also urged that the victims of Stalin's system should not be divided into national categories. Countless Russian Orthodox Christians have also become victims, and Poles and Russians should remember them together: 'Nothing unites more than common suffering when it is shared.'[36]

In 2012, the European Court of Human Rights announced its decision on the complaints of the victims' descendants: it stated that it could not rule retroactively on the events of 1940, since Russia did not accede to the Human Rights Convention until 1998. However, the military court in Moscow deliberately kept the circumstances of the massacre secret, which should be seen as a 'lack of humanity' towards the relatives. Moreover, the justification for the closure of the Moscow proceedings should not have been kept secret. The Russian media interpreted the verdict as a victory for Moscow: the court had not held Russia responsible for Stalin's crimes.

The lawyers of the Polish families lodged an appeal against the ruling from Strasbourg because they wanted to force the Moscow proceedings to be reopened – and failed. The Grand Chamber of the European Court of Human Rights even fell short in the first ruling in its final judgement in 2013: it could not detect any 'inhumane treatment' of the relatives by the Russian authorities. However, they were reprimanded because they had not sent the requested files to Strasbourg. The verdict had no consequences for Moscow. Russian politicians were highly satisfied – the case was closed for Moscow. Shortly afterwards, the Katyn documents, including Beria's draft of the assassination order, were deleted from the website of the Presidential Archives in Moscow.

Katyn remained an unpunished crime.

Epilogue

It is a paradox: the notorious liar and manipulator Joseph Goebbels once told the truth – in the highly controversial case of Katyn. This is the result of research by Polish and Russian historians who evaluated all relevant documents and testimonies. However, the first figures from the German Katyn report of 1943 had to be corrected, and other places of execution were added. And, of course, there were no 'Jewish perpetrators', as Goebbels' propaganda claimed. On the contrary: hundreds of representatives of the Jewish intelligentsia of Poland were among the victims.

The fact that Goebbels was so active in the Katyn case is the main argument for the Katyn revisionists, who have dominated the debate in Russia in recent years, with their version that the Germans were the perpetrators. As evidence for their thesis they cite the investigations of the NKVD on Katyn, especially the report of the Burdenko Commission controlled by the NKVD – and make a cardinal error, because it is in the nature of things that the NKVD came to the conclusion that it was free of any guilt, everything else would have been a self-incrimination. They also deny that the NKVD was an instrument of a totalitarian regime, in which the lie was one of the instruments of rulership.

Above all, the Katyn revisionists cannot conclusively answer a number of fundamental questions:

- Why did the Soviet leadership never inform the Polish government in exile about the camps 1-ON, 2-ON and 3-ON for the captured Poles near Smolensk, which allegedly existed until the summer of 1941?
- Why is there no documentation about these camps?
- Why have the letters to the prisoners since March 1940 been sent back to the senders as 'undeliverable'?
- How could the Germans have buried the murdered Polish POWs of the Ostashkov camp in Mednoye, if this village was controlled by the Wehrmacht only for a few hours of one day, namely on 20 October 1941, before the Red Army recaptured it?
- Why did Stalin block an investigation of the mass graves by the International Committee of the Red Cross in 1943, when the Germans were supposedly the perpetrators?

- Why was Katyn not mentioned in any of the books on German war crimes published in the Soviet Union after Stalin's death, not even in the *Great Soviet Encyclopaedia*?
- Why is there no Soviet novel and no feature film about Katyn, while the mass murders committed by Germans in other places became the subject of literature and cinema?
- Why is there not a single document proving German guilt in the archival material of the German Ministry of Propaganda, the SS task forces and the Army Group Centre, which fell into the hands of the Soviets in 1945 and are still in Moscow today?
- Why did Soviet prosecutor Rudenko in Nuremberg not file a formal protest against Katyn's removal from the list of German crimes?
- Why were the Soviet materials about Katyn kept secret, even though they allegedly contained evidence of German guilt?

Many individual questions have remained unanswered. The most important perhaps is: what is the reason for maintaining secret clauses for dozens of files from Russian archives? How can documents about a crime of 1940, as claimed, endanger Russia's security today? Instead of a reply, Moscow refers to London, where the files on the death of General Władysław Sikorski, the head of the Polish government in exile, in a plane crash off Gibraltar are also blocked.

But there are certainly files on his death in Moscow. It is now known that the Kremlin had its informants in Sikorski's cabinet. Did the legendary double agent Kim Philby, who was also in Gibraltar on that very day, even play a role? What did Philby report to Moscow about the internal analyses of the British and the Americans about Katyn, which he undoubtedly got to read?

Other deaths in connection with Katyn remained unsolved: did the Russian railway fitter Ivan Krivozertsev, witness to the transport of the Poles into Katyn Forest, hang himself in a southern English village or was his suicide faked by communist agents? What happened to the peasant Parfen Kiselev, who disappeared without a trace after his appearance before the Burdenko Commission? And the other residents of Katyn who were supposedly resettled?

Was the serious traffic accident of the Romanian medical examiner Alexandru Birkle shortly after his appearance before the Madden Committee just an unfortunate coincidence or was it a disguised assassination attempt? Had the heart attacks that his two colleagues, the Finn Arno Saxén and the Croatian Eduard Milosevich, had died of at the same time perhaps been caused by poisoning? And was the death of the daughter of their Danish colleague Helge Tramsen in Warsaw really an accident? Who ordered the assassination of Warsaw Prelate Stefan Niedzielak a few months before the great political turn of 1989?

How were forensics experts Marko Markov and František Hájek persuaded to distance themselves from the report of the International Medical Commission?

How exactly did Moscow's secret services deal with Smolensk Mayor Boris Menshagin, who did not let himself be broken, and with his deputy Boris Bazilevsky, who did not withstand the pressure? The files on the show trial in Leningrad, in which the German soldier Arno Dürre was accused of participating in the Katyn massacre, also await their examination.

The files on the intimidation and press campaigns controlled by Moscow have not yet been evaluated, as have the Gestapo files and the archive materials of the German Hitler opponents.

If these are all secondary aspects, then one main question still remains open for the Poles: where are the graves of the other victims of the 1940 executions? The total number of victims buried in Katyn, Mednoye and Pyatikhatki was 14,562, according to KGB leader Shelepin's letter to party leader Khrushchev. Shelepin names 7,305 other Poles who were shot at the time. In his letter to the Politburo, Beria even suggested the shooting of 25,700 Poles. Thus, nothing concrete is known about the places of execution, nor about the graves of several thousand Poles.

Polish historians have only found out that many of them were politicians, lawyers and scientists. Some were apparently buried in Bykovnia near Kiev, where according to Ukrainian historians more than 100,000 victims of terror under Lenin and Stalin were buried in mass graves. Others could lie in the Kuropaty forest near the Belarusian capital Minsk. But unlike the Ukrainian authorities, who are very cooperative, the Belarusian leadership has so far blocked the investigations.

Cooperation between Polish and Russian state institutions has also been halted. In 2015 Putin signed a law that rulings of international courts are no longer binding on Russia; it meant a fundamental break with Moscow's previous policy since the collapse of the Soviet Union. The Russian Ministry of Justice decreed that the human rights organisation 'Memorial' is covered by the Law on Foreign Agents, which affects all organisations receiving financial support from abroad. 'Memorial' has created the largest database of victims of Stalinism. Also in 2015, on the basis of this law, a public prosecutor, accompanied by police officers, stopped the screening of Wajda's film *Katyn* at the headquarters of 'Memorial' in St Petersburg. In the same year the Russian Post issued a stamp in honor of Stalinist Attorney General Rudenko, who played a central role in the Katyn manipulations and later had dissidents persecuted.

As long as the last graves are not known, as long as monuments are not erected for the last of the victims, the Katyn case will not be closed.

Endnotes

Chapter 1

1. *Polskie Dokumenty Dyplomatyczne 1939*. Wrzesień–grudzień. Ed. PISM. Warsaw 2007, p. 8.
2. *Zbrodnia katyńska. Polskie śledztwo*. Ed. Polska Fundacja Katyńska. Warsaw 2005, p. 102.
3. *Białe plamy-czarne plamy: sprawy trudne w polsko-rosyjskich stosunkach 1918–2008*. Ed. A. D. Rotfeld / A. V. Torkunow. Warsaw 2010, p. 447.
4. *Deutsche Politik in Polen 1939–1945*. Diensttagebuch von Generalgouverneur Hans Frank. Opladen 1980, p. 71.
5. *Z ziemi sowieckiej – z domu niewoli. Relacje, raporty, sprawozdania z londyńskiego archiwum prof. Stanisława Kota*. Warsaw 1995, p. 33.
6. Wincenty Urban: *Droga krzyżowa Archidiecezji Lwowskiej w latach II wojny światowej 1939–1945*. Wrocław 1983.
7. *Z ziemi sowieckiej*, p. 35.
8. *Pamięć i Sprawiedliwość*, 1.2009, pp. 50–55.
9. *Zeszyty Katyńskie*, 1(1990), p. 126.
10. *Pamięć i Sprawiedliwość*, pp. 47–70.
11. *Z ziemi sowieckiej*, p. 30.
12. Wanja W. Ronge: *Und dann mussten wir raus / I wtedy nas wywieźli. Wanderungen durch das Gedächtnis*. Berlin 2000, p. 50.
13. *Z ziemi sowieckiej*, p. 37.
14. *Z ziemi sowieckiej*, p. 34.
15. *Katyn. Despatches of Sir Owen O'Malley to the British Government*. Introd. L. FitzGibbon. London 1972, p. 8.

Chapter 2

1. *Katyn. Plenniki neobyavlennoy voiny*. Moscow 1999, p. 15.
2. *Katyn. Plenniki*, p. 158, 162, 168.
3. *Vestnik Katynskogo Memoriala*, 12(2012), p. 58.
4. *Zeszyty Katyńskie*, 12(2000), p. 30.
5. *Katyń. Dokumenty zbrodni*. Vol. 2. Ed. A. Gieysztor / R. Pichoja. Warsaw 1998, pp. 413–415.

6. Natalia Lebedeva: *Katyn – Prestuplenie protiv chelovechestva.* Moscow 1994, pp. 81–84, 89.
7. *Katyń 1940. Walka o prawdę.* Ed. W. Lis. Toruń 2012, p. 380.
8. *Katyń. Dokumenty*, vol. 1, p. 401.
9. *Pamiętniki znalezione w Katyniu.* Ed. Spotkania. Paris 1989, p. 41.
10. *Katyn. Plenniki*, p. 19.
11. Bronisław Młynarski: *W niewoli sowieckiej.* London 1974, p. 155.
12. *Katyn 1940–2000.* Dokumenty. Ed. N. I. Lebedeva. Moscow 2001, p. 30.
13. *Katyn. Plenniki*, p. 16, 169.
14. *Katyń. Dokumenty*, vol. 1. p. 435–437.
15. *Pamiętniki*, p. 41.
16. Lebedeva: *Katyn*, p. 84.
17. *Pamiętniki*, pp. 118, 178.
18. Lebedeva: *Katyn*, pp. 89–90, 94.
19. *Katynskaya drama Kozelsk, Starobelsk, Ostashkov. Sudba internirovannykh polskikh voyennosluzhashchikh.* Moscow 1991, pp. 139–140.
20. Allen Weinstein / Alexander Vassiliev: *The Haunted Wood. Soviet Espionage in America – the Stalin Era.* New York 1999, pp. 111–114.
21. Sluzhba vneshnej razvedki Rossiyskoy Federatsii – Zarubin Vassili Mikhailovich http://svr.gov.ru/history/zar.htm
22. Stanisław Swianiewicz: *W cieniu Katynia.* Warsaw 1990, p. 99.
23. Janusz Zawodny: *Katyń.* Paris 1989, pp. 116–117.
24. Zawodny, pp. 110–111.
25. Józef Czapski: *Wspomnienia starobielskie.* Warsaw 1990. p. 42.
26. *Katyn. Plenniki*, p. 26.
27. Lebedeva: Katyn, p. 91.
28. *Katyn. Plenniki*, p. 31.
29. Lebedeva: *Katyn*, p. 92.
30. *Katyń. Dokumenty*, vol. 1, p. 360.
31. *Katynskaya drama*, pp. 139–144.
32. *Katynskaya drama*, pp. 22–23.
33. Nikita Petrov: *Palachi. Oni vypolnyali zakazy Stalina.* Moscow 2011, pp. 23, 69, 95.
34. *Katyn 1940–2000*, p. 21.

Chapter 3
1. *Katynskaya drama*, p. 28.
2. *Katyn 1940–2000*, pp. 32–39.
3. *The Katyn Forest Massacre.* US Government Printing Office. Washington 1952, vol. IV, p. 607.
4. Swianiewicz, pp. 108–111.
5. *Amtliches Material zum Massenmord von Katyn.* Berlin 1943, p. 24.

6. Jędrzej Tucholski: *Kozielsk, Ostaszków, Starobielsk: lista ofiar.* Warsaw 1991, p. 40.
7. *Katynskaya drama*, p. 31.
8. Charków – Katyń – Twer – Bykownia. W 70. *Rocznicę zbrodni katyńskiej.* Toruń 2011, pp. 105–106.
9. *Novaya Polsha*, 1.2007, pp. 55–59.
10. *Novaya Polsha*, 4.2006, p. 50.
11. *Katyń. Dokumenty*, vol. 2., pp. 475, 482, 488, 492.
12. Petrov: *Palachi*, p. 82.
13. *Katyn 1940–2000*, pp. 35–36.
14. *Zeszyty Katyńskie*, 3.1994, pp. 35–37.
15. Petrov, *Palachi*, p. 196.
16. *Katyń. Dokumenty*, vol. 2, pp. 434–459.
17. *Novaya Polsha*, 1.2005, p. 50.
18. Oleg Zakirov: *Obcy element. Dramatyczne losy oficera KGB w walce o wyjaśnienie zbrodni katyńskiej.* Poznań 2010, p. 242.
19. *Moskovskie Novosti*, 17 June 1990, p. 3.
20. *Katyn 1940–2000*, p. 31.
21. Zawodny, p. 109.
22. *East European Jewish Affairs*, 23/1 (1993), pp. 49–55.
23. Petrov, *Palachi*, pp. 244–283.
24. *Novaya Polsha*, 4.2006, p. 50.
25. *Vestnik Katynskogo Memoriala*, 10(2010), pp. 10–11.
26. Sławomir Cenkiewicz: *Długie ramię Moskwy. Wywiad wojskowy Polski Ludowej 1943–1991.* Poznań 2011, p. 41.
27. *Katynskaya drama*, p. 35.
28. Józef Mackiewicz: *Katyń. Zbrodnia bez sądu i kary.* Warsaw 199., p. 51.
29. *Przegląd Historyczno-Wojskowy*, 3.2011, pp. 57–81.

Chapter 4

1. *Katyn 1940–2000*, p. 207.
2. Ivan Maisky: *Vospominaniya sovietskogo diplomata.* Moscow 1971, pp. 485–488.
3. Witold Wasilewski: *Ludobójstwo. Kłamstwo i walka o prawdę. Sprawa Katynia 1940–2014.* Łomianki 2014, pp. 28–29.
4. Evan McGilvory: *A Military Government in Exile. The Polish Government-in-Exile 1939–1945.* Solihull 2010, pp. 85–90.
5. Władysław Anders: *Bez ostatniego rozdziału. Wspomnienia z lat 1939–1946.* London 1949, pp. 88.
6. Anders, p. 138.
7. *Katyn 1940–2000*, p. 209.
8. *The Katyn Forest Massacre*, vol. IV, p. 942.
9. Józef Czapski: *Wspomnienia starobielskie.* Paris 1987, p. 19.

10. *Katynskaya drama*, pp. 31–32.

11. Sławomir Cenckiewicz: *Długie ramię Moskwy. Wywiad wojskowy Polski Ludowej 1943–1991*. Poznań 2011, pp. 41–46.

12. *Przegląd Historyczno-Wojskowy*, 3.2011, pp. 70–81.

13. Anders, p. 87.

14. Sławomir Koper: *Polskie pikiełko. Obrazy z życia elit emigracyjnych 1939–1945*. Warsaw 2012, p. 319.

15. Józef Czapski: *Na nieludzkiej ziemi*. Warsaw 1990, p. 98.

16. Anders, pp. 110–111.

17. *The Katyn Forest Massacre*, vol. VII, pp. 2042, 2073.

18. Stanislaw Kot: *Listy z Rosji do Gen. Sikorskiego*. London 1955, pp. 498–499.

19. *The Katyn Forest Massacre*, vol. VI, p. 1717.

20. Stanisław Kot: *Rozmowy z Kremlem*. London 1959, pp. 118–121.

21. Kot, *Rozmowy*, pp. 126–129.

22. Carer International Corp. 1973 https://www.youtube.com/watch?v=JW20VO8xkr4 4:05–4:23

23. Kot, *Rozmowy*, pp. 153–157.

24. Kot, *Rozmowy*, pp. 160, 162.

25. Anders, pp. 128–133.

26. Czapski, *Na nieludzkiej*, p. 159.

27. Eugenia Maresch: *Katyń 1940*. Warsaw 2012, pp. 16–17, 29.

28. *The Katyn Forest Massacre*, vol. VII, pp. 2043–2045, 2060, 2065.

29. The Ambassador in the Soviet Union (Standley) to the Secretary of State, 28 May 1942// Foreign Relations of the United States: Diplomatic Papers, 1942, Europe, Volume III, p. 148 https://history.state.gov/historicaldocuments/frus1942v03/d132

30. The Secretary of Embassy in Charge at Moscow (Thompson) to the Secretary of State, 4 February 1942 // Foreign Relations of the United States: Diplomatic Papers, 1942, Europe, Volume III, p. 106 https://history.state.gov/historicaldocuments/frus1942v03/d101

31. Mackiewicz, p. 66.

32. Anders, p. 163.

33. Kot, *Rozmowy*, p. 23.

34. Czapski, *Na nieludzkiej*, pp. 239–242.

35. Eleanor Roosevelt: *This I Remember*. New York 1949, p. 251.

36. Note from Eleanor Roosevelt to Sumner Welles Enclosing Letters from Individuals, Including Helena Sikorska, Regarding Welfare and Whereabouts of Polish Officers, 08/07/1942, http://research.archives.gov/description/6850465

37. *The Katyn Forest Massacre*, vol. VII, p. 2043.

38. *Zbrodnia katyńska*, p. IV.

39. *Katynskaya drama*, pp. 37–40.

40. *The Katyn Forest Massacre*, vol. III, pp. 416–417.

41. William H. Standley/ Arthur A. Ageton: *Admiral Ambassador to Russia*. Chicago 1955, p. 402.
42. Svetlana Alliluyeva: *Odin god docheri Stalina*. New York 1969, p. 77.

Chapter 5

 1. *The Nuremberg Trials Collection*, Vol. 17, 168th Day. Washington 1947–1949, p. 281.
 2. Maresch, p. 95.
 3. *Zbrodnia katyńska*, pp. 289–290.
 4. *Amtliches Material*, p. 26.
 5. Jerzy A. Wlazło: *Chłopak z Katynia*. Warsaw 2018, p. 18.
 6. *Vestnik Katynskogo Memoriala*, 10(2010), p. 33.
 7. Rudolf-Christoph Frhr. v. Gersdorff: *Soldat im Untergang*. Frankfurt/M. 1977, pp. 103, 140.
 8. Fabian v. Schlabrendorff: *Offiziere gegen Hitler*. Zürich 1951, pp. 52–54.
 9. Bodo Scheurig: *Henning von Tresckow. Eine Biographie*. Frankfurt/M. 1980, p. 114.
10. *Hitlers militärische Elite*. Ed. G. R. Ueberschär. Darmstadt 1998, pp. 259–260.
11. Schlabrendorff, *Offiziere*, p. 129.
12. Gersdorff, pp. 67, 71.
13. *NS-Verbrechen und der militärische Widerstand gegen Hitler*. Ed. G. R. Ueberschär. Darmstadt 2000, p. 193.
14. Scheurig, p. 140.
15. *NS-Verbrechen*, p. 84.
16. Gersdorff, pp. 119–121.
17. Gersdorff, p. 127.
18. Schlabrendorff, p. 116.
19. Schlabrendorff, pp. 116–124.
20. Gersdorff, p. 129.
21. Gersdorff, pp. 130–133, 140.
22. *Amtliches Material*, pp. 18, 21, 32–33, 92–94.
23. *Amtliches Material*, pp. 35–36.
24. Reinhart von Eichborn: *Der Fall Katyn. Zusammenfassende Darstellung*. 1952, pp. 22–23 (not published).
25. *Amtliches Material*, pp. 16, 88–92.
26. *Amtliches Material*, pp. 21–22, 26.
27. *Vestnik Katynskogo Memoriala*, 10(2010), pp. 32–39.
28. *Vestnik Katynskogo Memoriala*, 3(2004), pp. 51–94.
29. Schlabrendorff, pp. 119–120.
30. Boris Menshagin: *Vospominaniya: Smolensk ... Katyn ... Vladimirskaya tiurma*. Paris 1988, p. 130.
31. *Vestnik Katynskogo Memoriala*, 10(2010), pp. 31–38.
32. *Novy Zhurnal* [New York], 104(1971), p. 276.

33. *Amtliches Material*, pp. 38–47.

34. Tucholski, pp. 31–32, 35.

Chapter 6

1. *The Katyn Forest Massacre*, vol. V, pp. 1247–1249.

2. *Vierteljahrshefte für Zeitgeschichte*, 3(1982), p. 470.

3. *Deutsche Politik*, p. 156.

4. *Die Tagebücher von Joseph Goebbels*. Ed. E. Fröhlich. II, vol. 8. Munich 1993, p. 115.

5. Yuliya Buyanova: *Katynskoe delo: informatsionnaya borba SSSR i natsitskoy Germanii (1943–1945 gg.)*. Sankt-Peterburg 2011, p. 63.

6. *The Katyn Forest Massacre*, vol. VII, p. 2069.

7. *Raporty z ziem wcielonych do III Rzeszy (1942–1944)*. Ed. Z. Mazur, A. Pietrowicz, M. Rutkowska. Poznan 2004, p. 105.

8. *The Diaries of Sir Alexander Cadogan 1938–1945*. Ed. D. Dilks. London 1971, p. 521.

9. Winston Churchill: *The Second World War*. Vol. IV. London 1950, p. 759.

10. Material Relating to the Discovery of the Bodies of Polish Officers Near Smolensk and Polish–Soviet Relations, 04/1943, images 4–5 http://research.archives.gov/description/6850460

11. *Die Tagebücher*, II, vol. 8, p. 116.

12. *Polen – Juden – Schweizer*. Ed. P. Stauffer. Zürich 2004, pp. 187–191.

13. Rohan D'Olier Butler: *The Katyn Massacre and the Reactions in the Foreign Office. Memorandum by the Historical Adviser*. London 1973, p. 9.

14. *The Katyn Forest Massacre*, vol. IV, p. 678.

15. Report on alleged killing of 10,000 Polish officers by Russians in Smolensk area. OWI radio treatment, 04/19/1943 http://research.archives.gov/description/6851173

16. *The Katyn Forest Massacre*, vol. VII, pp. 1981, 1987–1988.

17. Outgoing Message No. 1095 from Military Intelligence Service to Military Attaché Cairo Indicating Gen. Strong's Interest in a Report about Katyn Affair only if German Complicity is Shown, 05/28/1943 http://research.archives.gov/description/6850508

18. Incoming Message No. 46 from Cairo to War and Military Intelligence Division (MILID) Concerning the Announcement in the German Radio about Polish Officers Found in Mass Graves Near Smolensk, 04/19/1943 http://research.archives.gov/description/6850507

19. George Sanford: *Katyn and the Soviet Massacre of 1940. Truth, justice and memory*. London / New York 2005, p. 169.

20. *Die Tagebücher*, Part II, vol. 8, p. 119.

21. *Berliner Börsenzeitung*, 15 April 1943; *Deutsche Allgemeine Zeitung*, 16 April 1943.

22. *Völkischer Beobachter*, 15/17 April 1943.

23. *Die Tagebücher*, II, vol. 8, p. 124.

24. *Perepiska Predsedatelya Sovieta Ministrov SSSR s prezidentami SShA i Premier-Ministrami Velikobritanii vo vremya Velikoi Otechestvennoi Voiny.* Izd. MID RF. Moscow 2005, p. 114.

25. Churchill, vol. IV, p. 761.

26. Sanford, p. 170.

27. *The Katyn Forest Massacre*, vol. IV, pp. 1223–1225.

28. *The Katyn Forest Massacre*, vol. VII, p. 2063.

29. Władysław Anders: *Zbrodnia katyńska w świetle dokumentów.* London 1950, pp. 91–92.

30. *The Katyn Forest Massacre*, vol. VII, p. 2064.

31. *The Katyn Forest Massacre*, vol. VII, p. 2067.

32. *Die Tagebücher*, II, vol. 8, pp. 174–175.

33. *Völkischer Beobachter*, 18 April 1943, p. 1.

34. *Kladderadatsch*, 23 May 1943, p. 6.

35. Jan K. Zawodny: *Death in the Forest. The Story of the Katyn Forest Massacre.* Notre Dame/Indiana 1972, pp. 38–39.

36. Message to President Franklin D. Roosevelt from Winston Churchill, 04/25/1943 http://research.archives.gov/description/6851134

37. Letter to President Franklin D. Roosevelt from Sumner Welles, 05/01/1943, images 4–5

38. Paul Stauffer, Die Schweiz und Katyn. Ed. Paul Stauffer *Polen – Juden – Schweizer.* Zurich 2004, pp. 188, 191.

39. Butler, p. 9.

40. *The Katyn Forest Massacre*, vol. VII, p. 2067.

41. Dennis Dunn: *Caught between Roosevelt and Stalin. America's Ambassadors to Moscow.* Lexington 1998, p. 311.

Chapter 7

1. *The Katyn Forest Massacre*, vol. V, p. 1499.

2. Ferdynand Goetel: Czasy wojny. Krakow 2005, pp. 99–111.

3. Kazimierz Skarżyński: *Katyń. Raport Polskiego Czerwonego Krzyża. Wyd. Wojciech Ziembiński.* Warsaw 1989, p. 17.

4. *Tygodnik Powszechny*, 22 September 2007, p. 13.

5. Skarżyński, pp. 30, 47.

6. Goetel, p. 104.

7. *Zbrodnia katyńska*, p. 208.

8. Czesław Madajczyk: *Dramat katyński.* Warsaw 1989, pp. 160–161.

9. *Tygodnik*, p. 13.

10. Skarżyński, p. 17.

11. *The Katyn Forest Massacre*, vol. III, p. 410

12. *Vierteljahrshefte für Zeitgeschichte*, 3(1982), p. 486.

13. Report – Katyn Forest Murders, 06/21/1948, images 142–145 http://research.archives.gov/description/6256905; Dossier on Katyn Forest Murders, 1948, images 18–19 http://research.archives.gov/description/6850550

14. *Zbrodnia katyńska*, pp. 307–309.
15. Dossier on Katyn Forest Murders, 1948, image 19 http://research.archives.gov/description/6850550
16. Jarosław Pałka: *General Stefan Mossor (1896–1957). Biografia wojskowa.* Warsaw 2008, pp. 155–159.
17. *Ostdeutscher Beobachter*, 20 April 1943, p. 3.
18. *Raporty*, pp. 105–106.
19. *Zeszyty Katyńskie*, 6(1996), p. 107.
20. *Die Tagebücher*, II, vol. 8, p. 124.
21. *Zeszyty Katyńskie*, 5(1995), pp. 25–26.
22. *The Katyn Forest Massacre*, vol. IV, p. 876.
23. *Goniec Codzienny*, 3 June 1943, p. 3.
24. Persönlicher Stab Reichsführer SS // Bundesarchiv, NS 19/1762, pp. 3, 5.
25. Leon Kozłowski: *Moje przeżycia.* Warsaw 2001.
26. Kozłowski, pp. 28–30, 42–43, 123–124, 151–157.
27. *Nowy Kurjer Warszawski*, 23 December 1941, p. 1.
28. *Raporty*, p. 105.
29. *Zeszyty Katyńskie*, 1(1990), p. 88.
30. *Raporty*, pp. 165, 432.
31. Madajczyk, pp. 160–161.
32. Skarżyński, pp. 15–17.
33. *Tygodnik Powszechny*, 13 January 2009, p. 8.
34. *The Katyn Forest Massacre*, vol. VI, p. 1627.
35. *The Katyn Forest Massacre*, vol. III, p. 399
36. Skarżyński, pp. 38–44.
37. Eugeniusz Cesary Król: *Polska i Polacy w propagandzie narodowego socjalizmu w Niemczech 1919–1945*, Warsaw 2006, p. 436.
38. *Die Tagebücher*, II, vol. 8, p. 190.
39. *Deutsche Politik*, p. 152.
40. *Vierteljahrshefte für Zeitgeschichte*, 3(1982), pp. 497–499.
41. *Zeszyty Katyńskie*, 1(1990), p. 113.
42. *The Daily Mirror*, 25 May 1943, p. 4.
43. *Raporty*, pp. 174–175.
44. Gersdorff, p. 142.

Chapter 8

1. Henri de Montfort: *Le Massacre de Katyn. Crime russe ou crime allemand?* Paris 1966, pp. 62–64.
2. *The Katyn Forest Massacre*, vol. V, pp. 1421–1422.
3. *Katyń. Una verità storica negata. La perizia di V. M. Palmieri.* Ed. Luigia Melillo. Napoli 2009, p. 20.
4. *The Katyn Forest Massacre*, vol. V, p. 1422.

5. *Zbrodnia katyńska*, p. 205.
6. *Amtliches Material*, p. 58–59.
7. *Katyn et la Suisse. Experts et expertises médicales dans les crises humanitaires.* Ed. D. Debons et al. Geneva 2009, p. 183.
8. Gersdorff, p. 142.
9. *Amtliches Material*, pp. 114–117.
10. *The Katyn Forest Massacre*, vol. V, p. 1599.
11. *Katyn et la Suisse*, pp. 183–185.
12. Anna E. Jessen: *Czaszka z Katynia. Opowieść o zbrodni.* Luboń 2019, p. 10.
13. *Schweizer Ärztezeitung*, 47.2003, p. 2511.
14. Katyń. Una verità, pp. 33–41.
15. *The Katyn Forest Massacre*, vol. V, p. 1409, 1614.
16. *Evropa mezi Nemeckem a Ruskem. Sborník prací k sedmdesátinám Jaroslava Valenty.* Prague 2000, pp. 509–514.
17. De massamoord bij Katyn, Nederlandsche Omroep, 28 May 1943 http://www.npogeschiedenis.nl/speler.WO_VPRO_046881.html
18. *Nieuwsblad van het Noorden*, 8 May 1943, p. 1.
19. Joris Dedeurwaarder: *Professor Speleers – een biografie.* Antwerpen 2002, p. 761.
20. *Polonia-Finlandia*, 3.2008, pp. 5–8.
21. Skarżyński, pp. 31, 47.
22. *The Katyn Forest Massacre*, vol. V, pp. 1562, 1567.
23. *Zeszyty Katyńskie*, 7(1997), pp. 105–106.
24. *The Katyn Forest Massacre*, vol. V, pp. 1465, 1564–1567.
25. Claudia Weber: *Krieg der Täter. Die Massenerschießungen von Katyń.* Hamburg 2015, p. 144.
26. E. Giménez Caballero: *La matanza de Katyn: visión sobre Rusia.* Madrid 1943, p. 39.
27. Giménez Caballero, pp. 7–19, 24, 31–36.
28. *Filip De Pilleeyn Studies*, (2007), p. 157.
29. Pierre Hubermont: *Khatyn ce n'est pas Katyn*, pp. 27, 38–43 (unpublished, Soma-Ceges/Brussels).
30. Pierre Hubermont: *J'étais à Katyn. Témoignage oculaire.* Brussels1943, p. 6.
31. *Le Matin*, 22 April 1943, p. 1; 5 June 1943, p. 1.
32. Fernand de Brinon: *France – Allemagne 1918–1934.* Paris 1934, pp. 217, 249.
33. *Je suis partout*, 30 April 1943, p. 1.
34. Fernand De Brinon visit to the SS Charlemagne Division, 1943 https://www.youtube.com/watch?v=QnkI6QrpDIo
35. *Je suis partout*, 9 July 1943, pp. 1–9.
36. *Le Petit Parisien*, 6 July 1943, p. 1.
37. *Die Tagebücher*, Part II, vol. 8, p. 458.
38. Stephen Sicari: *Pound's Epic Ambition: Dante and the Modern World.* New York 1991, p. 106.

39. *Inventario dell'archivio storico 1934–1970*. Ed. Benzoni / A. Ostinelli / S. Pizzettis. Rome 2007, p. 127.

40. Ezra Pound: *The Cantos*. New York 1981, LXXVII/42.

41. J. J. Wilhelm: *Ezra Pound: The Tragic Years, 1925–1972*, Pennsylvania, 1994, p. 231.

42. Ezra Pound, Soberly, in: *Radio Speeches of World War II*. Ed. L. W. Doob. Westport 1978, # 90 http://www.whale.to/b/pound.html#90_%28May_23,_ 1943%29_U.K.%28D6%29_

43. Official File Regarding Alleged Loss of Top Secret Document Concerning the Katyn Massacre, 1949–1954, image 175 http://research.archives.gov/description/ 6850555

44. John Nettles: *Jewels and Jackboots. Hitler's British Islands*. St. Mary/Jersey 2012.

45. Bern Despatch No. 8064 with Enclosures Regarding the Visit of Two American Officers Named J. H. Van Vliet and D. B. Stewart to Katyn, 05/02/1944, image 10 http://research.archives.gov/description/6850451

46. Krystyna Piórkowska: *English-speaking Witnesses to Katyn*. Warsaw 2012, p. 35.

47. Copy of a Report by Captain Stanley S. B. Gilder titled 'History of Visit Made to Katyn', 1944? http://research.archives.gov/description/6850521

48. *The Katyn Forest Massacre*, vol. I, pp. 6–9.

49. *The Katyn Forest Massacre*, vol. I, pp. 13–15.

50. Copy of a Report http://research.archives.gov/description/6850521

51. Gersdorff, p. 142.

52. Dossier on Katyn Forest Murders, 1948, images 184–185 http://research.archives. gov/description/6850549

53. Piórkowska, p. 52.

Chapter 9

1. *The Katyn Forest Massacre*, vol. VII, p. 2073.

2. David Mayers: *FDR's Ambassadors and the Diplomacy of Crisis: From the Rise of Hitler to the end of World War II*. Cambridge 2013, pp. 226–227.

3. Dunn, p. 184.

4. *The New York Times*, 29 November 1967, p. 47.

5. Germany, July 1941–1944 https://research.archives.gov/id/16608750 pp. 56–75, List of Key Nazis (10 December 1942).

6. Matthieu Durand: *'L'observateur' officieux. John Franklin Carter et son réseau de renseignement au service du président Roosevelt de 1941 à 1945*. Québec 2010, pp. 163–164.

7. Peter Conradi: *Hitler's Piano Player: The Rise and Fall of Ernst Hanfstaengl: Confidant of Hitler, Ally of FDR*. New York 2004, p. 7.

8. Alexander Werth: *The Year of Stalingrad*. London 1946, p. 403.

9. *The New York Times*, 4 October 1934, p. 1.

10. *The New York Times*, 14 March 1937, p. 14.

11. *Die Tagebücher* Part. I, vol. 4, pp. 47, 49, 53, 91.

12. Ernst Hanfstaengl: *15 Jahre mit Hitler. Zwischen Weißem und Braunem Haus.* Munich 1980, pp. 363–373.

13. Joseph E. Persico: *Roosevelt's Secret War. FDR and World War II Espionage.* New York 2002, pp. 193–194.

14. Persico, pp. 232–233.

15. *The Katyn Forest Massacre*, vol. VII, p. 2248.

16. Durand, pp. 171–172.

17. John Franklin Carter, Report on Hanfstaengl's Memorandum on Polish–Russian Relations, 28 April 1943, in: National Archives Catalog https://research.archives.gov/id/16619743 p. 74.

18. John Franklin Carter, May 1943 https://research.archives.gov/id/16619745, Report on Putzi's comments on the German Katyn incident propaganda, pp. 174–180.

19. Carter, John F., June – July 1943, p. 14 https://catalog.archives.gov/id/16619747

20. OSS – London Office (Mission and Personnel). Political Events of the Week 25–29 May p. 4 https://www.cia.gov/library/readingroom/document/cia-rdp13x00001r000100470002-1

21. Mark Stout, The Pond: Running Agents for State, War, and the CIA. The Hazards of Private Spy Operations, in: *Studies in Intelligence*, vol. 48, 3(2004), pp. 71, 74.

22. John V. Grombach: *The Great Liquidator.* New York 1980, pp. 107–108.

23. *Die Tagebücher*, II, vol. 8, p. 110.

24. Dorothy Thompson: *I Saw Hitler.* New York 1932, pp. 13–15.

25. *The Saturday Review of Literature*, 7 July 1934, p. 791.

26. *Time*, 12 June 1939.

27. *Die Tagebücher*, II, vol. 4. p. 51.

28. *Washington Star*, 30 April 1943; Richard Harwood: *Nuremberg and other War Crimes Trials.* Chapel Ascot 1978, p. 60.

29. *The New York Times*, 27 April 1943, p. 1; 9 May 1943, p. 34.

30. *The Washington Post*, 25 April 1943, p. B2.

31. *Chicago Tribune*, 28 April 1943, p. 18.

32. *Die Tagebücher*, II, vol. 7. p. 236.

33. *Völkischer Beobachter*, 15 April 1943, p. 1.

34. *Völkischer Beobachter*, 16 April 1943, p. 1.

35. *Die Grenz-Zeitung*, 16 April 1943, p. 2.

36. Quentin Reynolds: *The Curtain Rises.* New York 1944, p. 80.

37. *Life*, 4 October 1943, pp. 87–95.

38. Leonid Mlechin: *MID. Vneshnyaya politika Rossii. Tainaya diplomatika Kremlya.* Moscow 2011, p. 149.

39. Standley, p. 368.

40. Walter L. Hixson: *American Diplomacy of the Second World War.* New York 2003, p. 152.

41. *Churchill and Roosevelt. The Complete Correspondence.* Ed. Warren F. Kimball. Princeton 1984, vol. I, p. 421.

42. Elizabeth K. MacLean: *Presidential Address. The Outcast and His Critics: Joe Davies and George Kennan and Louis Brandeis.* Ohoi Academy of History 2001, p. 2. http://www.ohioacademyofhistory.org/2013/04/05/2001-proceedings/

43. Charles E. Bohlen: *Witness to History.* New York 1973, pp. 51–52.

44. *The New Yorker*, 25 February 1985, pp. 57–58.

45. Wilson D. Miscamble, George F. Kennan. A Life in the Foreign Service, in: *Foreign Service Journal*, 81(2004), p. 23; Thomas G. Paterson: *Meeting the Communist Threat: Truman to Reagan.* New York 1988, p. 122.

46. *Life*, 29 March 1943, pp. 44–48.

47. Joseph E. Davies: *Mission to Moscow.* New York 1941, pp. 67, 194–195, 269–270.

48. Dunn, pp. 71–72.

49. David H. Culbert: *Mission to Moscow.* Madison 1980, pp. 16–17.

50. *The New York Times*, 9 May 1943, p. E8.

51. *The New York Times*, 24 May 1943, p. 14.

52. Dunn, p. 62.

53. Standley, pp. 370–372.

54. *Life*, 29 March 1943, pp. 29, 40.

55. G. McJumsy/H. Hopkins: *Ally of the Poor and Defender of Democracy.* Cambridge/Mass. 1987, p. 293.

56. *The New York Times*, 25 May 1943, p. 8.

57. Standley, pp. 374–375.

58. Herbert Feis*: Churchill-Roosevelt-Stalin. The War They Waged and the Peace They Sought.* Princeton NJ 1957, pp. 131–133; Standley, pp. 375–376.

59. Standley, p. 380.

60. *Churchill and Roosevelt*, vol. II, p. 283.

61. *The Katyn Forest Massacre*, vol. VII, p. 2070.

62. Kimball MacLean, pp. 101, 119

63. *Katyn. Despatches*, pp. 22–29.

64. Maresch, p. 73.

65. Maresch, pp. 65–66.

66. Cadogan, *The Diaries*, p. 528.

67. Sanford, pp. 172–173, 180.

68. Message to President Franklin D. Roosevelt from Winston Churchill, 08/13/1943, ID 6851129 http://research.archives.gov/description/6851129

69. *Die Tagebücher*, II, vol. 8, p. 209.

70. *Katyn. Despatches*, p. 10.

71. Letter to President Franklin D. Roosevelt from Sumner Welles, 05/01/1943, images 4–5 http://research.archives.gov/description/6851130

72. *Die Tagebücher*, II, vol. 8, p. 178.
73. Philipp M. H. Bell, Censorship, Propaganda and Public Opinion: The Case of the Katyn Graves,1943, in: *Royal Historical Society*, Fifth Series, vol. 39 (1989), p. 77.
74. *The Times*, 30 April 1943, p. 5.
75. *Daily Worker*, 28 April 1943, p. 1.
76. Philip M. H. Bell: *John Bull and the Bear. British Public Opinion, Foreign Policy and the Soviet Union 1941–1945*. London 1990, pp. 114, 120–125.
77. Norman Davies: *Europe at War 1939–1945. No Simple Victory*. London 2007, p. 182.
78. Klemens von Klemperer: *German Resistance Against Hitler: The Search for Allies Abroad 1938–1945*. Oxford 1994, pp. 272–276.
79. Marie Vassiltchikov: *Berlin Diaries 1940–1945*, 1988, p. 99.
80. Germany, July 1941–1944, p. 75 https://research.archives.gov/id/16608750 pp. 56–75, List of Key Nazis (10 December 1942).
81. *Vierteljahrshefte für Zeitgeschichte*, 4(1992), p. 572
82. Persico, pp. 233–234, 279.
83. *The Katyn Forest Massacre*, vol. VII, pp. 2197–2198.
84. Persico, pp. 237–238.
85. Confidential, August 1958, pp. 15–19 http://www.oldmagazinearticles.com/1943-german-peace-feelers_pdf
86. Persico, p. 236.
87. Persico, pp. 67, 79.
88. *Vierteljahrshefte für Zeitgeschichte*, 4(1992), p. 620.
89. Heinz Höhne: *Canaris. Patriot im Zwielicht*. Munich 1976, pp. 462–464.
90. *Widerstand und Auswärtiges Amt. Diplomaten gegen Hitler*. Ed. J.E. Schulte u. M. Wala. Munich 2013, pp. 75–77.
91. Persico, p. 322.
92. Persico, p. 299.
93. Weinstein/Vassiliev, pp. 238-243.
94. Persico, p. 292.
95. Persico, p. 267.
96. *The Katyn Forest Massacre*, vol. VII, p. 2197, 2203.
97. Pismo sotrudnika NKVD Vassilya Mironova direktoru FBR Guveru (poslano anonimno) 1943 g. http://allin777.livejournal.com/262701.html
98. *Stalin i kholodnaya voina*. Ed. Institut vseobshchey istorii. Moscow 1998, p. 147–148.
99. Persico, p. 377.
100. John Earl Haynes / Harvey Klehr: *Venona – Decoding Soviet Espionage in America*. New Haven/Conn. 1999, p. 44.
101. Weinstein / Vassiliev, p. 239.
102. Persico, p. 377.

103. Klehr / Haynes, p. 225.
104. *Katyn 1940–2000*, pp. 214–215.
105. *The Katyn Forest Massacre*, vol. III, p. 498.
106. Piotr S. Wandycz: *The United States and Poland*. Cambridge MA 1980, p. 266.
107. Letter from J. Edgar Hoover to Honorable Adolf A. Berle Enclosing a Copy of a Pamphlet Titled 'Facts About the Severing of Relations Between the Soviet Government and the Polish Government in Exile', 12/31/1943 http://research. archives.gov/description/6850457
108. *The New York Times*, 9 September 1943, p. 27.
109. Tadeusz Katelbach: *Rok złych wróżb (1943)*. Łomianki 2005, p. 188.
110. The National Archives: Churchill and Stalin – Documents from the British Archives, 1943. No 48: Record of conversation at Soviet Embassy, Tehran, 1 December 1943, on the future of Poland. http://webarchive.nationalarchives.gov. uk/20031222065321/http://www.fco.gov.uk/Files/kfile/48-1.pdf
111. Persico, p. 273.
112. Churchill, vol. V: *Closing the Ring*. London 1951, pp. 373–374.
113. *The Katyn Forest Massacre*, vol. IV, p. 740.
114. Arthur Bliss Lane: *I Saw Poland Betrayed. An American Ambassador Reports to the American People*. Indianapolis NY 1948, p. 68.
115. John Lewis Gaddis: *George F. Kennan: An American Life*. London 2011, p. 182.
116. Cenckiewicz, pp. 41–46.

Chapter 10

1. *Zeszyty Katyńskie*, 23(2008), pp. 58–61.
2. Frank Fox: *God's Eye: Aerial Photography and the Katyń Massacre*. West Chester 1999. http://www.katyn-books.ru/archive/godseye/godseye-illustrations.htm
3. *Zeszyty Katyńskie*, 23(2008), p. 88.
4. *Zeszyty Katyńskie*, 23(2008), pp. 62–63.
5. Inessa Yazhborovskaya / Anatoli Yablokov / Valentina Parsadanova: *Katynsky sindrom v sovetsko-polskikh otnosheniyakh*. Moscow 2009, pp. 368–374.
6. *Katyn 1940–2000*, pp. 429–430.
7. *Zeszyty Katyńskie*, 23(2008), p. 65.
8. *Vestnik katynskogo memoriala*, 3.2004, pp. 9–18.
9. The Ambassador in the Soviet Union (Harriman) to the Secretary of State, 26 January 1944 // Foreign Relations of the United States: Diplomatic Papers, 1944, Europe, vol. III, p. 1239 https://history.state.gov/historicaldocuments/frus1944v03/d1155
10. Jerome Davis: *Behind Soviet Power. Stalin and the Russians*. West Haven, Conn. 1949, pp. 10, 12.
11. Davis, pp. 28–30, 41, 90, 99.

12. *Lubyanka, Stalin i MGB SSSR mart 1946 – mart 1953. Dokumenty*. Ed. V. N. Khaustov / V. P. Naumov / N. S. Plotnikova. Moscow 2007, pp. 211–212.

13. John Gibbons: *The Most Terrible Place in the World*. London 1943.

14. Richard E. Lauterbach: *These Are the Russians*. New York 1945, pp. 93, 103–109, 116–119.

15. Alexander G. Lovelace: Spies in the News: Soviet Espionage in the American Media During World War II and the Beginning of the Cold War, in: *The Journal of Slavic Military Studies*, 28:2(2015), p. 320.

16. Obyedkov, I. V., Ralph Parker – journalist ili razvedchik?, in: *Mezhdnarodnaya nauchno-prakticheskaya konferentsiya. Gumanitarnye osnovaniya sotsialnogo progressa*. Vol. 4. Moscow 2016, pp. 147–149.

17. *The New York Times*, 24 October 1943, p. 38.

18. S. Ani Mukherji, 'Like Another Planet to the Darker Americans': Black Cultural Work in the 1930s Moscow, in: *Africa in Europe: Studies in Transnational Practice in the Long Twentieth Century*. Ed. Eve Rosenhaft / Robbie Aitken. Liverpool 2013, p. 124.

19. *The Crisis*, September 1936, pp. 268–269.

20. Tim Tzouliadis: *The Forsaken: An American Tragedy in Stalin's Russia*. New York 2009, pp. 98–99.

21. John D. Stevens: *From the Back of the Foxhole: Black Correspondents in World War II*. Minneapolis 1973, p. 59.

22. *Wiadomości* [London], 28 November 1976, p. 1.

23. Edmund Stevens: *Russia is no Riddle*. New York 1945, p. 168.

24. Ray Moseley: *Reporting War. How Foreign Correspondents Risk Capture, Torture and Death to Cover World War II*. New Haven, CT 2017, p. 201.

25. Reynolds Quentin: *The Curtain Rises*. New York 1944, p. 46.

26. Alexander Werth: *Russia at War 1941–45*. London 1964, p. 637.

27. Harrison Salisbury, 'First Russian Impressions'. Harrison Salisbury Papers, Box 184. Rare Book and Manuscript Library. Columbia University [thanks to Dina Fainberg, City University of London, for sending the copies], p. 30.

28. Standley/ Ageton, p. 326.

29. Whitman Bassow: *The Moscow Correspondents. Reporting Russia from the Revolution to Glasnost*. New York 1988, p. 95.

30. Iosif Stalin: *On The Grand Alliance and the Need for a Second Front // Soviet War Documents: USSR Information Bulletin – Special Supplement*. Washington: Embassy of the Union of Soviet Socialist Republics, 3 October 1942, p. 32.

31. Duncan Hooper: *Writing the First Drafts of History. A Newsman's life, 1912–1990*. Collated and annotated by Ian Marshall. Balwyn/Victoria 1999, pp. 15–-16, 21, 23.

32. Lauterbach, pp. 182–183.

33. *Vierteljahreshefte für Zeitgeschichte*, 4.2000, p. 622.

34. David Mayers: *FDR's Ambassadors and the Diplomacy of Crisis: From the Rise of Hitler to the end of World War II*. Cambridge 2013, pp. 226–227.

35. Sudoplatov, *Spetsoperatsii*, p. 378.

36. Geoffrey Roberts, 'Do the Crows Still Roost in the Spasopeskovskaya Trees?' – The Wartime Correspondence of Kathleen Harriman, in: *The Harriman Magazine*. Ed Harriman Institute for Russian Studies at Columbia University. March 2015, p. 16.

37. E. Stevens, *Riddle*, p. 163.

38. *The Argus* [Melbourne], 9 June 1945, p. 16.

39. *Time*, 7 February 1944, p. 30.

40. Salisbury, *First Russian Impressions*, pp. 29, 32–33.

41. Homer Smith: *Black Man in Red Russia. A memoir.* Chicago 1964, p. 161.

42. Smith, p. 164.

43. Salisbury, *First Russian Impressions*, p. 35.

44. E. Stevens, *Riddle*, p. 170.

45. *Zeszyty Katyńskie*, 2(1992), pp. 113–114.

46. *The New York Times*, 27 January 1944, p. 3.

47. E. Stevens, *Riddle*, pp. 166–167.

48. *The Katyn Forest Massacre*, vol. VI, p. 1771.

49. *The Katyn Forest Massacre*, vol. VII, p. 2150.

50. Averell Harriman / Elie Abel: *Special Envoy to Churchill and Stalin 1941–1946.* New York 1975, p. 300.

51. Ivan Tolstoy, Nessostoyavshisya zagovor. *Radio Liberty*, 9 October 2014 http://www.svoboda.org/content/article/26644087.html

52. Werth, *Russia*, p. 662–663.

53. Lauterbach, pp. 308–315.

54. Davis, *Behind*, p. 100.

55. E. Stevens, *Riddle*, pp. 169–171.

56. *Daily Worker*, 27 January 1944, p. 4.

57. *Daily Worker*, 29 January 1944, p. 2.

58. *The Katyn Forest Massacre*, vol. II, p. 210.

59. *The Katyn Forest Massacre*, vol. II, pp. 210–212.

60. Salisbury, *First Russian Impressions*, p. 38.

61. Piórkowska, p. 99

62. *Altoona Mirror*, 28 January 1944, p. 152.

63. Hooper, p. 34.

64. *Daily Mirror*, 27 January 1944, p. 8.

65. *The Times*, 27 January 1944, p. 3.

66. *The Times*, 27 January 1944, p. 5.

67. Maresch, p. 222.

68. E. Stevens, p. 60.

69. *The New York Times*, 27 January 1944, p. 3.

70. Moscow Despatch No. 207 with Enclosure Regarding the Investigation of Soviet Authorities of the Massacre of Polish Soldiers in the Katyn Forest, Near Smolensk, 02/23/1944, images 3–8 http://research.archives.gov/description/6850474

71. Moscow Despatch No. 207, images 9–17.
72. Harriman / Abel, pp. 301–302.
73. Moscow Telegram No. 247 from W. Averell Harriman Regarding Trip to Smolensk and Examination of Evidence, 01/25/1944, File Unit 74ß.00116 http://research. archives.gov/description/6850473
74. Lauterbach, pp. 95–96.
75. Jan Kazimierz Zawodny: *Katyń*. Lublin/Paris 1989. pp. 139–140.
76. *Katyn Forest Murders*, Vol. 1 D229548, image 121, https://research.archives.gov/id/6850549?q=*:*
77. *Zeszyty Katyńskie*, 23(2008), p. 88.
78. *Polityka*, 18 February 1989, p. 14.
79. *Zeszyty Katyńskie*, 2(1992), pp. 113–114.
80. Yazhborovskaya, p. 357.
81. Sanford, p. 139
82. *Katyn. Desptaches*, p. 10.
83. Butler, pp. 28–33.
84. Butler, p. 9.
85. Laurence Rees: *World War II Behind Closed Doors: Stalin, the Nazis and the West*. New York 2010, p. 246.
86. Butler, pp. 9, 14–16.
87. Maresch, p. 244.
88. Laurence Rees: *World War II Behind Closed Doors: Stalin, the Nazis and the West*. New York 2010, p. 246.
89. Maresch, p. 245.
90. Jacek Tebinka, Dyplomacja brytyjska wobec sprawy katyńskiej w latach 1943–1945, in: *Z dziejów Polski i emigracji (1939–1989)*. Gorzów Wielkopolski 2003, p. 459.
91. *Die Tagebücher*, part II, vol. 11, p. 193.
92. *Goniec Krakowski*, 5 February 1944, p. 1.
93. *The Katyn Forest Massacre*, vol. VII, p. 2249.
94. Carter, John F., June–July 1944: Report on suggested fake speech by Hitler to aid invasion, 7 June 1944, in: National Archives Catalog https://research.archives.gov/id/16619776, pp. 10–13.
95. Persico, p. 330.
96. Durand, pp. 172–173.
97. *La Stampa*, 26 September 1951, p. 1.
98. *Sotsialistichesky Vestnik* [Paris], 6.1950, p. 114.
99. *Svoboda* [Munich], 4.1959, pp. 24–25.
100. Prawda o Katyniu. *Nakładem Związku Patriotów Polskich w ZSSR*. Moscow 1944.
101. William Lindsay White: *Report on the Russians*. London 1945, p. 18.

102. Gaddis, p. 46.

103. *American Journalism*, 3 July 2015, vol. 32(3), p. 327.

104. White, p. 105.

105. *The New York Times*, 10 December 1944, p. 35.

106. *The New York Times*, 18 March 1945, p. 43.

107. *American Journalism*, p. 318.

108. E. Stevens, *Riddle*, p. 295.

109. *American Journalism*, p. 324.

110. *American Journalism*, pp. 321, 324.

111. Ray Mosely: *Reporting War: How Foreign Correspondents Risked Capture, Torture and Death to Cover World War II*. New Haven 2017, p. 202.

112. Smith, pp. 163–164.

Chapter 11

1. *Vestnik Katynskogo Memoriala*, 7.2007, p. 115.

2. Petrov, *Palachi*, p. 274.

3. Pavel Sudoplatov: *Spetsoperatsii. Lubyanka i Kreml 1930–1950 gody*. Moscow 1997, p. 371.

4. Haynes/Klehr, p. 45.

5. *Vestnik Katynskogo Memoriala*, 10(2010), pp. 43–45.

6. *The Katyn Forest Massacre*, vol. V, p. 1577.

7. *Zeszyty Katyńskie*, 7(1997), pp. 157–158.

8. *Zeszyty Katyńskie*, 2(1992), pp. 88, 110.

9. *Zeszyty Katyńskie*, 7(1997), pp. 366–372.

10. *Zeszyty Katyńskie*, 19(2004), p. 84.

11. *Tygodnik Powszechny*, 22 September 2007, p. 11.

12. *Tygodnik Powszechny*, 13 January 2009, p. 8.

13. *The Katyn Forest Massacre*, vol. IV, p. 847.

14. Goetel, pp. 145–147.

15. Skarżyński, pp. 16, 80.

16. Butler, pp. 36–37.

17. *Zbrodnia katyńska*, pp. 199–245.

18. *Zeszyty Katyńskie*, 14(2002), pp. 7–9, 26–28.

19. *The Katyn Forest Massacre*, vol. V, pp. 1516–1517.

20. *Komunizm. System – ludzie – dokumentacja. Rocznik naukowy*, I.2012, p. 222.

21. Skarżyński, p. 59.

22. *Zeszyty Katyńskie*, 14(2002), pp. 7–9, 26–28.

23. Wojciech Materski: *Mord Katyński. Siedemdziesiąt lat drogi do prawdy*. Warsaw 2010, p. 49.

24. Skarżyński, p. 81.

25. Materski, pp. 50–51.
26. *Zeszyty Katyńskie*, 19(2004), pp. 87–92.
27. *Tko je tko u NDH: Hrvatska 1941–1945*. Zagreb 1997, pp. 275–276.
28. *Zeszyty Katyńskie*, 23(2008), p. 91.
29. *Istorichesko budeshche* [Sofia], 1–2/2004, p. 218.
30. *Katyn et la Suisse*, pp. 161–164.
31. *Katyn. Una verità*, p. 55.
32. *Katyn et la Suisse*, pp. 172–176.
33. Katyn Forest Massacre/State Security (STB) Activities, Doc. CIA-RDP80-00810A001000670008-9, pp. 2–4 https://www.cia.gov/library/readingroom/document/cia-rdp80-00810a001000670008-9
34. Report – Information on the Katyn Forest Incident, 05/01/1952, image 10 http://research.archives.gov/description/6256952
35. Katyn Forest Massacre/State Security, pp. 3–6.
36. *Polonia-Finlandia*, 3.2008, pp. 5–8.
37. *Katyn et la Suisse*, p. 183.
38. Joris Dedeurwaarder: *Professor Speleers – een biografie*. Antwerpen 2002, p. 792.
39. Despatch – Dr Hermann de Burlet, 05/07/1952 http://research.archives.gov/description/6882848
40. *Katyn et la Suisse*, pp. 77–92.
41. *Filip De Pillecyn Studies*, I (2005).
42. *Encyclopédie du Mouvement Wallon*, vol. II. Namur 2000, p. 820.
43. Barbara Berzel: *Die französische Literatur im Zeichen von Kollaboration und Faschismus*. Tübingen 2012, p. 193.
44. Ernesto Giménez Caballero: *Memorias de un dictador*. Barcelona 1981, p. 181.

Chapter 12
1. *Le Monde*, 21 January 1945, p. 2.
2. Claude Quetel: *L'effrayant docteur Petiot. Fou ou coupable?* Paris 2014, p. 7.
3. Memorandum by Mr F. B. Bourdillon of Research Department http://collection.europarchive.org/tna/20070206143611/http://fco.gov.uk/files/kfile/annexd.pdf
4. Telford Taylor: *The Anatomy of the Nuremberg Trials. A Personal Memoir*. London 1993, p. 467.
5. Piórkowska, pp. 87–88.
6. Copies of Correspondence, Reports and Other Records Relating to the Katyn Case, image 18 https://catalog.archives.gov/id/6850520
7. Noel Stock: *The Life of Ezra Pound*. New York 1970, p. 221.
8. Copy of a Report from Stockholm, Sweden Presenting Views on the Katyn Forest Massacre, 06/01/1944, image 1 http://research.archives.gov/description/6850526
9. *The New York Times*, 29 June 1945, p. 2.
10. Butler, p. 33.
11. Sanford, p. 186.

12. Koper, p. 370.

13. Taylor, p. 218.

14. Mr Justice Jackson. *Four Lectures in His Honour*. New York 1969, pp. 117–118.

15. Petrov, *Palachi*, p. 132.

16. *Daily Worker*, 21 May 1945, p. 1.

17. John Watkins: *Moscow Despatches: Inside Cold War Russia*. Ed. D. /W. Kaplan. Toronto 1987, p. 4.

18. John Jenks: *British Propaganda and News Media in the Cold War*. Edinburgh 2006, pp. 31–34.

19. George Orwell: *The Collected Essays, Journalism and Letters*. Vol. III. London 1968, p. 389.

20. Tatiana Stupnikova: *Nichego krome pravdy. Niurnberg-Moskva. Vospominaniya*. Moscow 1998, pp. 102–05.

21. Jurij Zoria: *Droga do prawdy o Katyniu*. Warsaw 1994, p. 63.

22. Nikita Petrov, Deutsche Kriegsgefangene unter der Justiz Stalins. Gerichtsprozesse gegen Kriegsgefangene der deutschen Armee in der UdSSR 1945–1952, in: *Gefangen in Russland*. Ed. St Karner, Vienna/Graz 1995, p. 192.

23. *Izvestia Sovietov deputatov trudiashchikhsya SSSR*, 29 December 1945, p. 5.

24. Personenrecherche II B 4-677 (141218/32), Deutsche Dienststelle für die Benachrichtigung der nächsten Angehörigen von Gefallenen der ehemaligen deutschen Wehrmacht. Berlin, 21 January 2015.

25. Pavel Luknitsky: *Leningrad deystvuyet ... Frontovoy dnevnik*. Vol 3. Leningrad 1968.

26. Yazhborovskaya, pp. 336–337.

27. *Pravda*, 5 January 1946, p. 5.

28. Leningradsky process, in: Istoria Rossii – Sovietsky Niurnberg http://histrf.ru/ biblioteka/Soviet-Nuremberg/Leningradsky-process.

29. Eichborn, p. 4.

30. *Die Zeit*, 22 July 1988, p. 10.

31. Gersdorff, p. 207.

32. Scheurig, pp. 163, 184.

33. Telephone conversation with his son Jürgen-Lewin von Schlabrendorff, 17 October 2014.

34. Heinz Höhne: *Canaris. Patriot im Zwielicht*. Munich 1976, pp. 462–464.

35. Fabian von Schlabrendorff: *Begegnungen in fünf Jahrzehnten*. Tübingen 1979, p. 351.

36. Michael Salter: *Nazi War Crimes, US Intelligence and Selective Prosecution at Nuremberg*. New York 2007, p. 321.

37. Persico, pp. 424–425.

38. Weinstein / Vassiliev, p. 250.

39. Salter, p. 337.

40. Fabian von Schlabrendorff, Relationship of the German General Staff with Hitler, in: Donovan, pp. 3–4 http://ebooks.library.cornell.edu/cgi/t/text/pageviewer-idx?c=nur;i dno=nur00655;view=image;seq=1

41. Literal Translation of Opinion on Indictment No. 1 Before the International Military Tribunal by Fabian von Schlabrendorff, in: Donovan, pp. 3–4 http://ebooks.library. cornell.edu/cgi/t/text/pageviewer-idx?c=nur;idno=nur02060;view=image;seq=1

42. Schlabrendorff, *Begegnungen*, p. 354.

43. General Donovan, Memorandum for Mr Justice Jackson / SECRET, in: Donovan, p. 1 http://ebooks.library.cornell.edu/cgi/t/text/pageviewer-idx?c=nur;idno=nur02066;vie w=image;seq=1

44. Dear Bob / The Katyn forest murder, in: Donovan, p. 1 http://library2.lawschool. cornell.edu/donovan/pdf/Batch_9/Vol_XIX_61_01_13.pdf

45. *The Katyn Forest Massacre*, vol. VII, p. 2277.

46. Salter, p. 349.

47. Taylor, p. 639.

48. Taylor, p. 469.

49. *The Katyn Forest Massacre*, vol. V, pp. 1541–1544.

50. Yazhborovskaya, p. 199.

51. *Zbrodnia Katyńska*, p. IV.

52. *Zeszyty Katyńskie*, 11(1999), p. 128.

53. Anders, pp. 402–403.

54. Peter Davison: *George Orwell – a Literary Life*. New York 1996, p. 161.

55. Orwell, *Collected Essays*, vol. IV, p. 238.

56. Montfort, p. 181.

57. Gersdorff, pp. 194–195.

58. Official File Regarding Alleged Loss of Top Secret Document Concerning the Katyn Massacre, 1949–1954, File Unit: Assistant Chief of Staff G2 333.9 p. 20, image 98, nr. 6 – 705689 http://research.archives.gov/description/6850555

59. Rudolph Frhr. V. Gersdorff, The Truth about 'Katyn', p. 1, 8 http://downloads. sturmpanzer.com/FMS/NARA_FMS_A917.pdf

60. Taylor, p. 471.

61. Gersdorff, *Soldat*, pp. 197–199.

62. *Die Zeit*, 22 July 1988, p. 10.

63. Norbert Frei: *Adenauer's Germany and the Nazi Past: The Politics of Amnesty and Integration*. New York 1997, p. 98.

64. Schlabrendorff, *Begegnungen*, pp. 351–353.

65. Taylor, p. 183.

66. *Zeszyty Katyńskie*, (23)2008, pp. 61, 94.

67. *Katynskaya drama*, pp. 160–162.

68. *Novaya Polsha*, 1.2007, p. 55.

69. Yazhborovskaya, pp. 336–337.

70. Yazhborovskaya, p. 356.

71. Butler, p. 20.

72. Yazhborovskaya, p. 356.

73. Interview of his daughter Sabine Koch in Leverkusen, 17 May 2016.

74. *The Nuremberg Trials Collection*, pp. 275–286.

75. *The Nuremberg Trials Collection*, pp. 297–308.

76. *The Nuremberg Trials Collection*, pp. 309–320.

77. Gersdorff, p. 199.

78. *The Nuremberg Trials Collection*, p. 324–331.

79. *Vestnik Katynskogo Memoriala*, 10(2010), p. 45.

80. Summary Report of Investigation Regarding Katyn Forest Murders, Headquarters, Sub-Region Nurnberg, Counter Intelligence Corps Region VI, image 7 https://catalog.archives.gov/id/6850506

81. *The Nuremberg Trials Collection*, p. 351.

82. *Katyn 1940–2000*, pp. 428, 438.

83. Menshagin, pp. 159–160.

84. Adam Basak: *Historia pewnej mistyfikacji. Zbrodnia Katyńska przed Trybunalem Norymberskim*. Wrocław, 1993, p 111.

85. Churchill, vol. IV, pp. 760–761.

86. *Der Spiegel*, 6 October 1986, p. 57.

87. Fall 1960: 12-16-1: The Defections of Dr John, by Delmege Trimble, p. 12 https://research.archives.gov/id/7283450

Chapter 13

1. *The Katyn Forest Massacre*, vol. VII, p. 2204.

2. Thomas Fleming: *The New Dealers' War: FDR and the War within World War II*. New York 2001, p. 550.

3. *The Katyn Forest Massacre*, vol. VII, pp. 2197, 2203–2204.

4. Arthur Bliss Lane: *I Saw Poland Betrayed. An American Ambassador Reports to the American People*. Indianapolis N.Y. 1948, p. 67.

5. Lane, pp. 303–304.

6. *The Katyn Forest Massacre*, vol. VII, pp. 2001–2002.

7. David McCullough: *Truman*. New York 1992, p. 451.

8. David Reynolds: *From World War to Cold War: Churchill, Roosevelt, and the International History of the 1940s*. Oxford 2006; Jonathan Walker: *Operation Unthinkable: The Third World War*. Stroud 2013.

9. *Zeszyty Katyńskie*, 12(2000), p. 89.

10. 000.5 (29 Jul 49) 1 January 1951 to 31 December 1951, Massacre of Polish Army Officers, image 203 http://research.archives.gov/description/7851352

11. *The Katyn Forest Massacre*, vol., VII, p. 2267

12. *New York Herald Tribune*, 3/4 July 1949; *Die Zeit*, 9 June 1949.

13. *The New York Times*, 11 July 1946, p. 22.

14. Lane, p. 255.

15. Elizabeth K. MacLean, Presidential Address. The Outcast and His Critics: Joe Davies and George Kennan and Louis Brandeis. Ohoi Academy of History 2001, p. 2. http://www.ohioacademyofhistory.org/2013/04/05/2001-proceedings/

16. *The Katyn Forest Massacre*, vol. VII, p. 2224.

17. Katyn Forest Murders, Vol. 1 D229548, images 60–87 https://research.archives.gov/id/6850549?q=*:*

18. Dossier on Katyn Forest Murders, 1948, image 179 http://research.archives.gov/description/6850549

19. Dossier on Katyn Forest Murders, 1948, images 60–87

20. Davis, *Behind*, pp. 90, 99, 118–119.

21. *Report on the Communist 'Peace Offensive'. A Campaign To Disarm and Defeat the United States*. Released by the Committee on Un-American Activities, US House of Representatives, Washington, DC, 1 April 1951, pp. 57, 59, 104, 107, 125, 135, 136, 147. https://archive.org/stream/reportoncommunis00unit/reportoncommunis00unit_djvu.txt

22. Investigation of Un-American Propaganda Activities in the United States – Louis F. Budenz. Revised Hearings before the House Un-American Activities Committee Seventy-Ninth Congress Second Session. Ashington 1946, p. 36.

23. *The Saturday Review*, 22 March 1947, p. 26.

24. Lovelace, p. 320.

25. Haynes / Klehr, p. 237.

26. *The New York Times*, 21 September 1950, p. 31.

27. *The Katyn Forest Massacre*, vol. III, pp. 225–309.

28. Memorandum from Matthew J. Connelly to Harry S. Truman, 02/06/1952 http://research.archives.gov/description/6851098

29. *The Katyn Forest Massacre*, vol. I, p. 15.

30. *The Katyn Forest Massacre*, vol. VII, pp. 2204–2205, 2214.

31. *Confidential*, August 1958, p. 57.

32. *The Katyn Forest Massacre*, vol. VII, p. 2249.

33. Standley / Ageton, pp. 401–411.

34. *The New York Times*, 20 February 2011, p. 26A.

35. *The Katyn Forest Massacre*, vol., VII, pp. 2127, 2134–2147.

36. *The Katyn Forest Massacre*, vol. VII, pp. 1972, 2223.

37. *The Katyn Forest Massacre*, vol., VII, pp. 2151–2152.

38. *The Katyn Forest Massacre*, vol., II, pp. 209, 213, 219.

39. *The Katyn Forest Massacre*, vol. VI., pp. 1785–1786.

40. *Time*, 23 February 1948.

41. *The Katyn Forest Massacre*, vol. VII., p. 2146.

42. *The Katyn Forest Massacre*, vol. VII., pp. 2070, 2146.

43. *Journalism History* 41:3 (Fall 2015), pp. 154–155.

44. *The New York Times*, 19 September 1954, p. 1.

45. Meeting with George Orwell; progress report from RIO(S); paper on Communist Strategy in South East Asia1949, The National Archives, FO 1110/189 http://discovery.nationalarchives.gov.uk/details/r/C242365

46. *The New York Review of Books*, 25 September 2003, pp. 7–15.
47. Ralph Parker: *Moscow Correspondent*. New York 1949, p. 25.
48. *Lubyanka, Stalin i MGB SSSR mart 1946 – mart 1953*. Dokumenty. Ed. V. N. Chaustov / V. P. Naumov / N. S. Plotnikova. Moscow 2007, p. 227.
49. *Baltimore Afro-African*, 27 September 1955, p. 6.
50. Edwin R. Bayley: *Joe McCarthy and the Press*. Madison WI 1981, p. 194.
51. *The Katyn Forest Massacre*, vol. II, pp. 143–146.
52. *Zeszyty Katyńskie*, 7(1997), pp. 366–367.
53. *The Katyn Forest Massacre*, vol. IV, pp. 605–606.
54. *Polonia-Finlandia*, 4.2008, p. 7.
55. *Katyn et la Suisse*, pp. 52–53.
56. *The Katyn Forest Massacre*, vol. V, pp. 1480, 1613, 1620.
57. *The Katyn Forest Massacre*, vol. III, pp. 317–318
58. *Katyn et la Suisse*, pp. 172–176.
59. *The Katyn Forest Massacre*, vol. V, pp. 1305, 1314.
60. Allen W. Dulles: *Germany's Underground*. New York 1947.
61. Events Leading up to Putsch of 20 July (1944) / Secret, in: Donovan Nuremberg Trials Collection, pp. 3–4 (ebooks.library.cornell.edu, Vol XCIII).
62. *The Saturday Evening Post*, 20 July 1946.
63. *Svoboda* [Munich], 4.1959, pp. 24–25.
64. *The Katyn Forest Massacre*, vol. VII, pp. 1940–1941.
65. *The Katyn Forest Massacre*, vol. VI, p. 1799.
66. '*I cease not to yowl*'. *Ezra Pound's Letters to Olivia Rossetti Agresti*. Ed Demetres / P. Tryphonopoulos / L. Surrette. Urbana/Chicago 1998, p. 82.
67. Carroll F. Terrell: *A Companion to the Cantos of Ezra Pound*. Vol. II. Berkeley 1984, p. 403.
68. Maresch, pp. 329–332.
69. Butler, p. 35.
70. Piórkowska, pp. 123–130.
71. Sanford, p. 178.
72. Butler, p. 12.
73. Butler, p. 19–20.
74. Maresch, p. 323.
75. *The Katyn Forest Massacre*, vol. VI, p. 1800.
76. *Selected Committee On the Katyn Forest Massacre: Final Report* (House Report No. 2505) 22 December 1952. Washington 1952.
77. Butler, p. 39.
78. *The Washington Post*, 12 November 1952, p. 1.
79. *The Washington Post*, 15 November 1952, p. 8
80. *Tko je tko u NDH: Hrvatska 1941–1945*. Zagreb 1997, pp. 275–276.
81. *Katyn et la Suisse*, pp. 172–176.

82. Ray J. Madden to Harry S. Truman and Matthew J. Connelly, with Attached Internal Notes, 01/19/1952 – 01/25/1952, image 4 http://research.archives.gov/description/6851099

83. Press Statement on Katyn Forst Massacre, State 188560, Origin EUR-12, 26 July 1978 http://aad.archives.gov/aad/createpdf?rid=187793&dt=2694&dl=2009

84. Rudolf, pp. 24–25.

85. Yazhborovskaya, pp. 336–337.

86. Conversation with Sabine Koch, 17 May 2016.

87. Report – Katyn Forest Incident, 05/22/1952, images 3, 8 http://research.archives.gov/description/6256922

88. *Evropa mezi Nemeckem a Ruskem*, pp. 513–515.

89. *Katyn et la Suisse*, p. 186.

90. Official File Regarding Alleged Loss of Top Secret Document Concerning the Katyn Massacre, 1949 – 1954,, images 171–178 http://research.archives.gov/description/6850555

91. Newly-discovered US witness report describes evidence of 1939 Katyn massacre http://www.foxnews.com/world/2014/01/09/newly-discovered-us-witness-report-describes-evidence-13-katyn-massacre/

92. Official File Regarding Alleged Loss of Top Secret Document Concerning the Katyn Massacre, 1949–1954 Prev 20, image 97, no. 705683 http://research.archives.gov/description/6850555

93. Report – Katyn Forest Murders, 06/21/1948, image 116 http://research.archives.gov/description/6256905

94. Dossier on Katyn Forest Murders, 1948, images 97–99 http://research.archives.gov/description/6850549

95. Ideological Special No. 71 Titled 'What the Katyn Hearings Have Brought Out So Far', 02/19/1952 http://research.archives.gov/description/6850536

Chapter 14

1. Przewoźnik/Adamska, p. 395.

2. Foreign Relations of the United States, 1952–1954, Eastern Europe; Soviet Union; Eastern Mediterranean, vol. VIII, p. 972 https://history.state.gov/historicaldocuments/frus1952-54v08/d499

3. Foreign Relations, vol. VIII, p. 986 https://history.state.gov/historicaldocuments/frus1952-54v08/d506

4. *Pravda*, 12 March 1952, p. 3.

5. *Rzeczpospolita*, 12 April 2000, p. 12.

6. Dossier on Katyn Forest Murders, 1948, image 19 http://research.archives.gov/description/6850550

7. Pałka, pp. 330–369.

8. *Komunizm*, I.2012, pp. 215–227.

9. *Trybuna Ludu*, 1 March 1952, p. 1.

10. *Szpilki*, 16 March 1952.

11. Current Intelligence Digest (7 August 1952) Doc. CIA-RDP79T01146A0011 00310001-6, p. 2 https://www.cia.gov/library/readingroom/document/cia-rdp79t 01146a001100310001-6

12. Report on the State Department in: http://tedlipien.com/blog/2015/06/24/wwii-voice-of-america-aired-stalin-propaganda-to-cover-up-his-role-in-katyn-massacre/

13. Longin Pastusiak: *Z tajników archiwów dyplomatycznych (Stosunki polsko-amerykańskie w latach 1948–1954)*. Toruń 2002, p. 48.

14. Zawodny, p.142.

15. *Komunizm*, I.2012, p. 215.

16. Bolesław Wójcicki: *Prawda o Katyniu*. Warsaw 1953, pp. 5–13, 68–91.

17. *Życie Radomskie*, 22 January 1952.

18. George F. Kennan: *Memoirs 1950–1963*. Vol. II. Boston 1972, p. 170.

19. Walter L. Hixson: *George F. Kennan. Cold War Iconoclast*. New York 1989, pp. 127–128.

20. Smith, p. 166.

21. Sergey Romanov, Katyn v 'dele Berii' http://katynfiles.com/content/romanov-katyn-beria-trial.html

22. Arkady Vaksberg: *Neraskrytye tainy*. Moscow 1993, pp. 80–85.

23. *Katyń. Dokumenty*, vol.. 2, p. 465.

24. Petrov, *Palachi*, pp. 201–201.

25. Ralf Parker http://www.kino-teatr.ru/kino/acter/m/sov/29143/foto/m2459/535819/

26. *The New York Times*, 29 May 1964, p. 29.

27. *Rzeczpospolita*, 9 April 2010, p. 10.

28. Paul Hollander: *Political Pilgrims. Western Intellectuals in the Search of the Good Society*. New Brunswick/London 1998, p. 166.

29. *Newsweek Historia*, 4.2015, p. 37.

30. *Zeszyty Katyńskie*, 2(1992), p. 144.

31. Yazhborovskaya, p. 213.

32. *Zeszyty Katyńskie*, 2(1992), p. 391.

33. *Karta* [Warsaw] 12(1994), p. 139.

34. *Gazeta Wyborcza*, 10 August 2009, p. 7.

35. *Sunday Times Magazine*, 28 May 1972, p. 5.

36. Materski, p. 67.

37. Svetlana Alliluyeva: *Twenty Letters to a Friend*. New York 1967, p. 207.

38. *The New Yorker*, 31 March 2014, pp. 30–37.

39. *The New York Times*, 23 July 1967, p. 10.

40. *The Times of India*, 24 July 1967, p. 6.

41. Menshagin, pp. 131–132, 142–143.

42. Zakirov, p. 201.

43. *The Washington Post*, 2 July 1974; *The New York Times*, 2 July 1974, p. 1.
44. Hubermont: *Khatyn*, p. 3.
45. *Sunday Times Magazine*, 28 May 1972, p. 5.
46. Maresch, p. 347.
47. The Butler Memorandum: Katyn in the Cold War (webarchive.nationalarchives. gov.uk)
48. Louis FitzGibbon: *Katyn Memorial*. Hove/Sussex 1976, p. 15.
49. Sanford, pp. 184, 211.
50. FitzGibbon, pp. 26–27, 30.
51. *The Economist*, 25 September 1976, p. 26.
52. Ronald Reagan Radio Broadcast: Katyn Forest, 11 February 1976. http://research. archives.gov/description/6743196
53. *Katyń. Dokumenty ludobójstwa*. Ed. ISP Polskiej Akademii Nauk. Warsaw 2001, p. 74.
54. Materski, pp. 68–69.
55. *Czarna księga cenzury PRL*. Vol. I. London 1977, p. 63.
56. *Zeszyty Katyńskie*, 5(1995), pp. 150–151.
57. *Biuletyn katyński*, 1 (33) 1991, pp. 1–3.
58. *Biuletyn Instytutu Pamięci Narodowej*, 4.2010, pp. 76–82.
59. Wasilewski, p. 234.
60. *Katyń 1940*. Walka, pp. 244–246.
61. *Tygodnik Powszechny*, 13 January 2009, p. 8.

Chapter 15

1. Yazhborovskaya, pp. 262, 279.
2. Jarema Maciszewski: *Katyń: wydrzeć prawdę*. Warsaw 1993, pp. 10–13.
3. Yazhborovskaya, p. 277.
4. Materski, p. 72.
5. *Tygodnik Powszechny*, 13 January 2009, p. 8.
6. Lebedeva: *Katyn – Prestuplenie*, pp. 4–6.
7. *Rosja a Katyń*. Ed. Ośrodek 'Karta'. Warsaw 2010, pp. 21–24.
8. Yazhborovskaya, pp. 264–265.
9. Valery Boldin: *Krushenie piedestala. Strikhi k portretu Gorbacheva*. Moscow 1995, p. 256.
10. *Katyń 1940*. Walka, pp. 244–247.
11. *Katynskaya drama*, p. 166.
12. *Moskovskie Novosti*, 6 August 1989, p. 6.
13. *Novaya Polsha*, 1.2005, pp. 50, 239.
14. Zakirov, pp. 201, 204, 222–224, 242.
15. *Novaya Polsha*, 1.2007, p. 58.
16. Zakirov, pp. 212, 237.

17. *Life*, 12 September 1960, p. 30.
18. Bassow, pp. 320–321.
19. Vladimir Abarinov: *Katynski labirint*. Moscow 1991, p. 29.
20. *Novaya Polsha*, 9.2000, pp. 63–69.
21. Lebedeva: *Katyn – Prestuplenie*, p. 306.
22. *Novaya Polsha*, 1.2007, pp. 55–59.
23. Yazhborovskaya, p. 308.
24. *Newsweek Historia*, [Warsaw], 4.2015, p. 37.
25. Yazhborovskaya, p. 355.
26. Boldin, pp. 257–261.
27. Sergei Strygin, L. M. Kaganovich o Katynskom dele, in: katyn.ru, 18 February 2010 http://www.katyn.ru/index.php?go=Pages&in=view&id=936
28. Zakirov, p. 251.
29. Boldin, p. 256.
30. Alexander Yakovlev: *Sumerki*. Moscow 2005, p. 422.
31. *Novaya Polsha*, 11.2005, p. 84.

Chapter 16

1. Materski, p. 79.
2. *Katyn*. Plenniki, p. 40.
3. *Novaya Polsha*, 1.2005, p. 50.
4. *Novaya Polsha*, 1.2007, pp. 55–59.
5. *Zeszyty Katyńskie* 5(1995), pp. 68–72.
6. *Zbrodnia katyńska*. Polskie śledztwo, p. 160.
7. *Katyń. Dokumenty*, vol. 2, pp. 453, 465.
8. Igor Petrov, Dva Olshanskikh borolis drug s drugom http://katynfiles.com/content/petrov-olshanskij.html
9. Uroki istorii XX veka, 24 dekabrya 2012 g. http://urokiistorii.ru/current/view/51657
10. Lovelace, p. 320.
11. Haynes / Klehr, p. 237.
12. Cheryl Heckler: *An Accidental Journalist. The Adventures of Edmund Stevens 1934–1945*. Columbia MO 2007, p. 250.
13. *The New York Times*, 27 May 1992, p. 14.
14. *The Christian Science Monitor*, 11 April 1995, p. 2.
15. Pavel Sudoplatov: *Tainye dni tainoy voiny i diplomatii*. Moscow 2001, p. 362.
16. Obyedkov, p. 151.
17. *Polska Agencja Prasowa* (PAP), 4 June 1995.
18. Materski, p. 88.
19. *Katyń 1940*. Walka, pp. 162–164.
20. *Rosja a Katyń*, pp. 117–118.
21. *Smolenskaya Gazeta*, 3 July 2007, p. 3.

22. *Pravo* [Moscow], 1.1998, pp. 77–79.

23. Yuri Mukhin: *Katynski detektiv.* Moscow 1996; *Antirossiyskaya podlost.* Moscow 2003.

24. Mukhin, *Antirossiyskaya*, pp. 5–10, 284, 444.

25. Elena Prudnikova / Ivan Chirigin; *Katyn. Lozh, stavshaya istoriey.* Moscow 2011.

26. *Nemtsy v Katyni. Dokumenty o rasstrele polskikh voyennoplennykh osenyu 1941.* Ed. R. Kosolapov. Moscow 2010, pp. 5–6.

27. *Nemtsy v Katyni.* p. 6.

28. *Tainy katynskoy tragedii. Materialy 'kruglogo stola'.* Moscow 2010, p. 159.

29. *Newsweek Historia* [Warsaw], 4.2015, p. 43.

30. *Rzeczpospolita*, 2 June 2010, p. 5.

31. *Novaya Gazeta*, 25 December 2009, p. 2.

32. *Katyń 1940.* Walka, pp. 182–185.

33. *Gazeta Wyborcza*, 8 April 2010, p. 3.

34. *Fakt* [Warsaw], 8 April 2010, p. 3.

35. *Osservatore Romano*, 18 July 2012, p. 1.

36. *Osservatore Romano*, 18 July 2012, p. 1.

Bibliography

Documents

Amtliches Material zum Massenmord von Katyn, Im Auftrage des Auswärtigen Amtes auf Grund urkundlichen Beweismaterials zusammengestellt, bearbeitet und herausgegeben von der Deutschen Informationsstelle. Berlin 1943 [*Whitebook of the German Ministry of Foreign Affairs*]

Anders, Władysław: *Zbrodnia katyńska w świetle dokumentów*, London 1950 [*Whitebook of the Polish government in exile*]

Bertram, Łukasz, Kłamstwa katyńskie, in: *Karta*, 66 (2011), pp. 80–99.

Butler, Rohan d'Olier: *The Katyn Massacre and the Reactions in the Foreign Office. Memorandum by the Historical Adviser.* London 1973 (webarchive.nationalarchives.gov.uk) [*Butler Memorandum*]

Case of Janowiec and others v. Russia. Applications nos. 55508/07 and 29520/09, European Court of Human Rights. Grand Chamber. Strasbourg 2013 (www.echr.coe.int).

Trial of the Major War Criminals before the International Military Tribunal Nuremberg, 14 November 1945 – 1 October 1946 (vol. XVII, 30 June – 2 July 1946)

Katyn 1940–2000, Dokumenty, Ed. N. I. Lebedeva. Moscow 2001.

Katyn, Despatches of Sir Owen O'Malley to the British Government, Introduced by Louis FitzGibbon. London 1972.

Katyń, Dokumenty zbrodni. T.1–4. Ed. A. Gieysztor, R. Pichoja, W. Materski. Warsaw 1995–2006.

Kot, Stanisław: *Rozmowy z Kremlem.* London 1959 [*Records of the Kremlin talks 1941/42*]

Skarżyński, Kazimierz: *Katyń. Raport Polskiego Czerwonego Krzyża.* Ed. Wojciech Ziembiński. Warsaw 1989 [*Report of the Polish Red Cross*]

Soobshcheniye Spetsialnoy Komissii po ustanovleniyu i rassledovaniyu obstoyatelstv rasstrela nemetsko-fashistskimi zakhvatchikami v Katynskom lesu voyennykh polskikh ofitserov, in: *Pravda*, 26 January 1944 [*Report of the Burdenko Commission*]

The Katyn Forest Massacre: Hearings Before the Select Committee to Conduct an Investigation of the Facts, Evidence, and Circumstances of the Katyn

Forest Massacre, Eighty-second Congress, First[-second] Session, on Investigation of the Murder of Thousands of Polish Officers in the Katyn Forest Near Smolensk, Russia. US Government Printing Office, 1952, vol. I–VII [*Report of the Madden Committee*]

Memoirs

Anders, Władysław: *Bez ostatniego rozdziału. Wspomnienia z lat 1939–1946.* London 1949.

Czapski, Józef: *Na nieludzkiej ziemi.* Warsaw 1990.

Giménez Caballero, Ernesto: *La matanza de Katyn: visión sobre Rusia.* Madrid 1943.

Goetel, Ferdynand: *Czasy wojny.* Cracow 2005.

Hubermont, Pierre: *Khatyn ce n'est pas Katyn,* 1976 (unpublished, Soma-Ceges/ Brussels).

Menshagin, Boris: *Vospominaniya: Smolensk ... Katyn ... Vladimirskaya tyurma.* Paris 1988.

Swianiewicz, Stanisław: *W cieniu Katynia.* Paris 1976.

Zakirov, Oleg: *Obcy element. Dramatyczne losy oficera KGB w walce o wyjaśnienie zbrodni katyńskiej.* Poznań 2010.

Studies

Buyanova, Yuliya: *Katynskoye delo: informatsionnaya borba SSSR i natsistskoi Germanii (1943–1945 gg.).* Sankt-Peterburg 2011.

Charków – Katyń – Twer – Bykownia. W 70. Rocznicę zbrodni katyńskiej. Zbiór studiów. Ed. A. Kola i J. Sziling. Toruń 2011.

Chwastyk-Kowalczyk, Jolanta: *Katyń, Dipisi, PKPR la łamach polskich czasopism uchodźczych.* Kielce 2011.

Fox, Frank: *God's Eye: Aerial Photography and the Katyn Forest Massacre.* West Chester PA. 1999.

Fox, John P., Der Fall Katyn und die NS-Propaganda, in: *Vierteljahrshefte für Zeitgeschichte,* 3(1982), pp. 462–499.

Katyń 1940. Walka o prawdę. Ed. Wojciech Lis. Toruń 2012.

Katyn. A Crime without Punishment. Ed. Anna M. Ciencala, Natalia S. Lebedeva, Wojciech Materski. New Haven/London 2007.

Katyn et la Suisse. Experts et expertises médicales dans les crises humanitaires. Ed. D. Debons et al. Geneva 2009.

Mackiewicz, Józef: *Katyń. Zbrodnia bez sądu i kary.* Warsaw 1997.

Maresch, Eugenia: *Katyn 1940: The Documentary Evidence of the West's Betrayal.* London 2010.

Materski, Wojciech: *Mord Katyński. Siedemdziesiąt lat drogi do prawdy.* Warsaw 2010.

Piórkowska, Krystyna: *English-speaking Witnesses to Katyn / Angielskojęzyczni świadkowie Katynia.* Warsaw 2012.

Przewoźnik, Andrzej/Adamska, Jolanta: *Zbrodnia prawda pamięć.* Warsaw 2010.

Rosja a Katyń. Ed. Ośrodek Karta. Warsaw 2010.

Sanford, George: *Katyn and the Soviet Massacre of 1940. Truth, Justice and Memory.* London/New York 2005.

Wasilewski, Witold: *Ludobójstwo. Kłamstwo i walka o prawdę. Sprawa Katynia 1940–2014.* Łomianki 2014.

Weber, Claudia: *Krieg der Täter. Die Massenerschießungen von Katyń.* Hamburg 2015.

Wolsza, Tomasz: *'To co wiedziałem przekracza swją grozą najśmielsze fantazje'. Wojenne i powojenne losy Polaków wizytujących Katyń w 1943 roku.* Warsaw 2015.

Yazhborovskaya, Inessa / Anatoli Yablokov / Valentina Parsadanova: *Katynsky sindrom v sovietsko-polskikh i rossiysko-polskikh otnosheniyakh.* Moscow 2009.

Zbrodnia Katyńska. Polskie śledztwo. Ed. Polska Fundacja Katyńska. Warsaw 2005.

Journals

Biuletyń Katyński, 1(1978) – 45(2000) [Krakow].

Vestnik Katynskogo Memoriala, 1(2002) – 14(2014) [Smolensk].

Zeszyty Katyńskie, 1(1990) – 26(2017) [Warsaw].

Register of People

Abramski, Jan
Ahrens, Friedrich
Alexeyeva, Anna
Alliluyeva, Svetlana
Anders, Władysław
Andropov, Yuri
Attlee, Clement

Babel, Isaac
Badylak, Walenty
Bazilevsky, Boris
Beria, Lavrentiy
Berling, Zygmunt
Bethell, Nicholas
Bierut, Bolesław
Biddle, Francis
Birkle, Alexandru
Blokhin, Vasily
Boldin, Valery
Borodenkov, Kirill
Brasillach, Robert
Brezhnev, Leonid
Brinon, Fernand de
Buhtz, Gerhard
Burdenko, Nikolai
Burlet, Herman de
Butler, Rohan d'Olier

Cadogan, Alexander
Canaris, Wilhelm
Carter, John Franklin
Cassidy, Henry C.

Churchill, Winston
Clark Kerr, Archibald
Conti, Leonardo
Curzon, George
Czapski, Józef

Davies, Joseph E.
Davis, Elmer
Davis, Jerome
De Pillecyn, Filip
Doe, John
Donovan, William
Dürre, Arno
Dulles, Allen W.
Dulles, John Foster

Earle, George H.
Eden, Anthony
Eichborn, Reinhart v.
Eisenhower, Dwight D.
Epstein, Julius

Falin, Valentin
Forte-Whiteman, Lovett
Franco, Francisco
Frank, Hans

George VI
Gersdorff, Rudolf-Christoph v.
Gibbons, John
Gierek, Edward
Gilder, Stanley

Voroshilov, Kliment
Vyshinsky, Andrey

Wajda, Andrzej
Wajda, Jakub
Wałęsa, Lech
Weizsäcker, Ernst v.
Werth, Alexander
Werth, Nicolas
White, William Lindsay
Wodziński, Marian
Wójcicki, Bolesław

Yakovlev, Alexander
Yeltsin, Boris

Zakirov, Oleg
Zarubin, Vasily
Zorya, Yuri
Zorya, Nikolai
Żywiecki, Ryszard

Index